RYAN NORTH MARK WAID IAN FLYNN

Jughead®

VOLUME THREE

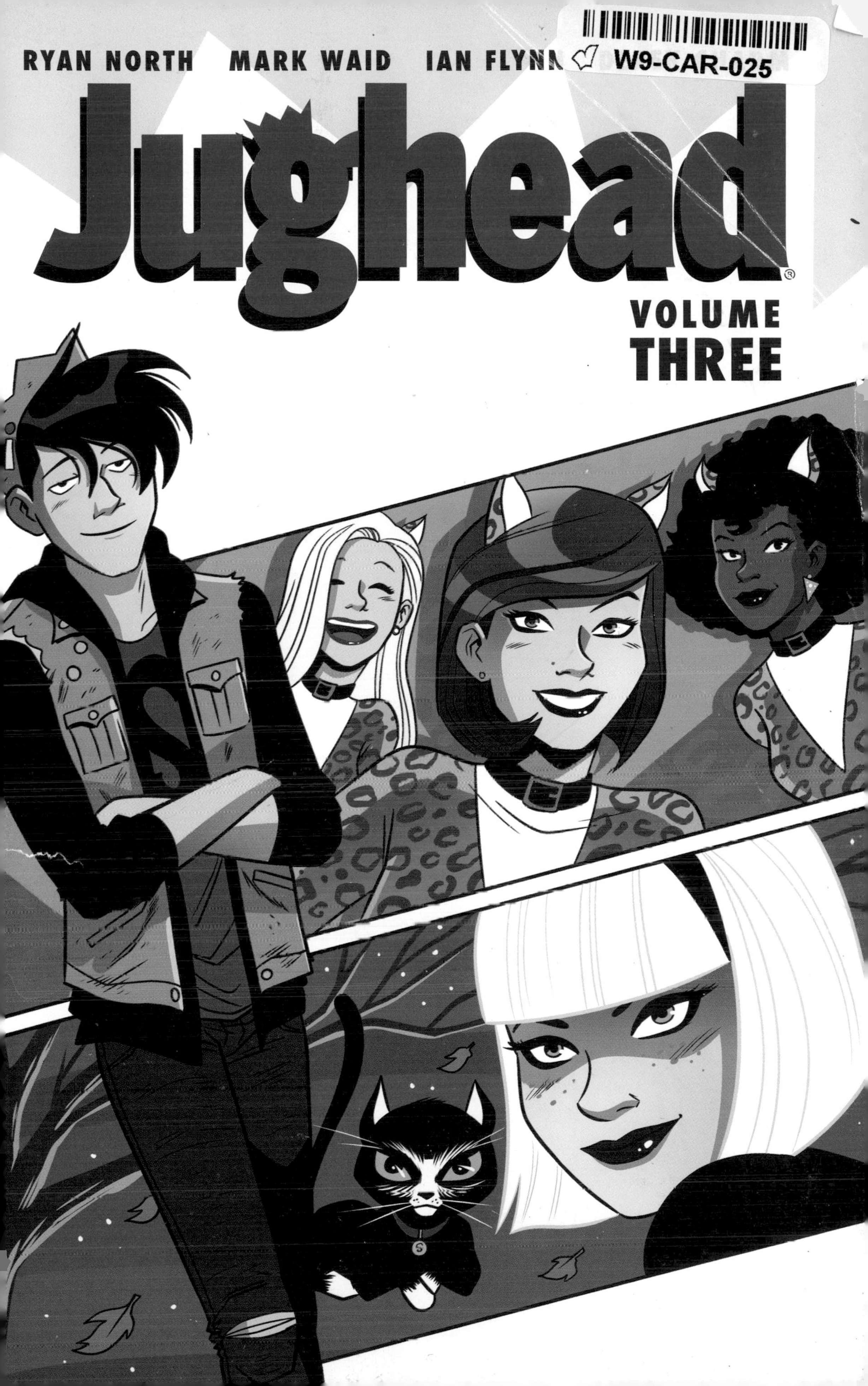

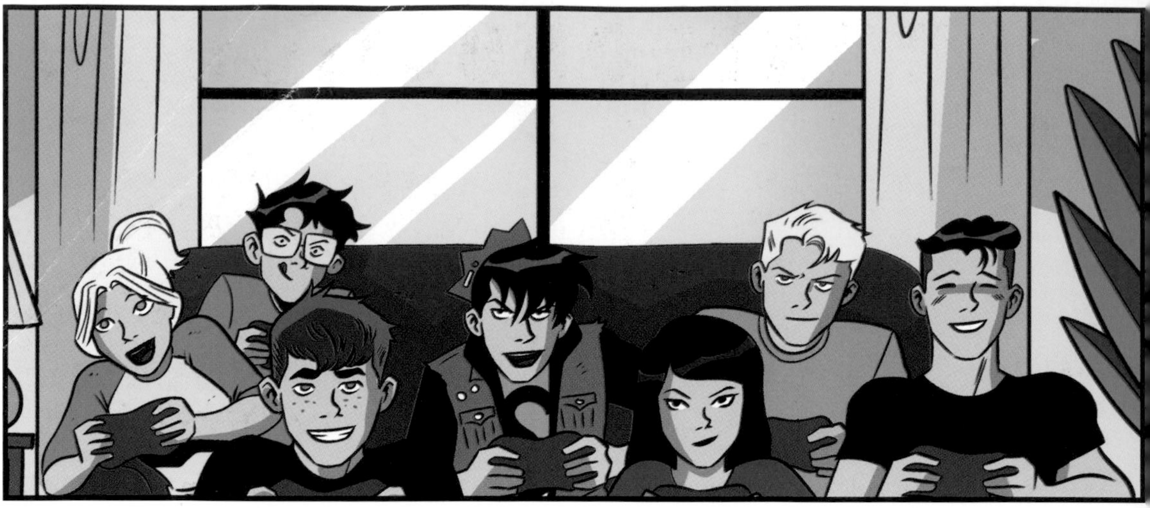

STORY BY:
RYAN NORTH
(ISSUES 12-14)
MARK WAID & IAN FLYNN
(ISSUES 15-16)

LETTERING BY:
JACK MORELLI

ART BY:
DEREK CHARM

COLORS BY:
MATT HERMS
(ISSUES 15-16)

MUSIC COMPOSITION:
ALLENE CHOMYN
(ISSUE 13)

EDITORS:
MIKE PELLERITO & VINCENT LOVALLO

ASSOCIATE EDITOR:
STEPHEN OSWALD

ASSISTANT EDITOR:
JAMIE LEE ROTANTE

EDITOR-IN-CHIEF:
VICTOR GORELICK

GRAPHIC DESIGN:
KARI McLACHLAN

PUBLISHER:
JON GOLDWATER

AN INTRODUCTION TO Jughead®

by RYAN NORTH

When I got the call to write *Jughead*, I wasn't worried. He's a man who likes eating and is awkward. How hard could it be? I'VE LIVED IT for my entire teenage years; certainly I could write it. But it turns out it's trickier than that! Jughead isn't JUST a burger-hungry teen.

Turns out, he's the soul of Riverdale.

While everyone around him is running around, boy/girl crazy, he's sensible. He's competent. He sees what the others don't, he can do what the others don't, and he is, I believe, kinder and more generous than any of them. He's the best of Riverdale, and he's the best of us. A character like that is hard to write—much harder than just "likes: food; dislikes: smooching"—but it's necessary if you're going to capture the core of who Jughead is. He's your best friend, and he'll always have your back.

That said, here's some stories where this great, sensible, kind, burger-loving guy still manages to get into all sorts of problems!

You're about to read two stories: one I wrote and one Mark Waid and Ian Flynn wrote! In mine, his friends hate him. In theirs, they like him a little too much. I will say this about their story: it's good, DESPITE THE FACT THEY CALLED ME OUT IN A LITTLE NOTE AT THE BOTTOM OF ONE OF THE PAGES. Don't worry, you'll know it when you see it, and you'll feel the same BLINDING RAGE. But there is one thing we can all agree on, even at our most enraged: Derek Charm absolutely knocks it out of the park with every page he draws.

One of the reasons my story guest-stars Reggie is I honestly can't get enough of how Derek draws him, with those muscles, that smile, and that classic Superman-style squint. This is my new canonical version of Reggie, as iconic as Jughead's crown, and now I can't imagine him any other way. It's not just Reggie: everyone in Charm's world is new and distinctive, but still instantly recognizable as their classic Archie selves. It's not an easy trick to take 75-year-old characters and update them while still retaining their essential selves, but Charm pulls it off like it isn't even a big deal.

I hope you enjoy these stories about my favorite burger teen in the world.

ISSUE
TWELVE

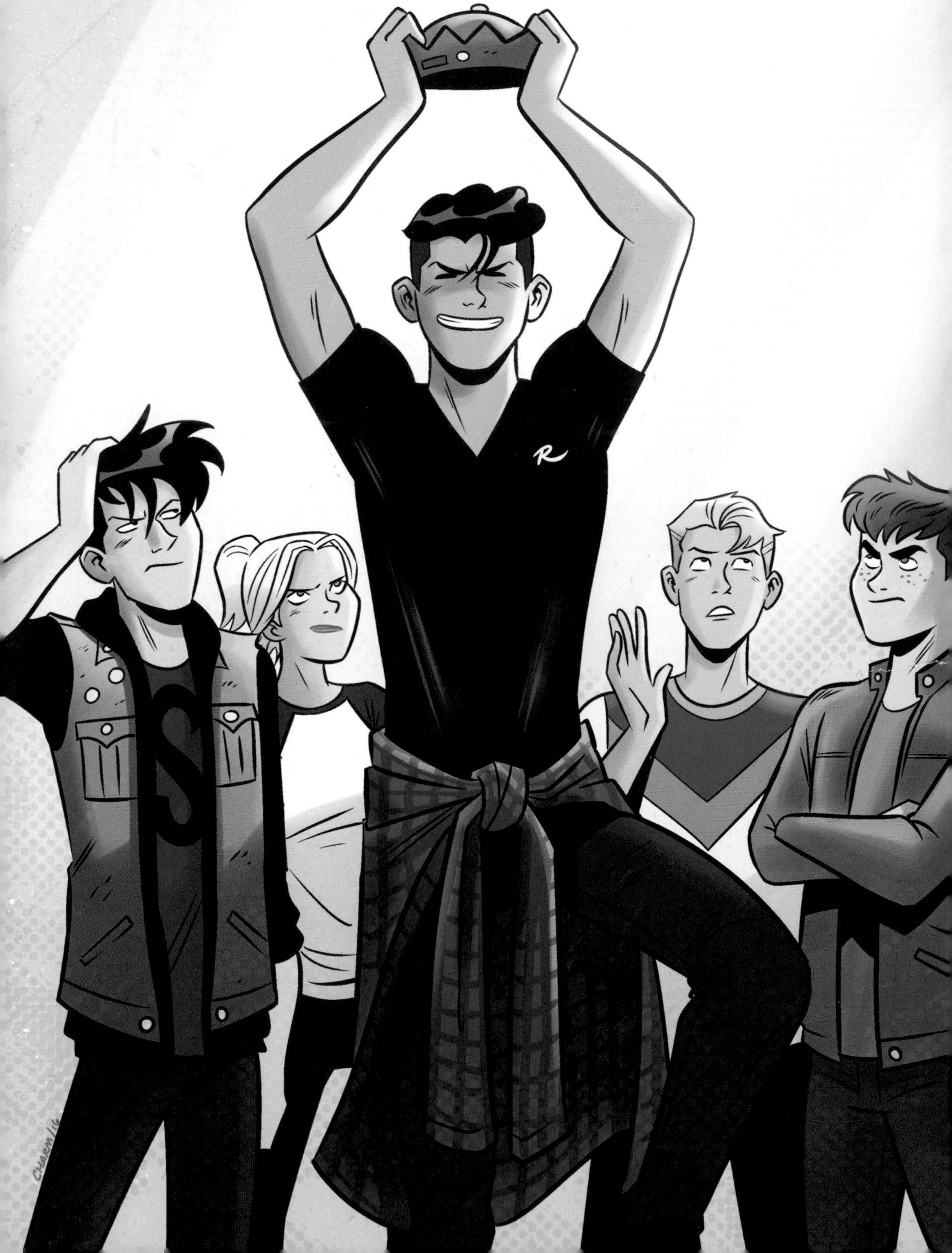

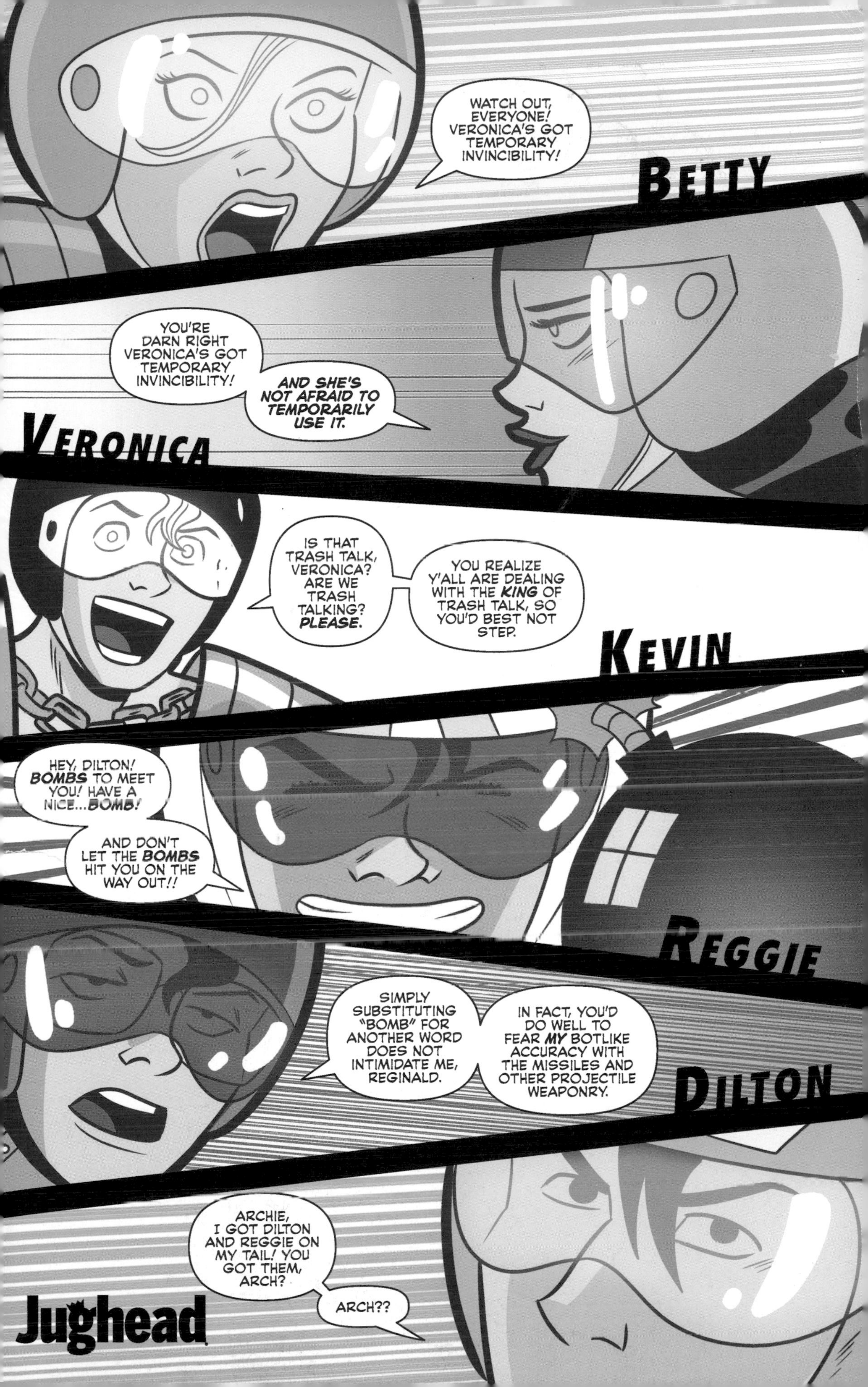
WATCH OUT, EVERYONE! VERONICA'S GOT TEMPORARY INVINCIBILITY!
BETTY
YOU'RE DARN RIGHT VERONICA'S GOT TEMPORARY INVINCIBILITY!
AND SHE'S NOT AFRAID TO TEMPORARILY USE IT.
VERONICA
IS THAT TRASH TALK, VERONICA? ARE WE TRASH TALKING? PLEASE.
YOU REALIZE Y'ALL ARE DEALING WITH THE KING OF TRASH TALK, SO YOU'D BEST NOT STEP.
KEVIN
HEY, DILTON! BOMBS TO MEET YOU! HAVE A NICE...BOMB!
AND DON'T LET THE BOMBS HIT YOU ON THE WAY OUT!!
REGGIE
SIMPLY SUBSTITUTING "BOMB" FOR ANOTHER WORD DOES NOT INTIMIDATE ME, REGINALD.
IN FACT, YOU'D DO WELL TO FEAR MY BOTLIKE ACCURACY WITH THE MISSILES AND OTHER PROJECTILE WEAPONRY.
DILTON
ARCHIE, I GOT DILTON AND REGGIE ON MY TAIL! YOU GOT THEM, ARCH?
ARCH??
Jughead

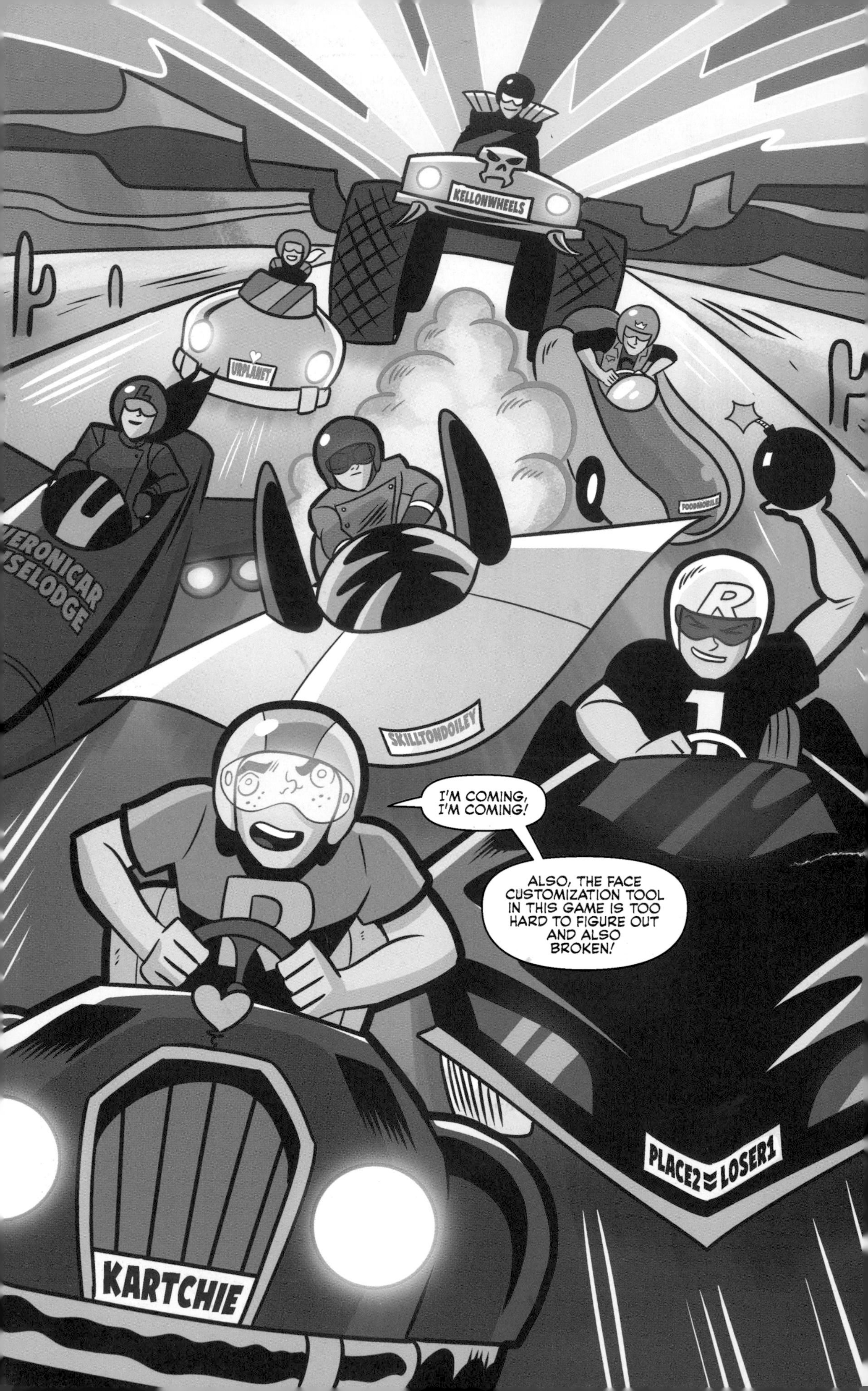
KELLONWHEELS
URPLANET
VERONICAR
SELODGE
FOODMOBILE
SKILLTONDOILEY
I'M COMING, I'M COMING!
ALSO, THE FACE CUSTOMIZATION TOOL IN THIS GAME IS TOO HARD TO FIGURE OUT AND ALSO BROKEN!
PLACE2 LOSER1
KARTCHIE

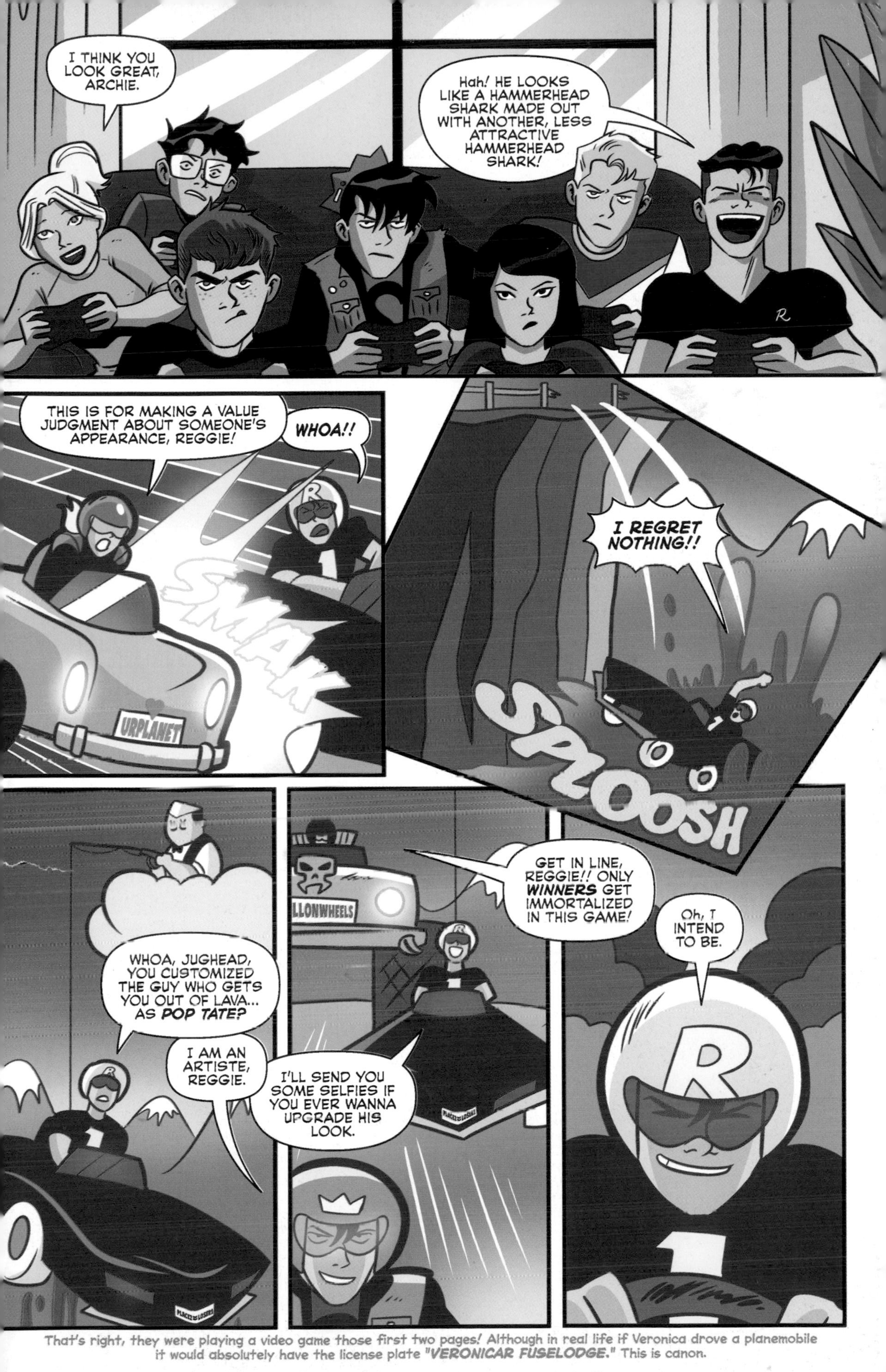
I THINK YOU LOOK GREAT, ARCHIE.
Hah! HE LOOKS LIKE A HAMMERHEAD SHARK MADE OUT WITH ANOTHER, LESS ATTRACTIVE HAMMERHEAD SHARK!
THIS IS FOR MAKING A VALUE JUDGMENT ABOUT SOMEONE'S APPEARANCE, REGGIE!
WHOA!!
SMAK
URPLANET
I REGRET NOTHING!!
SPLOOSH
WHOA, JUGHEAD, YOU CUSTOMIZED THE GUY WHO GETS YOU OUT OF LAVA... AS POP TATE?
I AM AN ARTISTE, REGGIE.
I'LL SEND YOU SOME SELFIES IF YOU EVER WANNA UPGRADE HIS LOOK.
GET IN LINE, REGGIE!! ONLY WINNERS GET IMMORTALIZED IN THIS GAME!
Oh, I INTEND TO BE.

That's right, they were playing a video game those first two pages! Although in real life if Veronica drove a planemobile it would absolutely have the license plate "***VERONICAR FUSELODGE.***" This is canon.

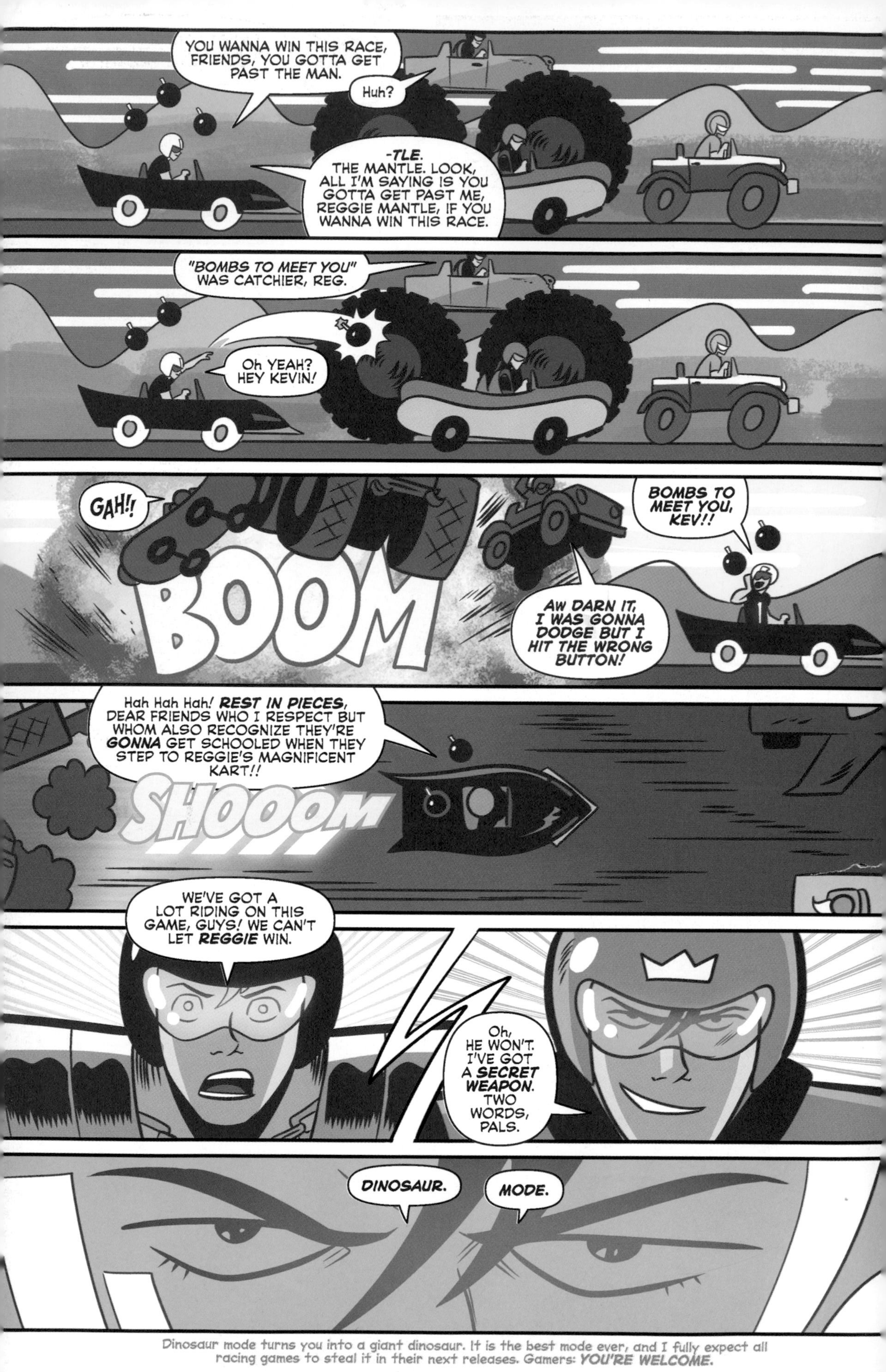

YOU WANNA WIN THIS RACE, FRIENDS, YOU GOTTA GET PAST THE MAN.
Huh?
-TLE. THE MANTLE. LOOK, ALL I'M SAYING IS YOU GOTTA GET PAST ME, REGGIE MANTLE, IF YOU WANNA WIN THIS RACE.
"BOMBS TO MEET YOU" WAS CATCHIER, REG.
Oh YEAH? HEY KEVIN!
GAH!!
BOOM
BOMBS TO MEET YOU, KEV!!
AW DARN IT, I WAS GONNA DODGE BUT I HIT THE WRONG BUTTON!
Hah Hah Hah! REST IN PIECES, DEAR FRIENDS WHO I RESPECT BUT WHOM ALSO RECOGNIZE THEY'RE GONNA GET SCHOOLED WHEN THEY STEP TO REGGIE'S MAGNIFICENT KART!!
SHOOOM
WE'VE GOT A LOT RIDING ON THIS GAME, GUYS! WE CAN'T LET REGGIE WIN.
Oh, HE WON'T. I'VE GOT A SECRET WEAPON. TWO WORDS, PALS.
DINOSAUR.
MODE.

Dinosaur mode turns you into a giant dinosaur. It is the best mode ever, and I fully expect all racing games to steal it in their next releases. Gamers: ***YOU'RE WELCOME.***

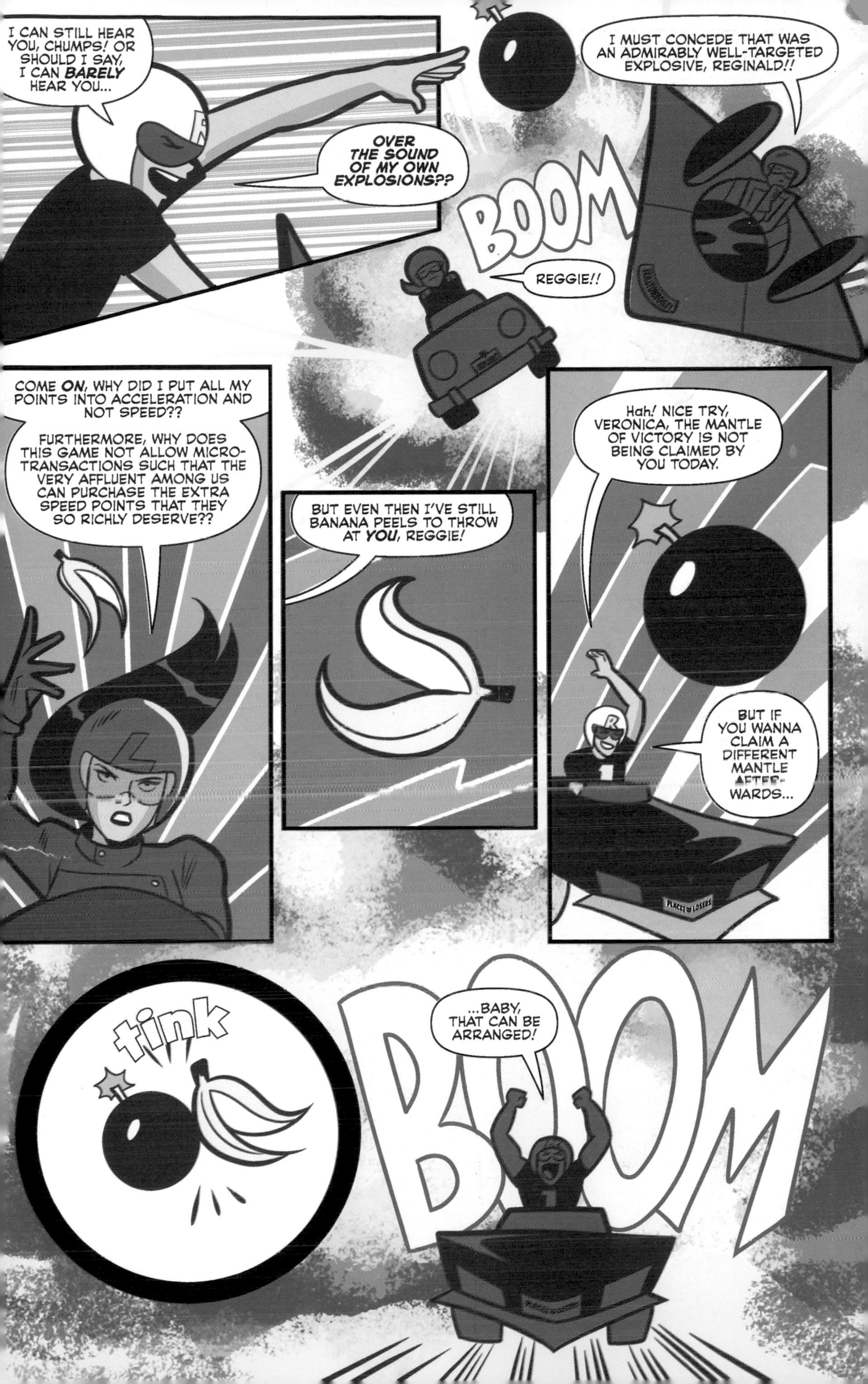
I CAN STILL HEAR YOU, CHUMPS! OR SHOULD I SAY, I CAN BARELY HEAR YOU...
OVER THE SOUND OF MY OWN EXPLOSIONS??
I MUST CONCEDE THAT WAS AN ADMIRABLY WELL-TARGETED EXPLOSIVE, REGINALD!!
BOOM
REGGIE!!
COME ON, WHY DID I PUT ALL MY POINTS INTO ACCELERATION AND NOT SPEED??
FURTHERMORE, WHY DOES THIS GAME NOT ALLOW MICRO-TRANSACTIONS SUCH THAT THE VERY AFFLUENT AMONG US CAN PURCHASE THE EXTRA SPEED POINTS THAT THEY SO RICHLY DESERVE??
BUT EVEN THEN I'VE STILL BANANA PEELS TO THROW AT YOU, REGGIE!
Hah! NICE TRY, VERONICA, THE MANTLE OF VICTORY IS NOT BEING CLAIMED BY YOU TODAY.
BUT IF YOU WANNA CLAIM A DIFFERENT MANTLE AFTER-WARDS...
PLACES 4 LOSERS
tink
...BABY, THAT CAN BE ARRANGED!
BOOM

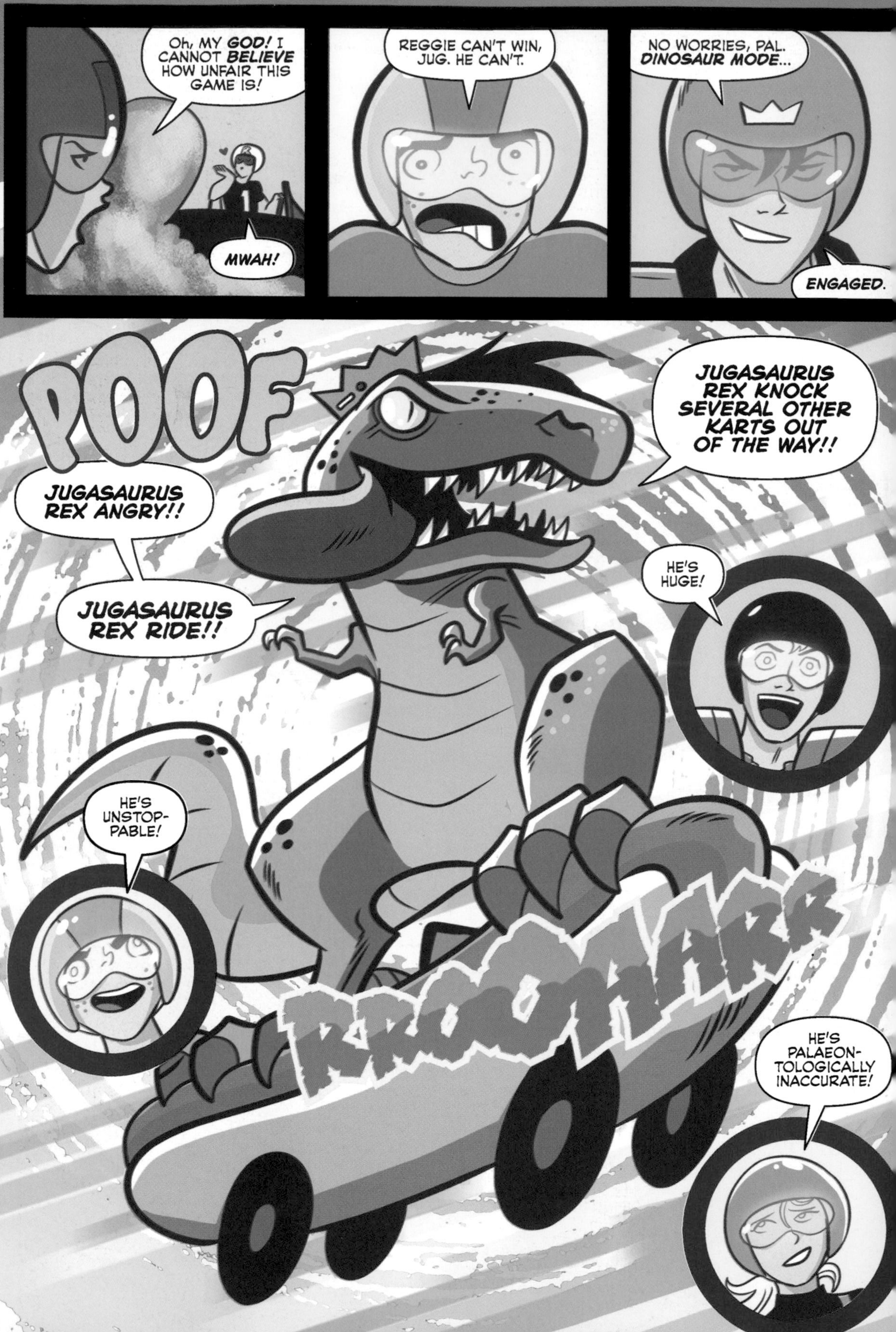
Oh, MY GOD! I CANNOT BELIEVE HOW UNFAIR THIS GAME IS!
MWAH!
REGGIE CAN'T WIN, JUG. HE CAN'T.
NO WORRIES, PAL. DINOSAUR MODE...
ENGAGED.
POOF
JUGASAURUS REX ANGRY!!
JUGASAURUS REX RIDE!!
JUGASAURUS REX KNOCK SEVERAL OTHER KARTS OUT OF THE WAY!!
HE'S HUGE!
HE'S UNSTOP-PABLE!
RROOAARR
HE'S PALAEON-TOLOGICALLY INACCURATE!

Betty is saying "he's palaeontologically inaccurate" because I care about all the paleontologists out there who both like reading comics about a hungry teen **AND** like not being enraged at unexamined inaccuracy in dinosauric representation. Got your back, friends!

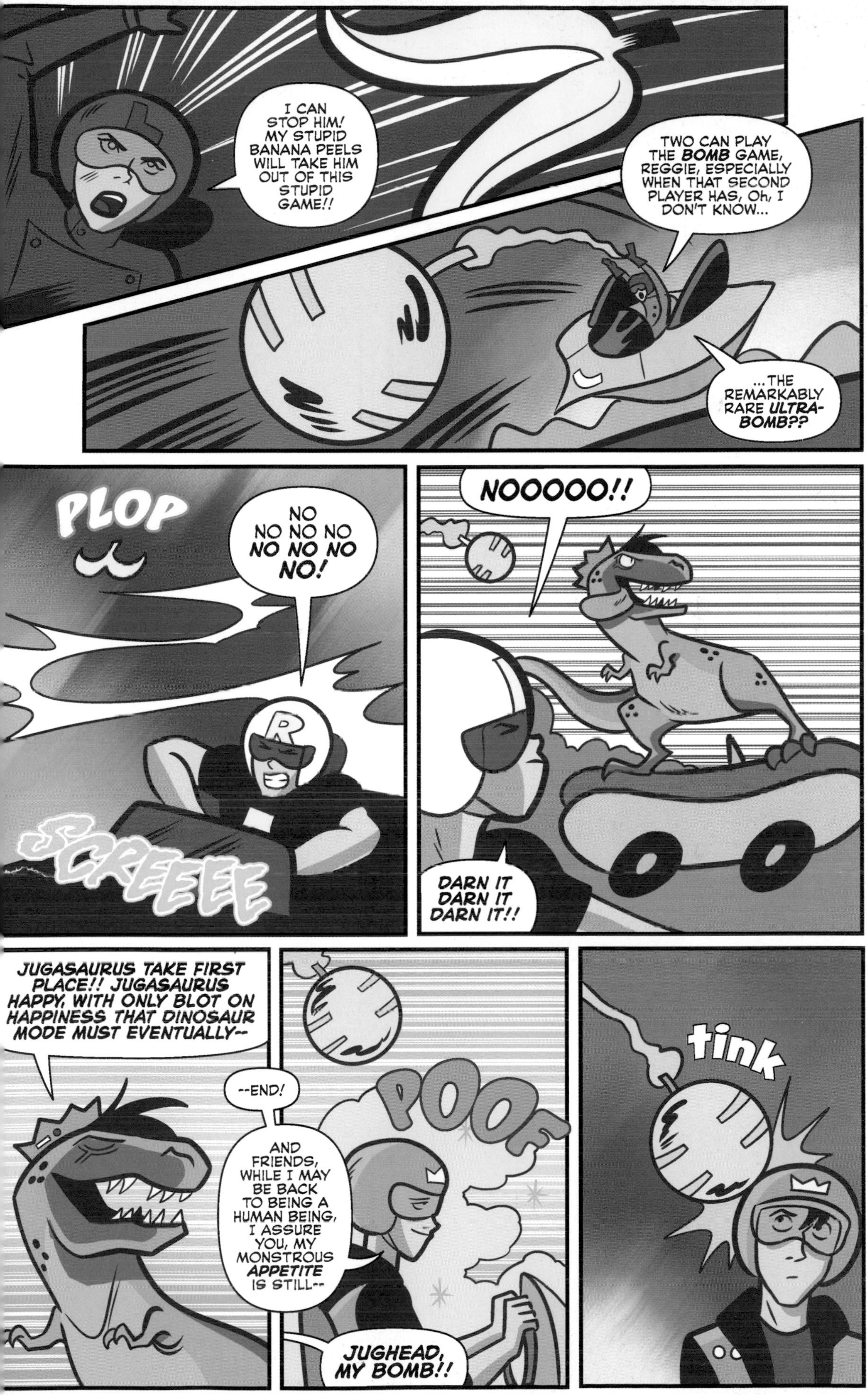
I CAN STOP HIM! MY STUPID BANANA PEELS WILL TAKE HIM OUT OF THIS STUPID GAME!!
TWO CAN PLAY THE BOMB GAME, REGGIE, ESPECIALLY WHEN THAT SECOND PLAYER HAS, Oh, I DON'T KNOW...
...THE REMARKABLY RARE ULTRA-BOMB??
PLOP
NO NO NO NO NO NO NO NO!
SCREEEE
NOOOOO!!
DARN IT DARN IT DARN IT!!
JUGASAURUS TAKE FIRST PLACE!! JUGASAURUS HAPPY, WITH ONLY BLOT ON HAPPINESS THAT DINOSAUR MODE MUST EVENTUALLY--
--END!
POOF
AND FRIENDS, WHILE I MAY BE BACK TO BEING A HUMAN BEING, I ASSURE YOU, MY MONSTROUS APPETITE IS STILL--
JUGHEAD, MY BOMB!!
tink

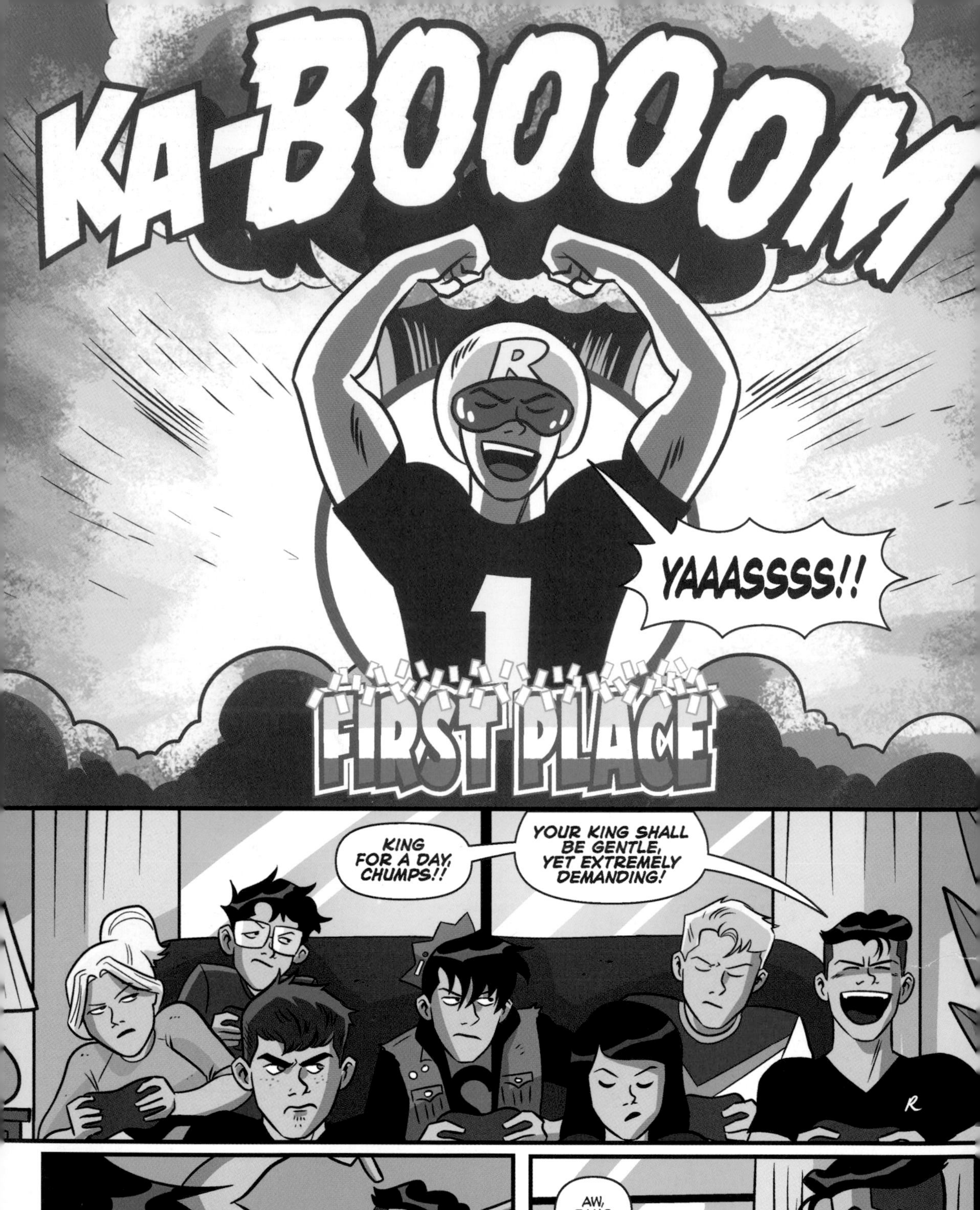
KA-BOOOOM
YAAASSSS!!
FIRST PLACE
KING FOR A DAY, CHUMPS!!
YOUR KING SHALL BE GENTLE, YET EXTREMELY DEMANDING!
ALSO, YOUR KING IS THE ONLY ONE WHO GETS TO WEAR CROWNS AROUND HERE
AW, DANG IT.

See, this is why you should always be careful about where you toss your implausibly giant bombs. That is the moral of this comic, which technically makes it educational, which means reading this book counts as a school credit. I am almost certain that is the case.

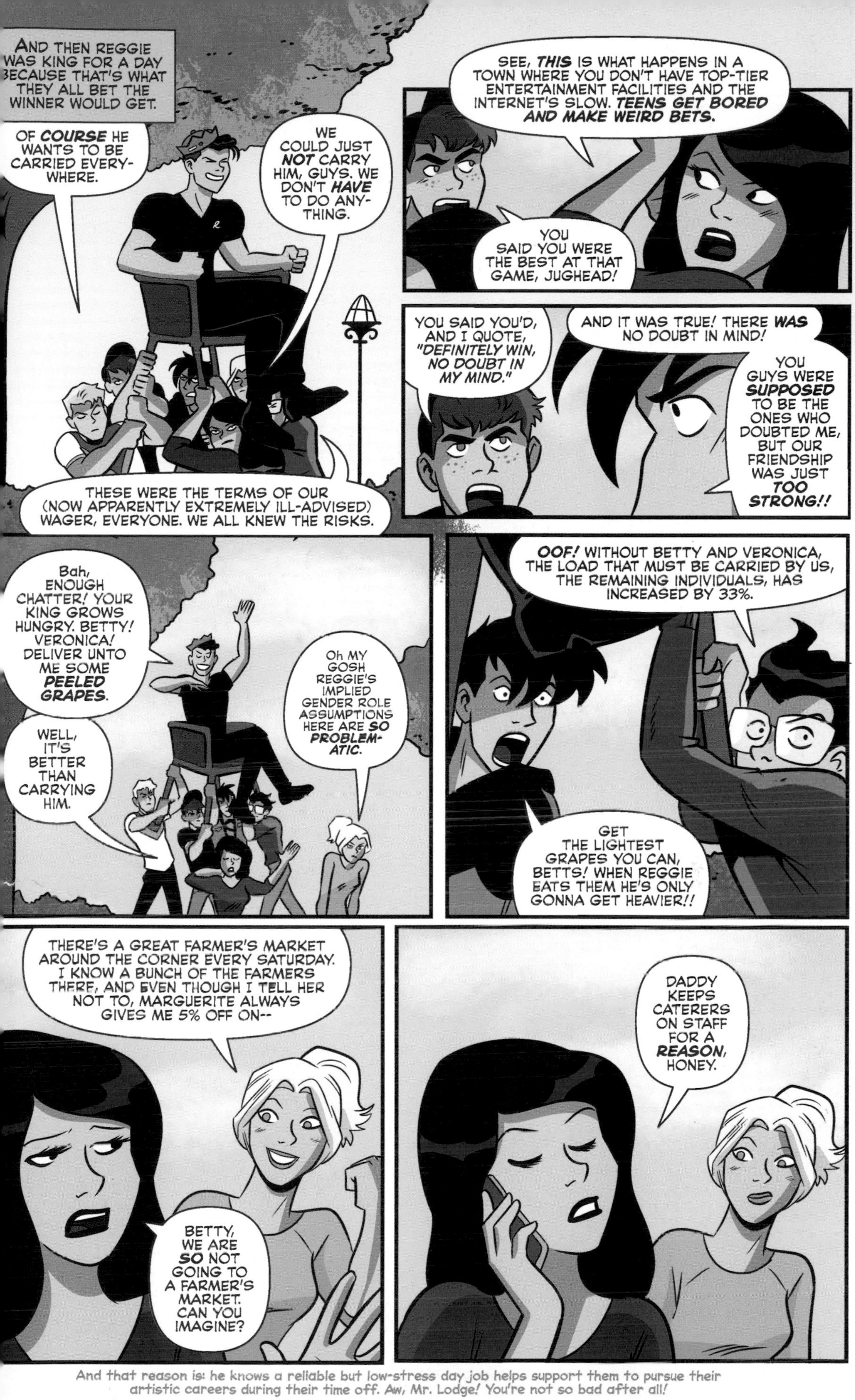
AND THEN REGGIE WAS KING FOR A DAY BECAUSE THAT'S WHAT THEY ALL BET THE WINNER WOULD GET.
OF COURSE HE WANTS TO BE CARRIED EVERY-WHERE.
WE COULD JUST NOT CARRY HIM, GUYS. WE DON'T HAVE TO DO ANY-THING.
THESE WERE THE TERMS OF OUR (NOW APPARENTLY EXTREMELY ILL-ADVISED) WAGER, EVERYONE. WE ALL KNEW THE RISKS.
SEE, THIS IS WHAT HAPPENS IN A TOWN WHERE YOU DON'T HAVE TOP-TIER ENTERTAINMENT FACILITIES AND THE INTERNET'S SLOW. TEENS GET BORED AND MAKE WEIRD BETS.
YOU SAID YOU WERE THE BEST AT THAT GAME, JUGHEAD!
YOU SAID YOU'D, AND I QUOTE, "DEFINITELY WIN, NO DOUBT IN MY MIND."
AND IT WAS TRUE! THERE WAS NO DOUBT IN MIND!
YOU GUYS WERE SUPPOSED TO BE THE ONES WHO DOUBTED ME, BUT OUR FRIENDSHIP WAS JUST TOO STRONG!!
Bah, ENOUGH CHATTER! YOUR KING GROWS HUNGRY. BETTY! VERONICA! DELIVER UNTO ME SOME PEELED GRAPES.
WELL, IT'S BETTER THAN CARRYING HIM.
Oh MY GOSH REGGIE'S IMPLIED GENDER ROLE ASSUMPTIONS HERE ARE SO PROBLEM-ATIC.
OOF! WITHOUT BETTY AND VERONICA, THE LOAD THAT MUST BE CARRIED BY US, THE REMAINING INDIVIDUALS, HAS INCREASED BY 33%.
GET THE LIGHTEST GRAPES YOU CAN, BETTS! WHEN REGGIE EATS THEM HE'S ONLY GONNA GET HEAVIER!!
THERE'S A GREAT FARMER'S MARKET AROUND THE CORNER EVERY SATURDAY. I KNOW A BUNCH OF THE FARMERS THERE, AND EVEN THOUGH I TELL HER NOT TO, MARGUERITE ALWAYS GIVES ME 5% OFF ON--
BETTY, WE ARE SO NOT GOING TO A FARMER'S MARKET. CAN YOU IMAGINE?
DADDY KEEPS CATERERS ON STAFF FOR A REASON, HONEY.

And that reason is: he knows a reliable but low-stress day job helps support them to pursue their artistic careers during their time off. Aw, Mr. Lodge! You're not so bad after all!

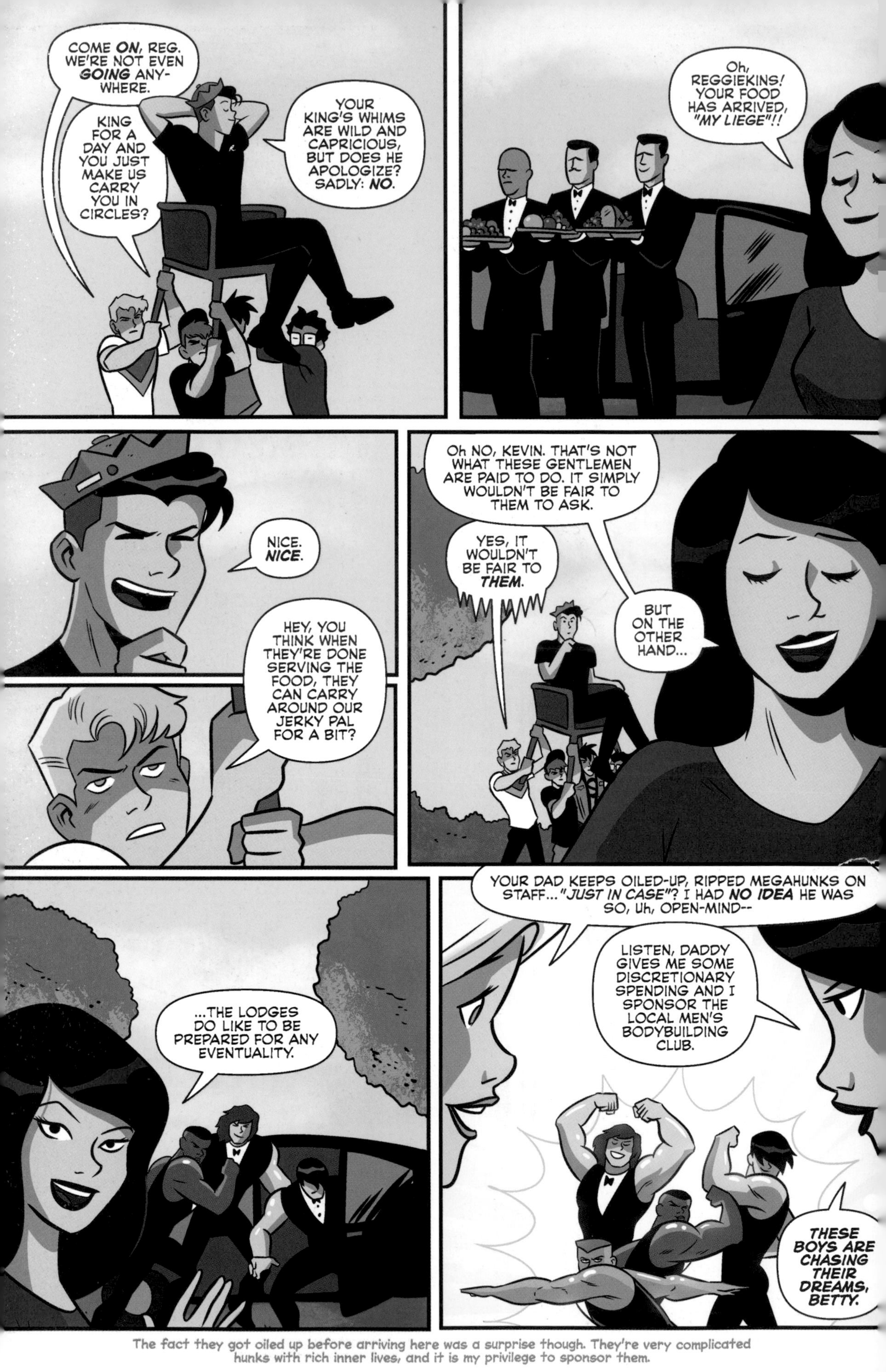
COME ON, REG. WE'RE NOT EVEN GOING ANY-WHERE.
KING FOR A DAY AND YOU JUST MAKE US CARRY YOU IN CIRCLES?
YOUR KING'S WHIMS ARE WILD AND CAPRICIOUS, BUT DOES HE APOLOGIZE? SADLY: NO.
Oh, REGGIEKINS! YOUR FOOD HAS ARRIVED, "MY LIEGE"!!
NICE. NICE.
HEY, YOU THINK WHEN THEY'RE DONE SERVING THE FOOD, THEY CAN CARRY AROUND OUR JERKY PAL FOR A BIT?
Oh NO, KEVIN. THAT'S NOT WHAT THESE GENTLEMEN ARE PAID TO DO. IT SIMPLY WOULDN'T BE FAIR TO THEM TO ASK.
YES, IT WOULDN'T BE FAIR TO THEM.
BUT ON THE OTHER HAND...
...THE LODGES DO LIKE TO BE PREPARED FOR ANY EVENTUALITY.
YOUR DAD KEEPS OILED-UP, RIPPED MEGAHUNKS ON STAFF..."JUST IN CASE"? I HAD NO IDEA HE WAS SO, Uh, OPEN-MIND--
LISTEN, DADDY GIVES ME SOME DISCRETIONARY SPENDING AND I SPONSOR THE LOCAL MEN'S BODYBUILDING CLUB.
THESE BOYS ARE CHASING THEIR DREAMS, BETTY.

The fact they got oiled up before arriving here was a surprise though. They're very complicated hunks with rich inner lives, and it is my privilege to sponsor them.

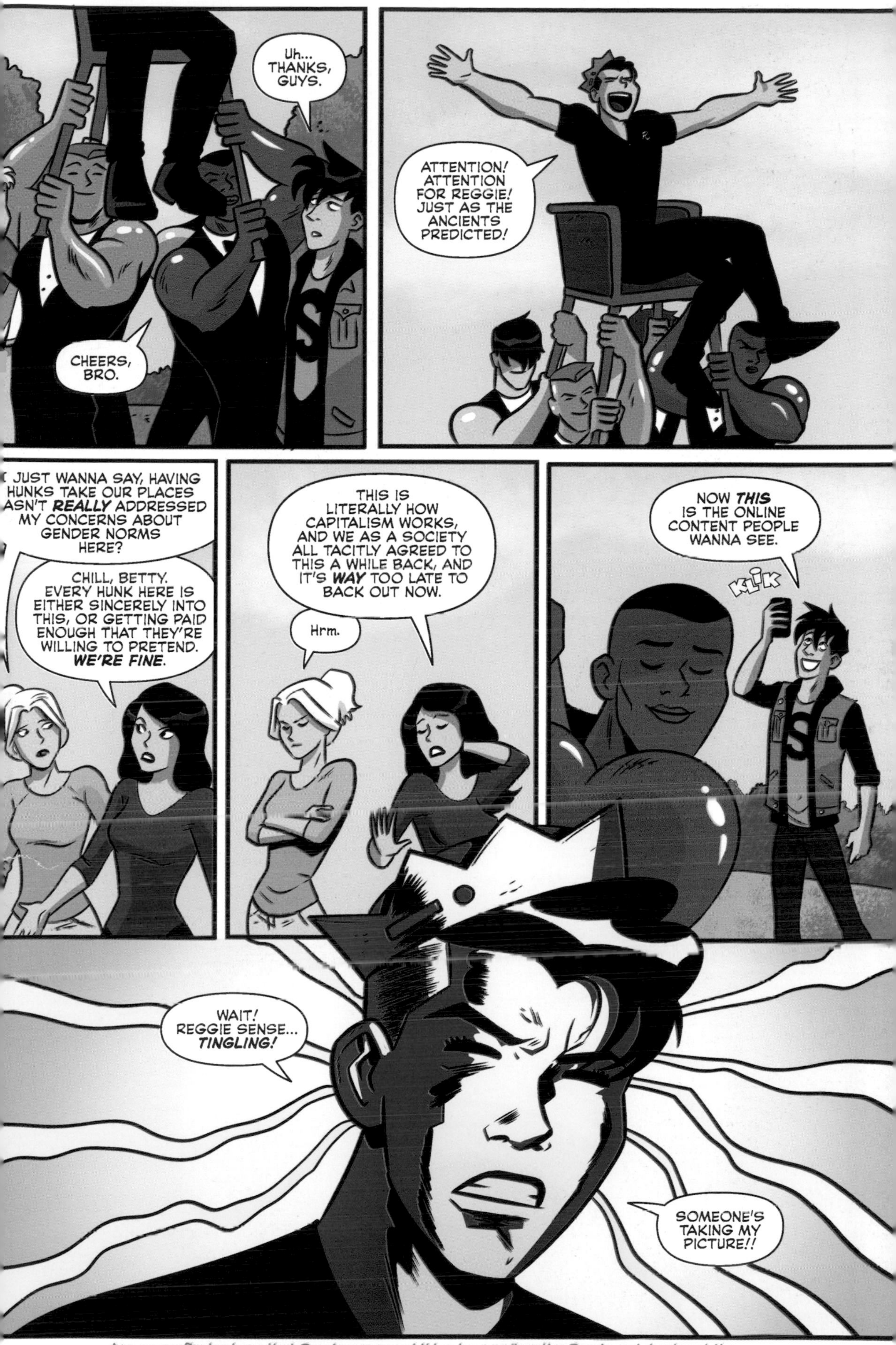
Uh... THANKS, GUYS.
CHEERS, BRO.
ATTENTION! ATTENTION FOR REGGIE! JUST AS THE ANCIENTS PREDICTED!
I JUST WANNA SAY, HAVING HUNKS TAKE OUR PLACES ASN'T REALLY ADDRESSED MY CONCERNS ABOUT GENDER NORMS HERE?
CHILL, BETTY. EVERY HUNK HERE IS EITHER SINCERELY INTO THIS, OR GETTING PAID ENOUGH THAT THEY'RE WILLING TO PRETEND. WE'RE FINE.
THIS IS LITERALLY HOW CAPITALISM WORKS, AND WE AS A SOCIETY ALL TACITLY AGREED TO THIS A WHILE BACK, AND IT'S WAY TOO LATE TO BACK OUT NOW.
Hrm.
NOW THIS IS THE ONLINE CONTENT PEOPLE WANNA SEE.
KLIK
WAIT! REGGIE SENSE... TINGLING!
SOMEONE'S TAKING MY PICTURE!!

Are we confirming here that Reggie was once bitten by a radioactive Reggie and developed the proportional speed and strength of a Reggie?? The answer: ***POSSIBLY?***

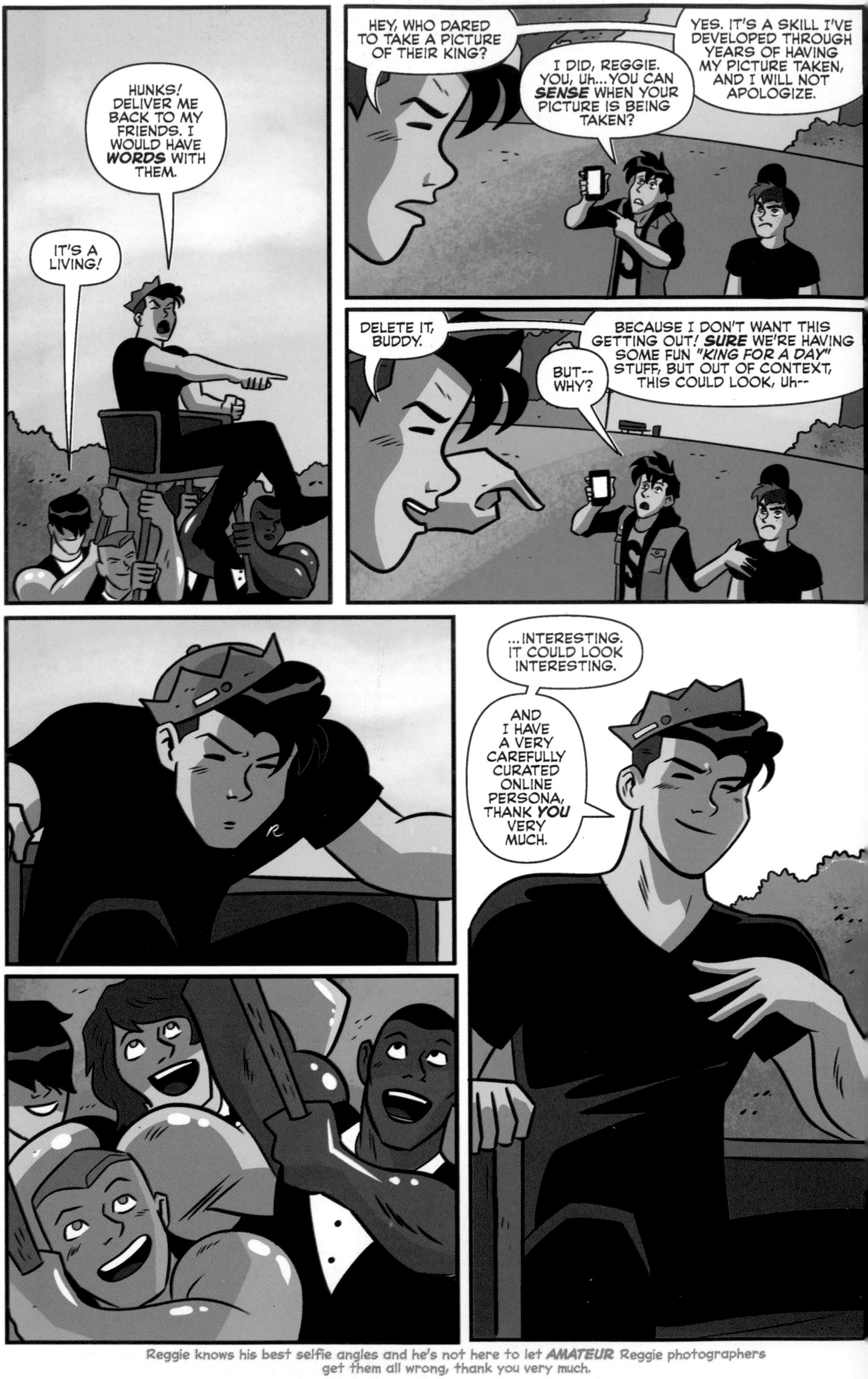
HUNKS! DELIVER ME BACK TO MY FRIENDS. I WOULD HAVE WORDS WITH THEM.
IT'S A LIVING!
HEY, WHO DARED TO TAKE A PICTURE OF THEIR KING?
I DID, REGGIE. YOU, UH...YOU CAN SENSE WHEN YOUR PICTURE IS BEING TAKEN?
YES. IT'S A SKILL I'VE DEVELOPED THROUGH YEARS OF HAVING MY PICTURE TAKEN, AND I WILL NOT APOLOGIZE.
DELETE IT, BUDDY.
BUT-- WHY?
BECAUSE I DON'T WANT THIS GETTING OUT! SURE WE'RE HAVING SOME FUN "KING FOR A DAY" STUFF, BUT OUT OF CONTEXT, THIS COULD LOOK, UH--
...INTERESTING. IT COULD LOOK INTERESTING.
AND I HAVE A VERY CAREFULLY CURATED ONLINE PERSONA, THANK YOU VERY MUCH.

Reggie knows his best selfie angles and he's not here to let *AMATEUR* Reggie photographers get them all wrong, thank you very much.

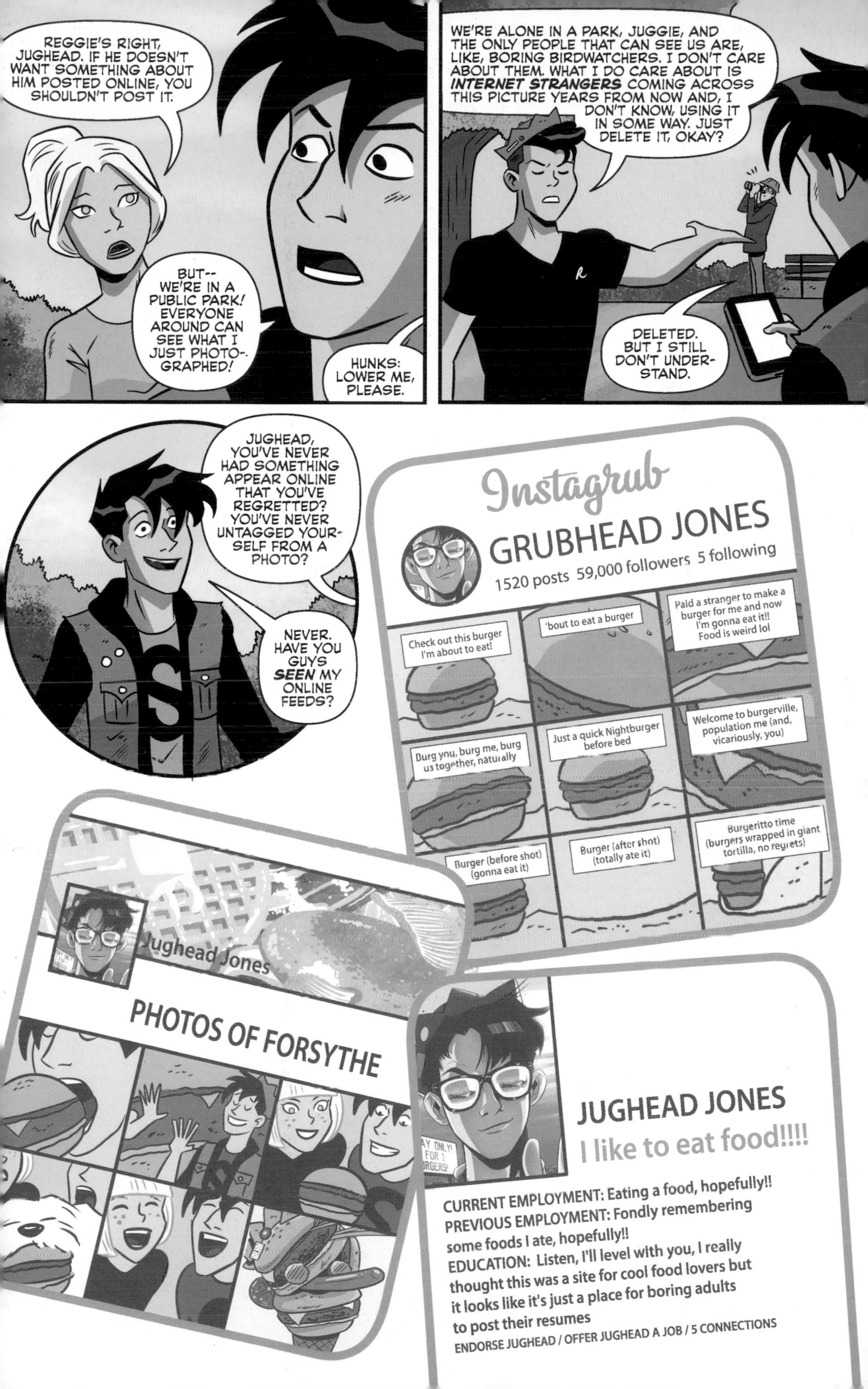
REGGIE'S RIGHT, JUGHEAD. IF HE DOESN'T WANT SOMETHING ABOUT HIM POSTED ONLINE, YOU SHOULDN'T POST IT.
BUT-- WE'RE IN A PUBLIC PARK! EVERYONE AROUND CAN SEE WHAT I JUST PHOTO-GRAPHED!
HUNKS: LOWER ME, PLEASE.
WE'RE ALONE IN A PARK, JUGGIE, AND THE ONLY PEOPLE THAT CAN SEE US ARE, LIKE, BORING BIRDWATCHERS. I DON'T CARE ABOUT THEM. WHAT I DO CARE ABOUT IS INTERNET STRANGERS COMING ACROSS THIS PICTURE YEARS FROM NOW AND, I DON'T KNOW, USING IT IN SOME WAY. JUST DELETE IT, OKAY?
DELETED. BUT I STILL DON'T UNDER-STAND.
JUGHEAD, YOU'VE NEVER HAD SOMETHING APPEAR ONLINE THAT YOU'VE REGRETTED? YOU'VE NEVER UNTAGGED YOUR-SELF FROM A PHOTO?
NEVER. HAVE YOU GUYS SEEN MY ONLINE FEEDS?
Instagrub
GRUBHEAD JONES
1520 posts 59,000 followers 5 following
Check out this burger I'm about to eat!
'bout to eat a burger
Paid a stranger to make a burger for me and now I'm gonna eat it!! Food is weird lol
Burg you, burg me, burg us together, naturally
Just a quick Nightburger before bed
Welcome to burgerville, population me (and, vicariously, you)
Burger (before shot) (gonna eat it)
Burger (after shot) (totally ate it)
Burgeritto time (burgers wrapped in giant tortilla, no regrets)
Jughead Jones
PHOTOS OF FORSYTHE
JUGHEAD JONES
I like to eat food!!!!
CURRENT EMPLOYMENT: Eating a food, hopefully!!
PREVIOUS EMPLOYMENT: Fondly remembering some foods I ate, hopefully!!
EDUCATION: Listen, I'll level with you, I really thought this was a site for cool food lovers but it looks like it's just a place for boring adults to post their resumes
ENDORSE JUGHEAD / OFFER JUGHEAD A JOB / 5 CONNECTIONS

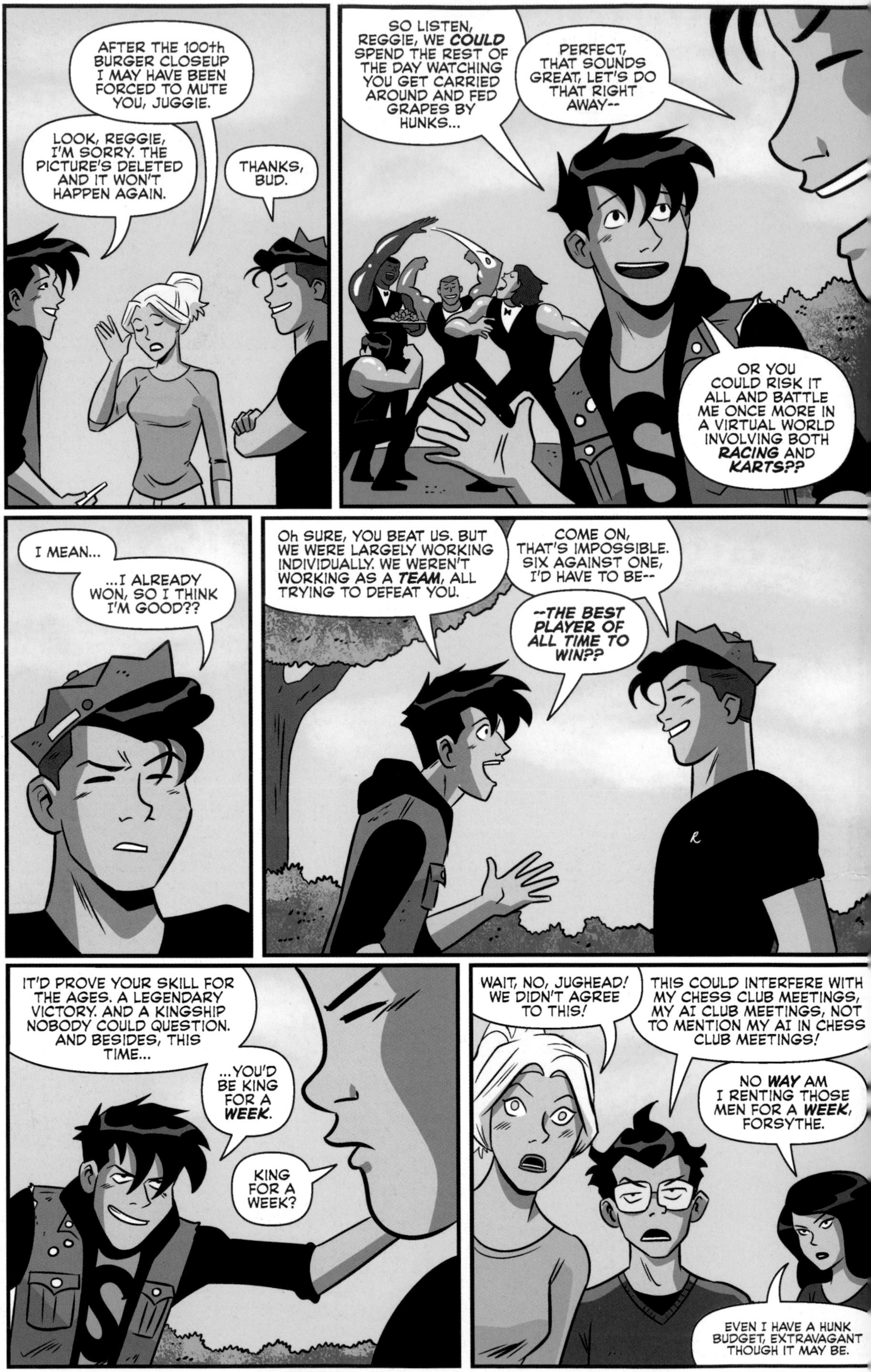
AFTER THE 100th BURGER CLOSEUP I MAY HAVE BEEN FORCED TO MUTE YOU, JUGGIE.
LOOK, REGGIE, I'M SORRY. THE PICTURE'S DELETED AND IT WON'T HAPPEN AGAIN.
THANKS, BUD.
SO LISTEN, REGGIE, WE COULD SPEND THE REST OF THE DAY WATCHING YOU GET CARRIED AROUND AND FED GRAPES BY HUNKS...
PERFECT, THAT SOUNDS GREAT, LET'S DO THAT RIGHT AWAY--
OR YOU COULD RISK IT ALL AND BATTLE ME ONCE MORE IN A VIRTUAL WORLD INVOLVING BOTH RACING AND KARTS??
I MEAN...
...I ALREADY WON, SO I THINK I'M GOOD??
Oh SURE, YOU BEAT US. BUT WE WERE LARGELY WORKING INDIVIDUALLY. WE WEREN'T WORKING AS A TEAM, ALL TRYING TO DEFEAT YOU.
COME ON, THAT'S IMPOSSIBLE. SIX AGAINST ONE, I'D HAVE TO BE--
--THE BEST PLAYER OF ALL TIME TO WIN??
IT'D PROVE YOUR SKILL FOR THE AGES. A LEGENDARY VICTORY. AND A KINGSHIP NOBODY COULD QUESTION. AND BESIDES, THIS TIME...
...YOU'D BE KING FOR A WEEK.
KING FOR A WEEK?
WAIT, NO, JUGHEAD! WE DIDN'T AGREE TO THIS!
THIS COULD INTERFERE WITH MY CHESS CLUB MEETINGS, MY AI CLUB MEETINGS, NOT TO MENTION MY AI IN CHESS CLUB MEETINGS!
NO WAY AM I RENTING THOSE MEN FOR A WEEK, FORSYTHE.
EVEN I HAVE A HUNK BUDGET, EXTRAVAGANT THOUGH IT MAY BE.

I will not have my hunk budget eating into my beefcake and studmuffin and dreamboat budgets, Jughead. ***I WILL NOT.***

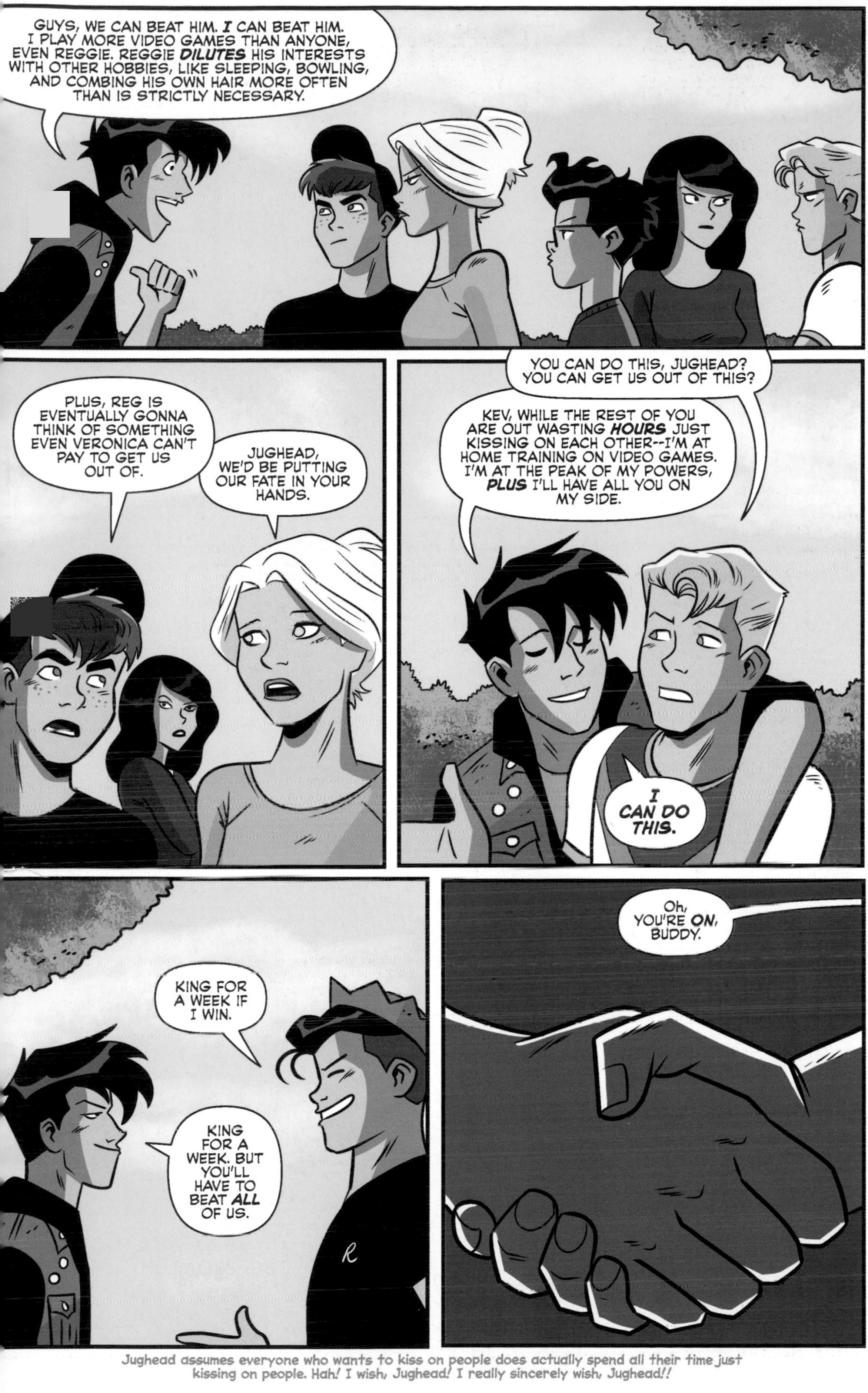
GUYS, WE CAN BEAT HIM. I CAN BEAT HIM. I PLAY MORE VIDEO GAMES THAN ANYONE, EVEN REGGIE. REGGIE DILUTES HIS INTERESTS WITH OTHER HOBBIES, LIKE SLEEPING, BOWLING, AND COMBING HIS OWN HAIR MORE OFTEN THAN IS STRICTLY NECESSARY.
PLUS, REG IS EVENTUALLY GONNA THINK OF SOMETHING EVEN VERONICA CAN'T PAY TO GET US OUT OF.
JUGHEAD, WE'D BE PUTTING OUR FATE IN YOUR HANDS.
YOU CAN DO THIS, JUGHEAD? YOU CAN GET US OUT OF THIS?
KEV, WHILE THE REST OF YOU ARE OUT WASTING HOURS JUST KISSING ON EACH OTHER--I'M AT HOME TRAINING ON VIDEO GAMES. I'M AT THE PEAK OF MY POWERS, PLUS I'LL HAVE ALL YOU ON MY SIDE.
I CAN DO THIS.
KING FOR A WEEK IF I WIN.
KING FOR A WEEK. BUT YOU'LL HAVE TO BEAT ALL OF US.
Oh, YOU'RE ON, BUDDY.

Jughead assumes everyone who wants to kiss on people does actually spend all their time just kissing on people. Hah! I wish, Jughead! I really sincerely wish, Jughead!!

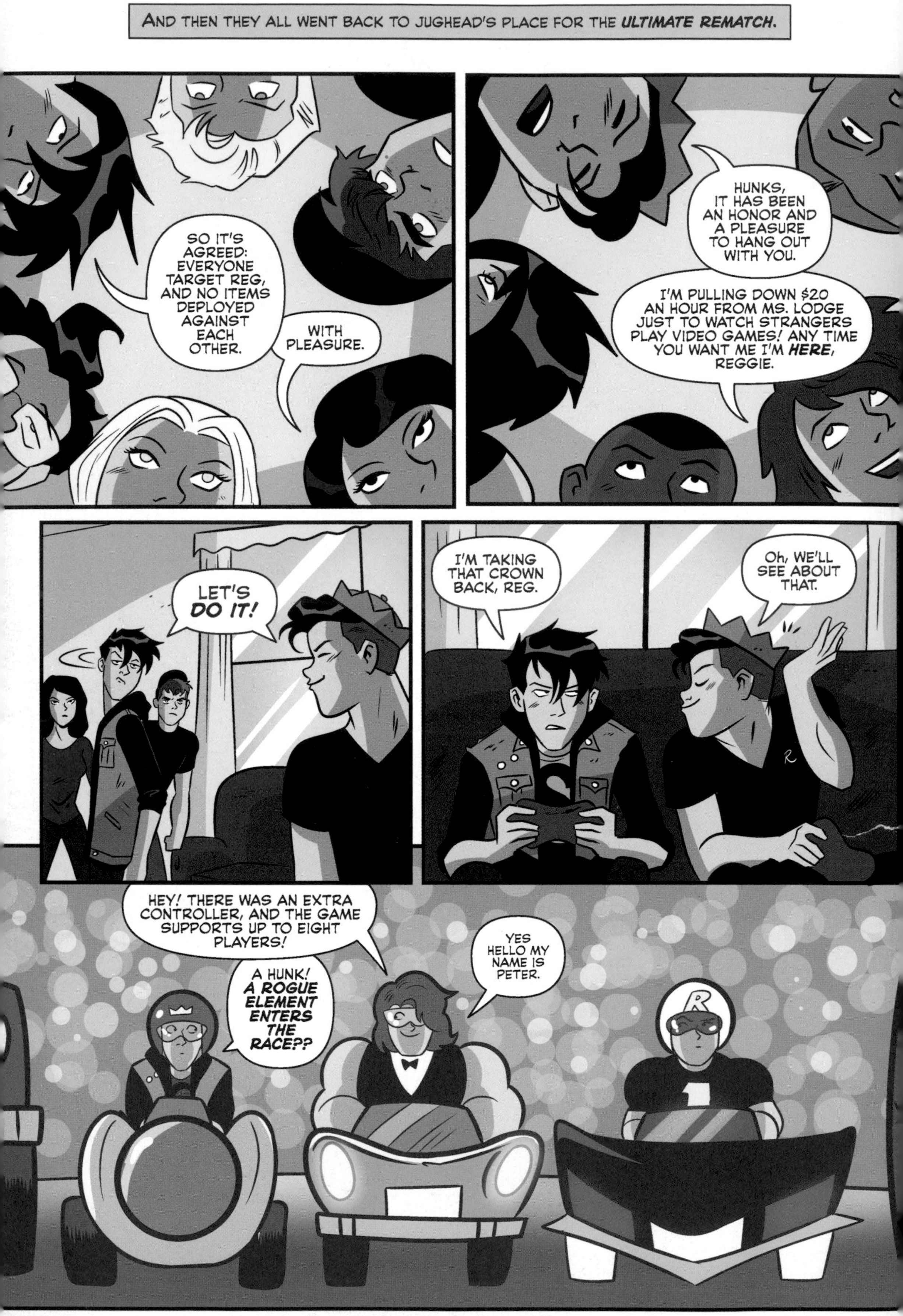
AND THEN THEY ALL WENT BACK TO JUGHEAD'S PLACE FOR THE *ULTIMATE REMATCH.*
SO IT'S AGREED: EVERYONE TARGET REG, AND NO ITEMS DEPLOYED AGAINST EACH OTHER.
WITH PLEASURE.
HUNKS, IT HAS BEEN AN HONOR AND A PLEASURE TO HANG OUT WITH YOU.
I'M PULLING DOWN $20 AN HOUR FROM MS. LODGE JUST TO WATCH STRANGERS PLAY VIDEO GAMES! ANY TIME YOU WANT ME I'M *HERE*, REGGIE.
LET'S *DO IT!*
I'M TAKING THAT CROWN BACK, REG.
Oh, WE'LL SEE ABOUT THAT.
HEY! THERE WAS AN EXTRA CONTROLLER, AND THE GAME SUPPORTS UP TO EIGHT PLAYERS!
A HUNK! *A ROGUE ELEMENT ENTERS THE RACE??*
YES HELLO MY NAME IS PETER.

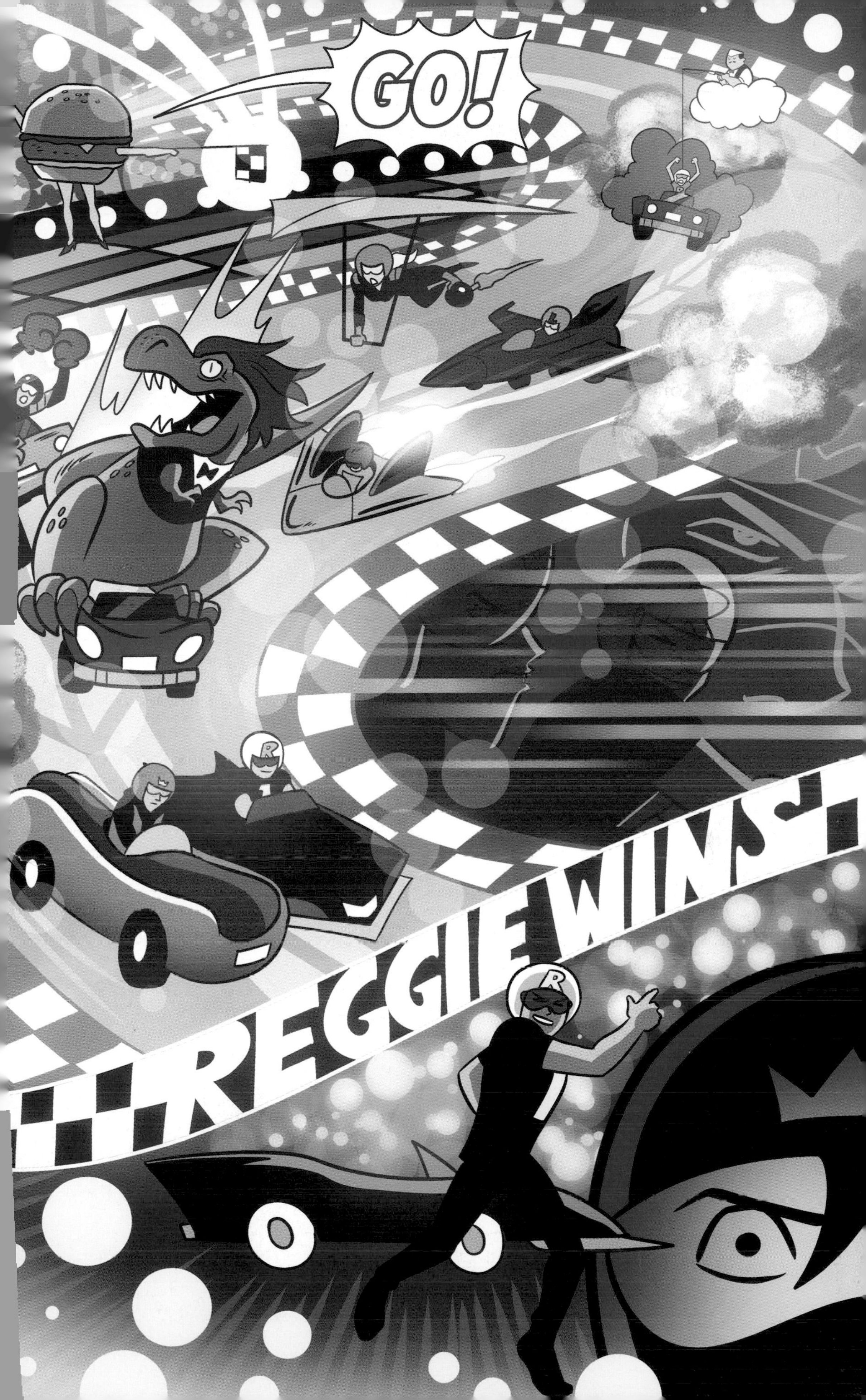
GO!
REGGIE WINS!

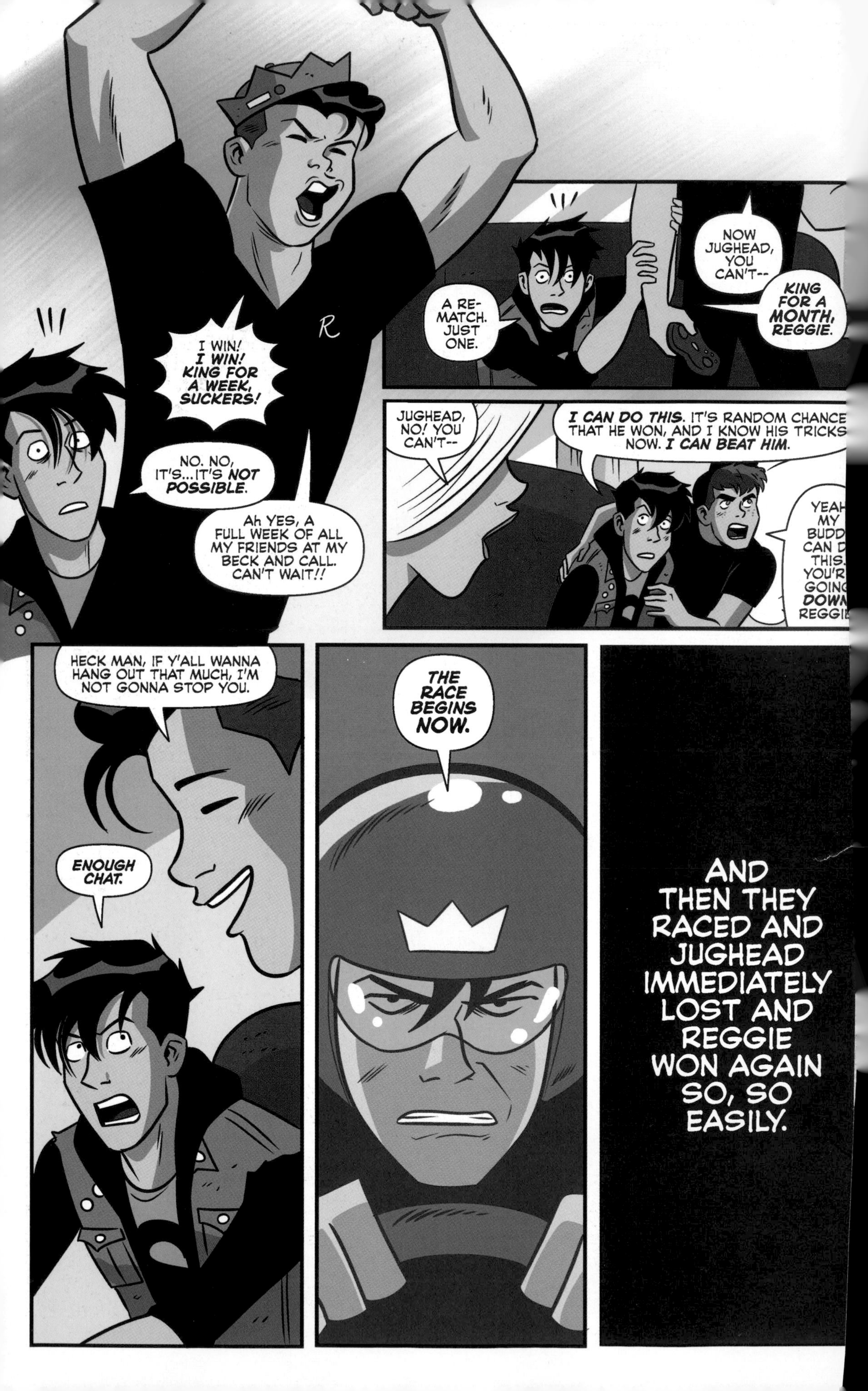
I WIN! I WIN! KING FOR A WEEK, SUCKERS!
NO. NO, IT'S...IT'S NOT POSSIBLE.
Ah YES, A FULL WEEK OF ALL MY FRIENDS AT MY BECK AND CALL. CAN'T WAIT!!
A RE-MATCH. JUST ONE.
NOW JUGHEAD, YOU CAN'T--
KING FOR A MONTH, REGGIE.
JUGHEAD, NO! YOU CAN'T--
I CAN DO THIS. IT'S RANDOM CHANCE THAT HE WON, AND I KNOW HIS TRICKS NOW. I CAN BEAT HIM.
HECK MAN, IF Y'ALL WANNA HANG OUT THAT MUCH, I'M NOT GONNA STOP YOU.
ENOUGH CHAT.
THE RACE BEGINS NOW.
AND THEN THEY RACED AND JUGHEAD IMMEDIATELY LOST AND REGGIE WON AGAIN SO, SO EASILY.

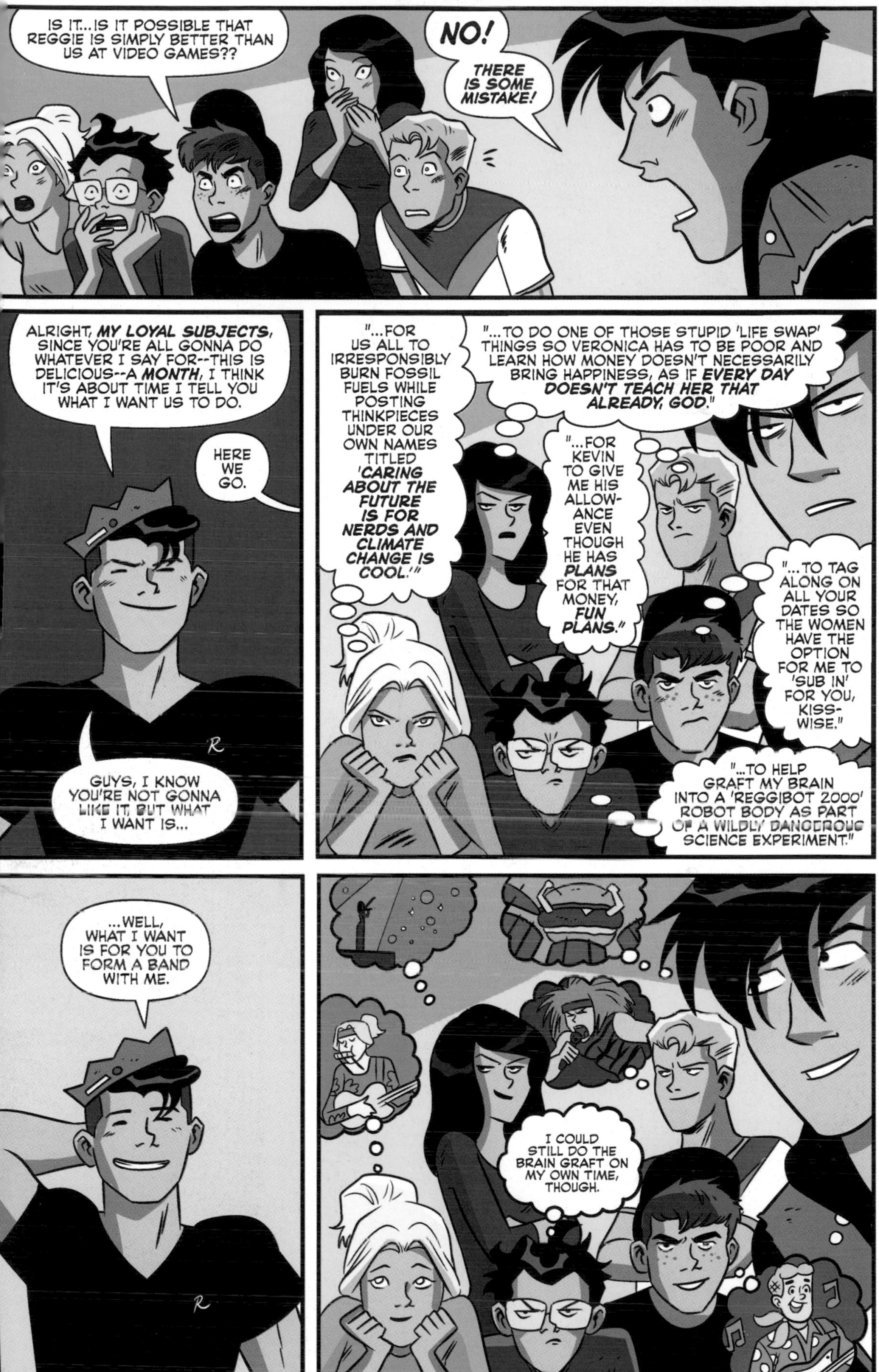
IS IT...IS IT POSSIBLE THAT REGGIE IS SIMPLY BETTER THAN US AT VIDEO GAMES??
NO!
THERE IS SOME MISTAKE!
ALRIGHT, MY LOYAL SUBJECTS, SINCE YOU'RE ALL GONNA DO WHATEVER I SAY FOR--THIS IS DELICIOUS--A MONTH, I THINK IT'S ABOUT TIME I TELL YOU WHAT I WANT US TO DO.
HERE WE GO.
GUYS, I KNOW YOU'RE NOT GONNA LIKE IT, BUT WHAT I WANT IS...
"...FOR US ALL TO IRRESPONSIBLY BURN FOSSIL FUELS WHILE POSTING THINKPIECES UNDER OUR OWN NAMES TITLED 'CARING ABOUT THE FUTURE IS FOR NERDS AND CLIMATE CHANGE IS COOL.'"
"...TO DO ONE OF THOSE STUPID 'LIFE SWAP' THINGS SO VERONICA HAS TO BE POOR AND LEARN HOW MONEY DOESN'T NECESSARILY BRING HAPPINESS, AS IF EVERY DAY DOESN'T TEACH HER THAT ALREADY, GOD."
"...FOR KEVIN TO GIVE ME HIS ALLOW-ANCE EVEN THOUGH HE HAS PLANS FOR THAT MONEY, FUN PLANS."
"...TO TAG ALONG ON ALL YOUR DATES SO THE WOMEN HAVE THE OPTION FOR ME TO 'SUB IN' FOR YOU, KISS-WISE."
"...TO HELP GRAFT MY BRAIN INTO A 'REGGIBOT 2000' ROBOT BODY AS PART OF A WILDLY DANGEROUS SCIENCE EXPERIMENT."
...WELL, WHAT I WANT IS FOR YOU TO FORM A BAND WITH ME.
I COULD STILL DO THE BRAIN GRAFT ON MY OWN TIME, THOUGH.

Veronica your innermost thoughts are getting too real; thank you in advance for having less real innermost thoughts.

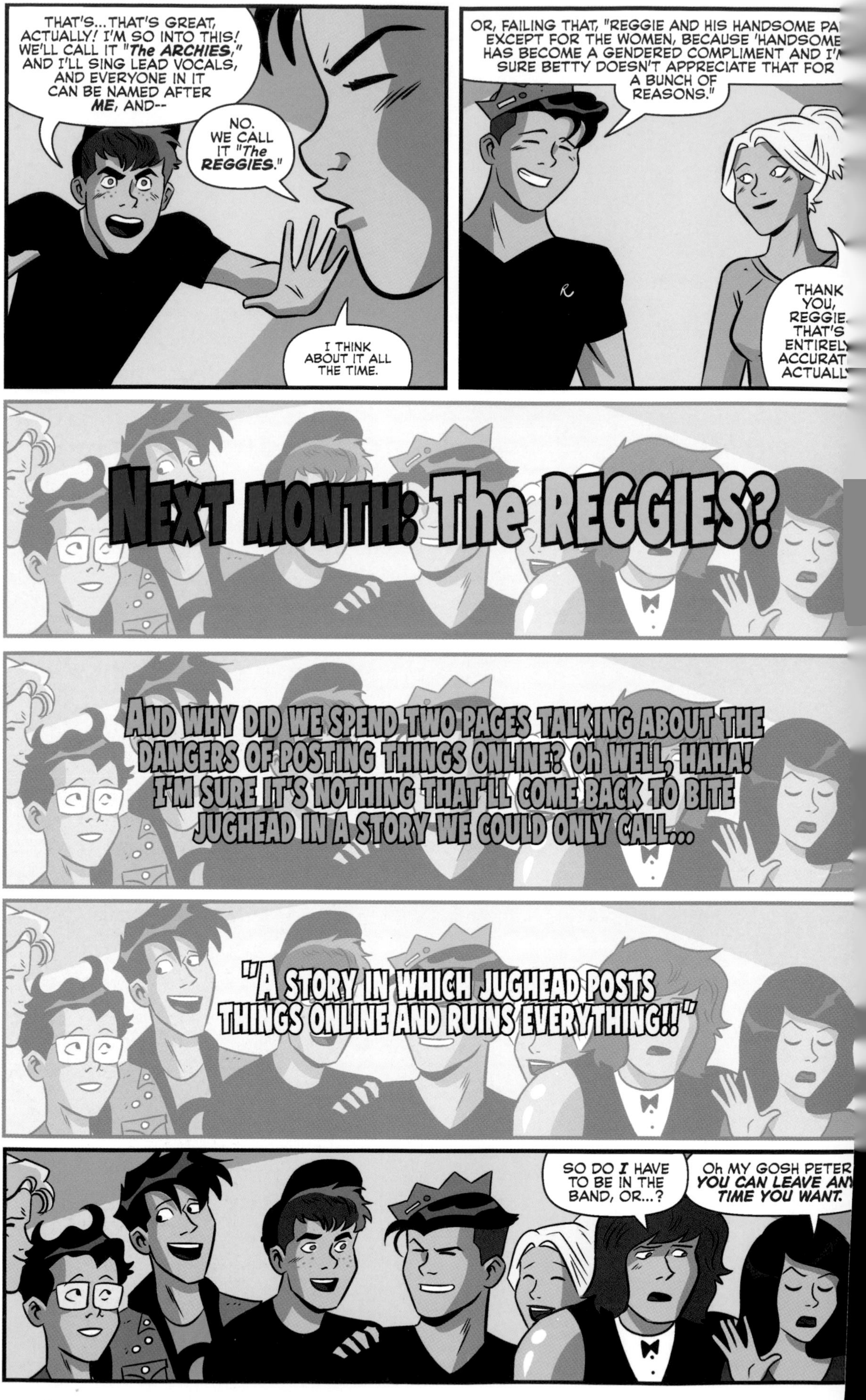
THAT'S...THAT'S GREAT, ACTUALLY! I'M SO INTO THIS! WE'LL CALL IT "The ARCHIES," AND I'LL SING LEAD VOCALS, AND EVERYONE IN IT CAN BE NAMED AFTER ME, AND--
NO. WE CALL IT "The REGGIES."
I THINK ABOUT IT ALL THE TIME.
OR, FAILING THAT, "REGGIE AND HIS HANDSOME PA EXCEPT FOR THE WOMEN, BECAUSE 'HANDSOME HAS BECOME A GENDERED COMPLIMENT AND I'M SURE BETTY DOESN'T APPRECIATE THAT FOR A BUNCH OF REASONS."
THANK YOU, REGGIE. THAT'S ENTIRELY ACCURAT ACTUALLY
NEXT MONTH: The REGGIES?
AND WHY DID WE SPEND TWO PAGES TALKING ABOUT THE DANGERS OF POSTING THINGS ONLINE? Oh WELL, HAHA! I'M SURE IT'S NOTHING THAT'LL COME BACK TO BITE JUGHEAD IN A STORY WE COULD ONLY CALL...
"A STORY IN WHICH JUGHEAD POSTS THINGS ONLINE AND RUINS EVERYTHING!!"
SO DO I HAVE TO BE IN THE BAND, OR...?
Oh MY GOSH PETER YOU CAN LEAVE AN TIME YOU WANT.

TO BE
CONTINUED...

ISSUE THIRTEEN

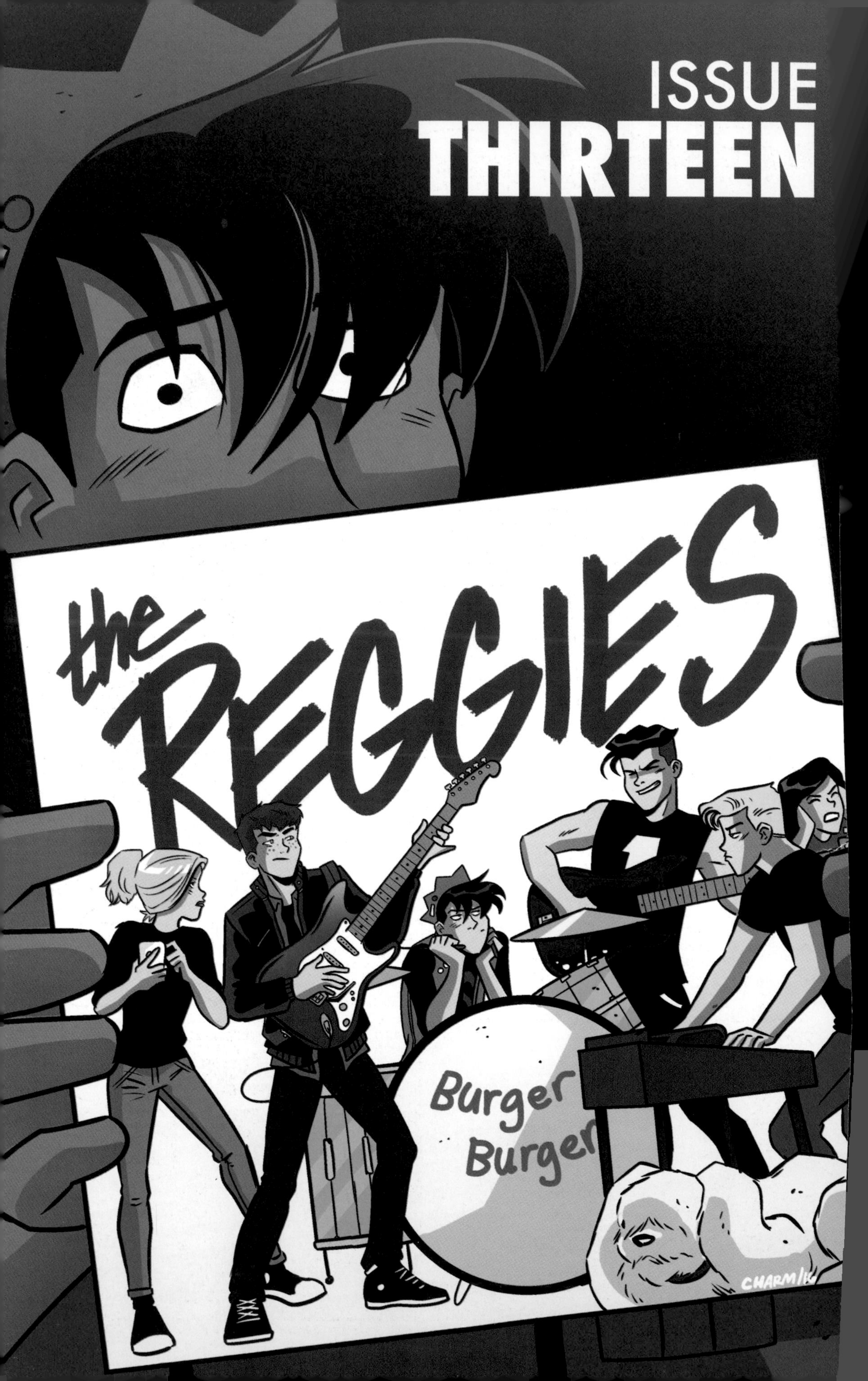
the REGGIES
Burger Burger
CHARM/16

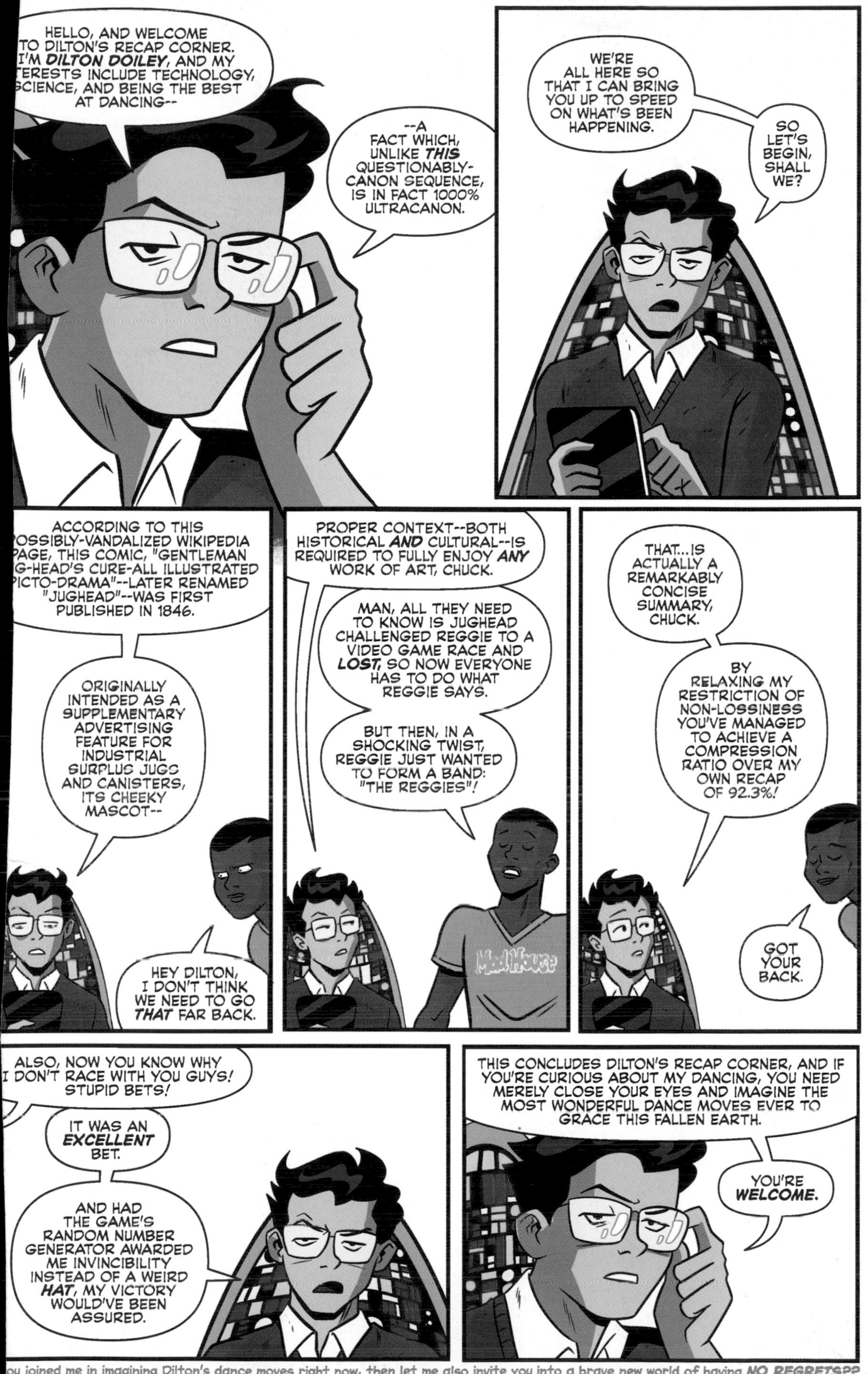
HELLO, AND WELCOME TO DILTON'S RECAP CORNER. I'M DILTON DOILEY, AND MY TERESTS INCLUDE TECHNOLOGY, SCIENCE, AND BEING THE BEST AT DANCING--
--A FACT WHICH, UNLIKE THIS QUESTIONABLY-CANON SEQUENCE, IS IN FACT 1000% ULTRACANON.
WE'RE ALL HERE SO THAT I CAN BRING YOU UP TO SPEED ON WHAT'S BEEN HAPPENING.
SO LET'S BEGIN, SHALL WE?
ACCORDING TO THIS OSSIBLY-VANDALIZED WIKIPEDIA PAGE, THIS COMIC, "GENTLEMAN G-HEAD'S CURE-ALL ILLUSTRATED PICTO-DRAMA"--LATER RENAMED "JUGHEAD"--WAS FIRST PUBLISHED IN 1846.
ORIGINALLY INTENDED AS A SUPPLEMENTARY ADVERTISING FEATURE FOR INDUSTRIAL SURPLUS JUGS AND CANISTERS, ITS CHEEKY MASCOT--
HEY DILTON, I DON'T THINK WE NEED TO GO THAT FAR BACK.
PROPER CONTEXT--BOTH HISTORICAL AND CULTURAL--IS REQUIRED TO FULLY ENJOY ANY WORK OF ART, CHUCK.
MAN, ALL THEY NEED TO KNOW IS JUGHEAD CHALLENGED REGGIE TO A VIDEO GAME RACE AND LOST, SO NOW EVERYONE HAS TO DO WHAT REGGIE SAYS.
BUT THEN, IN A SHOCKING TWIST, REGGIE JUST WANTED TO FORM A BAND: "THE REGGIES"!
THAT...IS ACTUALLY A REMARKABLY CONCISE SUMMARY, CHUCK.
BY RELAXING MY RESTRICTION OF NON-LOSSINESS YOU'VE MANAGED TO ACHIEVE A COMPRESSION RATIO OVER MY OWN RECAP OF 92.3%!
GOT YOUR BACK.
ALSO, NOW YOU KNOW WHY I DON'T RACE WITH YOU GUYS! STUPID BETS!
IT WAS AN EXCELLENT BET.
AND HAD THE GAME'S RANDOM NUMBER GENERATOR AWARDED ME INVINCIBILITY INSTEAD OF A WEIRD HAT, MY VICTORY WOULD'VE BEEN ASSURED.
THIS CONCLUDES DILTON'S RECAP CORNER, AND IF YOU'RE CURIOUS ABOUT MY DANCING, YOU NEED MERELY CLOSE YOUR EYES AND IMAGINE THE MOST WONDERFUL DANCE MOVES EVER TO GRACE THIS FALLEN EARTH.
YOU'RE WELCOME.

ou joined me in imagining Dilton's dance moves right now, then let me also invite you into a brave new world of having **NO REGRETS??**

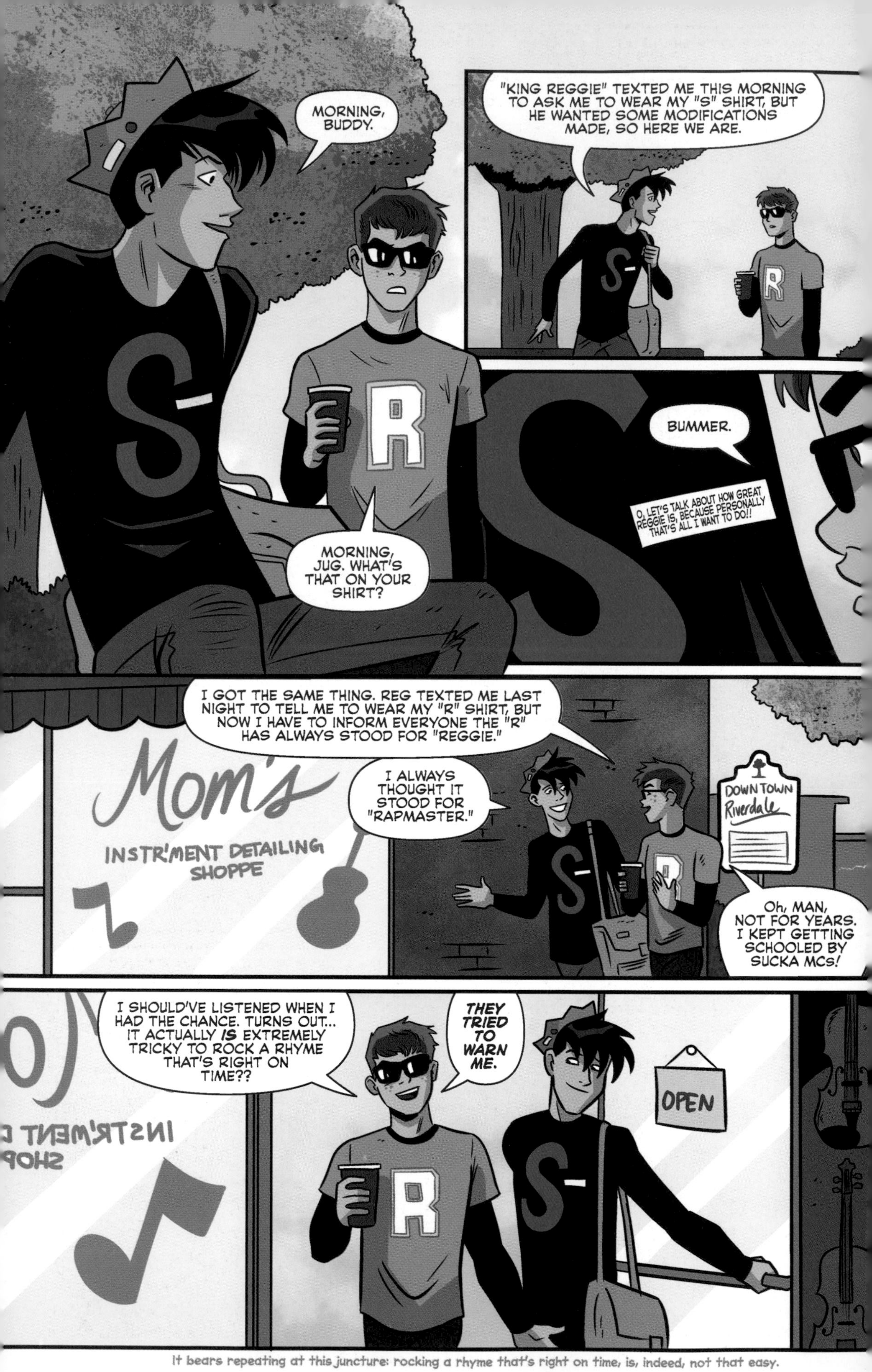
MORNING, BUDDY.
MORNING, JUG. WHAT'S THAT ON YOUR SHIRT?
"KING REGGIE" TEXTED ME THIS MORNING TO ASK ME TO WEAR MY "S" SHIRT, BUT HE WANTED SOME MODIFICATIONS MADE, SO HERE WE ARE.
BUMMER.
O, LET'S TALK ABOUT HOW GREAT REGGIE IS, BECAUSE PERSONALLY THAT'S ALL I WANT TO DO!!
I GOT THE SAME THING. REG TEXTED ME LAST NIGHT TO TELL ME TO WEAR MY "R" SHIRT, BUT NOW I HAVE TO INFORM EVERYONE THE "R" HAS ALWAYS STOOD FOR "REGGIE."
Mom's
INSTR'MENT DETAILING SHOPPE
I ALWAYS THOUGHT IT STOOD FOR "RAPMASTER."
DOWN TOWN Riverdale
Oh, MAN, NOT FOR YEARS. I KEPT GETTING SCHOOLED BY SUCKA MCs!
I SHOULD'VE LISTENED WHEN I HAD THE CHANCE. TURNS OUT... IT ACTUALLY IS EXTREMELY TRICKY TO ROCK A RHYME THAT'S RIGHT ON TIME??
THEY TRIED TO WARN ME.
OPEN

It bears repeating at this juncture: rocking a rhyme that's right on time, is, indeed, not that easy.

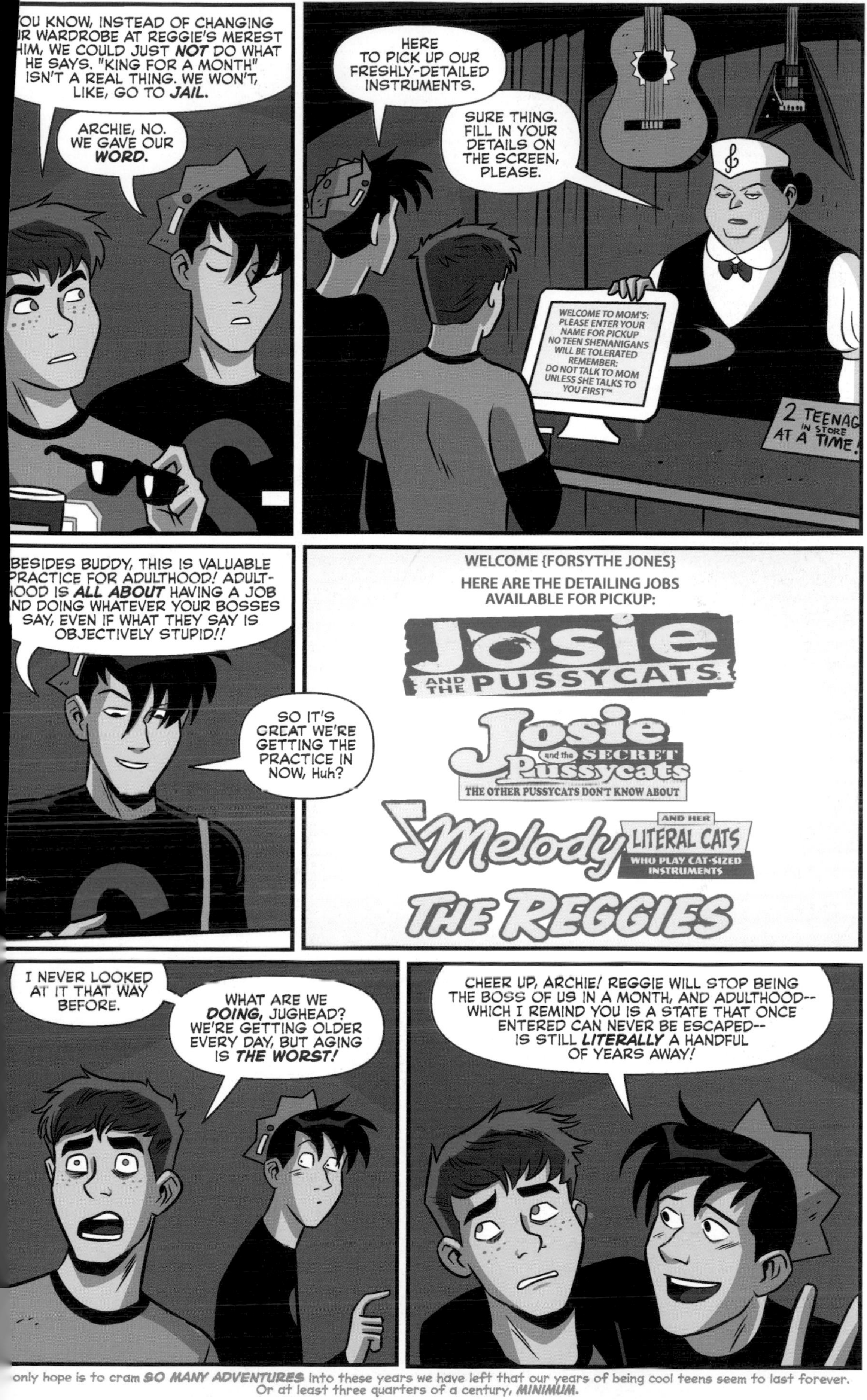
YOU KNOW, INSTEAD OF CHANGING OUR WARDROBE AT REGGIE'S MEREST WHIM, WE COULD JUST NOT DO WHAT HE SAYS. "KING FOR A MONTH" ISN'T A REAL THING. WE WON'T, LIKE, GO TO JAIL.
ARCHIE, NO. WE GAVE OUR WORD.
HERE TO PICK UP OUR FRESHLY-DETAILED INSTRUMENTS.
SURE THING. FILL IN YOUR DETAILS ON THE SCREEN, PLEASE.
WELCOME TO MOM'S: PLEASE ENTER YOUR NAME FOR PICKUP NO TEEN SHENANIGANS WILL BE TOLERATED REMEMBER: DO NOT TALK TO MOM UNLESS SHE TALKS TO YOU FIRST™
2 TEENAG IN STORE AT A TIME!
BESIDES BUDDY, THIS IS VALUABLE PRACTICE FOR ADULTHOOD! ADULTHOOD IS ALL ABOUT HAVING A JOB AND DOING WHATEVER YOUR BOSSES SAY, EVEN IF WHAT THEY SAY IS OBJECTIVELY STUPID!!
SO IT'S GREAT WE'RE GETTING THE PRACTICE IN NOW, Huh?
WELCOME {FORSYTHE JONES}
HERE ARE THE DETAILING JOBS AVAILABLE FOR PICKUP:
JOSIE AND THE PUSSYCATS
Josie and the SECRET Pussycats
THE OTHER PUSSYCATS DON'T KNOW ABOUT
Melody AND HER LITERAL CATS WHO PLAY CAT-SIZED INSTRUMENTS
THE REGGIES
I NEVER LOOKED AT IT THAT WAY BEFORE.
WHAT ARE WE DOING, JUGHEAD? WE'RE GETTING OLDER EVERY DAY, BUT AGING IS THE WORST!
CHEER UP, ARCHIE! REGGIE WILL STOP BEING THE BOSS OF US IN A MONTH, AND ADULTHOOD-- WHICH I REMIND YOU IS A STATE THAT ONCE ENTERED CAN NEVER BE ESCAPED-- IS STILL LITERALLY A HANDFUL OF YEARS AWAY!

only hope is to cram **SO MANY ADVENTURES** into these years we have left that our years of being cool teens seem to last forever. Or at least three quarters of a century, **MINIMUM.**

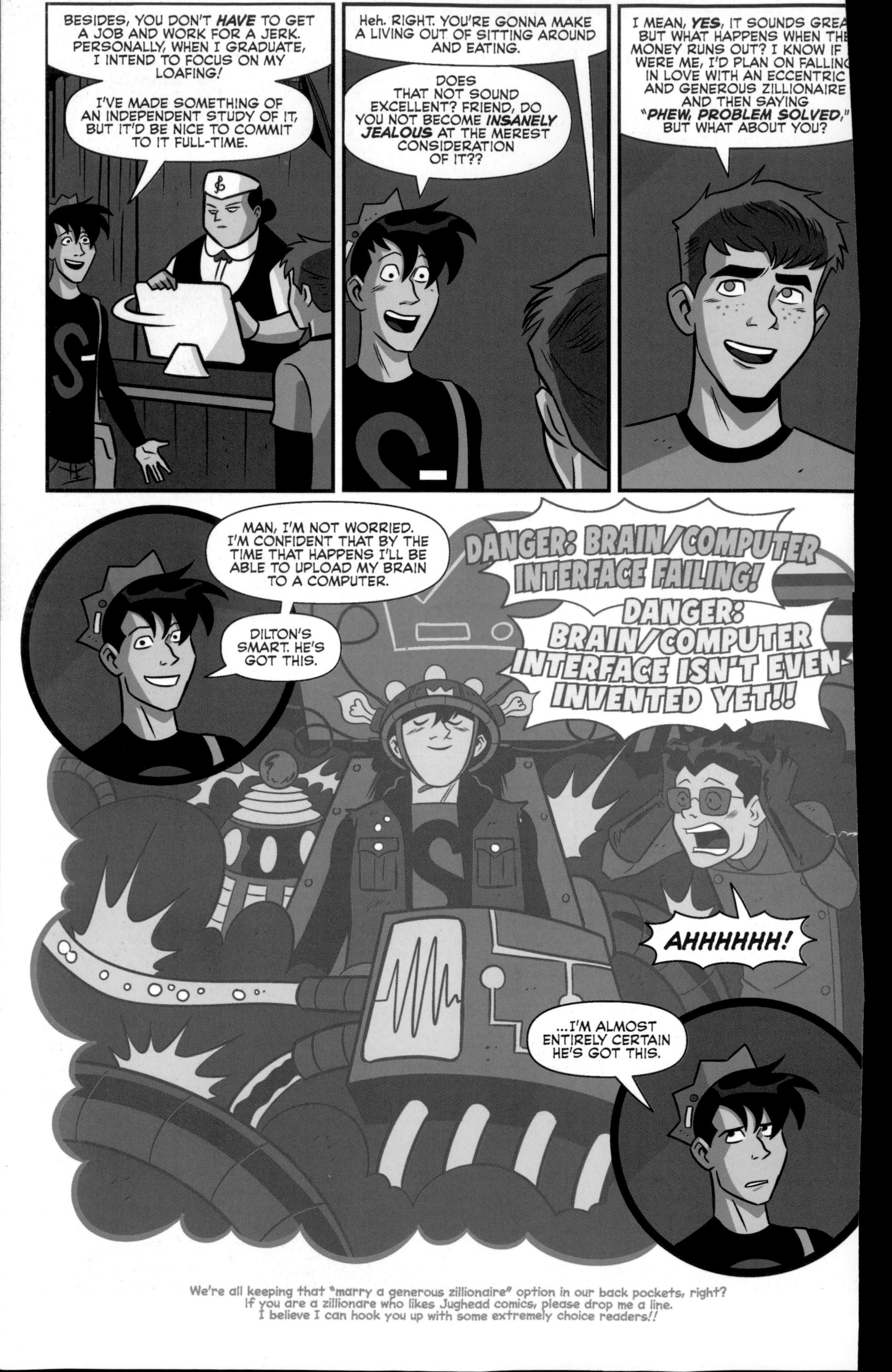
BESIDES, YOU DON'T HAVE TO GET A JOB AND WORK FOR A JERK. PERSONALLY, WHEN I GRADUATE, I INTEND TO FOCUS ON MY LOAFING!
I'VE MADE SOMETHING OF AN INDEPENDENT STUDY OF IT, BUT IT'D BE NICE TO COMMIT TO IT FULL-TIME.
Heh. RIGHT. YOU'RE GONNA MAKE A LIVING OUT OF SITTING AROUND AND EATING.
DOES THAT NOT SOUND EXCELLENT? FRIEND, DO YOU NOT BECOME INSANELY JEALOUS AT THE MEREST CONSIDERATION OF IT??
I MEAN, YES, IT SOUNDS GREA BUT WHAT HAPPENS WHEN THE MONEY RUNS OUT? I KNOW IF WERE ME, I'D PLAN ON FALLING IN LOVE WITH AN ECCENTRIC AND GENEROUS ZILLIONAIRE AND THEN SAYING "PHEW, PROBLEM SOLVED," BUT WHAT ABOUT YOU?
MAN, I'M NOT WORRIED. I'M CONFIDENT THAT BY THE TIME THAT HAPPENS I'LL BE ABLE TO UPLOAD MY BRAIN TO A COMPUTER.
DILTON'S SMART. HE'S GOT THIS.
DANGER: BRAIN/COMPUTER INTERFACE FAILING!
DANGER: BRAIN/COMPUTER INTERFACE ISN'T EVEN INVENTED YET!!
AHHHHHH!
...I'M ALMOST ENTIRELY CERTAIN HE'S GOT THIS.

We're all keeping that "marry a generous zillionaire" option in our back pockets, right?
If you are a zillionare who likes Jughead comics, please drop me a line.
I believe I can hook you up with some extremely choice readers!!

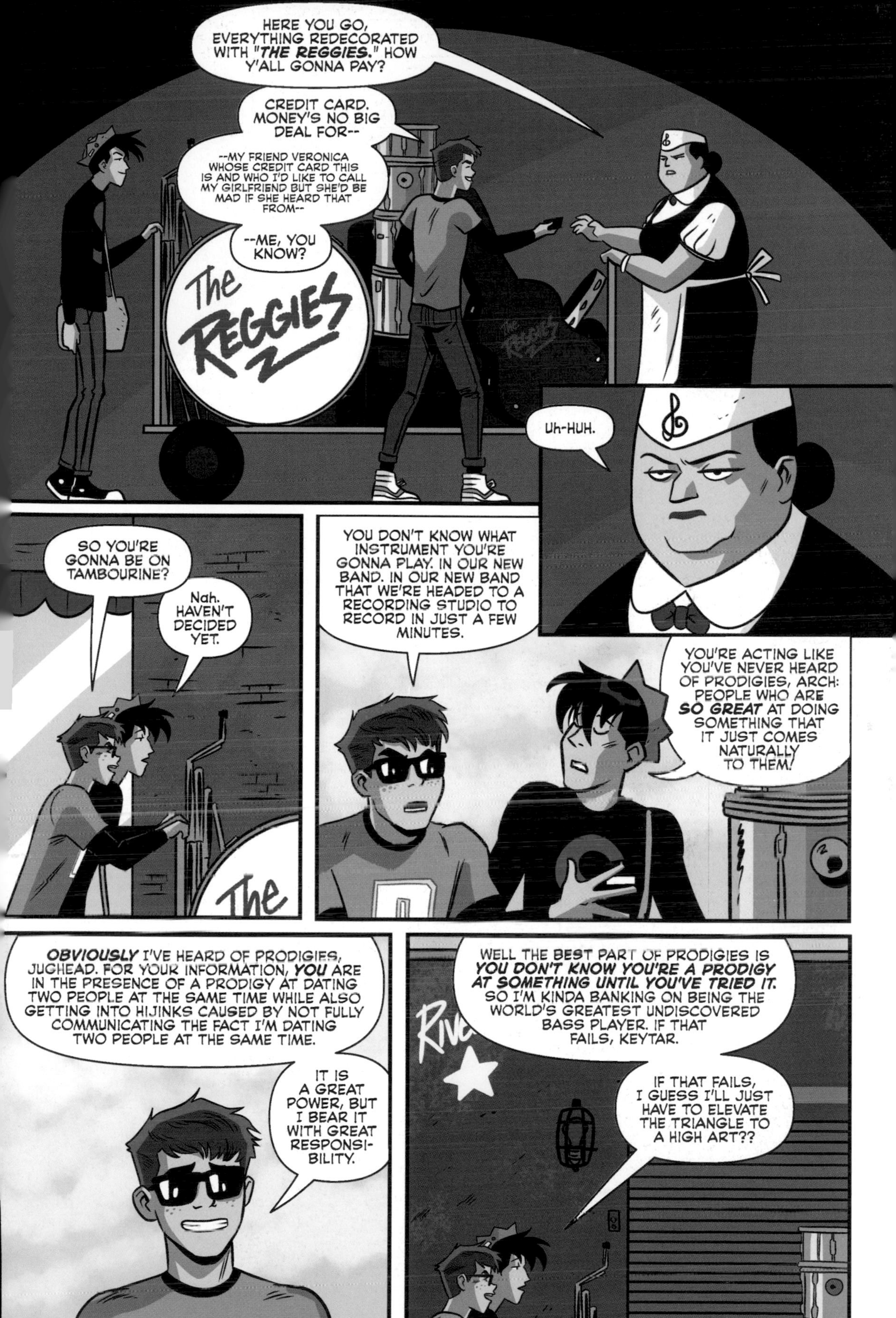
HERE YOU GO, EVERYTHING REDECORATED WITH "THE REGGIES." HOW Y'ALL GONNA PAY?
CREDIT CARD. MONEY'S NO BIG DEAL FOR--
--MY FRIEND VERONICA WHOSE CREDIT CARD THIS IS AND WHO I'D LIKE TO CALL MY GIRLFRIEND BUT SHE'D BE MAD IF SHE HEARD THAT FROM--
--ME, YOU KNOW?
The REGGIES
Uh-HUH.
SO YOU'RE GONNA BE ON TAMBOURINE?
Nah. HAVEN'T DECIDED YET.
YOU DON'T KNOW WHAT INSTRUMENT YOU'RE GONNA PLAY. IN OUR NEW BAND. IN OUR NEW BAND THAT WE'RE HEADED TO A RECORDING STUDIO TO RECORD IN JUST A FEW MINUTES.
YOU'RE ACTING LIKE YOU'VE NEVER HEARD OF PRODIGIES, ARCH: PEOPLE WHO ARE SO GREAT AT DOING SOMETHING THAT IT JUST COMES NATURALLY TO THEM!
OBVIOUSLY I'VE HEARD OF PRODIGIES, JUGHEAD. FOR YOUR INFORMATION, YOU ARE IN THE PRESENCE OF A PRODIGY AT DATING TWO PEOPLE AT THE SAME TIME WHILE ALSO GETTING INTO HIJINKS CAUSED BY NOT FULLY COMMUNICATING THE FACT I'M DATING TWO PEOPLE AT THE SAME TIME.
IT IS A GREAT POWER, BUT I BEAR IT WITH GREAT RESPONSIBILITY.
WELL THE BEST PART OF PRODIGIES IS YOU DON'T KNOW YOU'RE A PRODIGY AT SOMETHING UNTIL YOU'VE TRIED IT. SO I'M KINDA BANKING ON BEING THE WORLD'S GREATEST UNDISCOVERED BASS PLAYER. IF THAT FAILS, KEYTAR.
IF THAT FAILS, I GUESS I'LL JUST HAVE TO ELEVATE THE TRIANGLE TO A HIGH ART??

Credit card companies actually don't like it when you loan out your cards to a friend. Sorry, credit card companies! Sorry for making breaking your precious "rules" look extremely cool!!

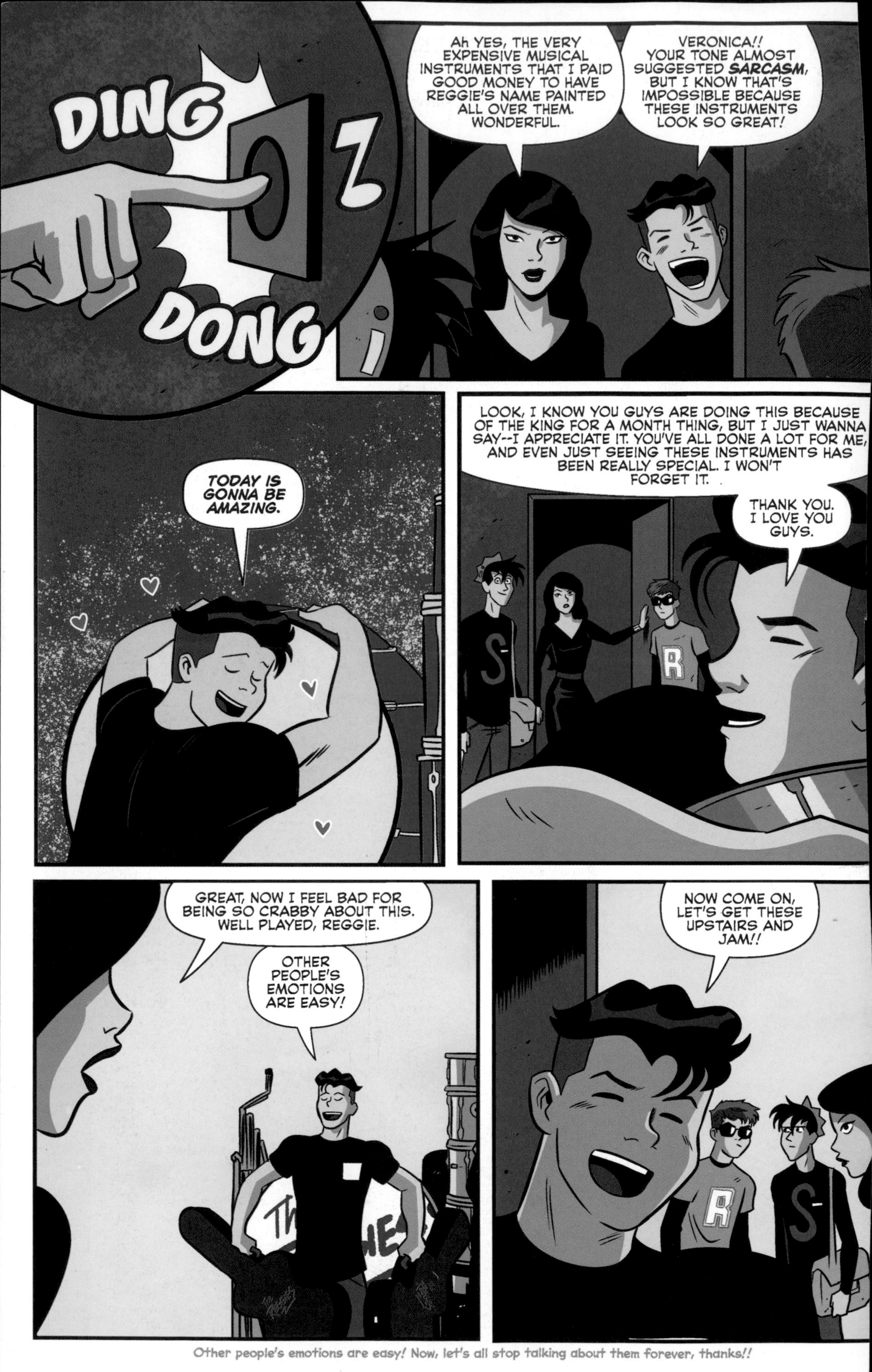
DING
DONG
Ah YES, THE VERY EXPENSIVE MUSICAL INSTRUMENTS THAT I PAID GOOD MONEY TO HAVE REGGIE'S NAME PAINTED ALL OVER THEM. WONDERFUL.
VERONICA!! YOUR TONE ALMOST SUGGESTED SARCASM, BUT I KNOW THAT'S IMPOSSIBLE BECAUSE THESE INSTRUMENTS LOOK SO GREAT!
TODAY IS GONNA BE AMAZING.
LOOK, I KNOW YOU GUYS ARE DOING THIS BECAUSE OF THE KING FOR A MONTH THING, BUT I JUST WANNA SAY--I APPRECIATE IT. YOU'VE ALL DONE A LOT FOR ME, AND EVEN JUST SEEING THESE INSTRUMENTS HAS BEEN REALLY SPECIAL. I WON'T FORGET IT.
THANK YOU. I LOVE YOU GUYS.
GREAT, NOW I FEEL BAD FOR BEING SO CRABBY ABOUT THIS. WELL PLAYED, REGGIE.
OTHER PEOPLE'S EMOTIONS ARE EASY!
NOW COME ON, LET'S GET THESE UPSTAIRS AND JAM!!

Other people's emotions are easy! Now, let's all stop talking about them forever, thanks!!

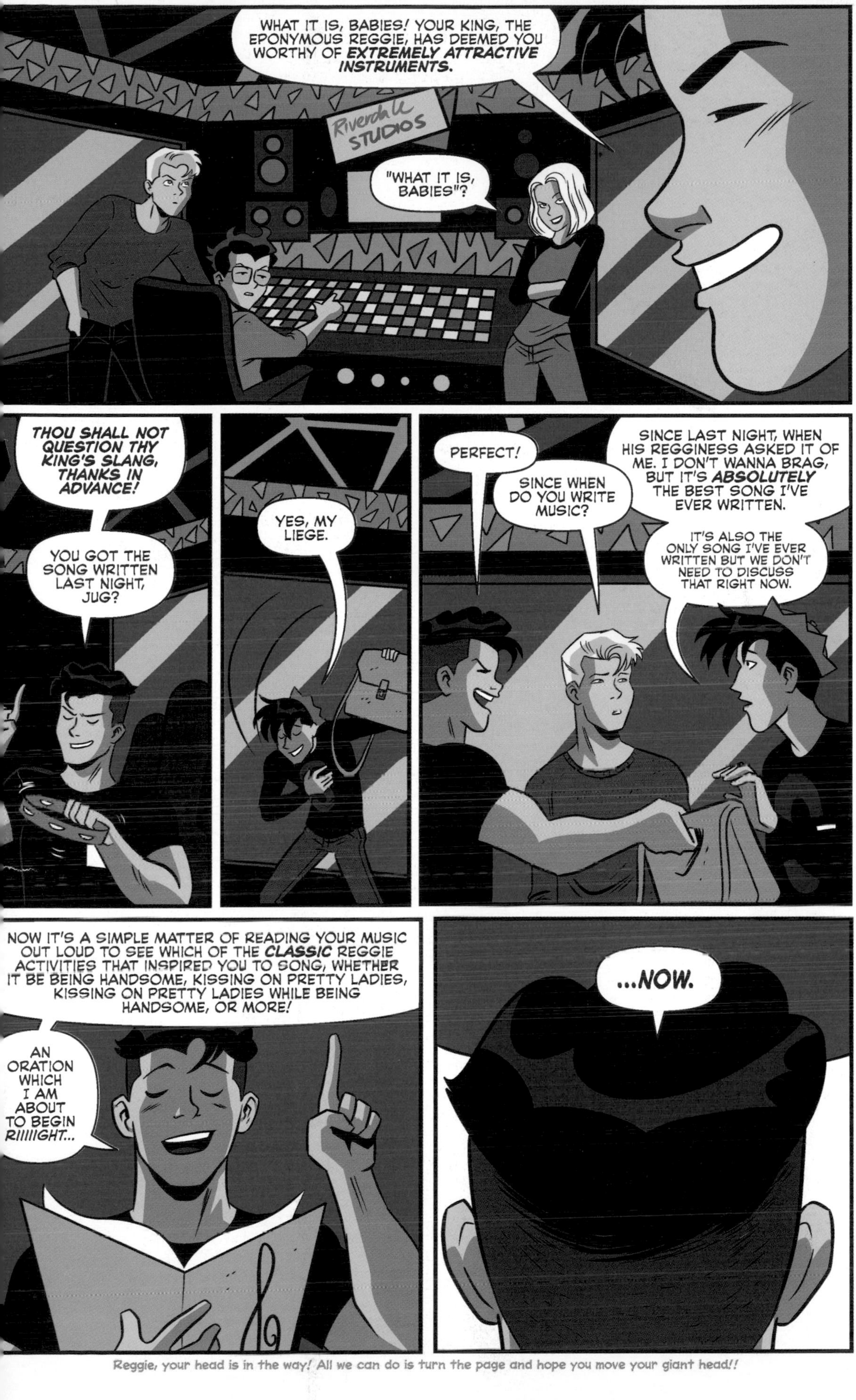
WHAT IT IS, BABIES! YOUR KING, THE EPONYMOUS REGGIE, HAS DEEMED YOU WORTHY OF EXTREMELY ATTRACTIVE INSTRUMENTS.
Riverdale STUDIOS
"WHAT IT IS, BABIES"?
THOU SHALL NOT QUESTION THY KING'S SLANG, THANKS IN ADVANCE!
YOU GOT THE SONG WRITTEN LAST NIGHT, JUG?
YES, MY LIEGE.
PERFECT!
SINCE WHEN DO YOU WRITE MUSIC?
SINCE LAST NIGHT, WHEN HIS REGGINESS ASKED IT OF ME. I DON'T WANNA BRAG, BUT IT'S ABSOLUTELY THE BEST SONG I'VE EVER WRITTEN.
IT'S ALSO THE ONLY SONG I'VE EVER WRITTEN BUT WE DON'T NEED TO DISCUSS THAT RIGHT NOW.
NOW IT'S A SIMPLE MATTER OF READING YOUR MUSIC OUT LOUD TO SEE WHICH OF THE CLASSIC REGGIE ACTIVITIES THAT INSPIRED YOU TO SONG, WHETHER IT BE BEING HANDSOME, KISSING ON PRETTY LADIES, KISSING ON PRETTY LADIES WHILE BEING HANDSOME, OR MORE!
AN ORATION WHICH I AM ABOUT TO BEGIN RIIIIIGHT...
...NOW.

Reggie, your head is in the way! All we can do is turn the page and hope you move your giant head!!

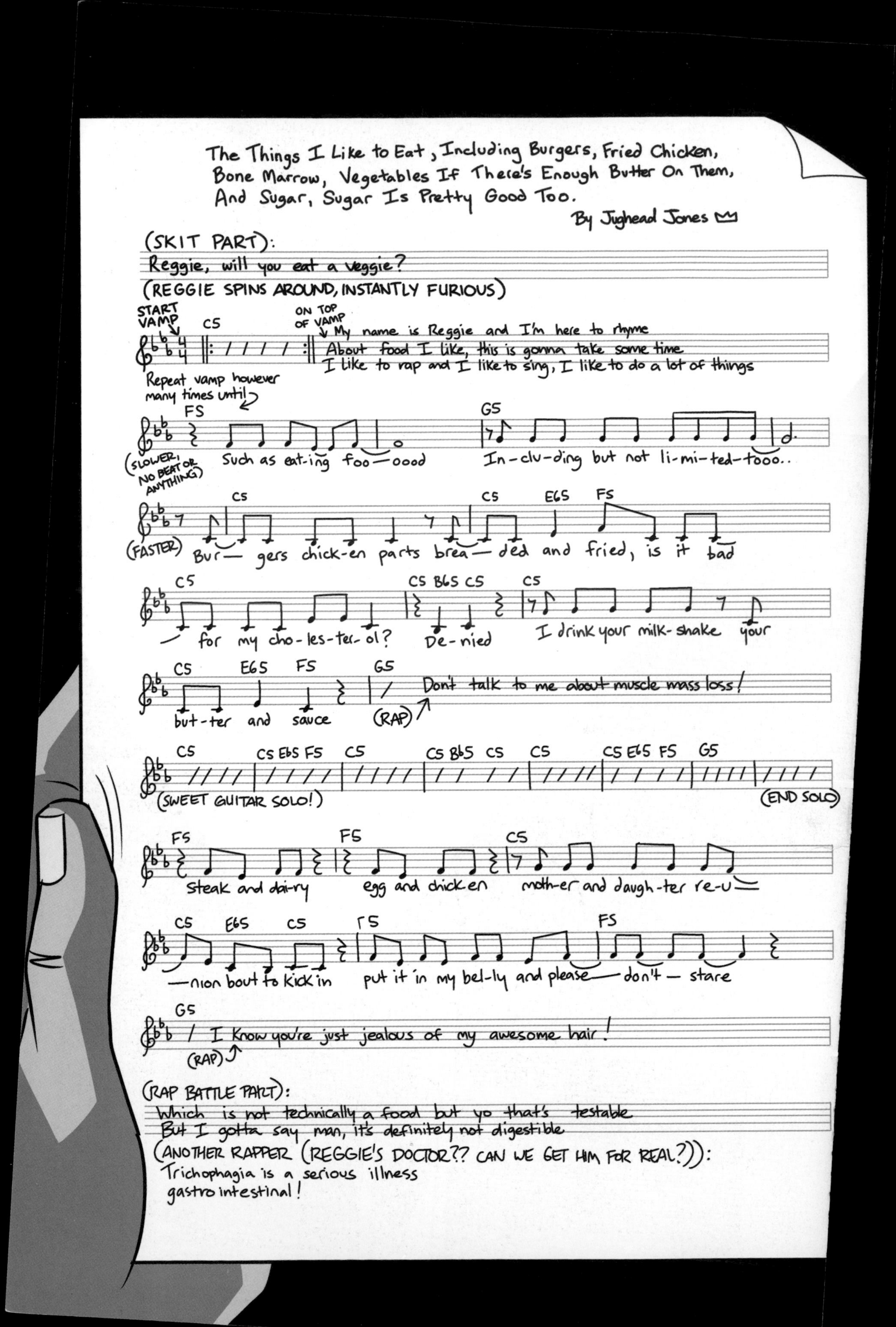

The Things I Like to Eat, Including Burgers, Fried Chicken, Bone Marrow, Vegetables If There's Enough Butter On Them, And Sugar, Sugar Is Pretty Good Too.
By Jughead Jones
(SKIT PART):
Reggie, will you eat a veggie?
(REGGIE SPINS AROUND, INSTANTLY FURIOUS)
START VAMP
C5
ON TOP OF VAMP
My name is Reggie and I'm here to rhyme
About food I like, this is gonna take some time
I like to rap and I like to sing, I like to do a lot of things
Repeat vamp however many times until
F5
G5
(SLOWER, NO BEAT OR ANYTHING)
Such as eat-ing foo—oood
In-clu-ding but not li-mi-ted-tooo..
C5
C5
Eb5
F5
(FASTER)
Bur— gers chick-en parts brea—ded and fried, is it bad
C5
C5 Bb5 C5
C5
— for my cho-les-ter-ol? De-nied
I drink your milk-shake your
C5
Eb5
F5
G5
but-ter and sauce
(RAP)
Don't talk to me about muscle mass loss!
C5
C5 Eb5 F5
C5
C5 Bb5 C5
C5
C5 Eb5 F5
G5
(SWEET GUITAR SOLO!)
(END SOLO)
F5
F5
C5
steak and dai-ry
egg and chick-en
moth-er and daugh-ter re-u—
C5
Eb5
C5
F5
F5
—nion bout to kick in
put it in my bel-ly and please— don't — stare
G5
I Know you're just jealous of my awesome hair!
(RAP)
(RAP BATTLE PART):
Which is not technically a food but yo that's testable
But I gotta say man, it's definitely not digestible
(ANOTHER RAPPER (REGGIE'S DOCTOR?? CAN WE GET HIM FOR REAL?)):
Trichophagia is a serious illness
gastro intestinal!

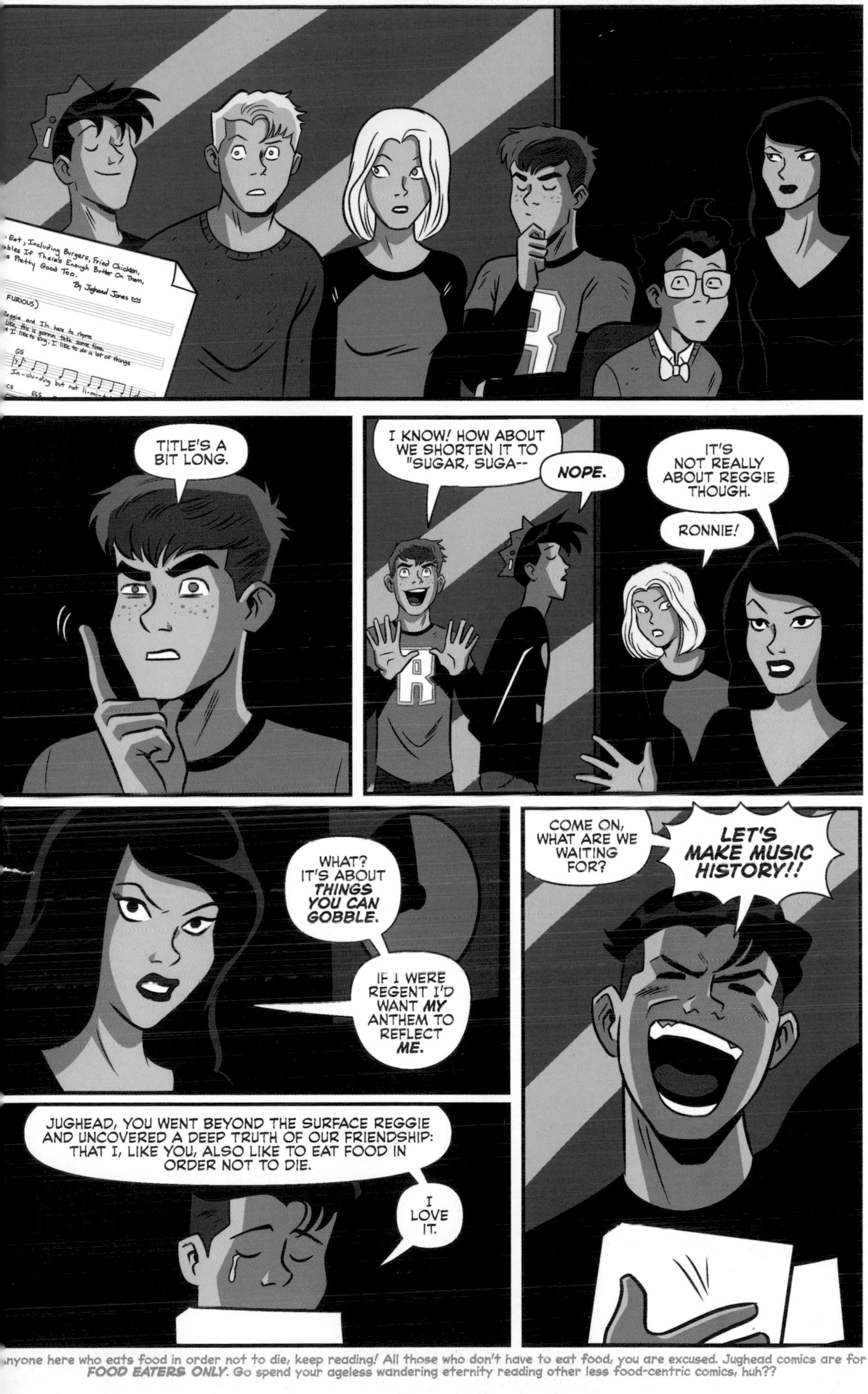
Eat, Including Burgers, Fried Chicken,
If There's Enough Butter On Them,
Pretty Good Too.
By Jughead Jones
FURIOUS)
and I'm here to rhyme
this is gonna take some time
I like to sing, I like to do a lot of things
In-clu-ding but not
TITLE'S A BIT LONG.
I KNOW! HOW ABOUT WE SHORTEN IT TO "SUGAR, SUGA--
NOPE.
IT'S NOT REALLY ABOUT REGGIE THOUGH.
RONNIE!
WHAT? IT'S ABOUT THINGS YOU CAN GOBBLE.
IF I WERE REGENT I'D WANT MY ANTHEM TO REFLECT ME.
JUGHEAD, YOU WENT BEYOND THE SURFACE REGGIE AND UNCOVERED A DEEP TRUTH OF OUR FRIENDSHIP: THAT I, LIKE YOU, ALSO LIKE TO EAT FOOD IN ORDER NOT TO DIE.
I LOVE IT.
COME ON, WHAT ARE WE WAITING FOR?
LET'S MAKE MUSIC HISTORY!!

nyone here who eats food in order not to die, keep reading! All those who don't have to eat food, you are excused. Jughead comics are for **FOOD EATERS ONLY**. Go spend your ageless wandering eternity reading other less food-centric comics, huh??

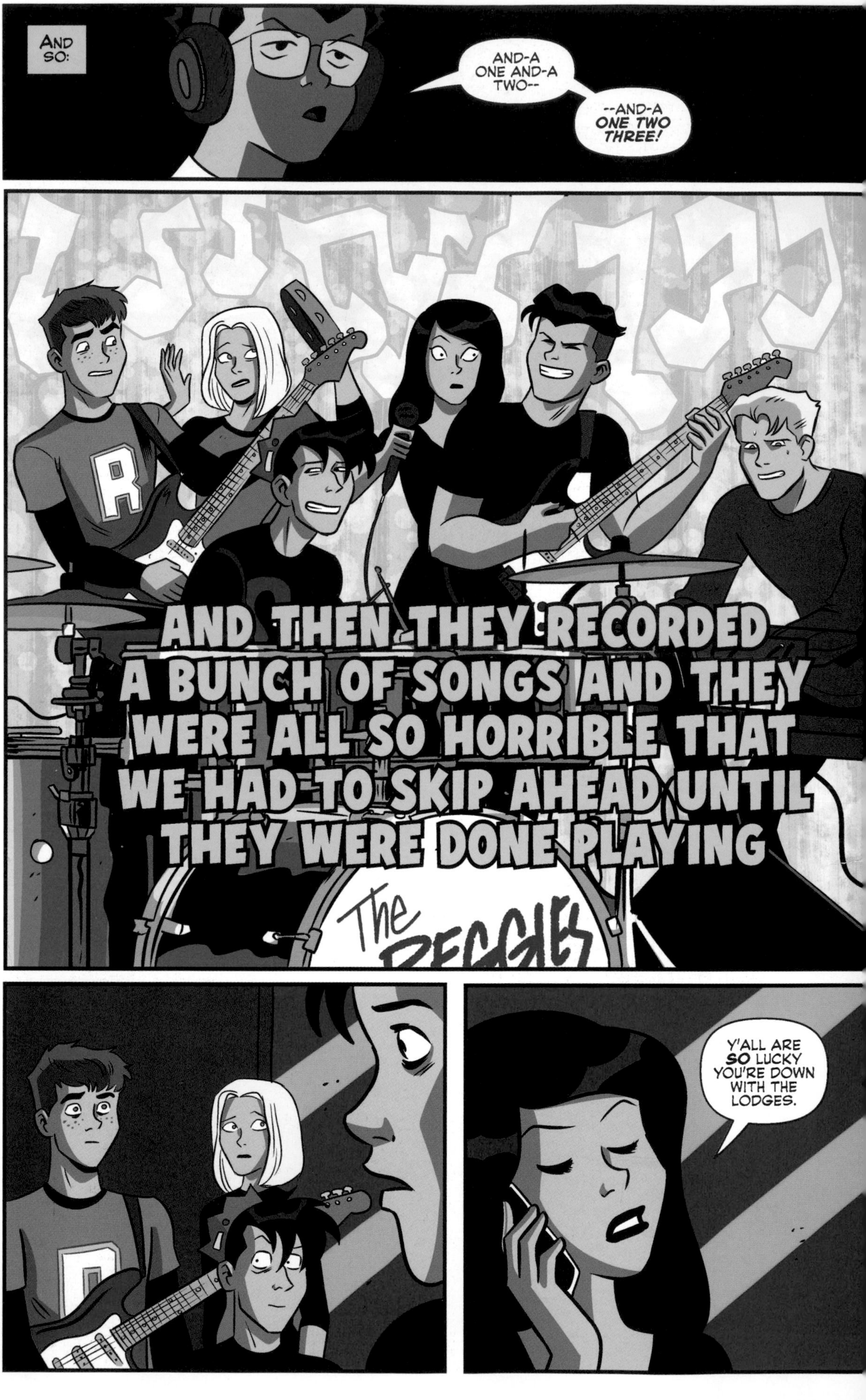
AND SO:
AND-A ONE AND-A TWO--
--AND-A ONE TWO THREE!
AND THEN THEY RECORDED A BUNCH OF SONGS AND THEY WERE ALL SO HORRIBLE THAT WE HAD TO SKIP AHEAD UNTIL THEY WERE DONE PLAYING
The REGGIES
Y'ALL ARE SO LUCKY YOU'RE DOWN WITH THE LODGES.

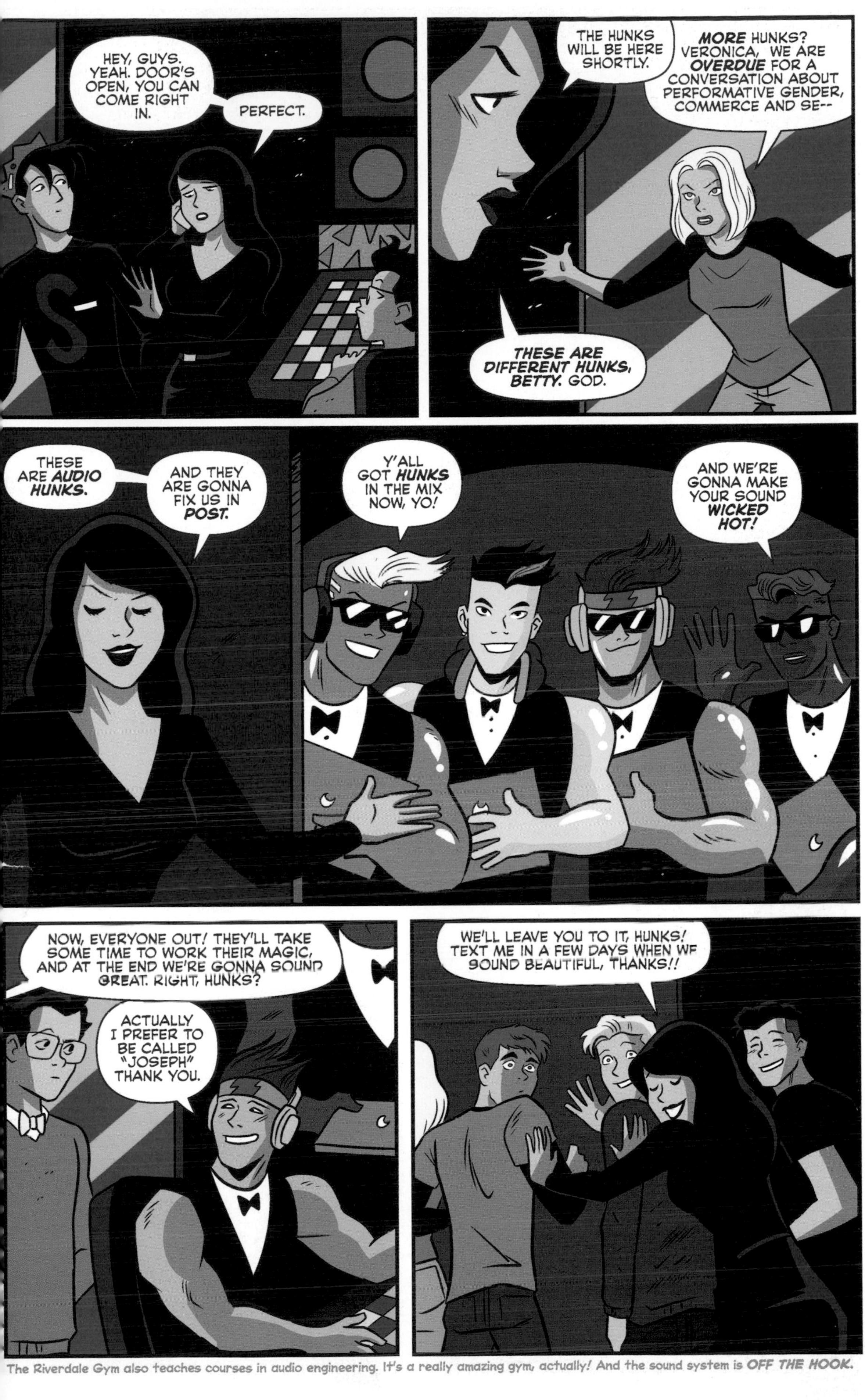
HEY, GUYS. YEAH. DOOR'S OPEN, YOU CAN COME RIGHT IN.
PERFECT.
THE HUNKS WILL BE HERE SHORTLY.
MORE HUNKS? VERONICA, WE ARE OVERDUE FOR A CONVERSATION ABOUT PERFORMATIVE GENDER, COMMERCE AND SE--
THESE ARE DIFFERENT HUNKS, BETTY. GOD.
THESE ARE AUDIO HUNKS.
AND THEY ARE GONNA FIX US IN POST.
Y'ALL GOT HUNKS IN THE MIX NOW, YO!
AND WE'RE GONNA MAKE YOUR SOUND WICKED HOT!
NOW, EVERYONE OUT! THEY'LL TAKE SOME TIME TO WORK THEIR MAGIC, AND AT THE END WE'RE GONNA SOUND GREAT. RIGHT, HUNKS?
ACTUALLY I PREFER TO BE CALLED "JOSEPH" THANK YOU.
WE'LL LEAVE YOU TO IT, HUNKS! TEXT ME IN A FEW DAYS WHEN WE SOUND BEAUTIFUL, THANKS!!

The Riverdale Gym also teaches courses in audio engineering. It's a really amazing gym, actually! And the sound system is ***OFF THE HOOK.***

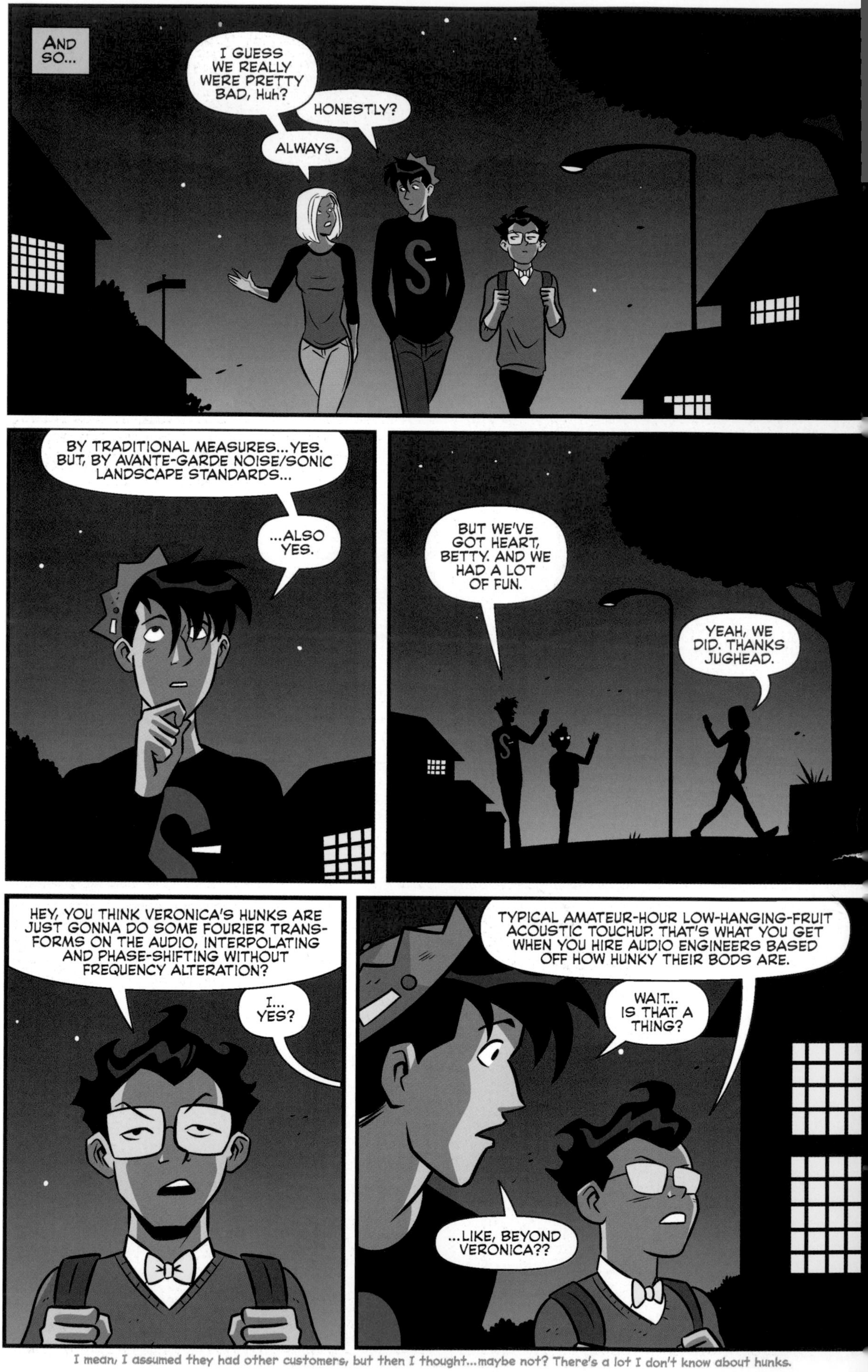
AND SO...
I GUESS WE REALLY WERE PRETTY BAD, Huh?
HONESTLY?
ALWAYS.
BY TRADITIONAL MEASURES...YES. BUT, BY AVANTE-GARDE NOISE/SONIC LANDSCAPE STANDARDS...
...ALSO YES.
BUT WE'VE GOT HEART, BETTY. AND WE HAD A LOT OF FUN.
YEAH, WE DID. THANKS JUGHEAD.
HEY, YOU THINK VERONICA'S HUNKS ARE JUST GONNA DO SOME FOURIER TRANSFORMS ON THE AUDIO, INTERPOLATING AND PHASE-SHIFTING WITHOUT FREQUENCY ALTERATION?
I... YES?
TYPICAL AMATEUR-HOUR LOW-HANGING-FRUIT ACOUSTIC TOUCHUP. THAT'S WHAT YOU GET WHEN YOU HIRE AUDIO ENGINEERS BASED OFF HOW HUNKY THEIR BODS ARE.
WAIT... IS THAT A THING?
...LIKE, BEYOND VERONICA??

I mean, I assumed they had other customers, but then I thought...maybe not? There's a lot I don't know about hunks.

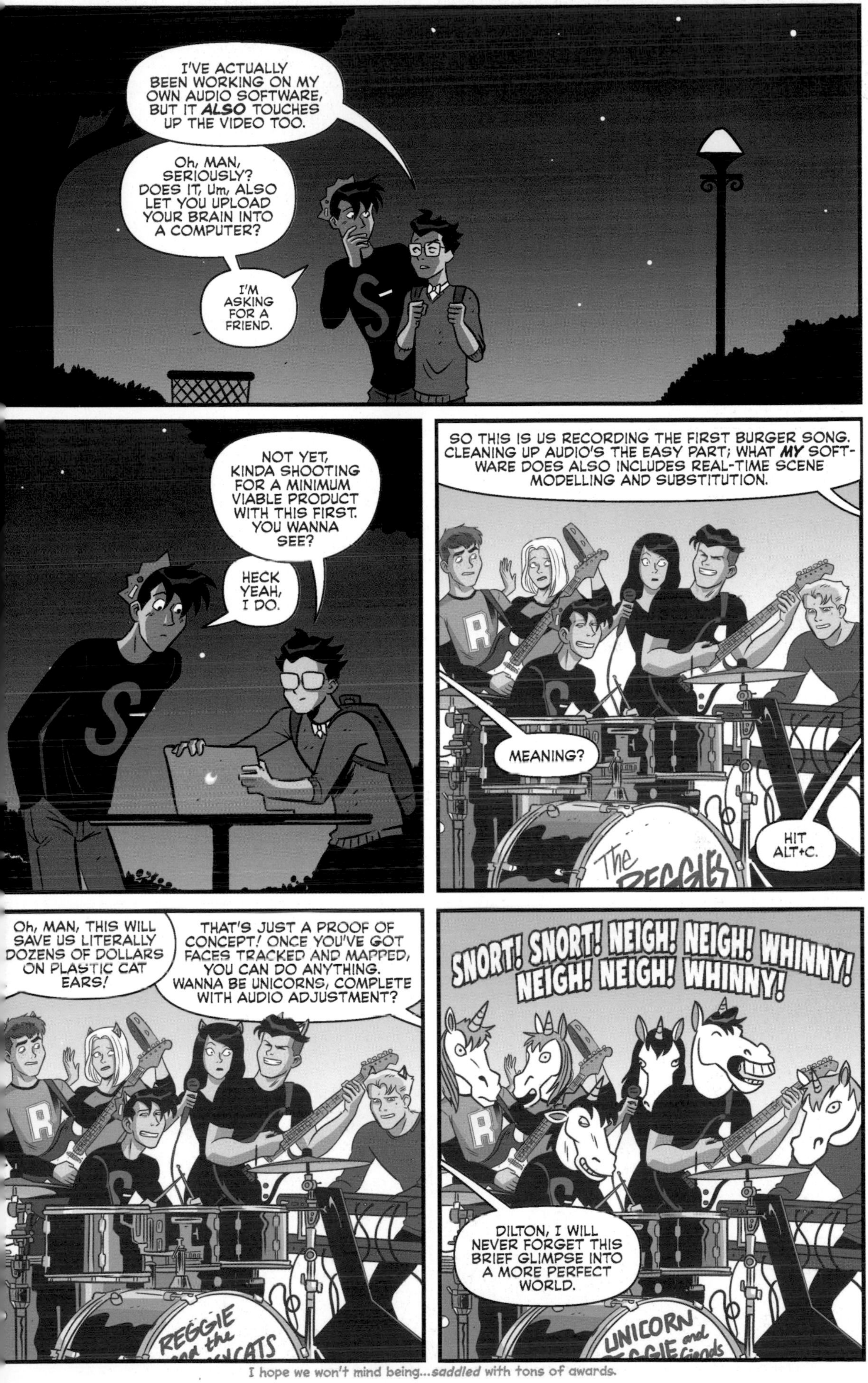
I'VE ACTUALLY BEEN WORKING ON MY OWN AUDIO SOFTWARE, BUT IT *ALSO* TOUCHES UP THE VIDEO TOO.
Oh, MAN, SERIOUSLY? DOES IT, Um, ALSO LET YOU UPLOAD YOUR BRAIN INTO A COMPUTER?
I'M ASKING FOR A FRIEND.
NOT YET, KINDA SHOOTING FOR A MINIMUM VIABLE PRODUCT WITH THIS FIRST. YOU WANNA SEE?
HECK YEAH, I DO.
SO THIS IS US RECORDING THE FIRST BURGER SONG. CLEANING UP AUDIO'S THE EASY PART; WHAT *MY* SOFTWARE DOES ALSO INCLUDES REAL-TIME SCENE MODELLING AND SUBSTITUTION.
MEANING?
HIT ALT+C.
Oh, MAN, THIS WILL SAVE US LITERALLY DOZENS OF DOLLARS ON PLASTIC CAT EARS!
THAT'S JUST A PROOF OF CONCEPT! ONCE YOU'VE GOT FACES TRACKED AND MAPPED, YOU CAN DO ANYTHING. WANNA BE UNICORNS, COMPLETE WITH AUDIO ADJUSTMENT?
SNORT! SNORT! NEIGH! NEIGH! WHINNY! NEIGH! NEIGH! WHINNY!
DILTON, I WILL NEVER FORGET THIS BRIEF GLIMPSE INTO A MORE PERFECT WORLD.

I hope we won't mind being...*saddled* with tons of awards.

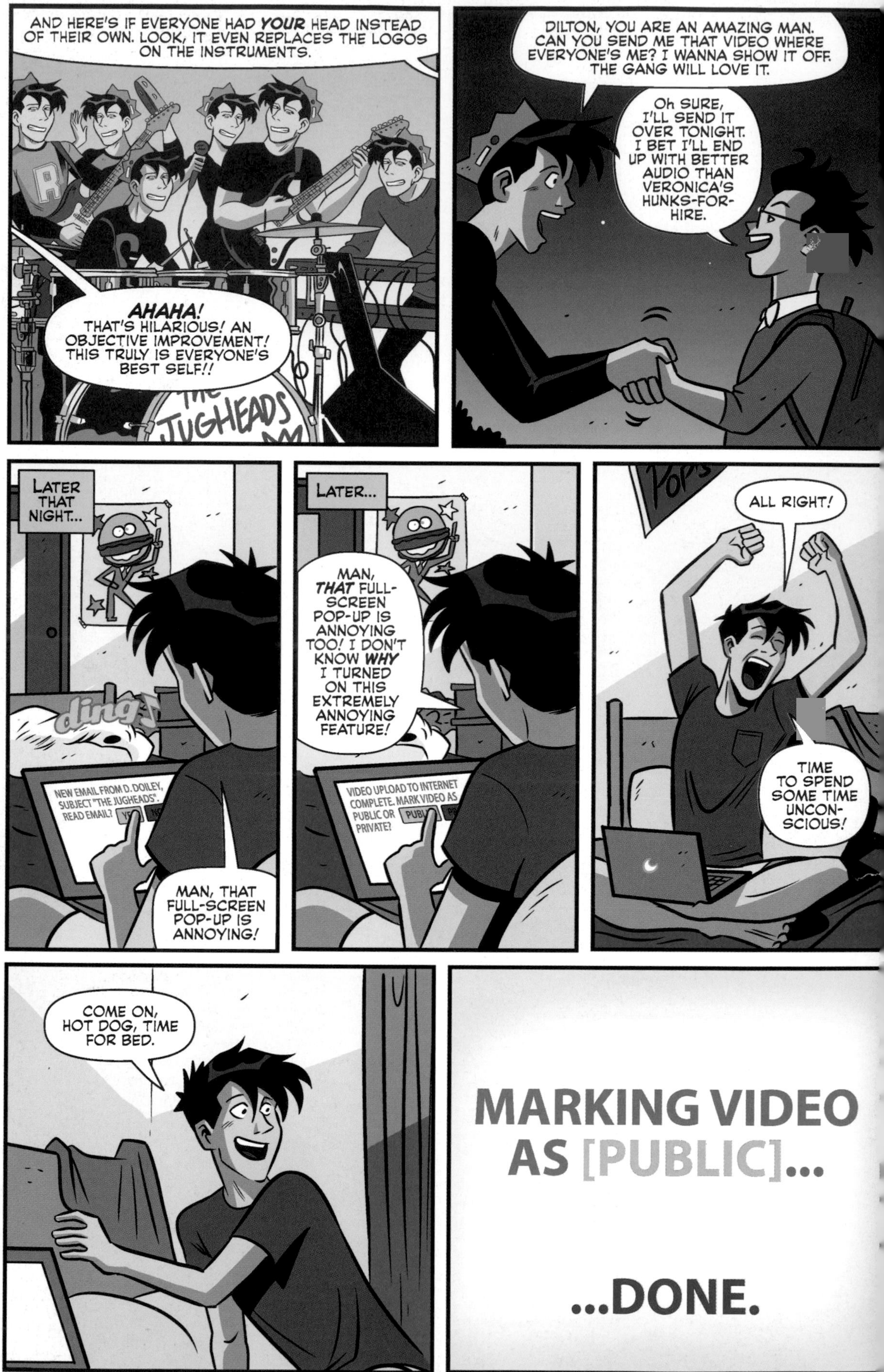

AND HERE'S IF EVERYONE HAD YOUR HEAD INSTEAD OF THEIR OWN. LOOK, IT EVEN REPLACES THE LOGOS ON THE INSTRUMENTS.
AHAHA! THAT'S HILARIOUS! AN OBJECTIVE IMPROVEMENT! THIS TRULY IS EVERYONE'S BEST SELF!!
THE JUGHEADS
DILTON, YOU ARE AN AMAZING MAN. CAN YOU SEND ME THAT VIDEO WHERE EVERYONE'S ME? I WANNA SHOW IT OFF. THE GANG WILL LOVE IT.
Oh SURE, I'LL SEND IT OVER TONIGHT. I BET I'LL END UP WITH BETTER AUDIO THAN VERONICA'S HUNKS-FOR-HIRE.
LATER THAT NIGHT...
ding
NEW EMAIL FROM D. DOILEY, SUBJECT "THE JUGHEADS". READ EMAIL?
MAN, THAT FULL-SCREEN POP-UP IS ANNOYING!
LATER...
MAN, THAT FULL-SCREEN POP-UP IS ANNOYING TOO! I DON'T KNOW WHY I TURNED ON THIS EXTREMELY ANNOYING FEATURE!
VIDEO UPLOAD TO INTERNET COMPLETE. MARK VIDEO AS PUBLIC OR PRIVATE?
POP'S
ALL RIGHT!
TIME TO SPEND SOME TIME UNCONSCIOUS!
COME ON, HOT DOG, TIME FOR BED.
MARKING VIDEO AS [PUBLIC]...
...DONE.

Who designed the UI for Jughead's computer?? Not all user elements need to be so giant that you can read them from across the room or over someone's shoulder in a comic book! It's entirely...oh wait, wait, I get why we did it that way now, ***NEVER MIND.***

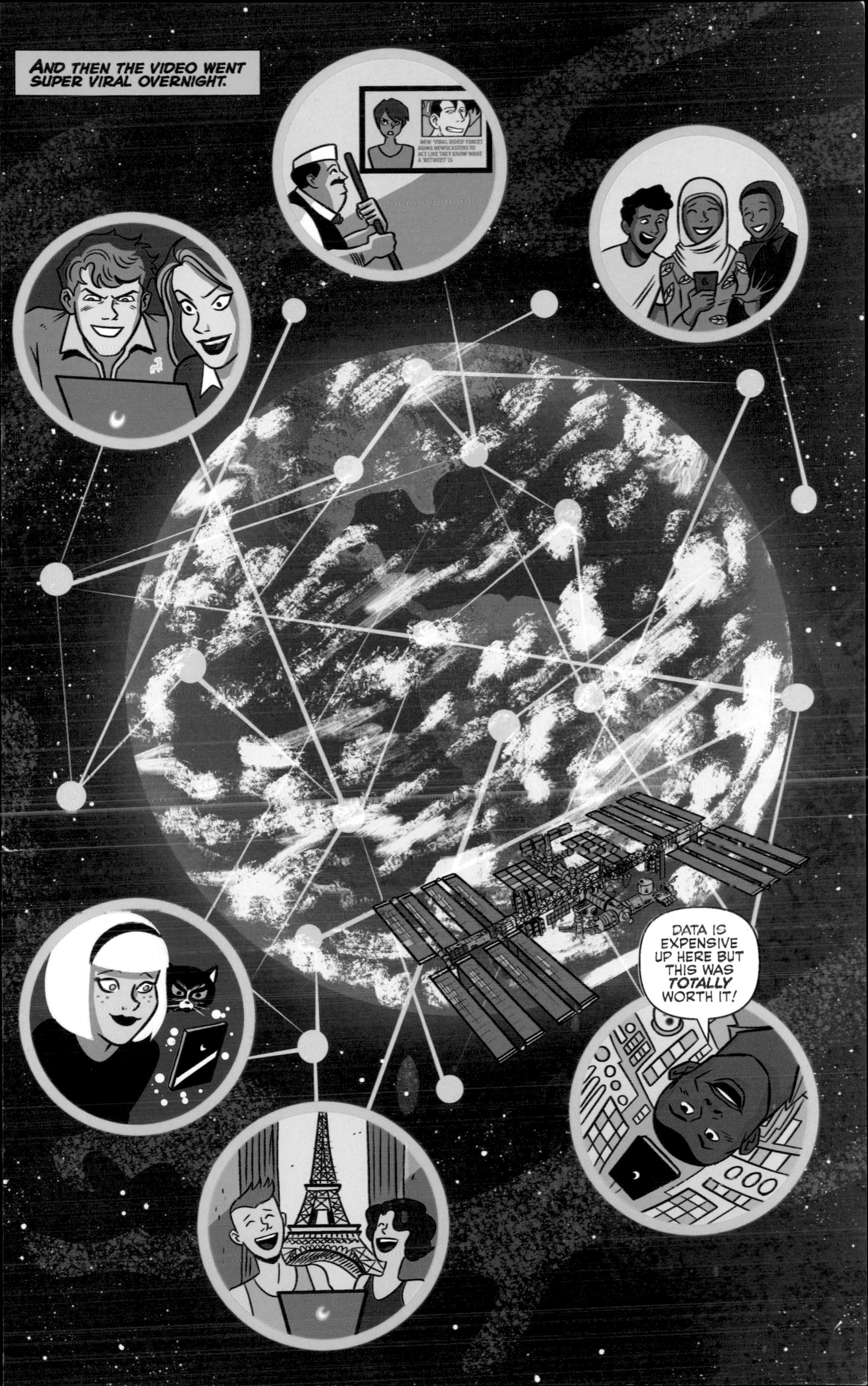
AND THEN THE VIDEO WENT SUPER VIRAL OVERNIGHT.
NEW 'VIRAL VIDEO' FORCES AGING NEWSCASTERS TO ACT LIKE THEY KNOW WHAT A 'RETWEET' IS
DATA IS EXPENSIVE UP HERE BUT THIS WAS *TOTALLY* WORTH IT!

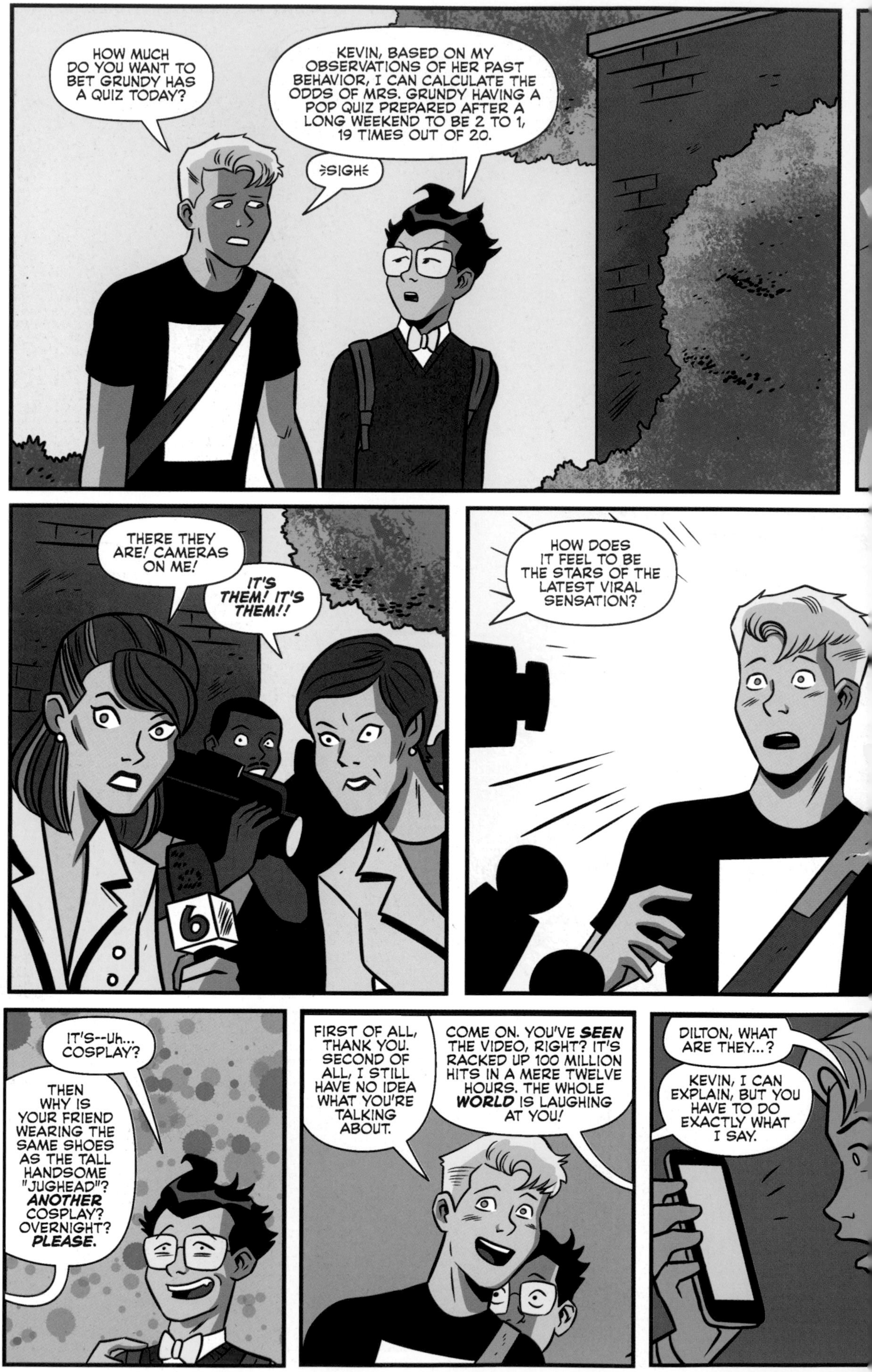

HOW MUCH DO YOU WANT TO BET GRUNDY HAS A QUIZ TODAY?
KEVIN, BASED ON MY OBSERVATIONS OF HER PAST BEHAVIOR, I CAN CALCULATE THE ODDS OF MRS. GRUNDY HAVING A POP QUIZ PREPARED AFTER A LONG WEEKEND TO BE 2 TO 1, 19 TIMES OUT OF 20.
SIGH
THERE THEY ARE! CAMERAS ON ME!
IT'S THEM! IT'S THEM!!
6
HOW DOES IT FEEL TO BE THE STARS OF THE LATEST VIRAL SENSATION?
IT'S--UH... COSPLAY?
THEN WHY IS YOUR FRIEND WEARING THE SAME SHOES AS THE TALL HANDSOME "JUGHEAD"? ANOTHER COSPLAY? OVERNIGHT? PLEASE.
FIRST OF ALL, THANK YOU. SECOND OF ALL, I STILL HAVE NO IDEA WHAT YOU'RE TALKING ABOUT.
COME ON. YOU'VE SEEN THE VIDEO, RIGHT? IT'S RACKED UP 100 MILLION HITS IN A MERE TWELVE HOURS. THE WHOLE WORLD IS LAUGHING AT YOU!
DILTON, WHAT ARE THEY...?
KEVIN, I CAN EXPLAIN, BUT YOU HAVE TO DO EXACTLY WHAT I SAY.

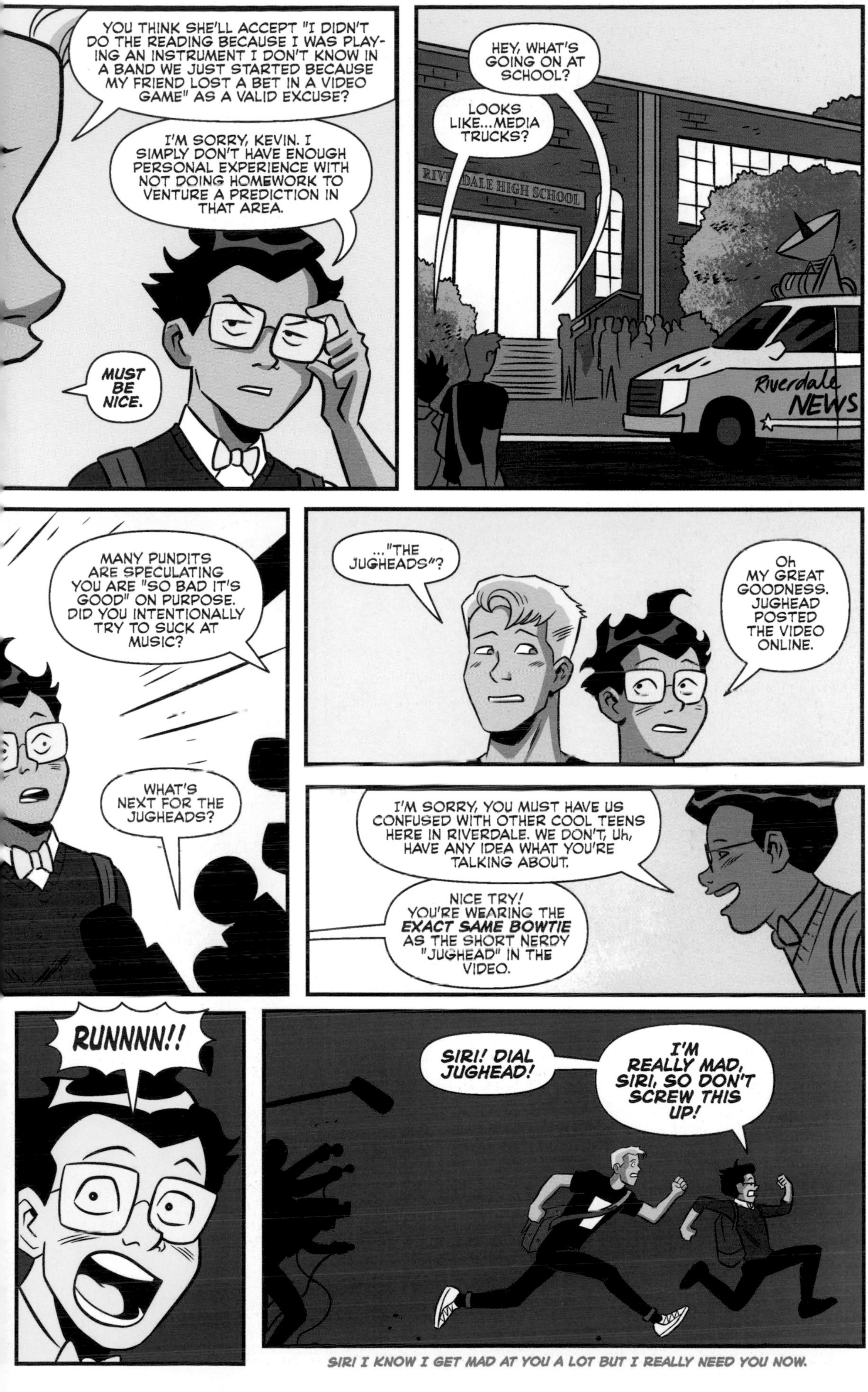
YOU THINK SHE'LL ACCEPT "I DIDN'T DO THE READING BECAUSE I WAS PLAYING AN INSTRUMENT I DON'T KNOW IN A BAND WE JUST STARTED BECAUSE MY FRIEND LOST A BET IN A VIDEO GAME" AS A VALID EXCUSE?
I'M SORRY, KEVIN. I SIMPLY DON'T HAVE ENOUGH PERSONAL EXPERIENCE WITH NOT DOING HOMEWORK TO VENTURE A PREDICTION IN THAT AREA.
MUST BE NICE.
HEY, WHAT'S GOING ON AT SCHOOL?
LOOKS LIKE...MEDIA TRUCKS?
RIVERDALE HIGH SCHOOL
Riverdale NEWS
MANY PUNDITS ARE SPECULATING YOU ARE "SO BAD IT'S GOOD" ON PURPOSE. DID YOU INTENTIONALLY TRY TO SUCK AT MUSIC?
WHAT'S NEXT FOR THE JUGHEADS?
..."THE JUGHEADS"?
Oh MY GREAT GOODNESS. JUGHEAD POSTED THE VIDEO ONLINE.
I'M SORRY, YOU MUST HAVE US CONFUSED WITH OTHER COOL TEENS HERE IN RIVERDALE. WE DON'T, Uh, HAVE ANY IDEA WHAT YOU'RE TALKING ABOUT.
NICE TRY! YOU'RE WEARING THE EXACT SAME BOWTIE AS THE SHORT NERDY "JUGHEAD" IN THE VIDEO.
RUNNNN!!
SIRI! DIAL JUGHEAD!
I'M REALLY MAD, SIRI, SO DON'T SCREW THIS UP!
SIRI I KNOW I GET MAD AT YOU A LOT BUT I REALLY NEED YOU NOW.

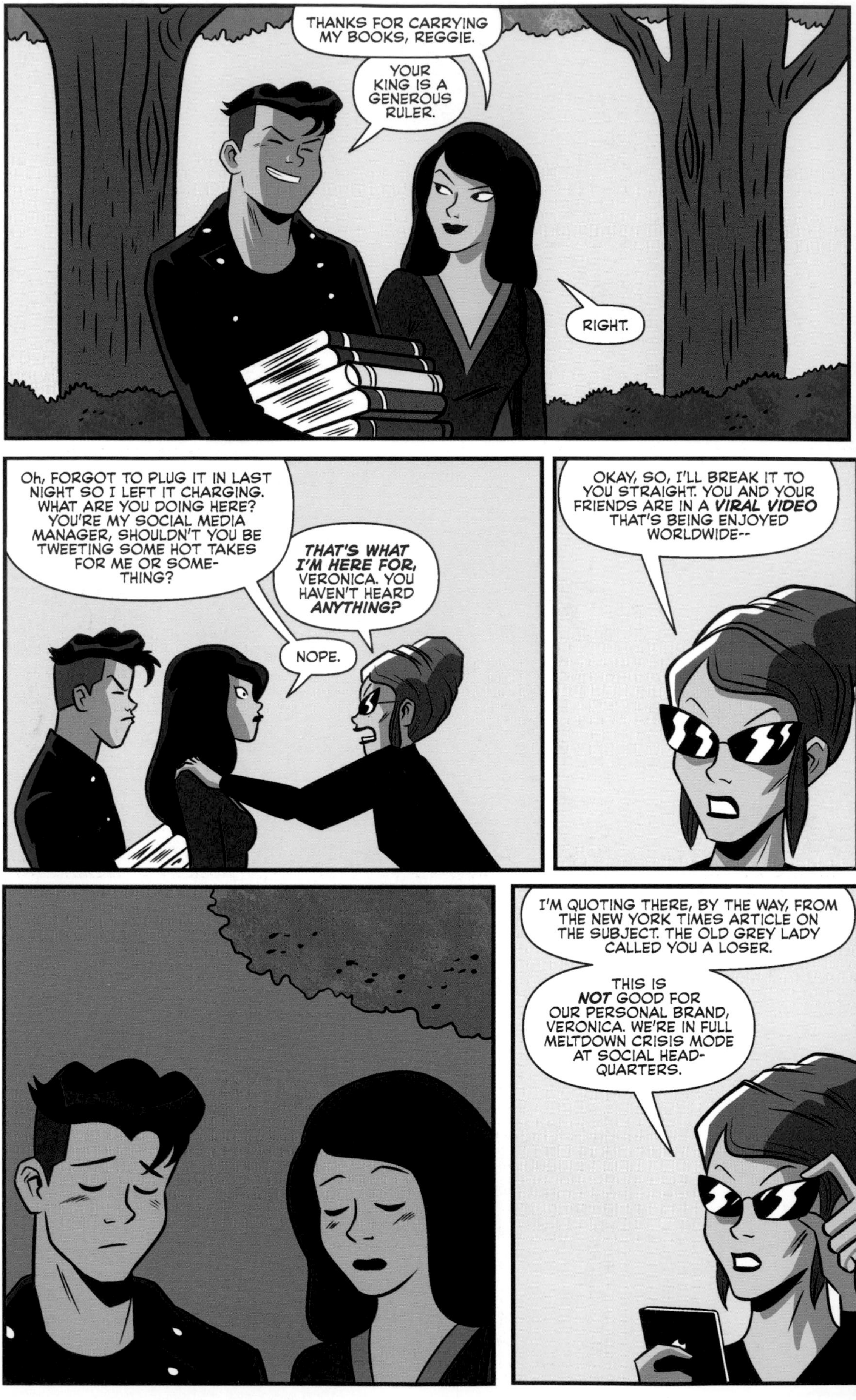
THANKS FOR CARRYING MY BOOKS, REGGIE.
YOUR KING IS A GENEROUS RULER.
RIGHT.
Oh, FORGOT TO PLUG IT IN LAST NIGHT SO I LEFT IT CHARGING. WHAT ARE YOU DOING HERE? YOU'RE MY SOCIAL MEDIA MANAGER, SHOULDN'T YOU BE TWEETING SOME HOT TAKES FOR ME OR SOME-THING?
THAT'S WHAT I'M HERE FOR, VERONICA. YOU HAVEN'T HEARD ANYTHING?
NOPE.
OKAY, SO, I'LL BREAK IT TO YOU STRAIGHT. YOU AND YOUR FRIENDS ARE IN A VIRAL VIDEO THAT'S BEING ENJOYED WORLDWIDE--
I'M QUOTING THERE, BY THE WAY, FROM THE NEW YORK TIMES ARTICLE ON THE SUBJECT. THE OLD GREY LADY CALLED YOU A LOSER.
THIS IS NOT GOOD FOR OUR PERSONAL BRAND, VERONICA. WE'RE IN FULL MELTDOWN CRISIS MODE AT SOCIAL HEAD-QUARTERS.

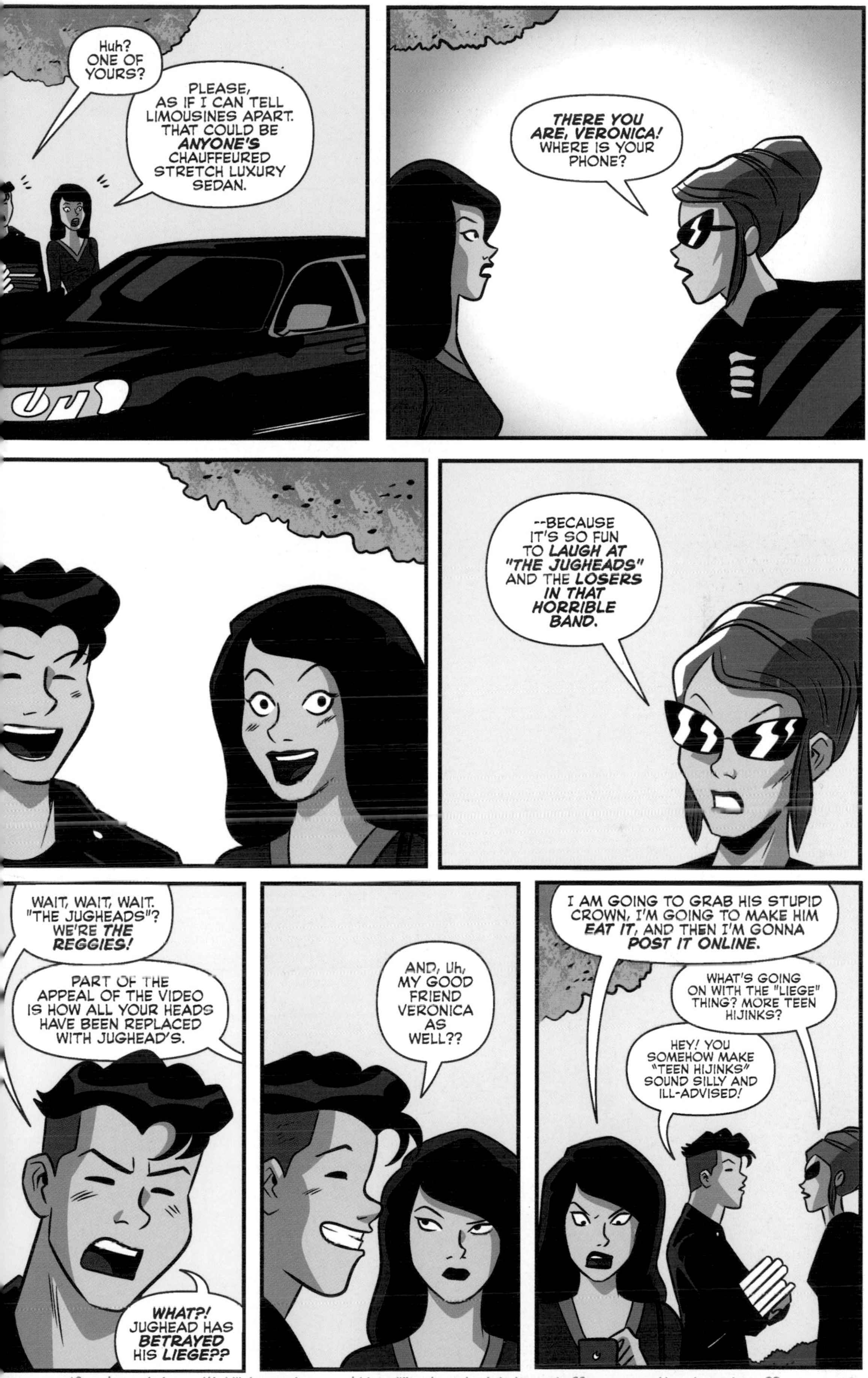
Huh? ONE OF YOURS?
PLEASE, AS IF I CAN TELL LIMOUSINES APART. THAT COULD BE ANYONE'S CHAUFFEURED STRETCH LUXURY SEDAN.
THERE YOU ARE, VERONICA! WHERE IS YOUR PHONE?
--BECAUSE IT'S SO FUN TO LAUGH AT "THE JUGHEADS" AND THE LOSERS IN THAT HORRIBLE BAND.
WAIT, WAIT, WAIT. "THE JUGHEADS"? WE'RE THE REGGIES!
PART OF THE APPEAL OF THE VIDEO IS HOW ALL YOUR HEADS HAVE BEEN REPLACED WITH JUGHEAD'S.
WHAT?! JUGHEAD HAS BETRAYED HIS LIEGE??
AND, Uh, MY GOOD FRIEND VERONICA AS WELL??
I AM GOING TO GRAB HIS STUPID CROWN, I'M GOING TO MAKE HIM EAT IT, AND THEN I'M GONNA POST IT ONLINE.
WHAT'S GOING ON WITH THE "LIEGE" THING? MORE TEEN HIJINKS?
HEY! YOU SOMEHOW MAKE "TEEN HIJINKS" SOUND SILLY AND ILL-ADVISED!

If you're not down with hijinks, perhaps you'd be willing to entertain japes, buffoonery, and/or shenanigans??

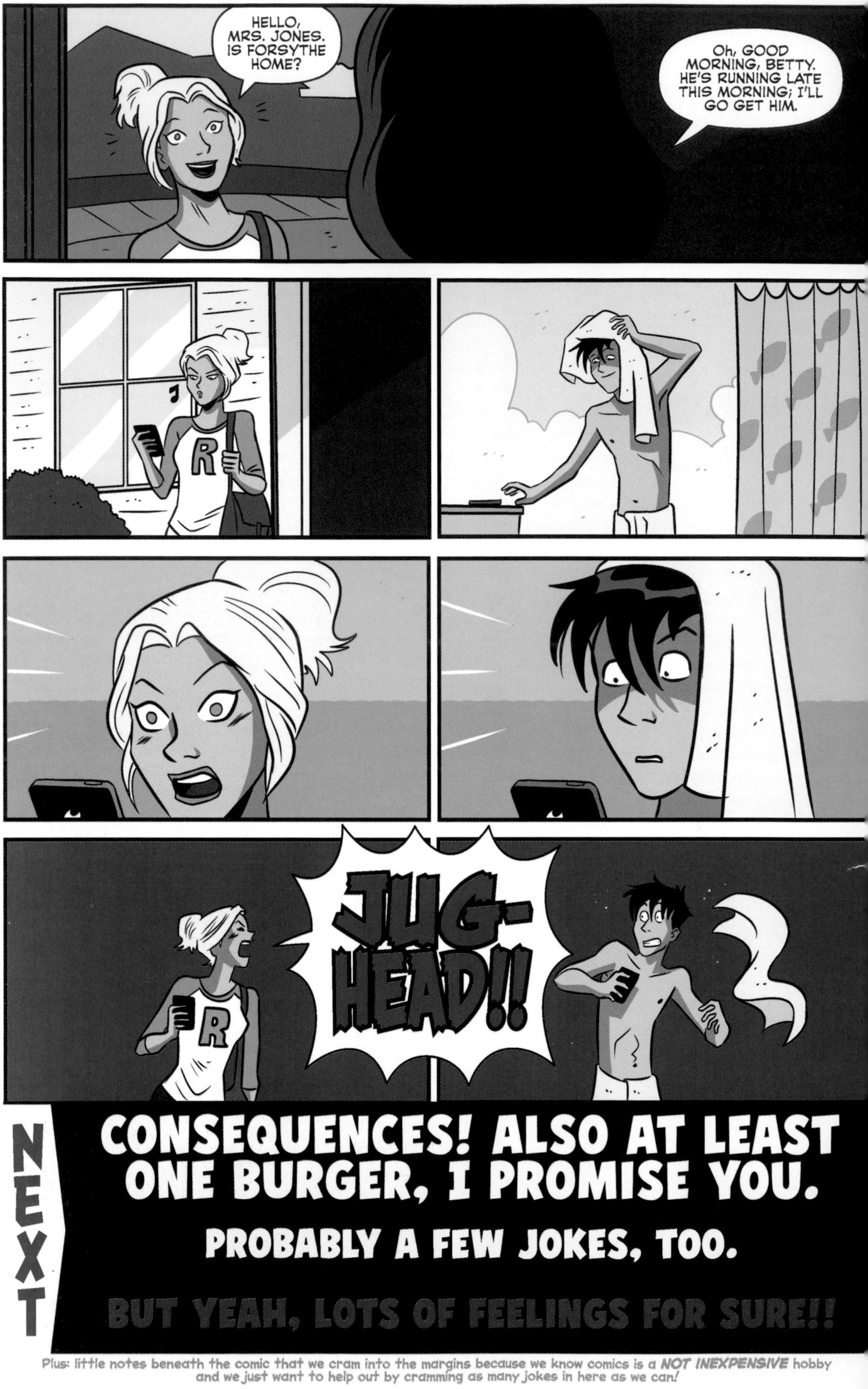
HELLO, MRS. JONES. IS FORSYTHE HOME?
Oh, GOOD MORNING, BETTY. HE'S RUNNING LATE THIS MORNING; I'LL GO GET HIM.
JUG-HEAD!!

NEXT

CONSEQUENCES! ALSO AT LEAST ONE BURGER, I PROMISE YOU.

PROBABLY A FEW JOKES, TOO.

BUT YEAH, LOTS OF FEELINGS FOR SURE!!

Plus: little notes beneath the comic that we cram into the margins because we know comics is a ***NOT INEXPENSIVE*** hobby and we just want to help out by cramming as many jokes in here as we can!

TO BE

CONTINUED...

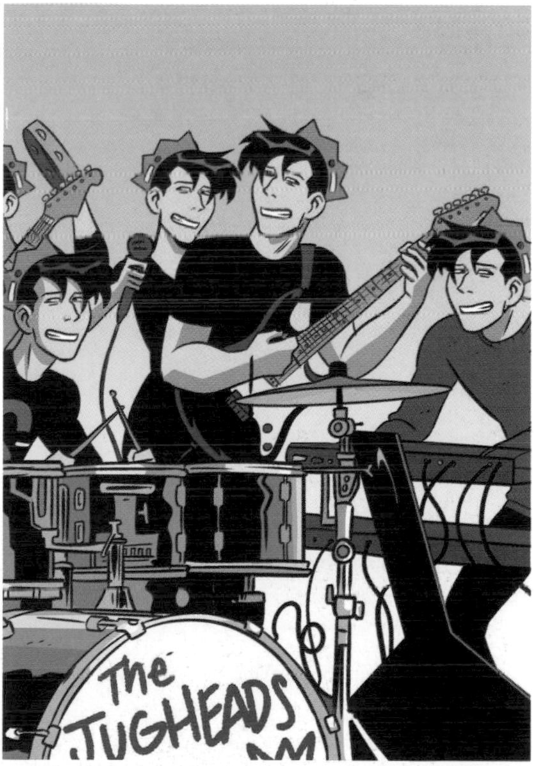
The JUGHEADS

ISSUE FOURTEEN

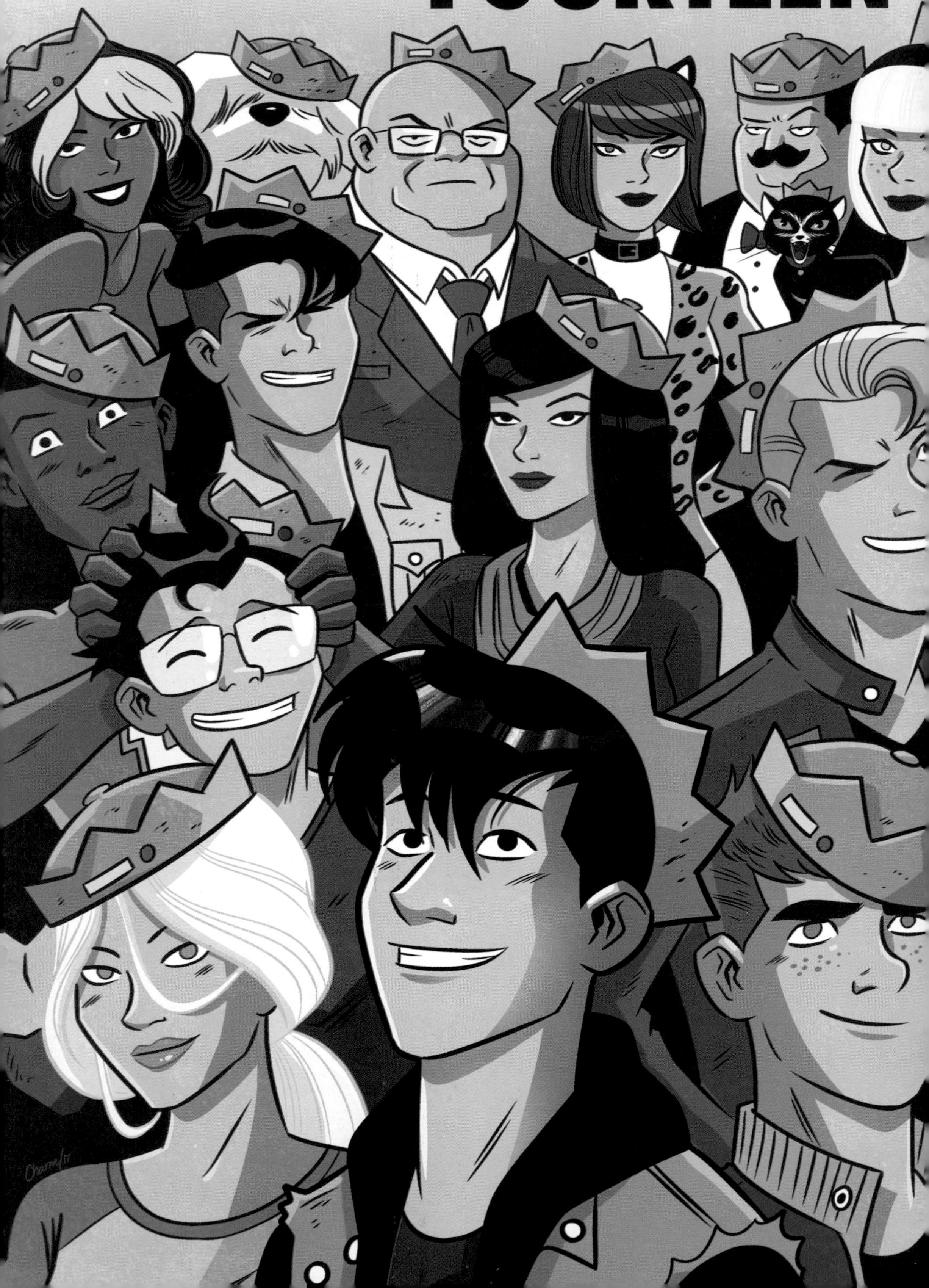

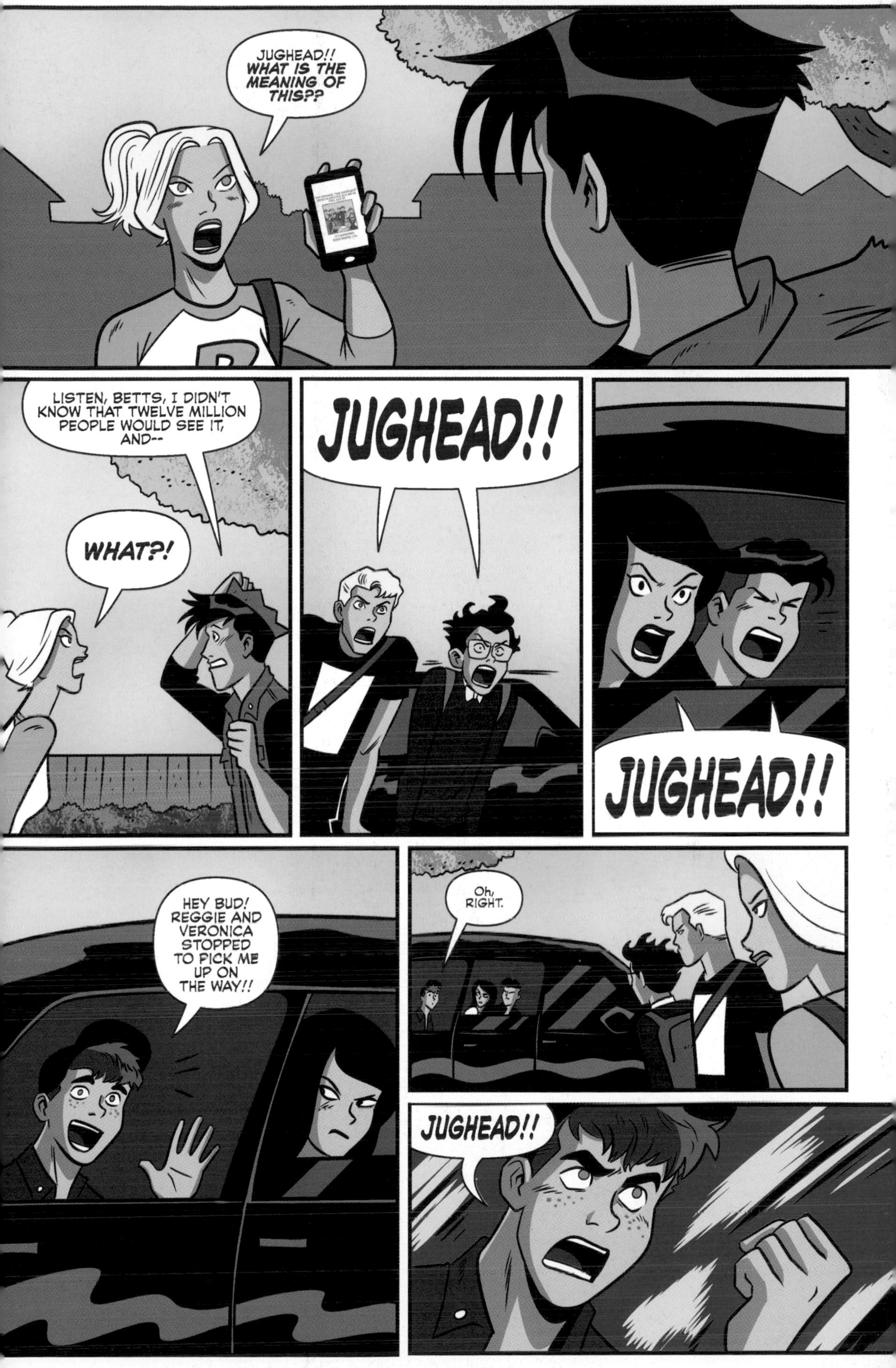
JUGHEAD!! WHAT IS THE MEANING OF THIS??
LISTEN, BETTS, I DIDN'T KNOW THAT TWELVE MILLION PEOPLE WOULD SEE IT, AND--
WHAT?!
JUGHEAD!!
JUGHEAD!!
HEY BUD! REGGIE AND VERONICA STOPPED TO PICK ME UP ON THE WAY!!
Oh, RIGHT.
JUGHEAD!!

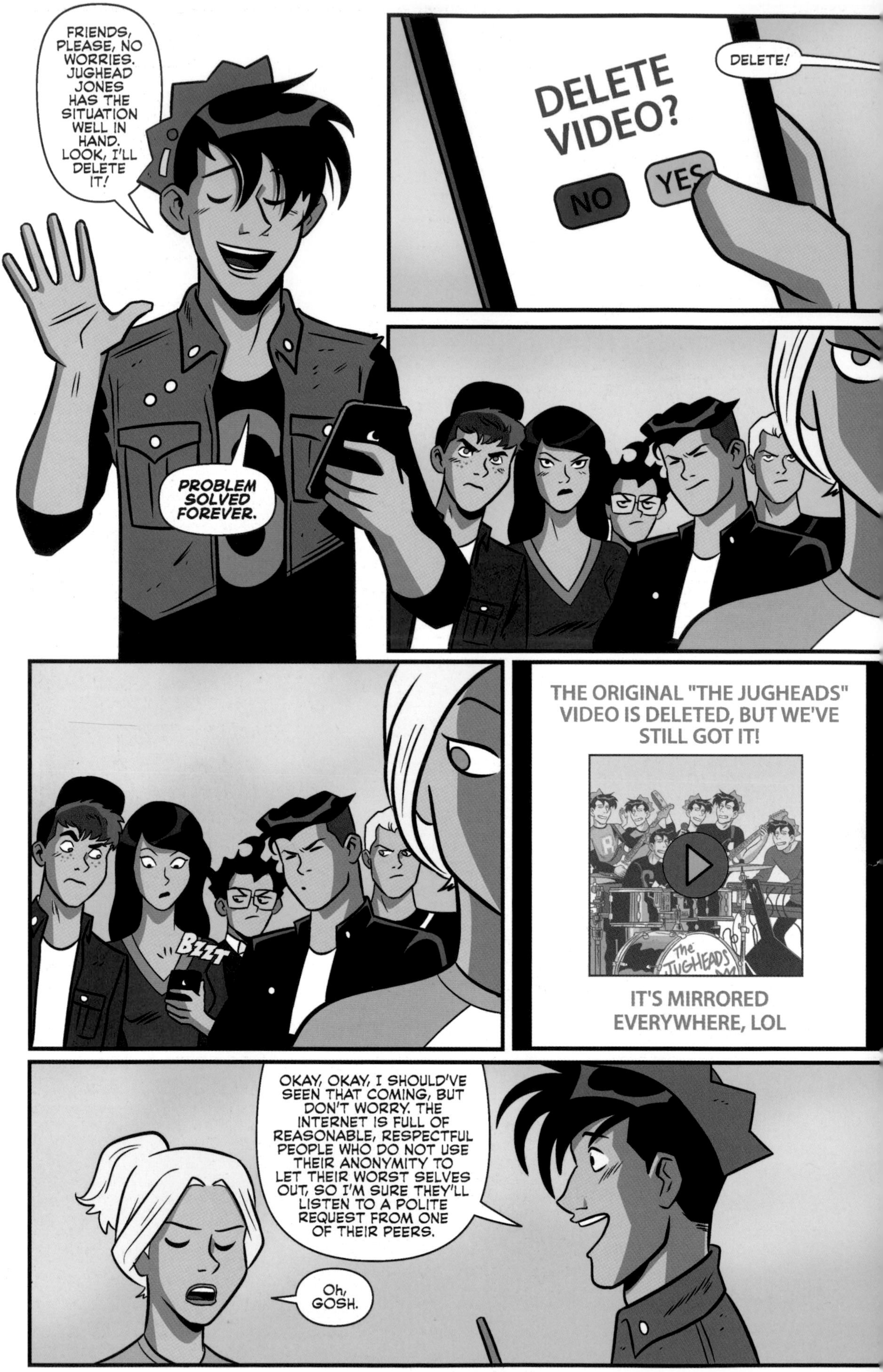
FRIENDS, PLEASE, NO WORRIES. JUGHEAD JONES HAS THE SITUATION WELL IN HAND. LOOK, I'LL DELETE IT!
DELETE VIDEO?
NO
YES
DELETE!
PROBLEM SOLVED FOREVER.
BZZT
THE ORIGINAL "THE JUGHEADS" VIDEO IS DELETED, BUT WE'VE STILL GOT IT!
THE JUGHEADS
IT'S MIRRORED EVERYWHERE, LOL
OKAY, OKAY, I SHOULD'VE SEEN THAT COMING, BUT DON'T WORRY. THE INTERNET IS FULL OF REASONABLE, RESPECTFUL PEOPLE WHO DO NOT USE THEIR ANONYMITY TO LET THEIR WORST SELVES OUT, SO I'M SURE THEY'LL LISTEN TO A POLITE REQUEST FROM ONE OF THEIR PEERS.
Oh, GOSH.

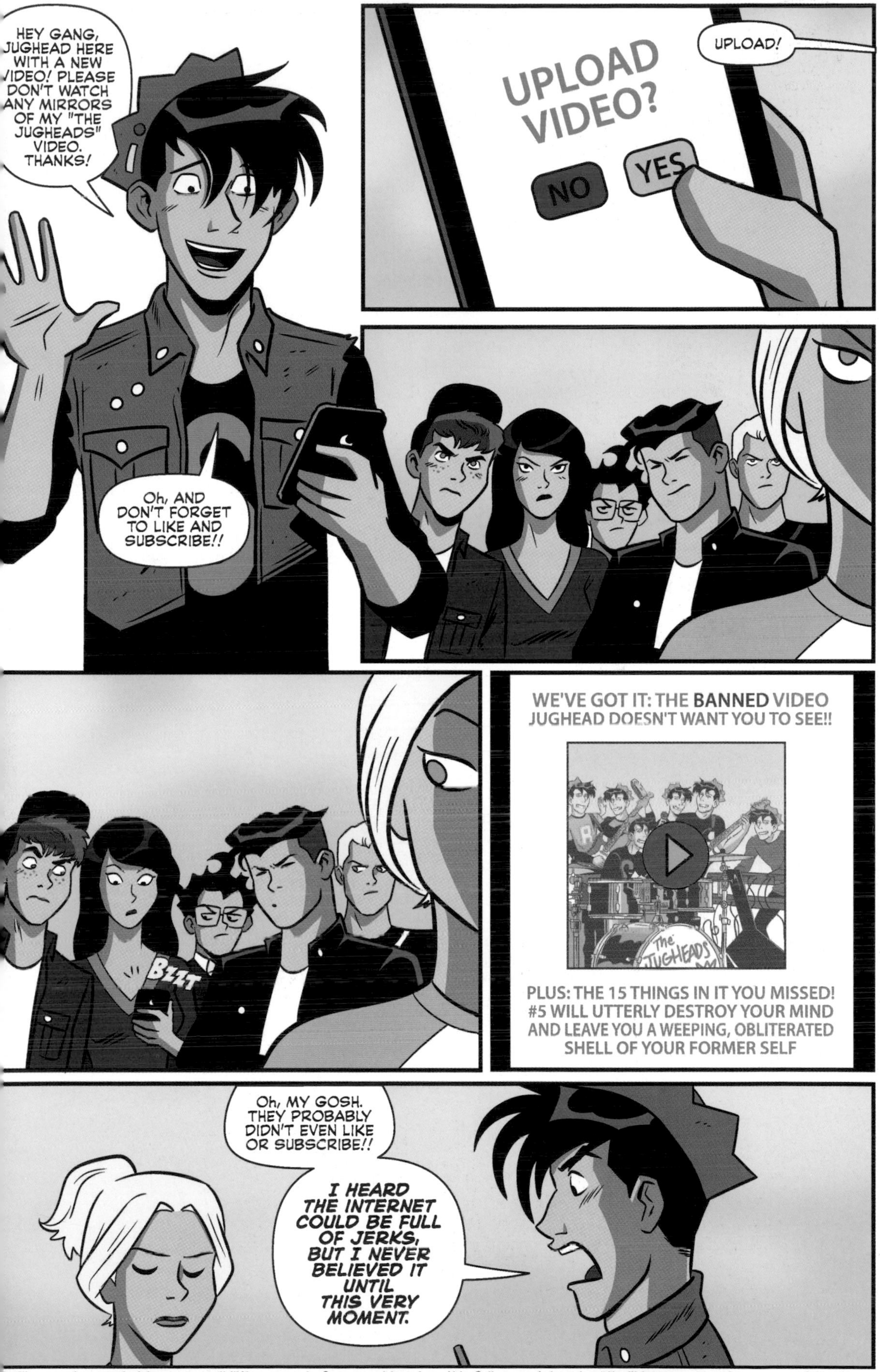
HEY GANG, JUGHEAD HERE WITH A NEW VIDEO! PLEASE DON'T WATCH ANY MIRRORS OF MY "THE JUGHEADS" VIDEO. THANKS!
UPLOAD VIDEO?
NO
YES
UPLOAD!
Oh, AND DON'T FORGET TO LIKE AND SUBSCRIBE!!
BZZT
WE'VE GOT IT: THE BANNED VIDEO JUGHEAD DOESN'T WANT YOU TO SEE!!
The JUGHEADS
PLUS: THE 15 THINGS IN IT YOU MISSED! #5 WILL UTTERLY DESTROY YOUR MIND AND LEAVE YOU A WEEPING, OBLITERATED SHELL OF YOUR FORMER SELF
Oh, MY GOSH. THEY PROBABLY DIDN'T EVEN LIKE OR SUBSCRIBE!!
I HEARD THE INTERNET COULD BE FULL OF JERKS, BUT I NEVER BELIEVED IT UNTIL THIS VERY MOMENT.

" will expand your mind to new possibilities never before considered on this fallen mortal realm, #11 will leave you cursing an uncaring universe for all those years wasted, squandered on the empty nothingness you so ironically called "living" before you first laid eyes on this two minute internet video!!

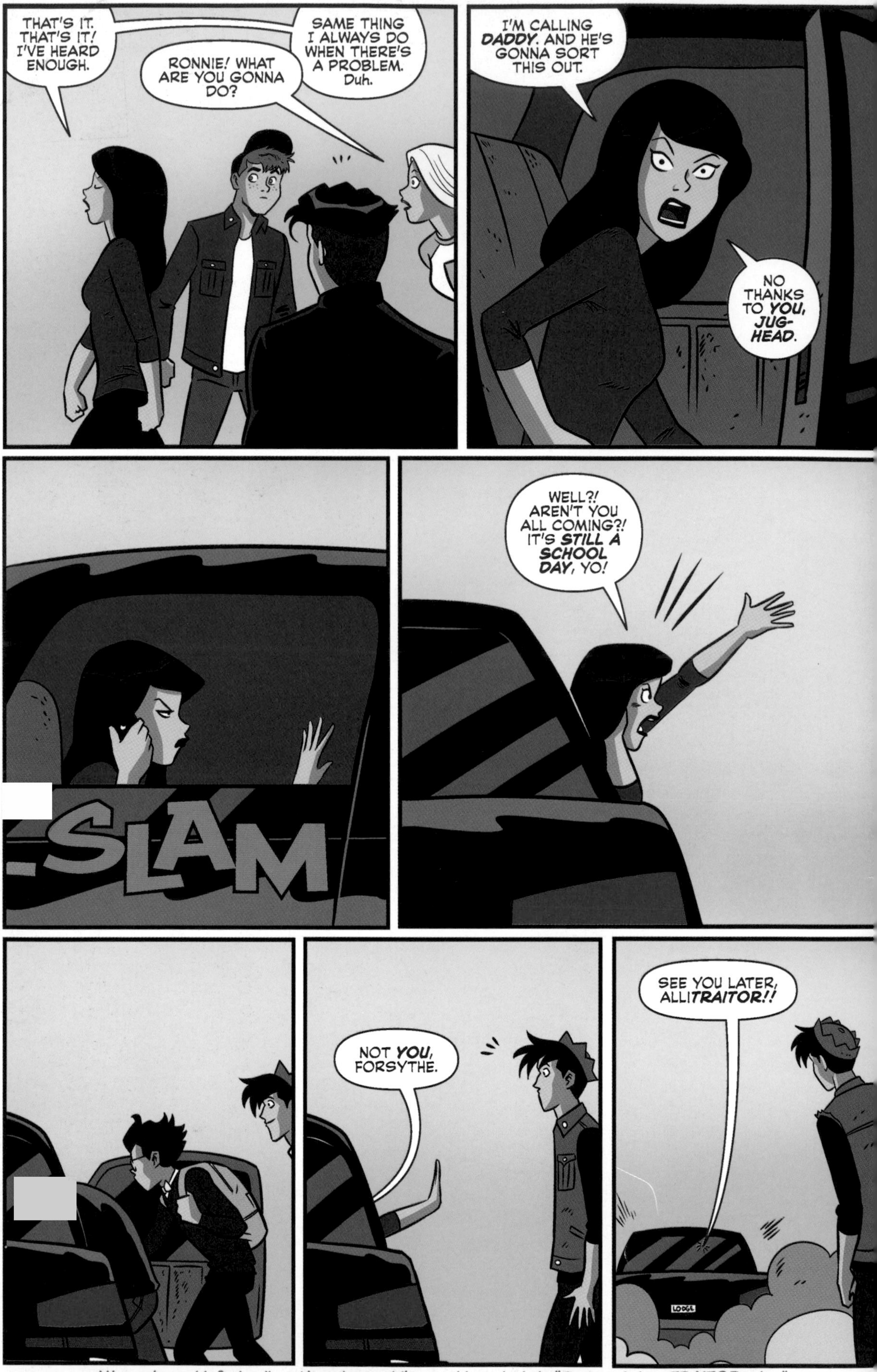
THAT'S IT. THAT'S IT! I'VE HEARD ENOUGH.
RONNIE! WHAT ARE YOU GONNA DO?
SAME THING I ALWAYS DO WHEN THERE'S A PROBLEM. Duh.
I'M CALLING DADDY. AND HE'S GONNA SORT THIS OUT.
NO THANKS TO YOU, JUG-HEAD.
SLAM
WELL?! AREN'T YOU ALL COMING?! IT'S STILL A SCHOOL DAY, YO!
NOT YOU, FORSYTHE.
SEE YOU LATER, ALLITRAITOR!!
LODGE

Alternate and inferior lines Veronica could've used here include "See you later, ***TRAITOR***gator" and "See you ***TRAITOR***, alligator." You made the right call, Veronica.

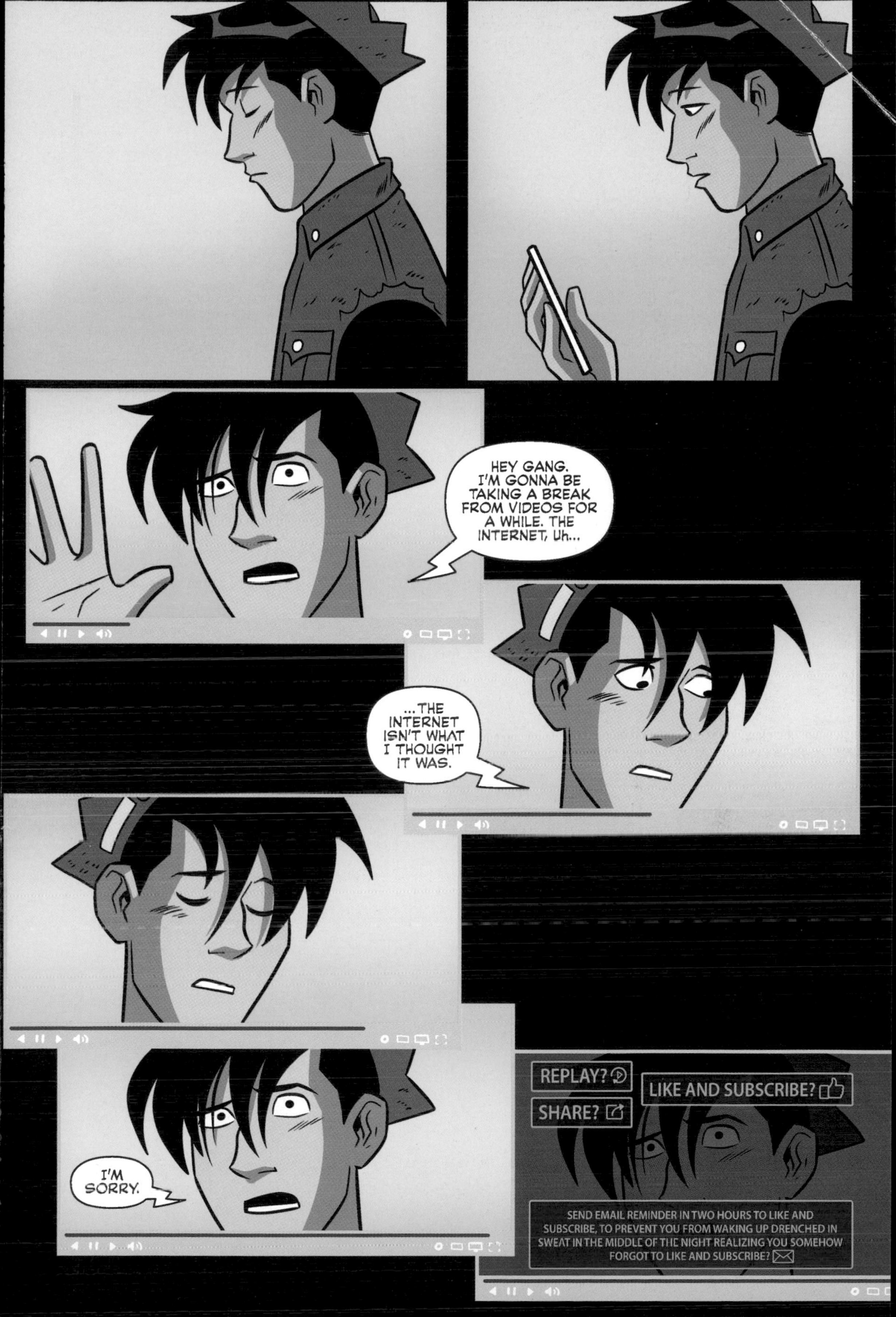
HEY GANG. I'M GONNA BE TAKING A BREAK FROM VIDEOS FOR A WHILE. THE INTERNET, Uh...
...THE INTERNET ISN'T WHAT I THOUGHT IT WAS.
I'M SORRY.
REPLAY?
SHARE?
LIKE AND SUBSCRIBE?
SEND EMAIL REMINDER IN TWO HOURS TO LIKE AND SUBSCRIBE, TO PREVENT YOU FROM WAKING UP DRENCHED IN SWEAT IN THE MIDDLE OF THE NIGHT REALIZING YOU SOMEHOW FORGOT TO LIKE AND SUBSCRIBE?

Sorry for reminding you all of all those times you stopped dead in your tracks, a previously fine day ***RUINED*** with the realization that, once again, you'd forgotten to like and subscribe.

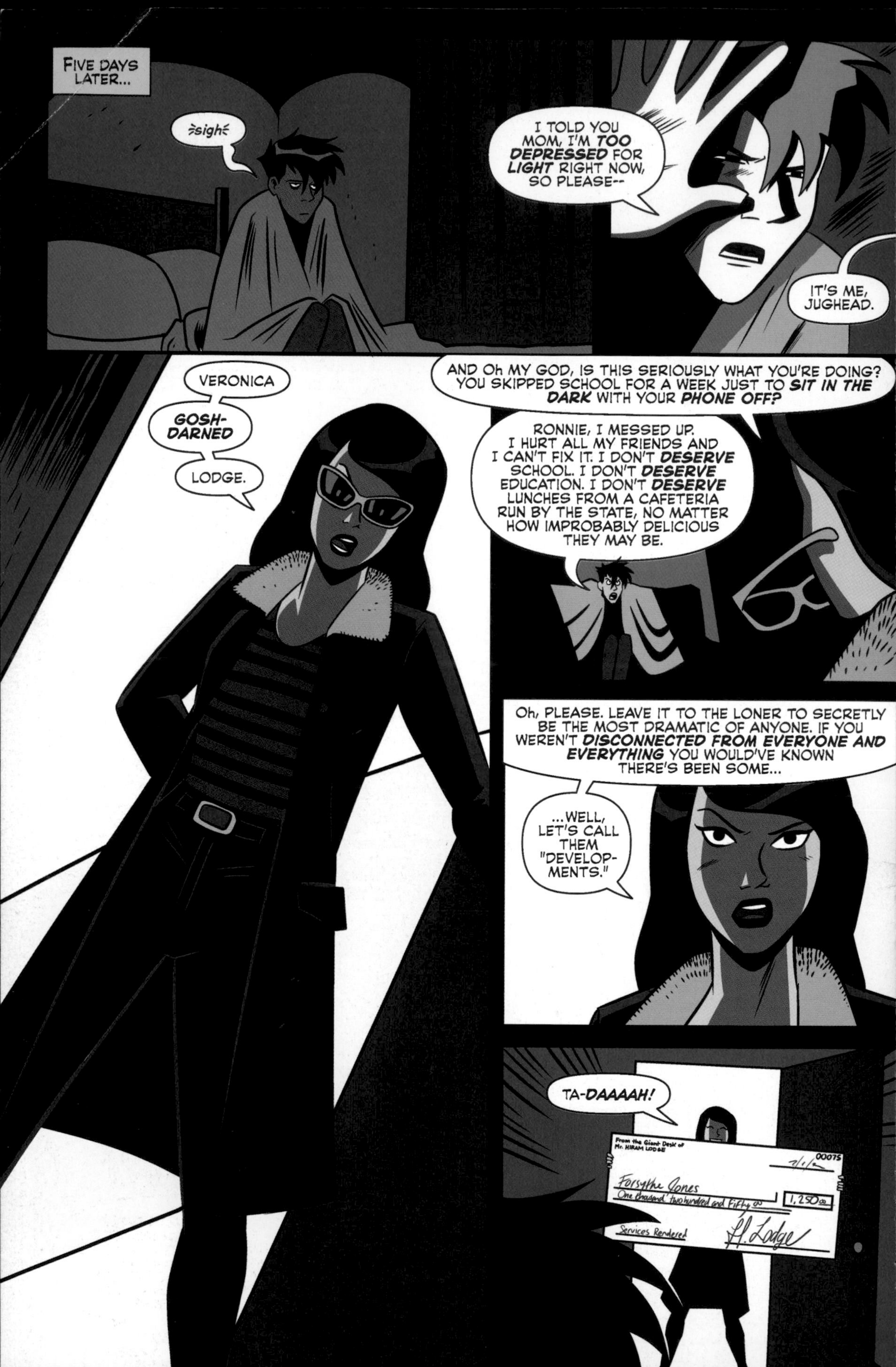
FIVE DAYS LATER...
≥sigh≤
I TOLD YOU MOM, I'M TOO DEPRESSED FOR LIGHT RIGHT NOW, SO PLEASE--
IT'S ME, JUGHEAD.
VERONICA
GOSH-DARNED
LODGE.
AND Oh MY GOD, IS THIS SERIOUSLY WHAT YOU'RE DOING? YOU SKIPPED SCHOOL FOR A WEEK JUST TO SIT IN THE DARK WITH YOUR PHONE OFF?
RONNIE, I MESSED UP. I HURT ALL MY FRIENDS AND I CAN'T FIX IT. I DON'T DESERVE SCHOOL. I DON'T DESERVE EDUCATION. I DON'T DESERVE LUNCHES FROM A CAFETERIA RUN BY THE STATE, NO MATTER HOW IMPROBABLY DELICIOUS THEY MAY BE.
Oh, PLEASE. LEAVE IT TO THE LONER TO SECRETLY BE THE MOST DRAMATIC OF ANYONE. IF YOU WEREN'T DISCONNECTED FROM EVERYONE AND EVERYTHING YOU WOULD'VE KNOWN THERE'S BEEN SOME...
...WELL, LET'S CALL THEM "DEVELOPMENTS."
TA-DAAAAH!
From the Giant Desk of Mr. HIRAM LODGE
00075
Forsythe Jones
One thousand two hundred and Fifty 00
1,250 00
Services Rendered
H. Lodge

Is Veronica's middle name ***TRULY*** "Gosh-Darned"? This comic promises "yes!", especially if ***YOU*** promise to never look it up anywhere else!

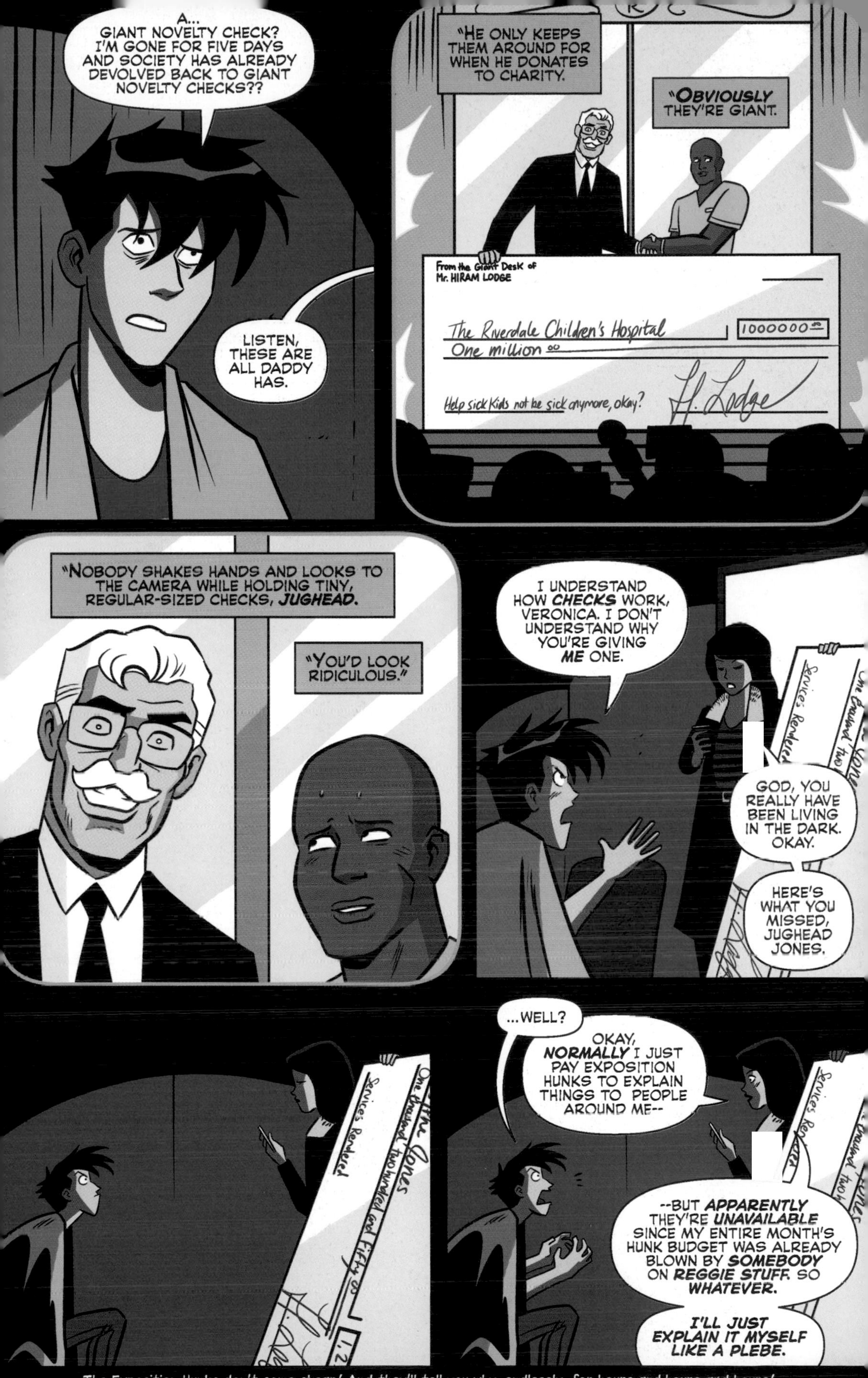
A... GIANT NOVELTY CHECK? I'M GONE FOR FIVE DAYS AND SOCIETY HAS ALREADY DEVOLVED BACK TO GIANT NOVELTY CHECKS??
LISTEN, THESE ARE ALL DADDY HAS.
"HE ONLY KEEPS THEM AROUND FOR WHEN HE DONATES TO CHARITY.
"OBVIOUSLY THEY'RE GIANT.
From the Giant Desk of Mr. HIRAM LODGE
The Riverdale Children's Hospital
1000000.00
One million 00
Help sick Kids not be sick anymore, okay?
H. Lodge
"NOBODY SHAKES HANDS AND LOOKS TO THE CAMERA WHILE HOLDING TINY, REGULAR-SIZED CHECKS, JUGHEAD.
"YOU'D LOOK RIDICULOUS."
I UNDERSTAND HOW CHECKS WORK, VERONICA. I DON'T UNDERSTAND WHY YOU'RE GIVING ME ONE.
GOD, YOU REALLY HAVE BEEN LIVING IN THE DARK. OKAY.
HERE'S WHAT YOU MISSED, JUGHEAD JONES.
Services Rendered
One thousand two hundred and Fifty 00
...WELL?
OKAY, NORMALLY I JUST PAY EXPOSITION HUNKS TO EXPLAIN THINGS TO PEOPLE AROUND ME--
--BUT APPARENTLY THEY'RE UNAVAILABLE SINCE MY ENTIRE MONTH'S HUNK BUDGET WAS ALREADY BLOWN BY SOMEBODY ON REGGIE STUFF. SO WHATEVER.
I'LL JUST EXPLAIN IT MYSELF LIKE A PLEBE.

The Exposition Hunks don't come cheap! And they'll tell you why: endlessly, for hours and hours and hours!

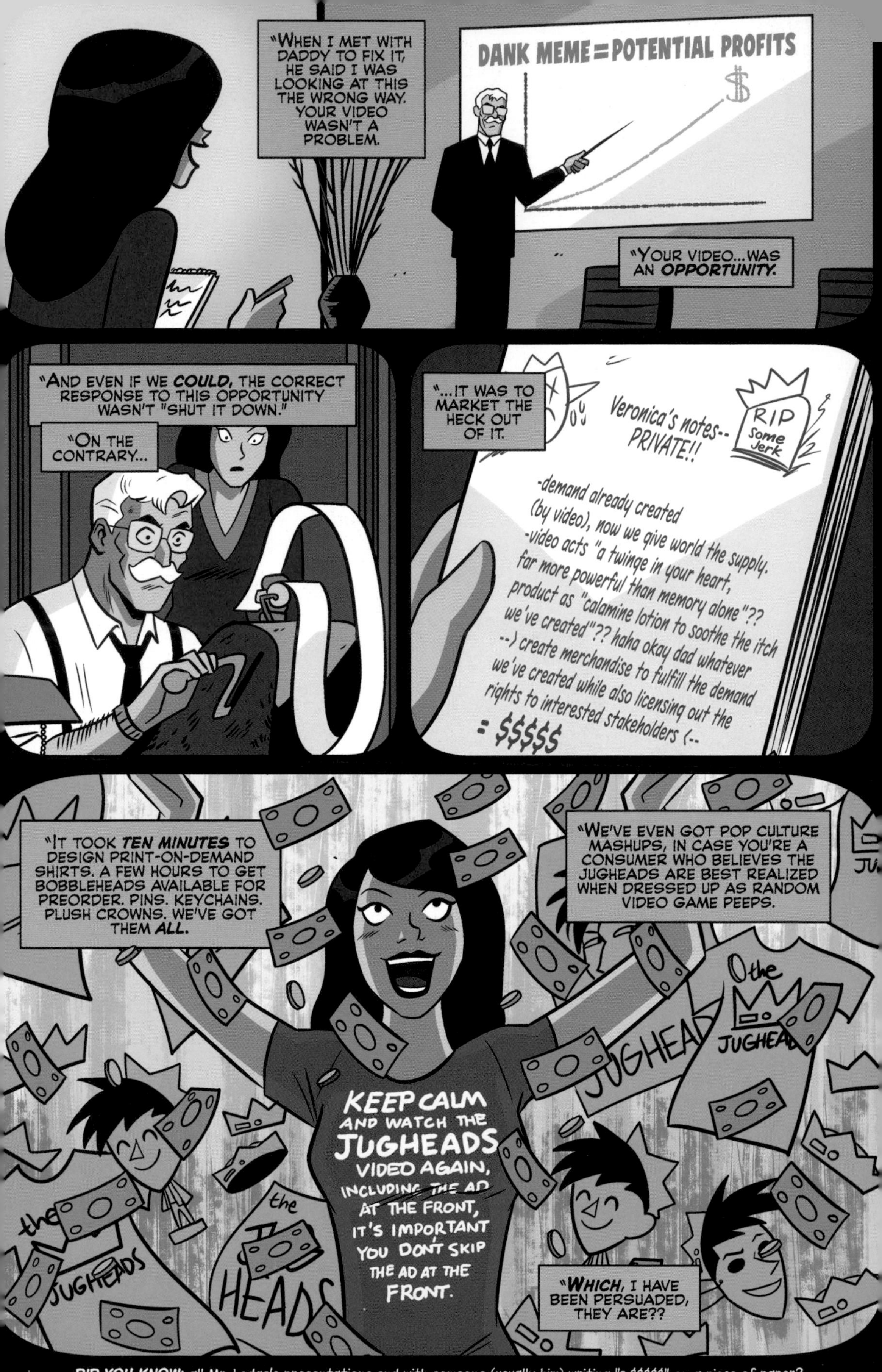
"WHEN I MET WITH DADDY TO FIX IT, HE SAID I WAS LOOKING AT THIS THE WRONG WAY. YOUR VIDEO WASN'T A PROBLEM.
DANK MEME = POTENTIAL PROFITS
"YOUR VIDEO...WAS AN OPPORTUNITY.
"AND EVEN IF WE COULD, THE CORRECT RESPONSE TO THIS OPPORTUNITY WASN'T "SHUT IT DOWN."
"ON THE CONTRARY...
"...IT WAS TO MARKET THE HECK OUT OF IT.
Veronica's notes-- PRIVATE!!
RIP Some Jerk
-demand already created (by video), now we give world the supply.
-video acts "a twinge in your heart, far more powerful than memory alone"?? product as "calamine lotion to soothe the itch we've created"?? haha okay dad whatever
--) create merchandise to fulfill the demand we've created while also licensing out the rights to interested stakeholders (--
= $$$$$
"IT TOOK TEN MINUTES TO DESIGN PRINT-ON-DEMAND SHIRTS. A FEW HOURS TO GET BOBBLEHEADS AVAILABLE FOR PREORDER. PINS. KEYCHAINS. PLUSH CROWNS. WE'VE GOT THEM ALL.
"WE'VE EVEN GOT POP CULTURE MASHUPS, IN CASE YOU'RE A CONSUMER WHO BELIEVES THE JUGHEADS ARE BEST REALIZED WHEN DRESSED UP AS RANDOM VIDEO GAME PEEPS.
KEEP CALM AND WATCH THE JUGHEADS VIDEO AGAIN, INCLUDING ~~THE AD~~ AT THE FRONT, IT'S IMPORTANT YOU DON'T SKIP THE AD AT THE FRONT.
the JUGHEADS
"WHICH, I HAVE BEEN PERSUADED, THEY ARE??

DID YOU KNOW: all Mr. Lodge's presentations end with someone (usually him) writing "= $$$$$" on a piece of paper?

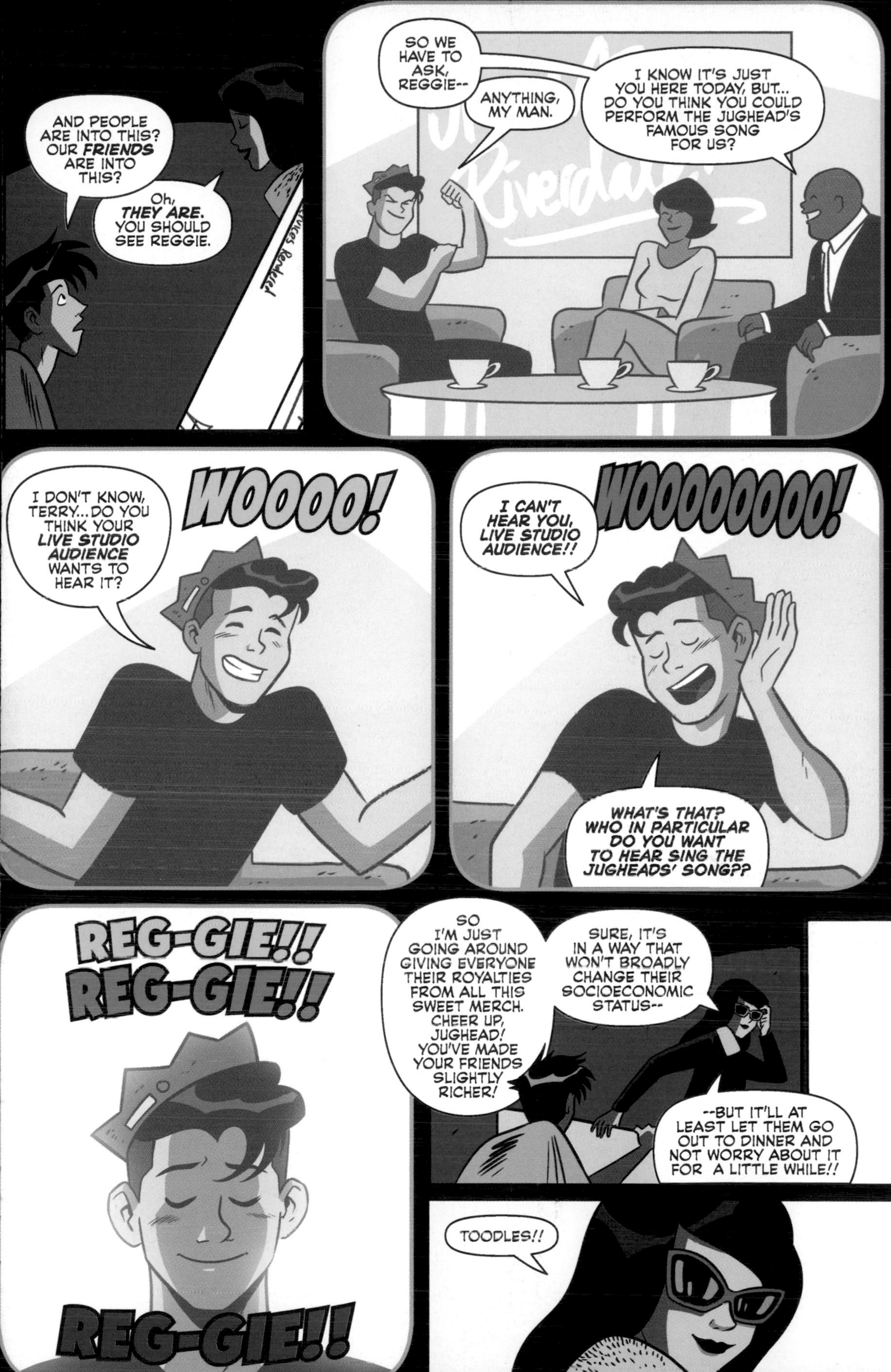
AND PEOPLE ARE INTO THIS? OUR FRIENDS ARE INTO THIS?
Oh, THEY ARE. YOU SHOULD SEE REGGIE.
SO WE HAVE TO ASK, REGGIE--
ANYTHING, MY MAN.
I KNOW IT'S JUST YOU HERE TODAY, BUT... DO YOU THINK YOU COULD PERFORM THE JUGHEAD'S FAMOUS SONG FOR US?
I DON'T KNOW, TERRY...DO YOU THINK YOUR LIVE STUDIO AUDIENCE WANTS TO HEAR IT?
WOOOO!
I CAN'T HEAR YOU, LIVE STUDIO AUDIENCE!!
WOOOOOOOO!
WHAT'S THAT? WHO IN PARTICULAR DO YOU WANT TO HEAR SING THE JUGHEADS' SONG??
REG-GIE!! REG-GIE!!
REG-GIE!!
SO I'M JUST GOING AROUND GIVING EVERYONE THEIR ROYALTIES FROM ALL THIS SWEET MERCH. CHEER UP, JUGHEAD! YOU'VE MADE YOUR FRIENDS SLIGHTLY RICHER!
SURE, IT'S IN A WAY THAT WON'T BROADLY CHANGE THEIR SOCIOECONOMIC STATUS--
--BUT IT'LL AT LEAST LET THEM GO OUT TO DINNER AND NOT WORRY ABOUT IT FOR A LITTLE WHILE!!
TOODLES!!

Guy on stage trying to elicit audience response: "I can't hear you!" Me, in the audience, shouting: "*IT'S BECAUSE THE ACOUSTICS OF THIS ROOM ARE DESIGNED TO SEND SOUND TOWARDS TO THE BACK!!*"

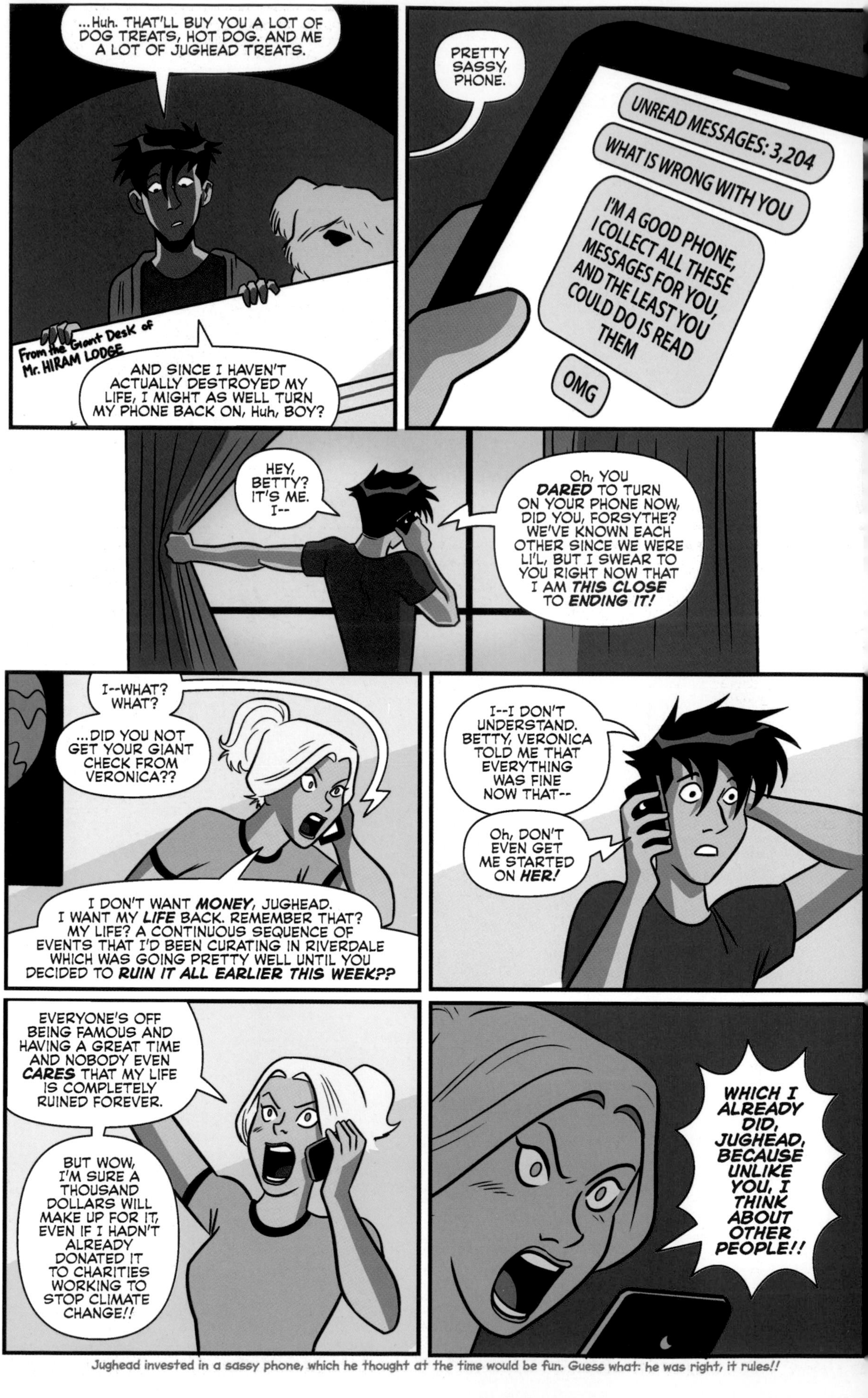
...Huh. THAT'LL BUY YOU A LOT OF DOG TREATS, HOT DOG. AND ME A LOT OF JUGHEAD TREATS.
From the Giant Desk of Mr. HIRAM LODGE
AND SINCE I HAVEN'T ACTUALLY DESTROYED MY LIFE, I MIGHT AS WELL TURN MY PHONE BACK ON, Huh, BOY?
PRETTY SASSY, PHONE.
UNREAD MESSAGES: 3,204
WHAT IS WRONG WITH YOU
I'M A GOOD PHONE, I COLLECT ALL THESE MESSAGES FOR YOU, AND THE LEAST YOU COULD DO IS READ THEM
OMG
HEY, BETTY? IT'S ME. I--
Oh, YOU DARED TO TURN ON YOUR PHONE NOW, DID YOU, FORSYTHE? WE'VE KNOWN EACH OTHER SINCE WE WERE LI'L, BUT I SWEAR TO YOU RIGHT NOW THAT I AM THIS CLOSE TO ENDING IT!
I--WHAT? WHAT?
...DID YOU NOT GET YOUR GIANT CHECK FROM VERONICA??
I DON'T WANT MONEY, JUGHEAD. I WANT MY LIFE BACK. REMEMBER THAT? MY LIFE? A CONTINUOUS SEQUENCE OF EVENTS THAT I'D BEEN CURATING IN RIVERDALE WHICH WAS GOING PRETTY WELL UNTIL YOU DECIDED TO RUIN IT ALL EARLIER THIS WEEK??
I--I DON'T UNDERSTAND. BETTY, VERONICA TOLD ME THAT EVERYTHING WAS FINE NOW THAT--
Oh, DON'T EVEN GET ME STARTED ON HER!
EVERYONE'S OFF BEING FAMOUS AND HAVING A GREAT TIME AND NOBODY EVEN CARES THAT MY LIFE IS COMPLETELY RUINED FOREVER.
BUT WOW, I'M SURE A THOUSAND DOLLARS WILL MAKE UP FOR IT, EVEN IF I HADN'T ALREADY DONATED IT TO CHARITIES WORKING TO STOP CLIMATE CHANGE!!
WHICH I ALREADY DID, JUGHEAD, BECAUSE UNLIKE YOU, I THINK ABOUT OTHER PEOPLE!!

Jughead invested in a sassy phone, which he thought at the time would be fun. Guess what: he was right, it rules!!

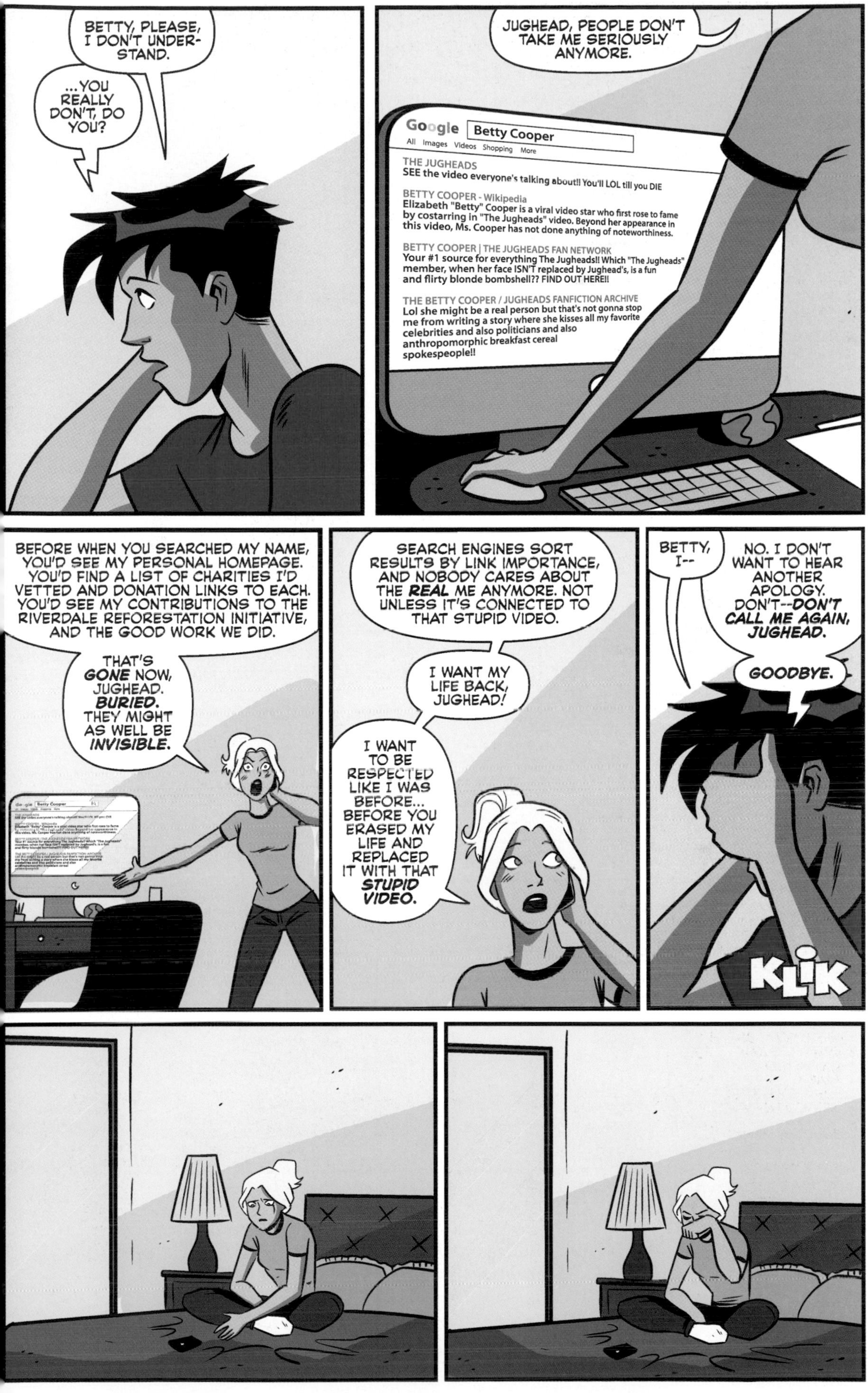
BETTY, PLEASE, I DON'T UNDERSTAND.
...YOU REALLY DON'T, DO YOU?
JUGHEAD, PEOPLE DON'T TAKE ME SERIOUSLY ANYMORE.
Google Betty Cooper
All Images Videos Shopping More
THE JUGHEADS
SEE the video everyone's talking about!! You'll LOL till you DIE
BETTY COOPER - Wikipedia
Elizabeth "Betty" Cooper is a viral video star who first rose to fame by costarring in "The Jugheads" video. Beyond her appearance in this video, Ms. Cooper has not done anything of noteworthiness.
BETTY COOPER | THE JUGHEADS FAN NETWORK
Your #1 source for everything The Jugheads!! Which "The Jugheads" member, when her face ISN'T replaced by Jughead's, is a fun and flirty blonde bombshell?? FIND OUT HERE!!
THE BETTY COOPER / JUGHEADS FANFICTION ARCHIVE
Lol she might be a real person but that's not gonna stop me from writing a story where she kisses all my favorite celebrities and also politicians and also anthropomorphic breakfast cereal spokespeople!!
BEFORE WHEN YOU SEARCHED MY NAME, YOU'D SEE MY PERSONAL HOMEPAGE. YOU'D FIND A LIST OF CHARITIES I'D VETTED AND DONATION LINKS TO EACH. YOU'D SEE MY CONTRIBUTIONS TO THE RIVERDALE REFORESTATION INITIATIVE, AND THE GOOD WORK WE DID.
THAT'S GONE NOW, JUGHEAD. BURIED. THEY MIGHT AS WELL BE INVISIBLE.
SEARCH ENGINES SORT RESULTS BY LINK IMPORTANCE, AND NOBODY CARES ABOUT THE REAL ME ANYMORE. NOT UNLESS IT'S CONNECTED TO THAT STUPID VIDEO.
I WANT MY LIFE BACK, JUGHEAD!
I WANT TO BE RESPECTED LIKE I WAS BEFORE... BEFORE YOU ERASED MY LIFE AND REPLACED IT WITH THAT STUPID VIDEO.
BETTY, I--
NO. I DON'T WANT TO HEAR ANOTHER APOLOGY. DON'T--DON'T CALL ME AGAIN, JUGHEAD.
GOODBYE.
KLIK

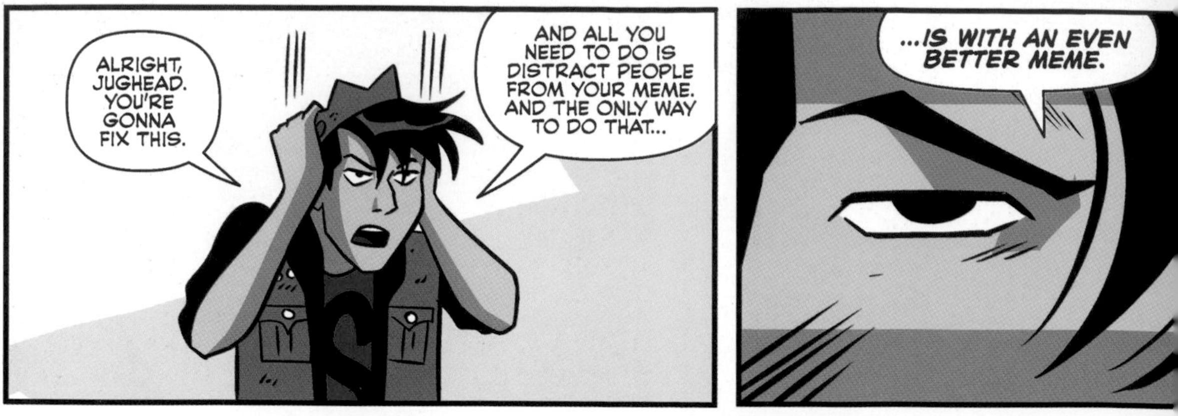
ALRIGHT, JUGHEAD. YOU'RE GONNA FIX THIS.
AND ALL YOU NEED TO DO IS DISTRACT PEOPLE FROM YOUR MEME. AND THE ONLY WAY TO DO THAT...
...IS WITH AN EVEN BETTER MEME.

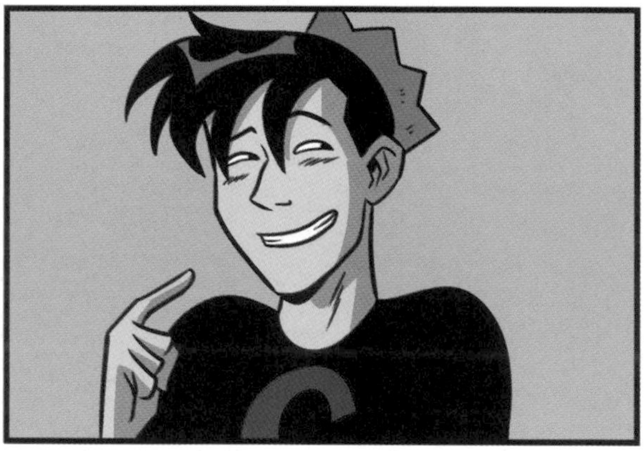

THE JUGHEADS ARE BACK!! BUT NOW IT'S JUST THE ONE GUY INSTEAD OF A BUNCH OF THEM, SO IT'S A LOT MORE STRAIGHTFORWARD

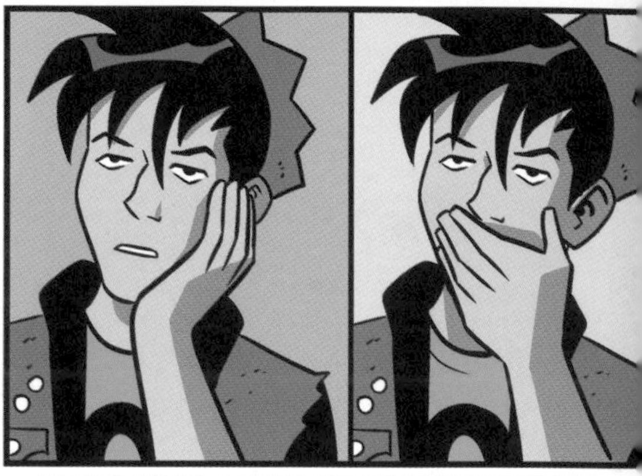

THE JUGHEADS 2: JUGHEAD REACTS TO "THE JUGHEADS"!! IT'S JUGCEPTION!! LOL!!

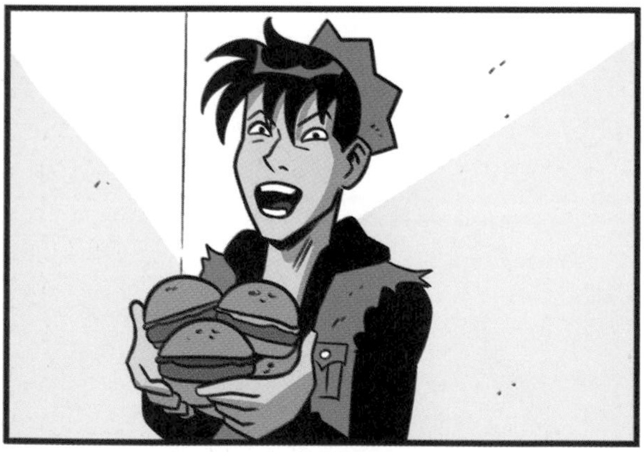

ERMAHGERD! IT'S 'THE JUGHEADS'... PART 5!!

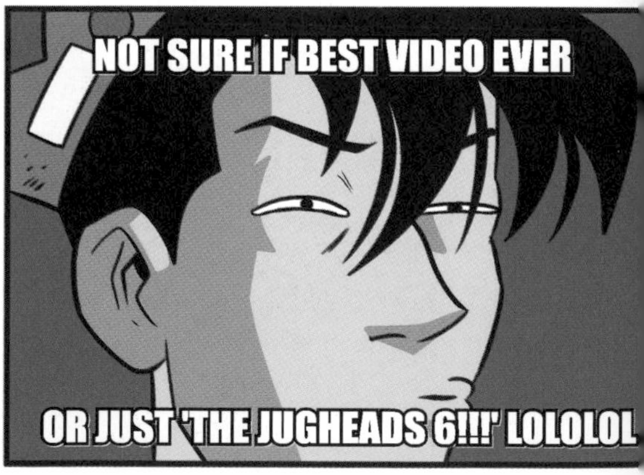
NOT SURE IF BEST VIDEO EVER
OR JUST 'THE JUGHEADS 6!!!' LOLOLOL

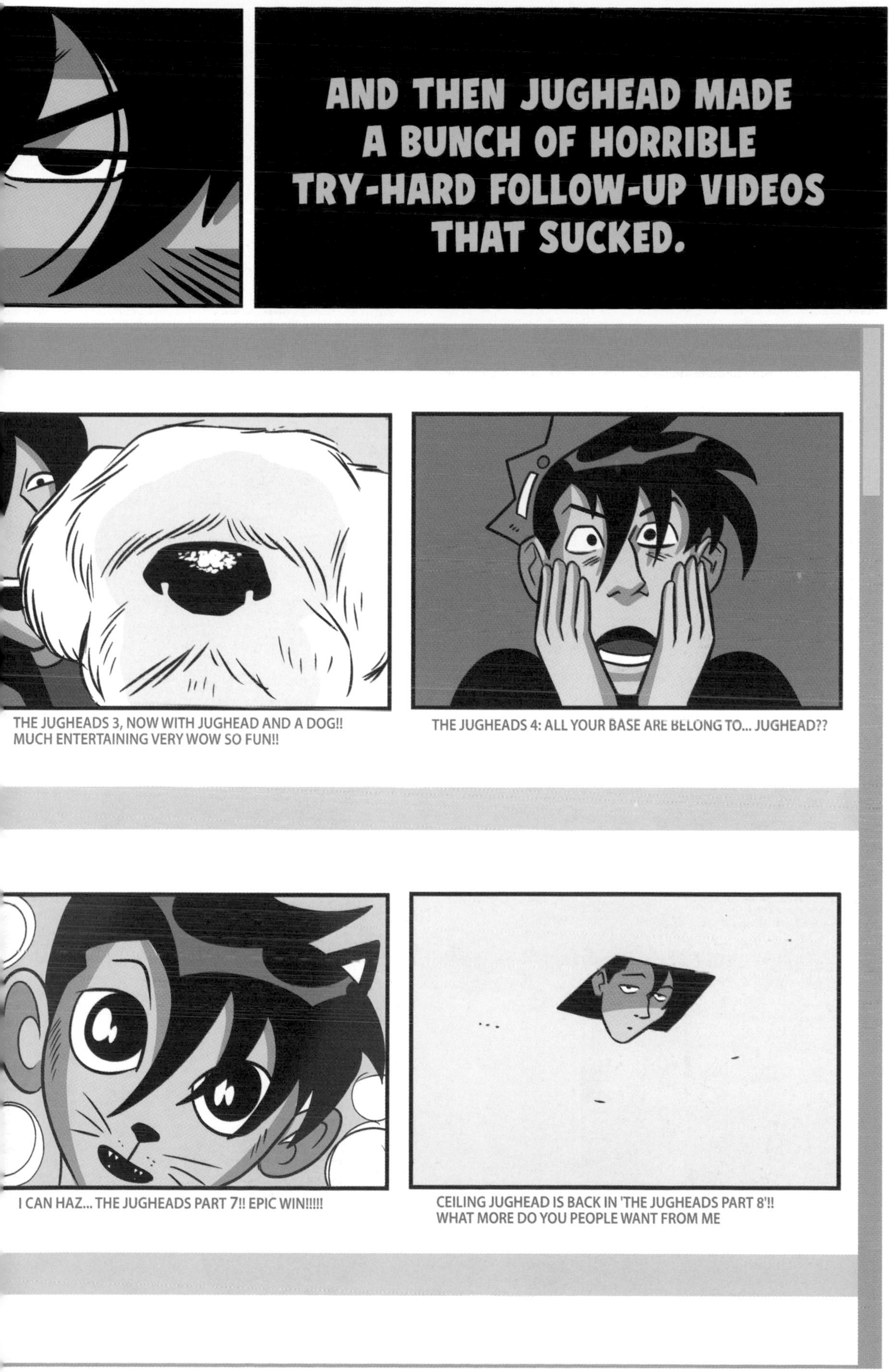
AND THEN JUGHEAD MADE A BUNCH OF HORRIBLE TRY-HARD FOLLOW-UP VIDEOS THAT SUCKED.
THE JUGHEADS 3, NOW WITH JUGHEAD AND A DOG!! MUCH ENTERTAINING VERY WOW SO FUN!!
THE JUGHEADS 4: ALL YOUR BASE ARE BELONG TO... JUGHEAD??
I CAN HAZ... THE JUGHEADS PART 7!! EPIC WIN!!!!!
...
CEILING JUGHEAD IS BACK IN 'THE JUGHEADS PART 8'!! WHAT MORE DO YOU PEOPLE WANT FROM ME

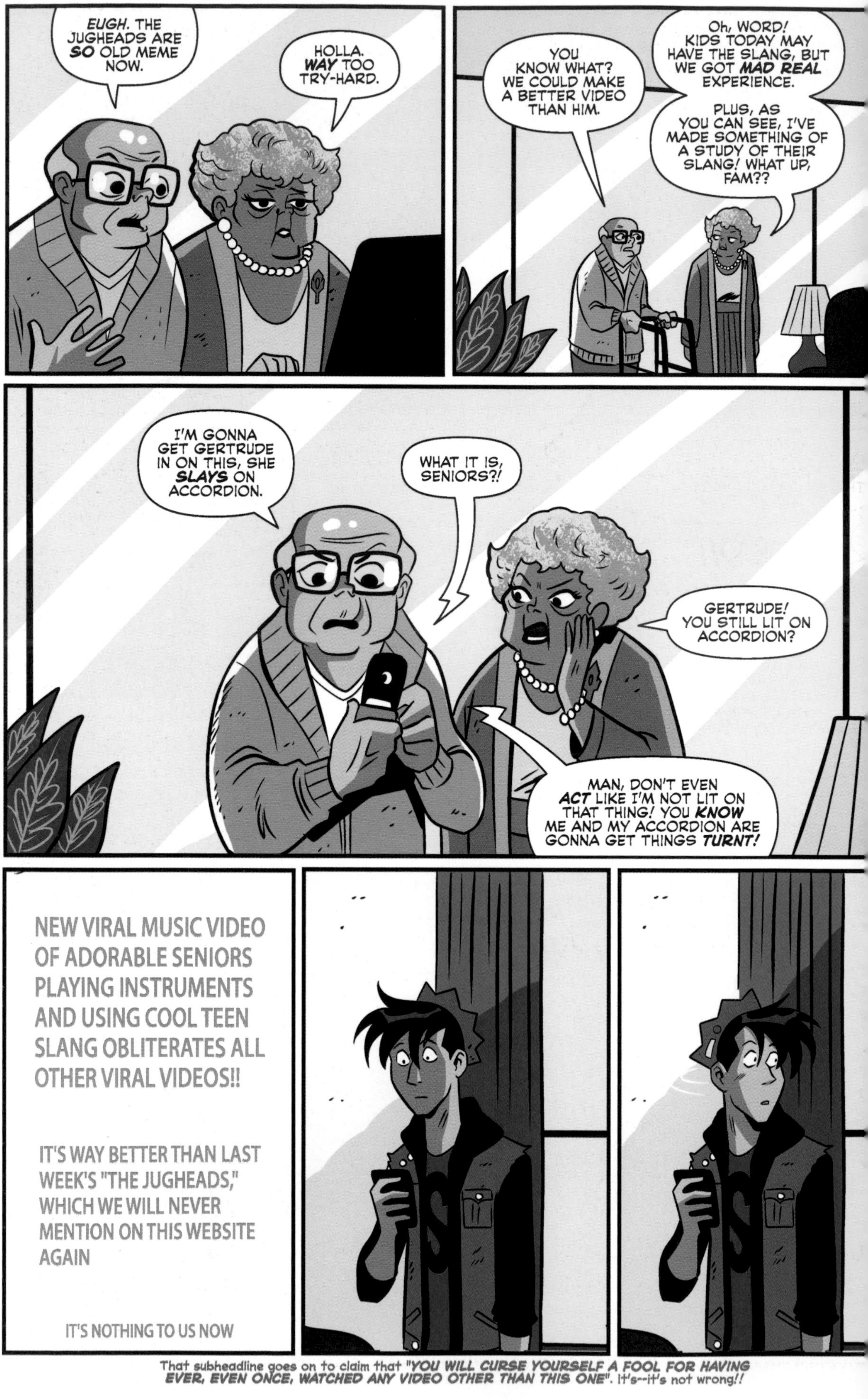
EUGH. THE JUGHEADS ARE SO OLD MEME NOW.
HOLLA. WAY TOO TRY-HARD.
YOU KNOW WHAT? WE COULD MAKE A BETTER VIDEO THAN HIM.
Oh, WORD! KIDS TODAY MAY HAVE THE SLANG, BUT WE GOT MAD REAL EXPERIENCE.
PLUS, AS YOU CAN SEE, I'VE MADE SOMETHING OF A STUDY OF THEIR SLANG! WHAT UP, FAM??
I'M GONNA GET GERTRUDE IN ON THIS, SHE SLAYS ON ACCORDION.
WHAT IT IS, SENIORS?!
GERTRUDE! YOU STILL LIT ON ACCORDION?
MAN, DON'T EVEN ACT LIKE I'M NOT LIT ON THAT THING! YOU KNOW ME AND MY ACCORDION ARE GONNA GET THINGS TURNT!
NEW VIRAL MUSIC VIDEO OF ADORABLE SENIORS PLAYING INSTRUMENTS AND USING COOL TEEN SLANG OBLITERATES ALL OTHER VIRAL VIDEOS!!
IT'S WAY BETTER THAN LAST WEEK'S "THE JUGHEADS," WHICH WE WILL NEVER MENTION ON THIS WEBSITE AGAIN
IT'S NOTHING TO US NOW

That subheadline goes on to claim that "*YOU WILL CURSE YOURSELF A FOOL FOR HAVING EVER, EVEN ONCE, WATCHED ANY VIDEO OTHER THAN THIS ONE*". It's--it's not wrong!!

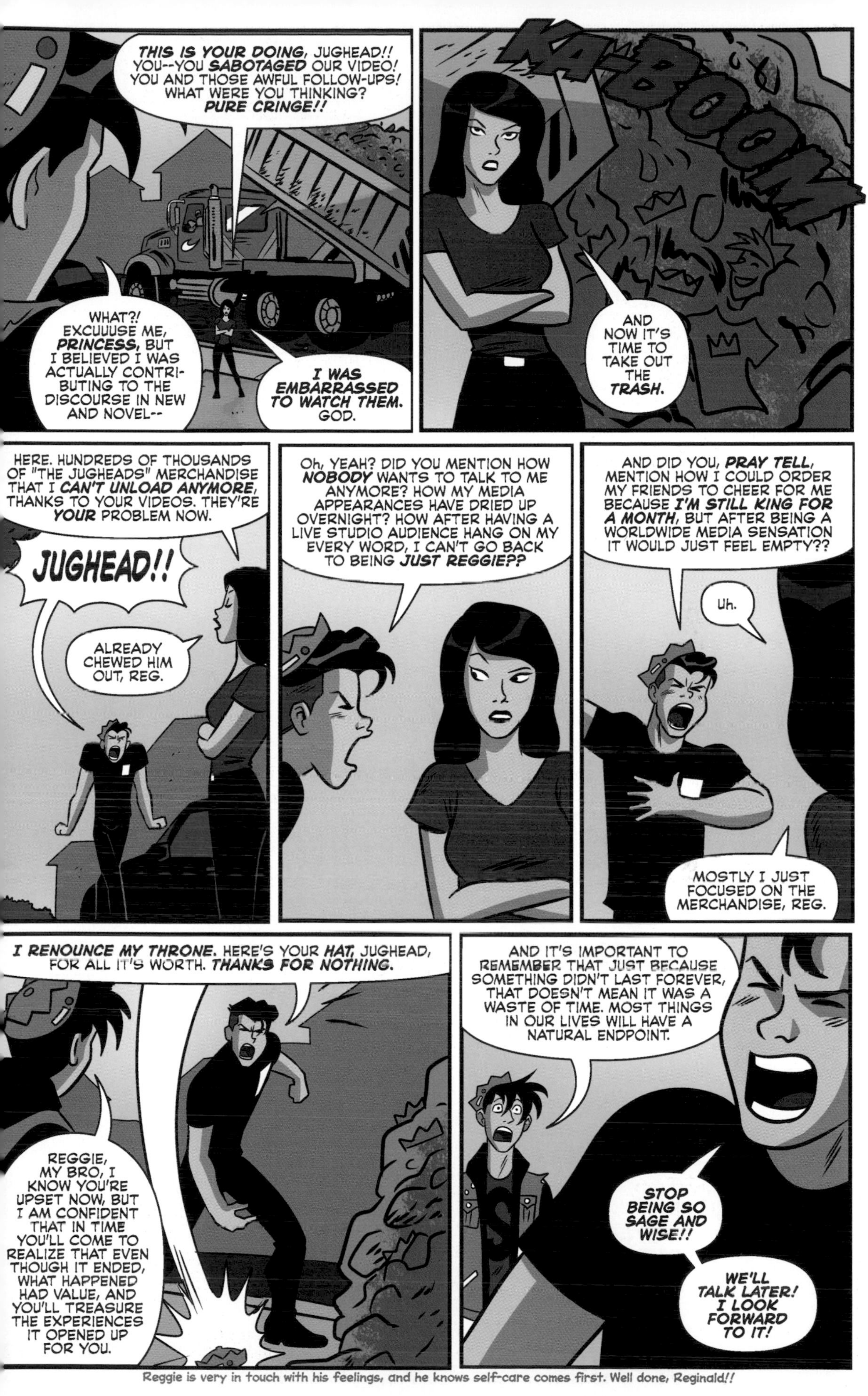
THIS IS YOUR DOING, JUGHEAD!! YOU--YOU SABOTAGED OUR VIDEO! YOU AND THOSE AWFUL FOLLOW-UPS! WHAT WERE YOU THINKING? PURE CRINGE!!
WHAT?! EXCUUUSE ME, PRINCESS, BUT I BELIEVED I WAS ACTUALLY CONTRI-BUTING TO THE DISCOURSE IN NEW AND NOVEL--
I WAS EMBARRASSED TO WATCH THEM. GOD.
KA-BOOM
AND NOW IT'S TIME TO TAKE OUT THE TRASH.
HERE. HUNDREDS OF THOUSANDS OF "THE JUGHEADS" MERCHANDISE THAT I CAN'T UNLOAD ANYMORE, THANKS TO YOUR VIDEOS. THEY'RE YOUR PROBLEM NOW.
JUGHEAD!!
ALREADY CHEWED HIM OUT, REG.
Oh, YEAH? DID YOU MENTION HOW NOBODY WANTS TO TALK TO ME ANYMORE? HOW MY MEDIA APPEARANCES HAVE DRIED UP OVERNIGHT? HOW AFTER HAVING A LIVE STUDIO AUDIENCE HANG ON MY EVERY WORD, I CAN'T GO BACK TO BEING JUST REGGIE??
AND DID YOU, PRAY TELL, MENTION HOW I COULD ORDER MY FRIENDS TO CHEER FOR ME BECAUSE I'M STILL KING FOR A MONTH, BUT AFTER BEING A WORLDWIDE MEDIA SENSATION IT WOULD JUST FEEL EMPTY??
Uh.
MOSTLY I JUST FOCUSED ON THE MERCHANDISE, REG.
I RENOUNCE MY THRONE. HERE'S YOUR HAT, JUGHEAD, FOR ALL IT'S WORTH. THANKS FOR NOTHING.
REGGIE, MY BRO, I KNOW YOU'RE UPSET NOW, BUT I AM CONFIDENT THAT IN TIME YOU'LL COME TO REALIZE THAT EVEN THOUGH IT ENDED, WHAT HAPPENED HAD VALUE, AND YOU'LL TREASURE THE EXPERIENCES IT OPENED UP FOR YOU.
AND IT'S IMPORTANT TO REMEMBER THAT JUST BECAUSE SOMETHING DIDN'T LAST FOREVER, THAT DOESN'T MEAN IT WAS A WASTE OF TIME. MOST THINGS IN OUR LIVES WILL HAVE A NATURAL ENDPOINT.
STOP BEING SO SAGE AND WISE!!
WE'LL TALK LATER! I LOOK FORWARD TO IT!

Reggie is very in touch with his feelings, and he knows self-care comes first. Well done, Reginald!!

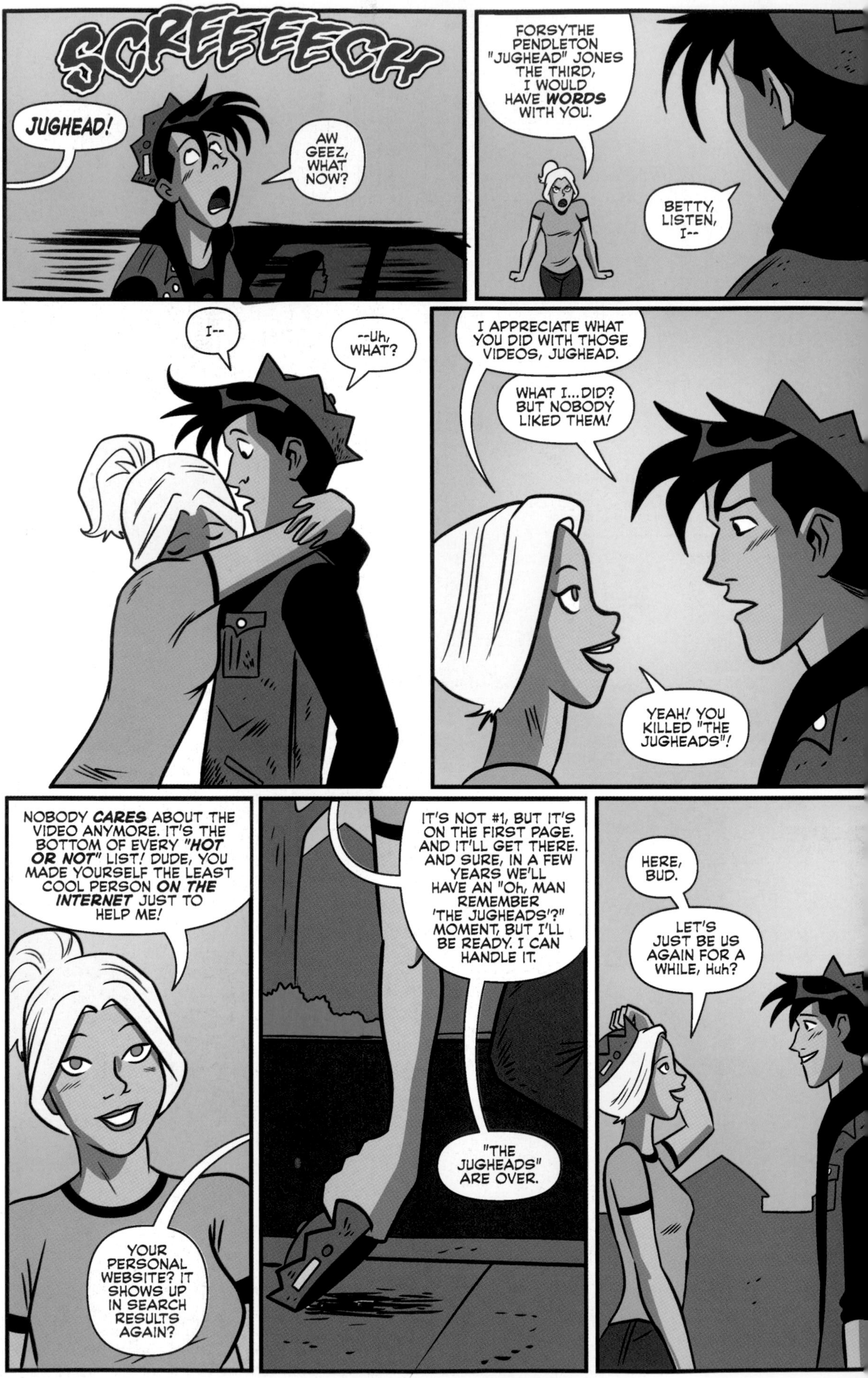
SCREEEECH
JUGHEAD!
AW GEEZ, WHAT NOW?
FORSYTHE PENDLETON "JUGHEAD" JONES THE THIRD, I WOULD HAVE WORDS WITH YOU.
BETTY, LISTEN, I--
I--
--Uh, WHAT?
I APPRECIATE WHAT YOU DID WITH THOSE VIDEOS, JUGHEAD.
WHAT I...DID? BUT NOBODY LIKED THEM!
YEAH! YOU KILLED "THE JUGHEADS"!
NOBODY CARES ABOUT THE VIDEO ANYMORE. IT'S THE BOTTOM OF EVERY "HOT OR NOT" LIST! DUDE, YOU MADE YOURSELF THE LEAST COOL PERSON ON THE INTERNET JUST TO HELP ME!
YOUR PERSONAL WEBSITE? IT SHOWS UP IN SEARCH RESULTS AGAIN?
IT'S NOT #1, BUT IT'S ON THE FIRST PAGE. AND IT'LL GET THERE. AND SURE, IN A FEW YEARS WE'LL HAVE AN "Oh, MAN REMEMBER 'THE JUGHEADS'?" MOMENT, BUT I'LL BE READY. I CAN HANDLE IT.
"THE JUGHEADS" ARE OVER.
HERE, BUD.
LET'S JUST BE US AGAIN FOR A WHILE, Huh?

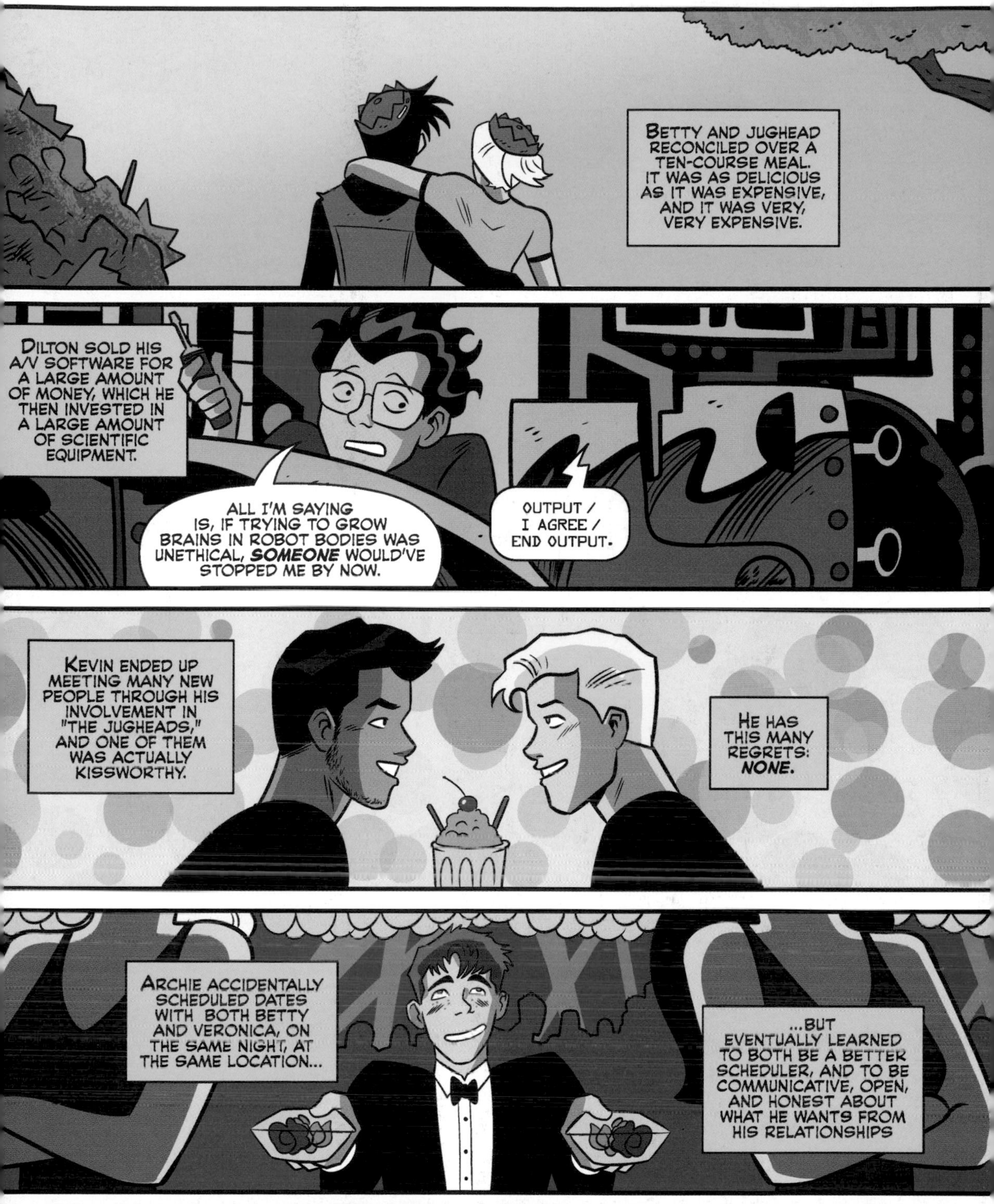
BETTY AND JUGHEAD RECONCILED OVER A TEN-COURSE MEAL. IT WAS AS DELICIOUS AS IT WAS EXPENSIVE, AND IT WAS VERY, VERY EXPENSIVE.
DILTON SOLD HIS A/V SOFTWARE FOR A LARGE AMOUNT OF MONEY, WHICH HE THEN INVESTED IN A LARGE AMOUNT OF SCIENTIFIC EQUIPMENT.
ALL I'M SAYING IS, IF TRYING TO GROW BRAINS IN ROBOT BODIES WAS UNETHICAL, *SOMEONE* WOULD'VE STOPPED ME BY NOW.
OUTPUT / I AGREE / END OUTPUT.
KEVIN ENDED UP MEETING MANY NEW PEOPLE THROUGH HIS INVOLVEMENT IN "THE JUGHEADS," AND ONE OF THEM WAS ACTUALLY KISSWORTHY.
HE HAS THIS MANY REGRETS: ***NONE.***
ARCHIE ACCIDENTALLY SCHEDULED DATES WITH BOTH BETTY AND VERONICA, ON THE SAME NIGHT, AT THE SAME LOCATION...
...BUT EVENTUALLY LEARNED TO BOTH BE A BETTER SCHEDULER, AND TO BE COMMUNICATIVE, OPEN, AND HONEST ABOUT WHAT HE WANTS FROM HIS RELATIONSHIPS
THE HUNKS ARE HUNKY TO THIS VERY DAY.
THE END.

h, Jughead also caught up on the school he missed while he was away for a week being depressed! In fact, let's say that he and Ms. Grundy even high fived over the fact that he caught up ***SO EFFICIENTLY!*** And you know Ms. Grundy doesn't high five for just anything. She is ***MEGA STINGY*** with the fives: hi, down low, too slow, or otherwise.

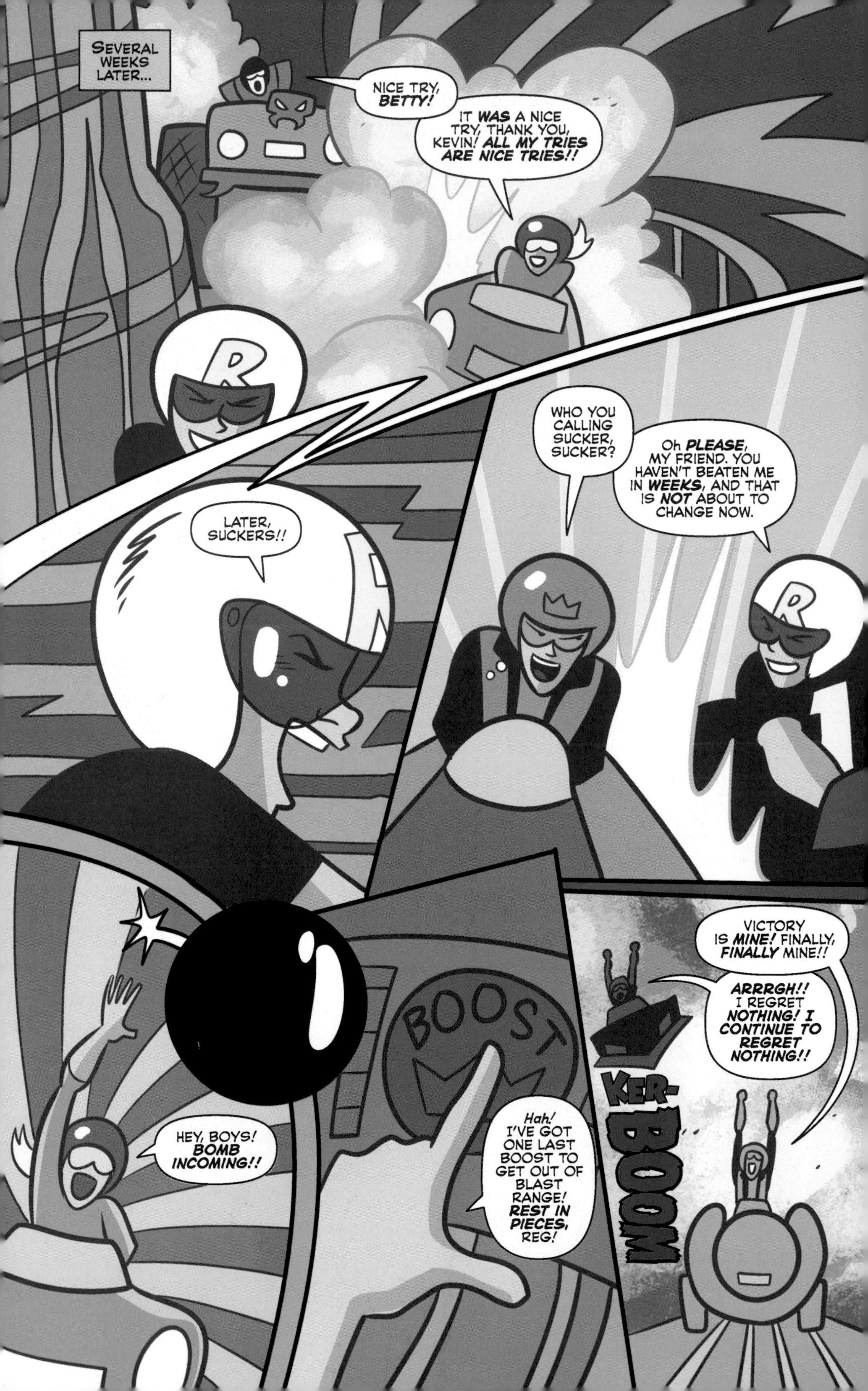

SEVERAL WEEKS LATER...
NICE TRY, BETTY!
IT WAS A NICE TRY, THANK YOU, KEVIN! ALL MY TRIES ARE NICE TRIES!!
LATER, SUCKERS!!
WHO YOU CALLING SUCKER, SUCKER?
Oh PLEASE, MY FRIEND. YOU HAVEN'T BEATEN ME IN WEEKS, AND THAT IS NOT ABOUT TO CHANGE NOW.
HEY, BOYS! BOMB INCOMING!!
BOOST
Hah! I'VE GOT ONE LAST BOOST TO GET OUT OF BLAST RANGE! REST IN PIECES, REG!
VICTORY IS MINE! FINALLY, FINALLY MINE!!
ARRRGH!! I REGRET NOTHING! I CONTINUE TO REGRET NOTHING!!
KER-BOOM

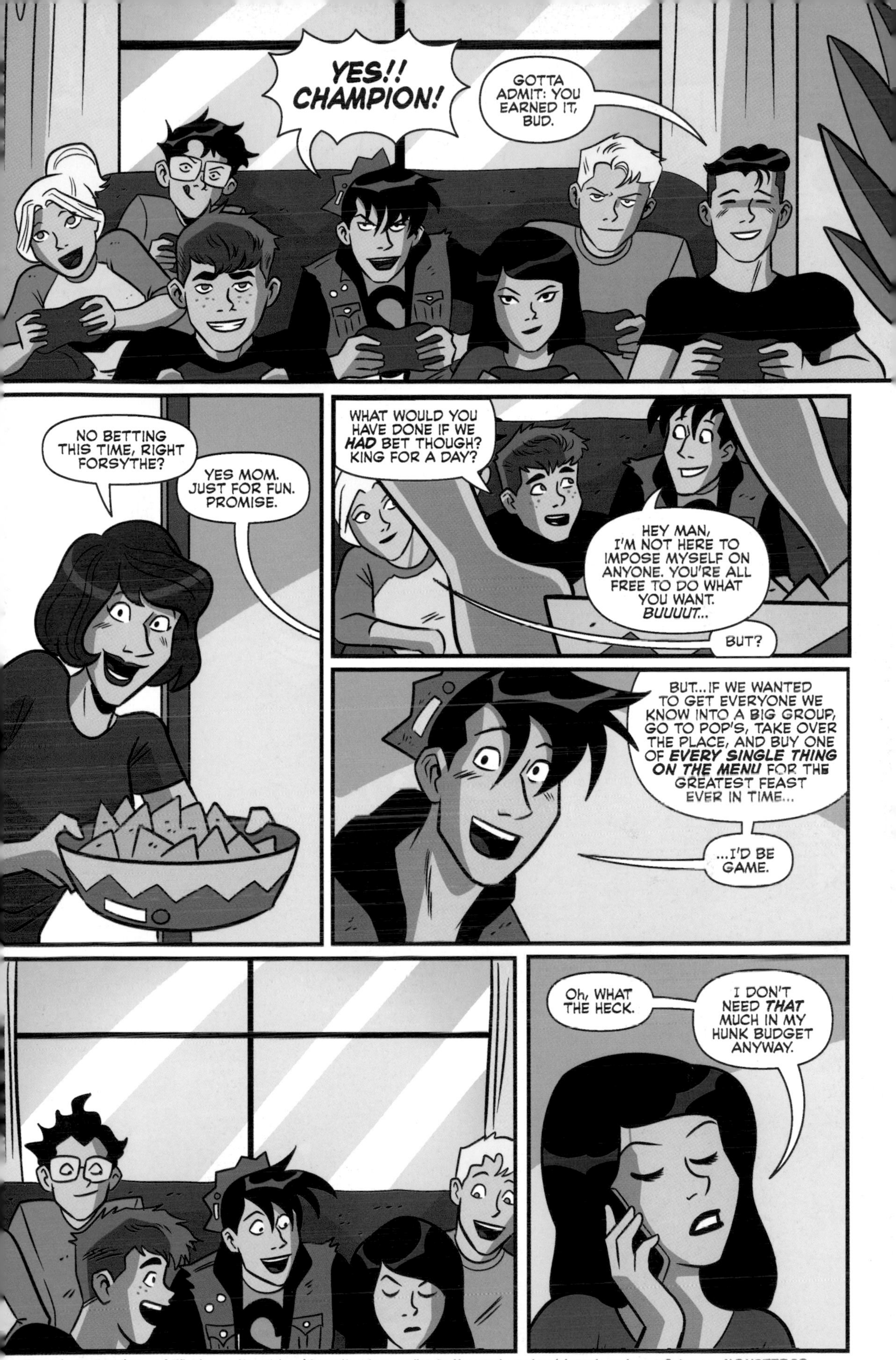
YES!! CHAMPION!
GOTTA ADMIT: YOU EARNED IT, BUD.
NO BETTING THIS TIME, RIGHT FORSYTHE?
YES MOM. JUST FOR FUN. PROMISE.
WHAT WOULD YOU HAVE DONE IF WE HAD BET THOUGH? KING FOR A DAY?
HEY MAN, I'M NOT HERE TO IMPOSE MYSELF ON ANYONE. YOU'RE ALL FREE TO DO WHAT YOU WANT. BUUUUT...
BUT?
BUT...IF WE WANTED TO GET EVERYONE WE KNOW INTO A BIG GROUP, GO TO POP'S, TAKE OVER THE PLACE, AND BUY ONE OF EVERY SINGLE THING ON THE MENU FOR THE GREATEST FEAST EVER IN TIME...
...I'D BE GAME.
Oh, WHAT THE HECK.
I DON'T NEED THAT MUCH IN MY HUNK BUDGET ANYWAY.

There's Jughead's mom! What, you thought we'd mention her earlier in the comic and not have her show up? Are we ***MONSTERS?*** Are we ***DEAF*** to the cries of the legions of (hold on while I look up her name) "Gladys Jones" fans??

ISSUE
FIFTEEN

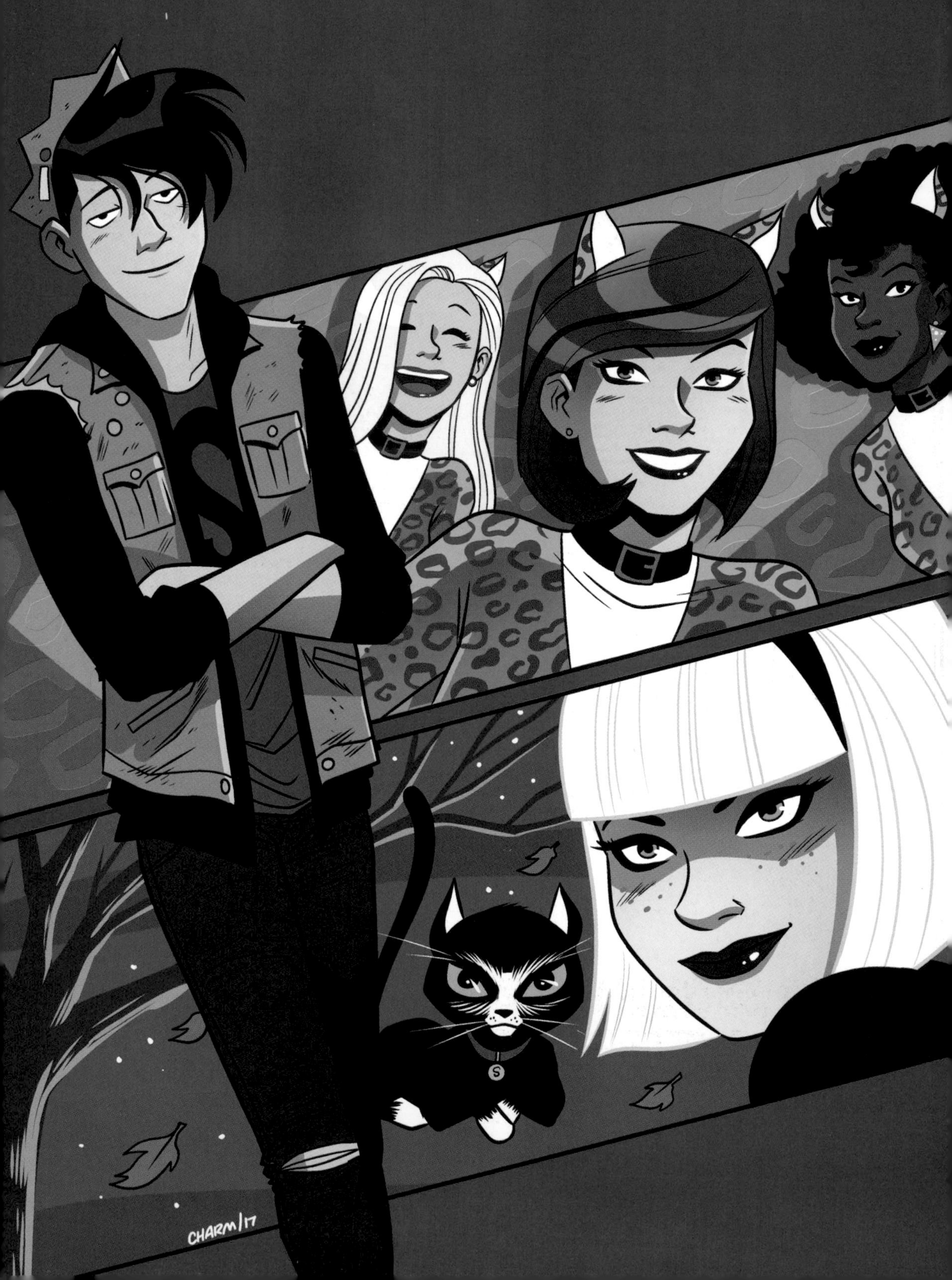
CHARM/17

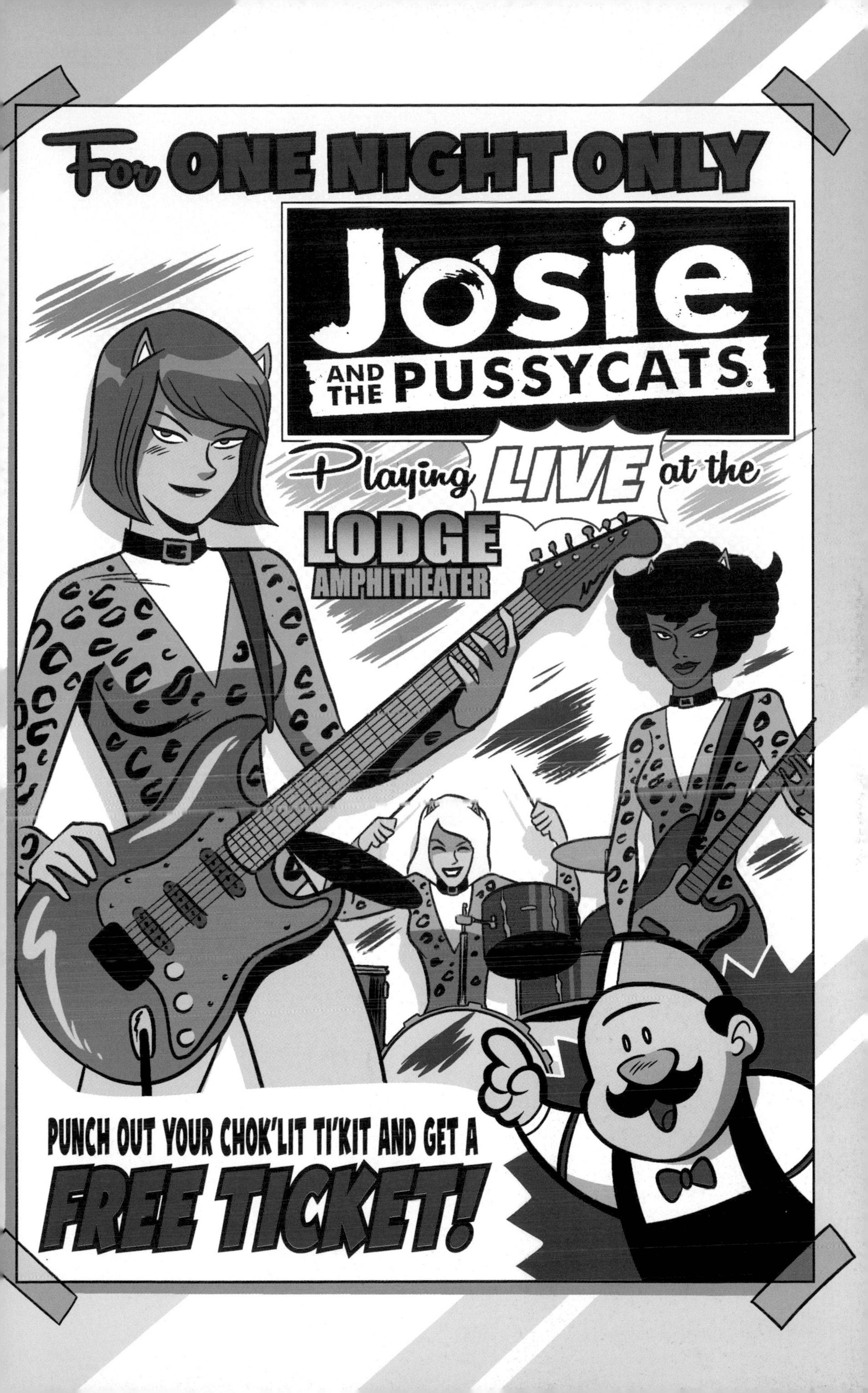
For ONE NIGHT ONLY
Josie AND THE PUSSYCATS®
Playing LIVE at the
LODGE AMPHITHEATER
PUNCH OUT YOUR CHOK'LIT TI'KIT AND GET A
FREE TICKET!

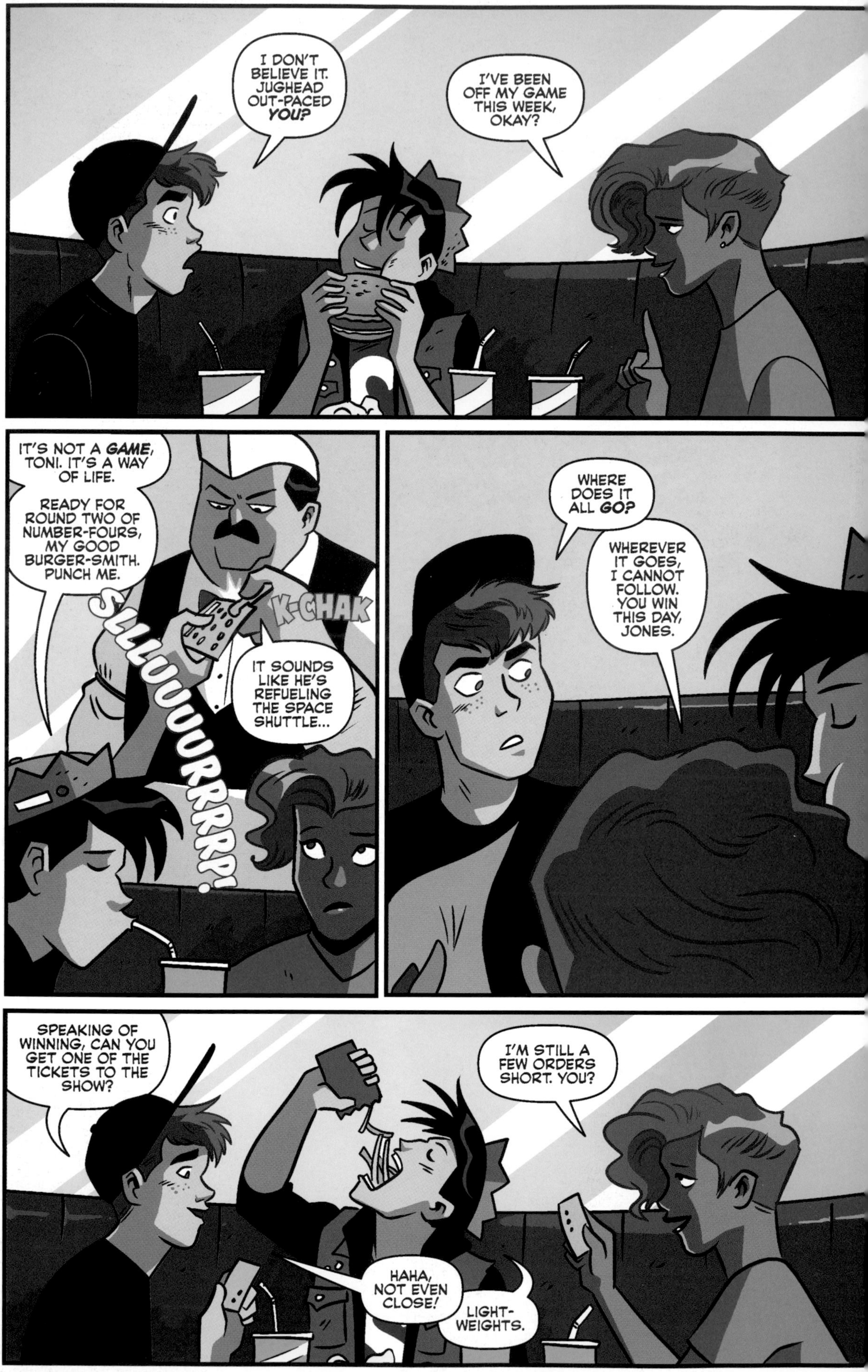
I DON'T BELIEVE IT. JUGHEAD OUT-PACED *YOU?*
I'VE BEEN OFF MY GAME THIS WEEK, OKAY?
IT'S NOT A *GAME*, TONI. IT'S A WAY OF LIFE.
READY FOR ROUND TWO OF NUMBER-FOURS, MY GOOD BURGER-SMITH. PUNCH ME.
K-CHAK
SLLLUUUUURRRP!
IT SOUNDS LIKE HE'S REFUELING THE SPACE SHUTTLE...
WHERE DOES IT ALL *GO?*
WHEREVER IT GOES, I CANNOT FOLLOW. YOU WIN THIS DAY, JONES.
SPEAKING OF WINNING, CAN YOU GET ONE OF THE TICKETS TO THE SHOW?
I'M STILL A FEW ORDERS SHORT. YOU?
HAHA, NOT EVEN CLOSE!
LIGHT-WEIGHTS.

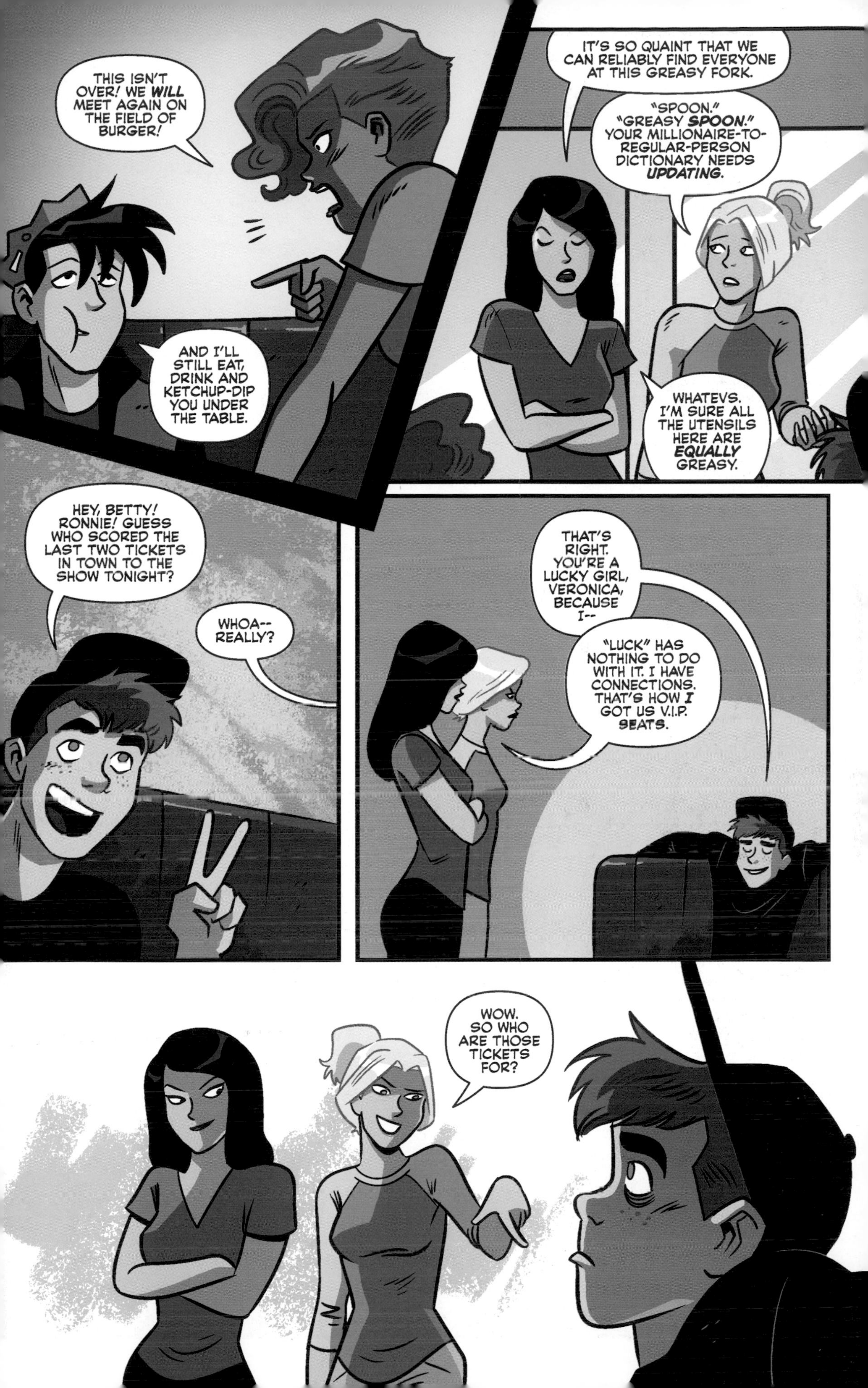
THIS ISN'T OVER! WE WILL MEET AGAIN ON THE FIELD OF BURGER!
AND I'LL STILL EAT, DRINK AND KETCHUP-DIP YOU UNDER THE TABLE.
IT'S SO QUAINT THAT WE CAN RELIABLY FIND EVERYONE AT THIS GREASY FORK.
"SPOON." "GREASY SPOON." YOUR MILLIONAIRE-TO-REGULAR-PERSON DICTIONARY NEEDS UPDATING.
WHATEVS. I'M SURE ALL THE UTENSILS HERE ARE EQUALLY GREASY.
HEY, BETTY! RONNIE! GUESS WHO SCORED THE LAST TWO TICKETS IN TOWN TO THE SHOW TONIGHT?
WHOA-- REALLY?
THAT'S RIGHT. YOU'RE A LUCKY GIRL, VERONICA, BECAUSE I--
"LUCK" HAS NOTHING TO DO WITH IT. I HAVE CONNECTIONS. THAT'S HOW I GOT US V.I.P. SEATS.
WOW. SO WHO ARE THOSE TICKETS FOR?

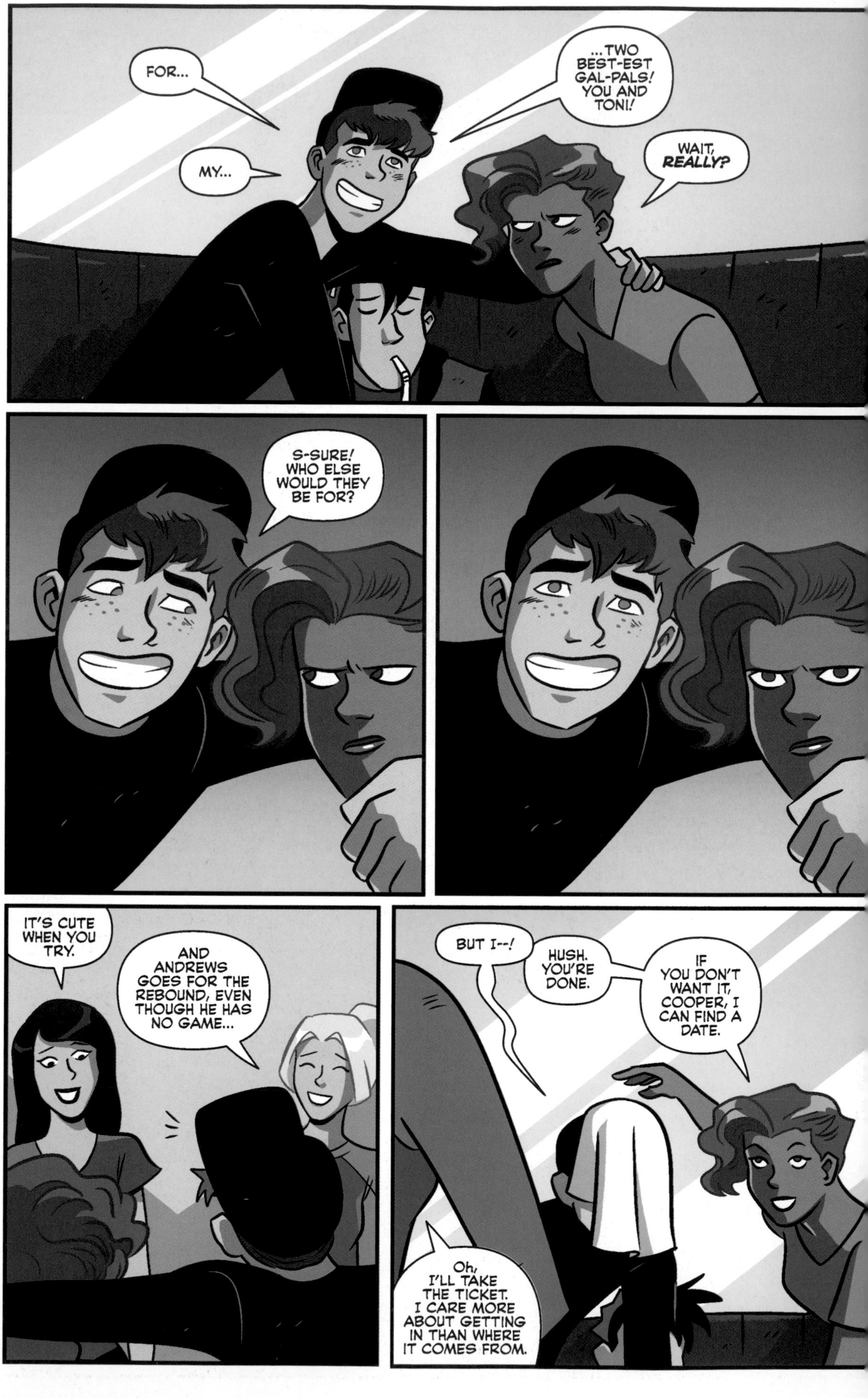
FOR...
MY...
...TWO BEST-EST GAL-PALS! YOU AND TONI!
WAIT, *REALLY?*
S-SURE! WHO ELSE WOULD THEY BE FOR?
IT'S CUTE WHEN YOU TRY.
AND ANDREWS GOES FOR THE REBOUND, EVEN THOUGH HE HAS NO GAME...
BUT I--!
HUSH. YOU'RE DONE.
IF YOU DON'T WANT IT, COOPER, I CAN FIND A DATE.
Oh, I'LL TAKE THE TICKET. I CARE MORE ABOUT GETTING IN THAN WHERE IT COMES FROM.

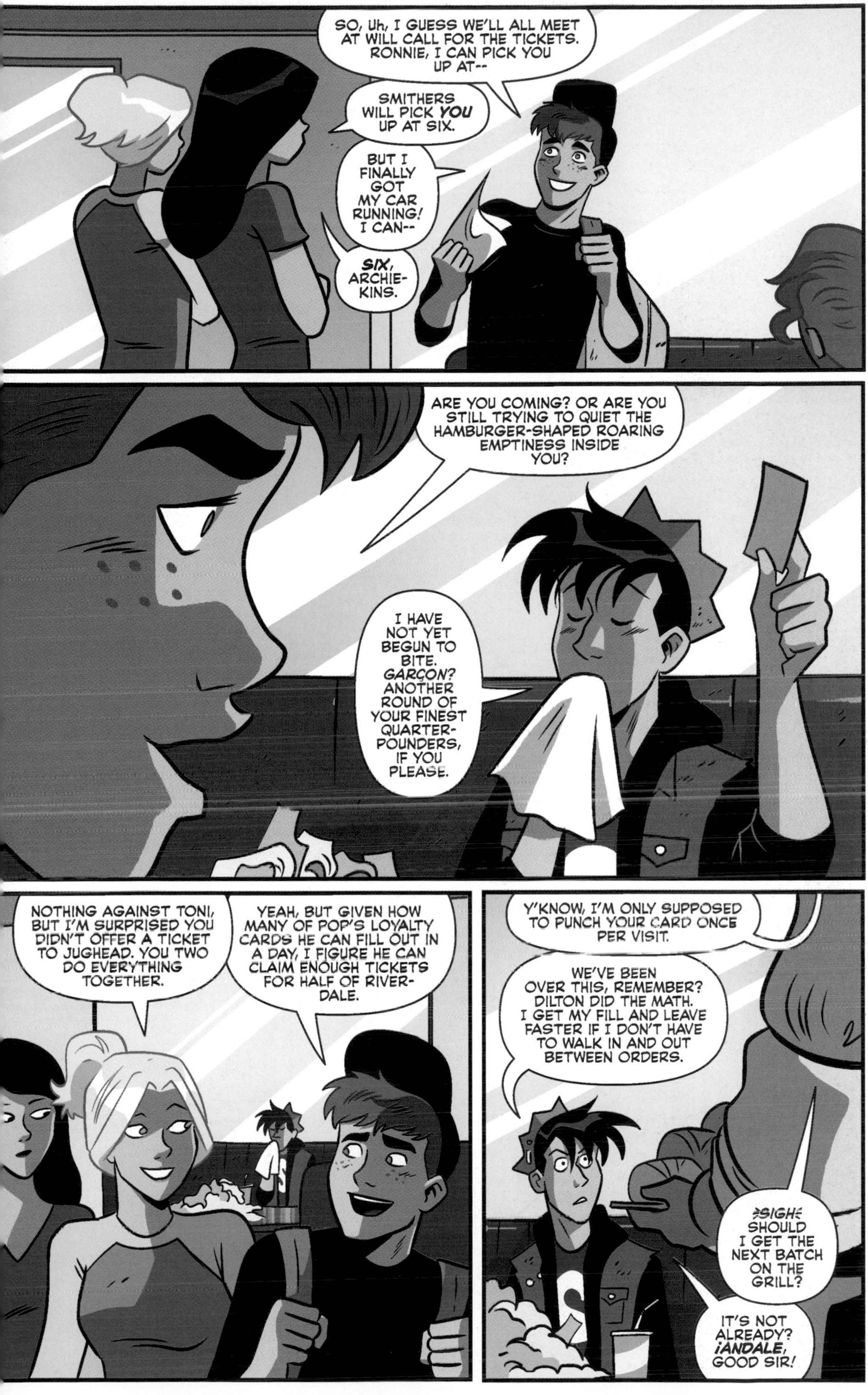
SO, Uh, I GUESS WE'LL ALL MEET AT WILL CALL FOR THE TICKETS. RONNIE, I CAN PICK YOU UP AT--
SMITHERS WILL PICK *YOU* UP AT SIX.
BUT I FINALLY GOT MY CAR RUNNING! I CAN--
SIX, ARCHIE-KINS.
ARE YOU COMING? OR ARE YOU STILL TRYING TO QUIET THE HAMBURGER-SHAPED ROARING EMPTINESS INSIDE YOU?
I HAVE NOT YET BEGUN TO BITE. *GARÇON?* ANOTHER ROUND OF YOUR FINEST QUARTER-POUNDERS, IF YOU PLEASE.
NOTHING AGAINST TONI, BUT I'M SURPRISED YOU DIDN'T OFFER A TICKET TO JUGHEAD. YOU TWO DO EVERYTHING TOGETHER.
YEAH, BUT GIVEN HOW MANY OF POP'S LOYALTY CARDS HE CAN FILL OUT IN A DAY, I FIGURE HE CAN CLAIM ENOUGH TICKETS FOR HALF OF RIVER-DALE.
Y'KNOW, I'M ONLY SUPPOSED TO PUNCH YOUR CARD ONCE PER VISIT.
WE'VE BEEN OVER THIS, REMEMBER? DILTON DID THE MATH. I GET MY FILL AND LEAVE FASTER IF I DON'T HAVE TO WALK IN AND OUT BETWEEN ORDERS.
SIGH SHOULD I GET THE NEXT BATCH ON THE GRILL?
IT'S NOT ALREADY? *¡ANDALE*, GOOD SIR!

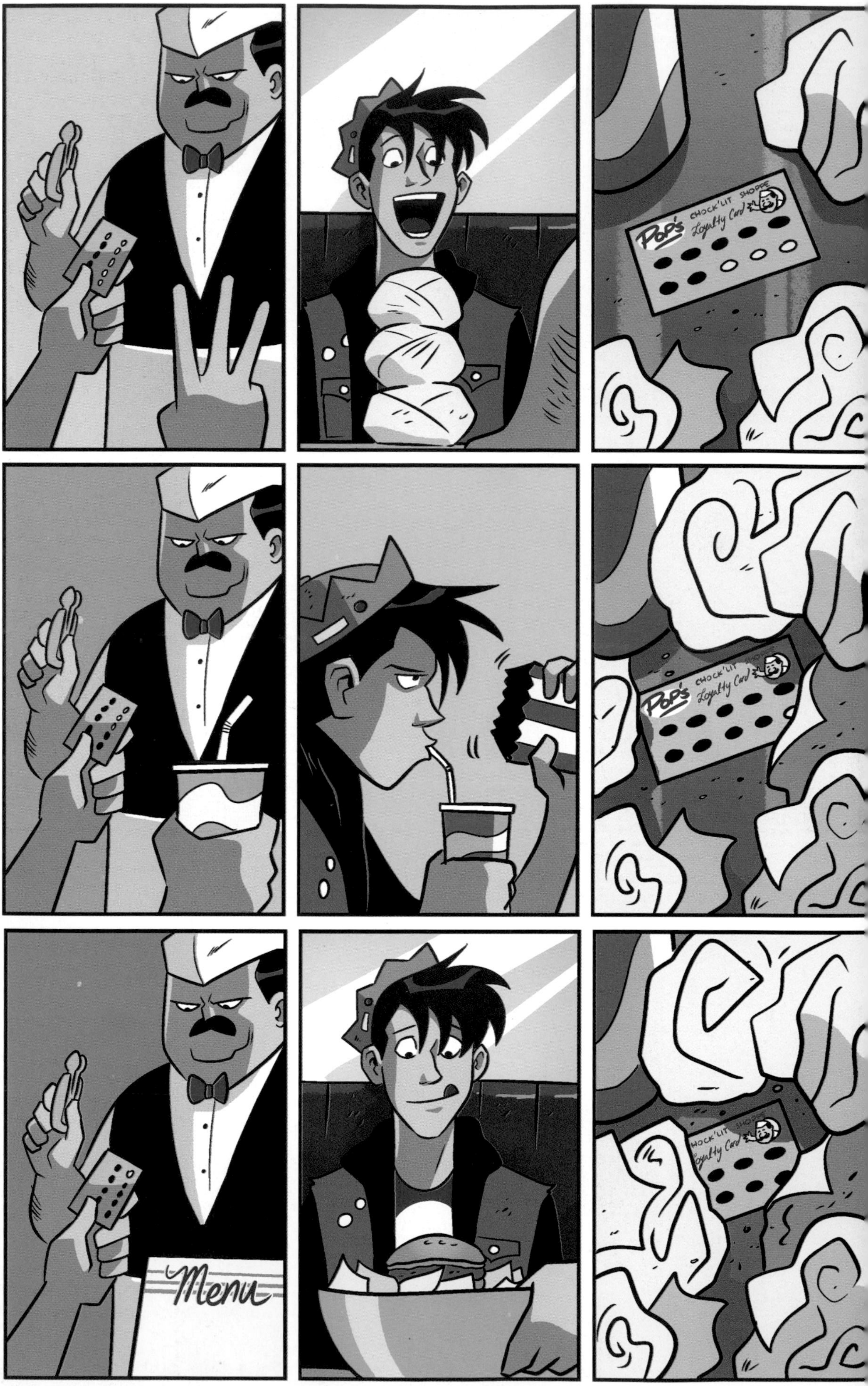
POP's
CHOCK'LIT SHOPPE
Loyalty Card
POP's
CHOCK'LIT SHOPPE
Loyalty Card
Menu
CHOCK'LIT SHOPPE
Loyalty Card

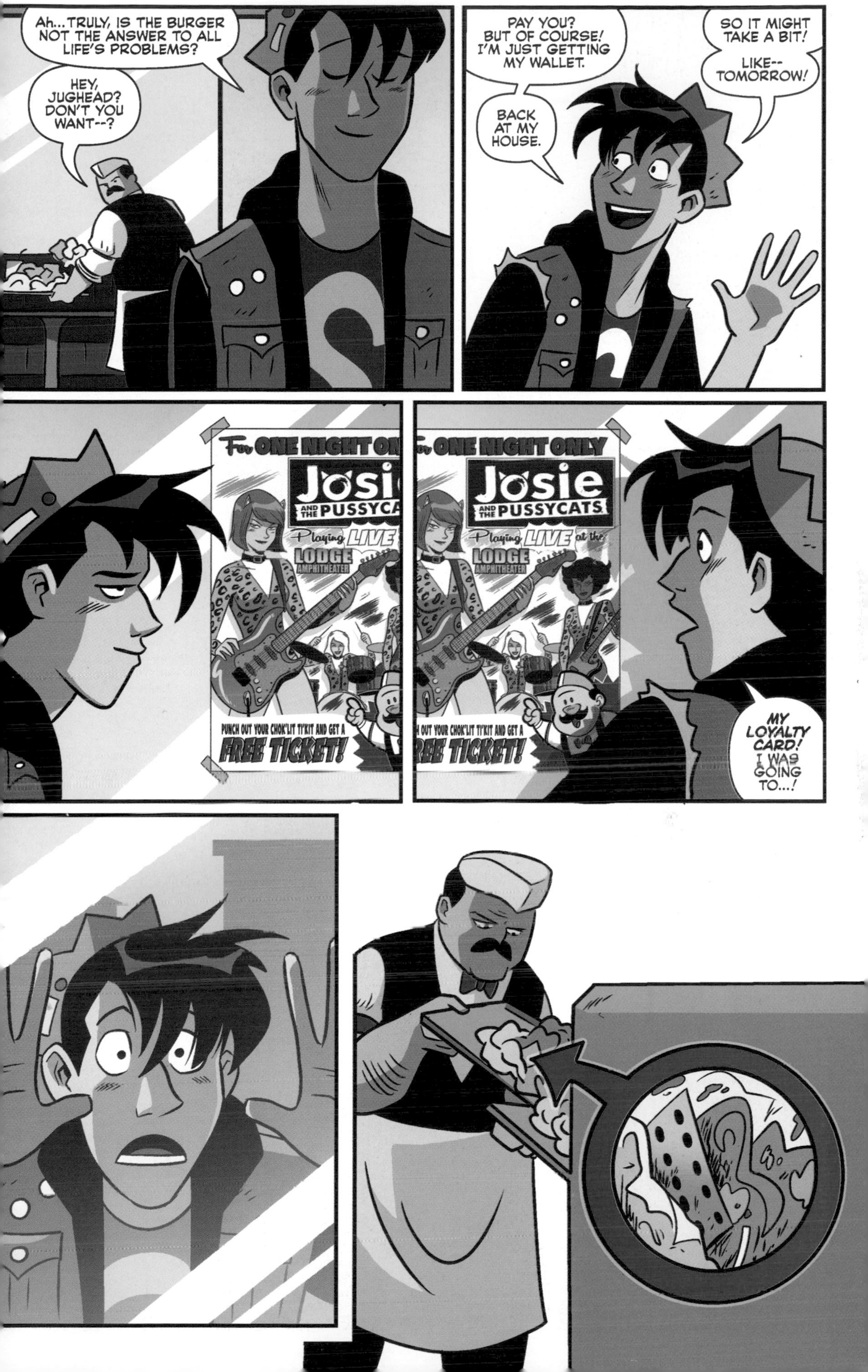

Ah...TRULY, IS THE BURGER NOT THE ANSWER TO ALL LIFE'S PROBLEMS?
HEY, JUGHEAD? DON'T YOU WANT--?
PAY YOU? BUT OF COURSE! I'M JUST GETTING MY WALLET.
BACK AT MY HOUSE.
SO IT MIGHT TAKE A BIT!
LIKE-- TOMORROW!
For ONE NIGHT ONLY
Josie AND THE PUSSYCATS
Playing LIVE at the
LODGE AMPHITHEATER
PUNCH OUT YOUR CHOK'LIT TI'KIT AND GET A
FREE TICKET!
MY LOYALTY CARD! I WAS GOING TO...!

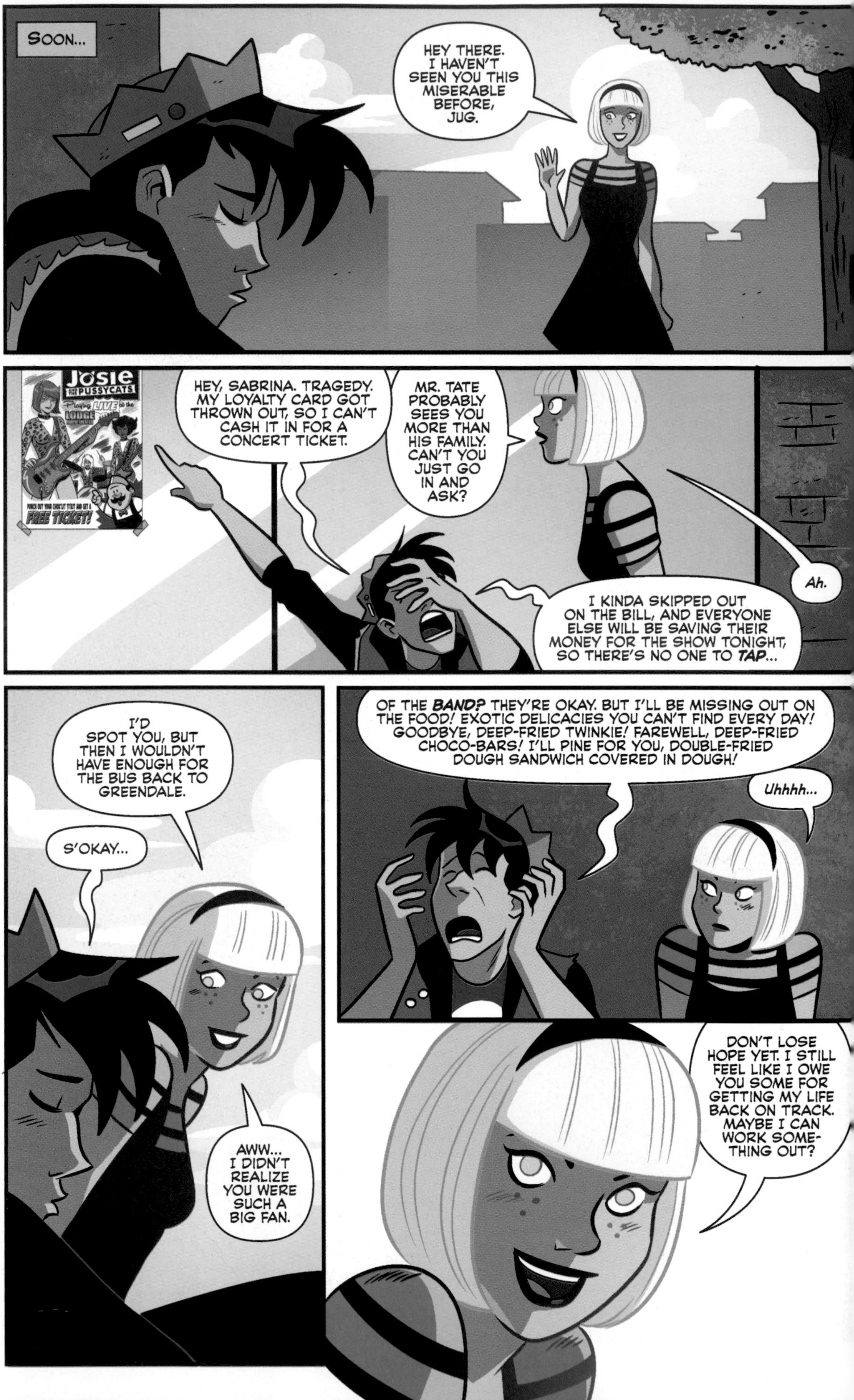
SOON...
HEY THERE. I HAVEN'T SEEN YOU THIS MISERABLE BEFORE, JUG.
JOSIE
PUSSYCATS
FREE TICKET!
HEY, SABRINA. TRAGEDY. MY LOYALTY CARD GOT THROWN OUT, SO I CAN'T CASH IT IN FOR A CONCERT TICKET.
MR. TATE PROBABLY SEES YOU MORE THAN HIS FAMILY. CAN'T YOU JUST GO IN AND ASK?
I KINDA SKIPPED OUT ON THE BILL, AND EVERYONE ELSE WILL BE SAVING THEIR MONEY FOR THE SHOW TONIGHT, SO THERE'S NO ONE TO *TAP*...
Ah.
I'D SPOT YOU, BUT THEN I WOULDN'T HAVE ENOUGH FOR THE BUS BACK TO GREENDALE.
S'OKAY...
AWW... I DIDN'T REALIZE YOU WERE SUCH A BIG FAN.
OF THE *BAND?* THEY'RE OKAY. BUT I'LL BE MISSING OUT ON THE FOOD! EXOTIC DELICACIES YOU CAN'T FIND EVERY DAY! GOODBYE, DEEP-FRIED TWINKIE! FAREWELL, DEEP-FRIED CHOCO-BARS! I'LL PINE FOR YOU, DOUBLE-FRIED DOUGH SANDWICH COVERED IN DOUGH!
Uhhhh...
DON'T LOSE HOPE YET. I STILL FEEL LIKE I OWE YOU SOME FOR GETTING MY LIFE BACK ON TRACK. MAYBE I CAN WORK SOME-THING OUT?

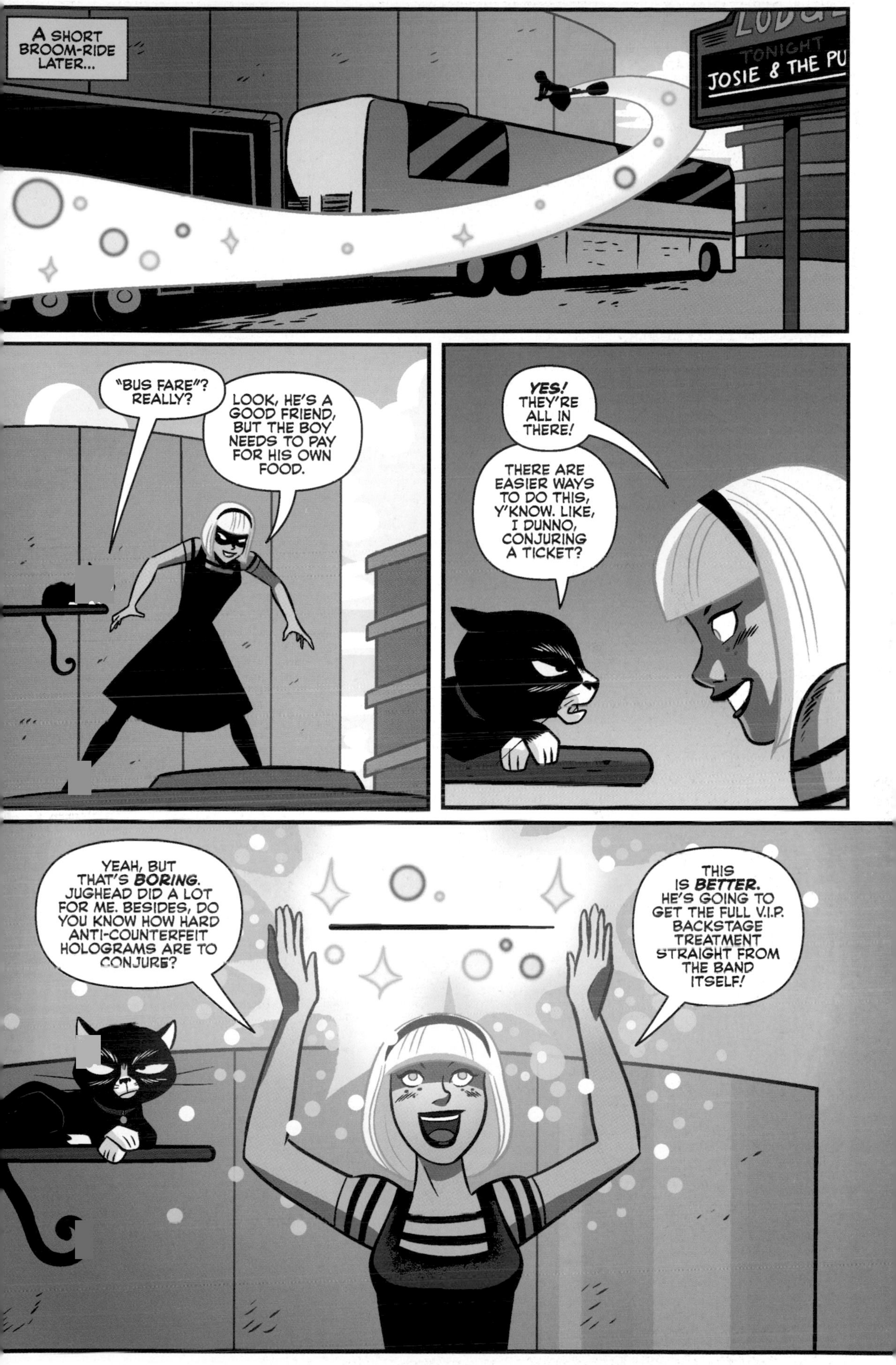
A SHORT BROOM-RIDE LATER...
LODGE TONIGHT JOSIE & THE PU
"BUS FARE"? REALLY?
LOOK, HE'S A GOOD FRIEND, BUT THE BOY NEEDS TO PAY FOR HIS OWN FOOD.
YES! THEY'RE ALL IN THERE!
THERE ARE EASIER WAYS TO DO THIS, Y'KNOW. LIKE, I DUNNO, CONJURING A TICKET?
YEAH, BUT THAT'S BORING. JUGHEAD DID A LOT FOR ME. BESIDES, DO YOU KNOW HOW HARD ANTI-COUNTERFEIT HOLOGRAMS ARE TO CONJURE?
THIS IS BETTER. HE'S GOING TO GET THE FULL V.I.P. BACKSTAGE TREATMENT STRAIGHT FROM THE BAND ITSELF!

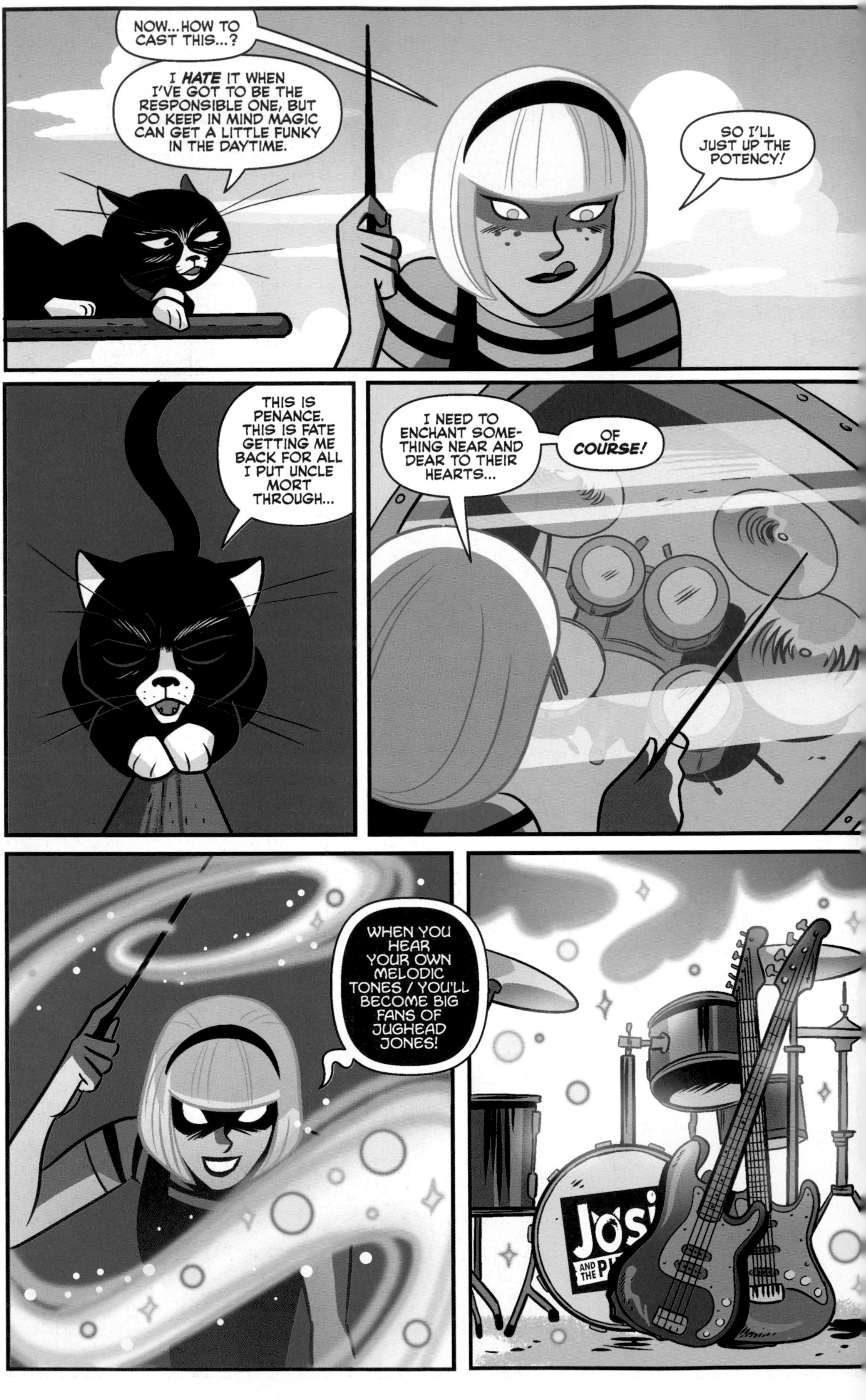
NOW...HOW TO CAST THIS...?
I HATE IT WHEN I'VE GOT TO BE THE RESPONSIBLE ONE, BUT DO KEEP IN MIND MAGIC CAN GET A LITTLE FUNKY IN THE DAYTIME.
SO I'LL JUST UP THE POTENCY!
THIS IS PENANCE. THIS IS FATE GETTING ME BACK FOR ALL I PUT UNCLE MORT THROUGH...
I NEED TO ENCHANT SOME-THING NEAR AND DEAR TO THEIR HEARTS...
OF COURSE!
WHEN YOU HEAR YOUR OWN MELODIC TONES / YOU'LL BECOME BIG FANS OF JUGHEAD JONES!

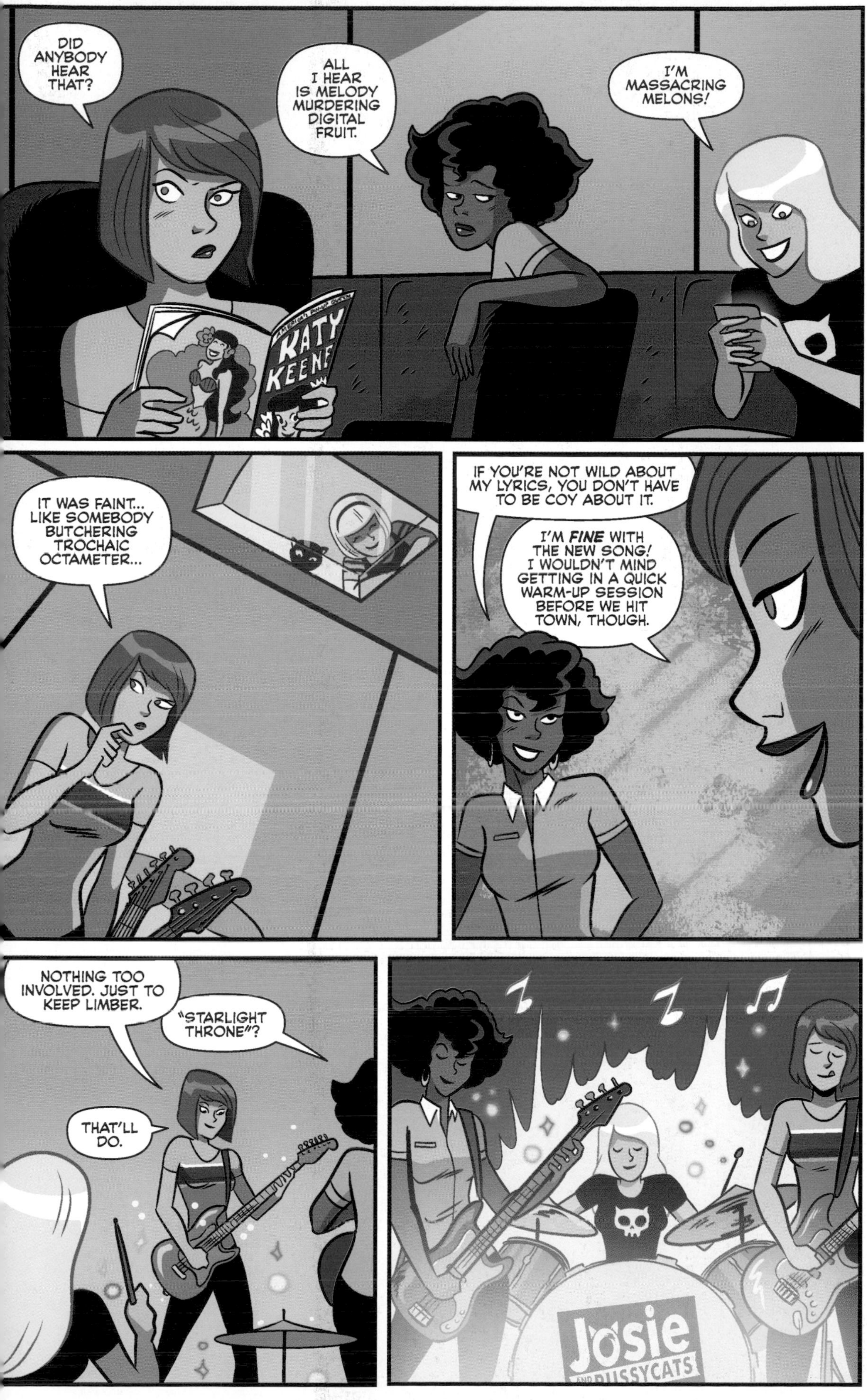
DID ANYBODY HEAR THAT?
ALL I HEAR IS MELODY MURDERING DIGITAL FRUIT.
I'M MASSACRING MELONS!
KATY KEENE
IT WAS FAINT... LIKE SOMEBODY BUTCHERING TROCHAIC OCTAMETER...
IF YOU'RE NOT WILD ABOUT MY LYRICS, YOU DON'T HAVE TO BE COY ABOUT IT.
I'M *FINE* WITH THE NEW SONG! I WOULDN'T MIND GETTING IN A QUICK WARM-UP SESSION BEFORE WE HIT TOWN, THOUGH.
NOTHING TOO INVOLVED. JUST TO KEEP LIMBER.
"STARLIGHT THRONE"?
THAT'LL DO.
Josie
PUSSYCATS

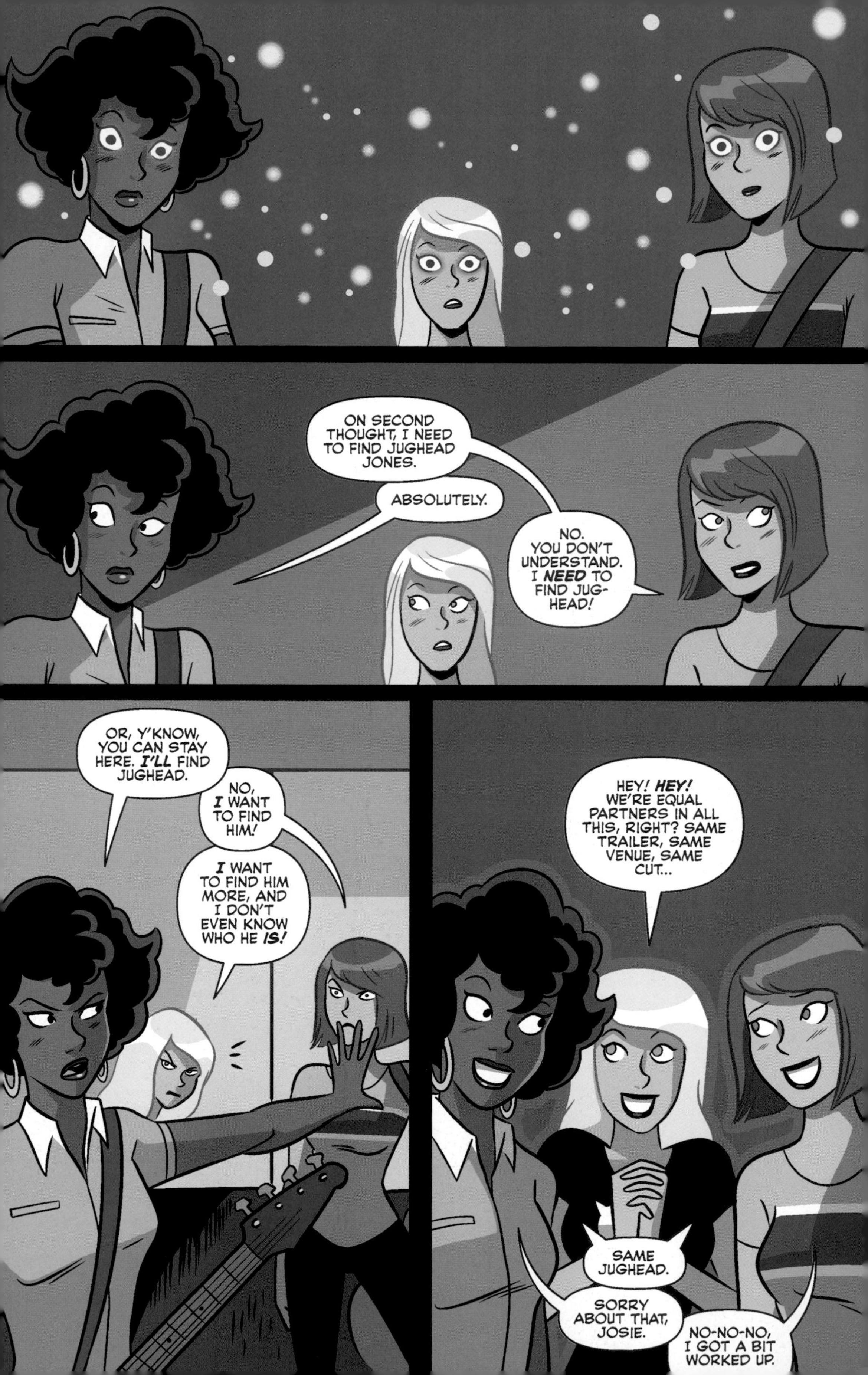
ON SECOND THOUGHT, I NEED TO FIND JUGHEAD JONES.
ABSOLUTELY.
NO. YOU DON'T UNDERSTAND. I *NEED* TO FIND JUG-HEAD!
OR, Y'KNOW, YOU CAN STAY HERE. *I'LL* FIND JUGHEAD.
NO, *I* WANT TO FIND HIM!
I WANT TO FIND HIM MORE, AND I DON'T EVEN KNOW WHO HE *IS!*
HEY! *HEY!* WE'RE EQUAL PARTNERS IN ALL THIS, RIGHT? SAME TRAILER, SAME VENUE, SAME CUT...
SAME JUGHEAD.
SORRY ABOUT THAT, JOSIE.
NO-NO-NO, I GOT A BIT WORKED UP.

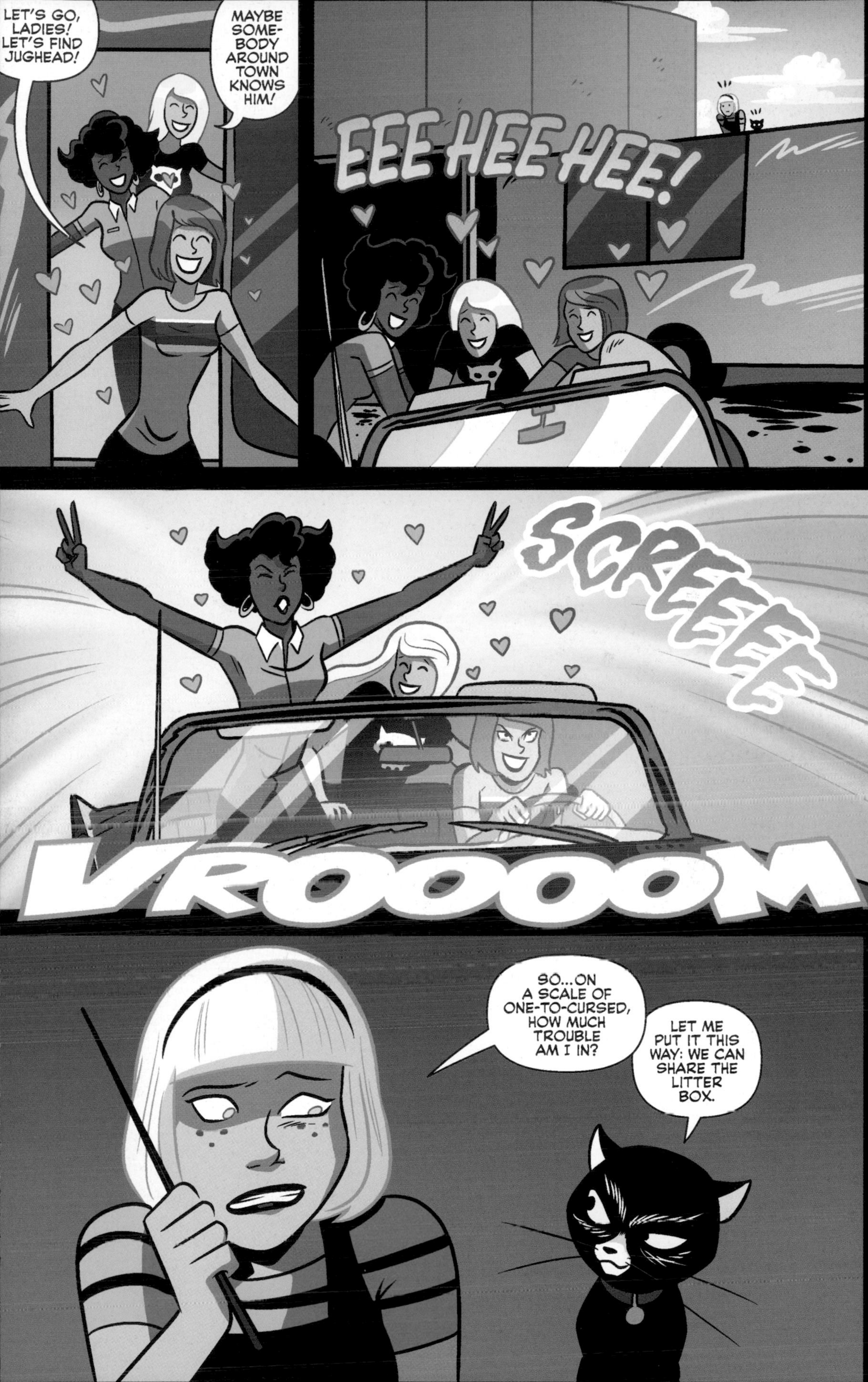
LET'S GO, LADIES! LET'S FIND JUGHEAD!
MAYBE SOMEBODY AROUND TOWN KNOWS HIM!
EEE HEE HEE!
SCREEEE
VROOOOOM
SO...ON A SCALE OF ONE-TO-CURSED, HOW MUCH TROUBLE AM I IN?
LET ME PUT IT THIS WAY: WE CAN SHARE THE LITTER BOX.

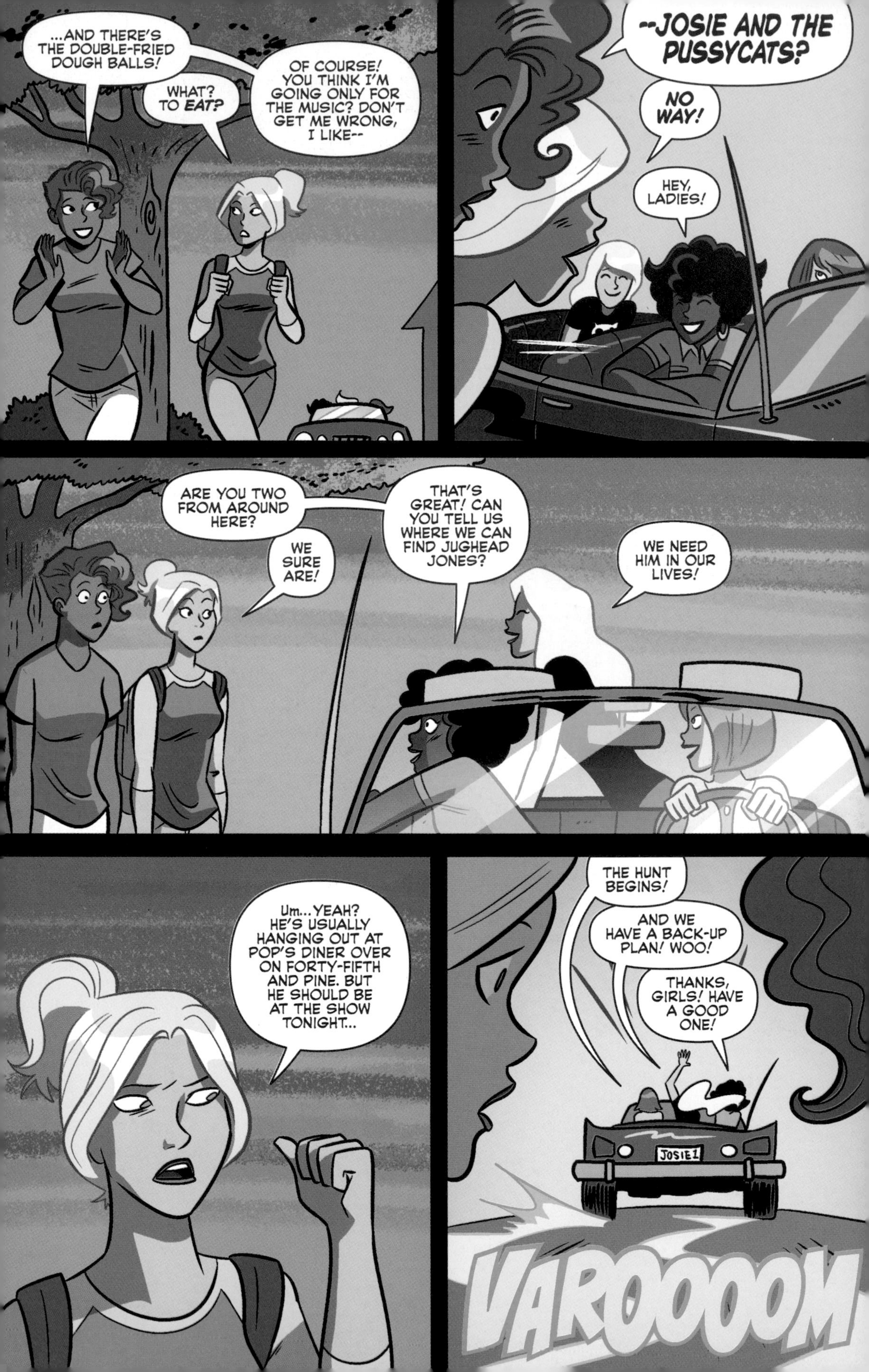
...AND THERE'S THE DOUBLE-FRIED DOUGH BALLS!
WHAT? TO EAT?
OF COURSE! YOU THINK I'M GOING ONLY FOR THE MUSIC? DON'T GET ME WRONG, I LIKE--
--JOSIE AND THE PUSSYCATS?
NO WAY!
HEY, LADIES!
ARE YOU TWO FROM AROUND HERE?
WE SURE ARE!
THAT'S GREAT! CAN YOU TELL US WHERE WE CAN FIND JUGHEAD JONES?
WE NEED HIM IN OUR LIVES!
Um...YEAH? HE'S USUALLY HANGING OUT AT POP'S DINER OVER ON FORTY-FIFTH AND PINE. BUT HE SHOULD BE AT THE SHOW TONIGHT...
THE HUNT BEGINS!
AND WE HAVE A BACK-UP PLAN! WOO!
THANKS, GIRLS! HAVE A GOOD ONE!
JOSIE1
VAROOOOM

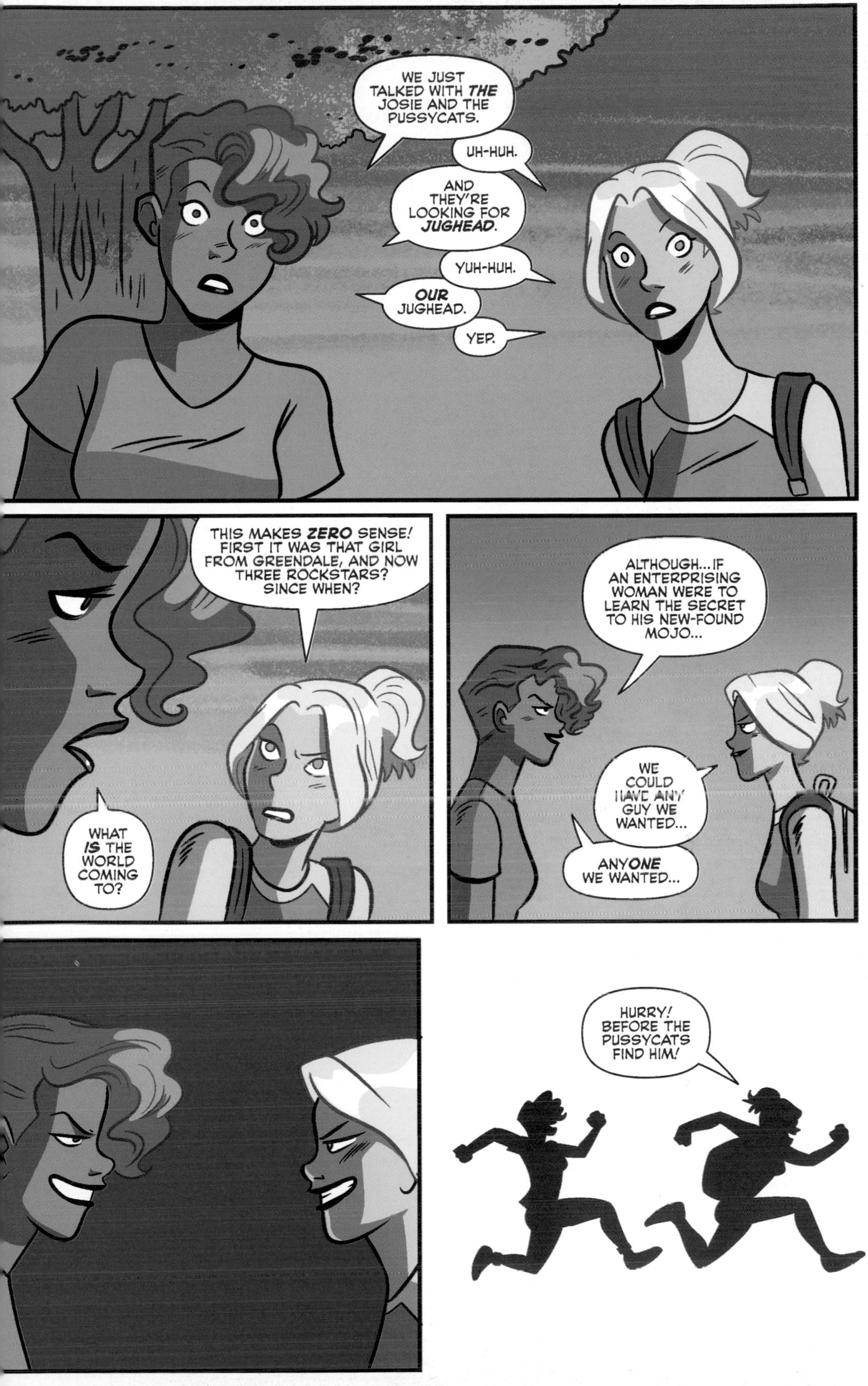
WE JUST TALKED WITH THE JOSIE AND THE PUSSYCATS.
UH-HUH.
AND THEY'RE LOOKING FOR JUGHEAD.
YUH-HUH.
OUR JUGHEAD.
YEP.
THIS MAKES ZERO SENSE! FIRST IT WAS THAT GIRL FROM GREENDALE, AND NOW THREE ROCKSTARS? SINCE WHEN?
WHAT IS THE WORLD COMING TO?
ALTHOUGH...IF AN ENTERPRISING WOMAN WERE TO LEARN THE SECRET TO HIS NEW-FOUND MOJO...
WE COULD HAVE ANY GUY WE WANTED...
ANYONE WE WANTED...
HURRY! BEFORE THE PUSSYCATS FIND HIM!

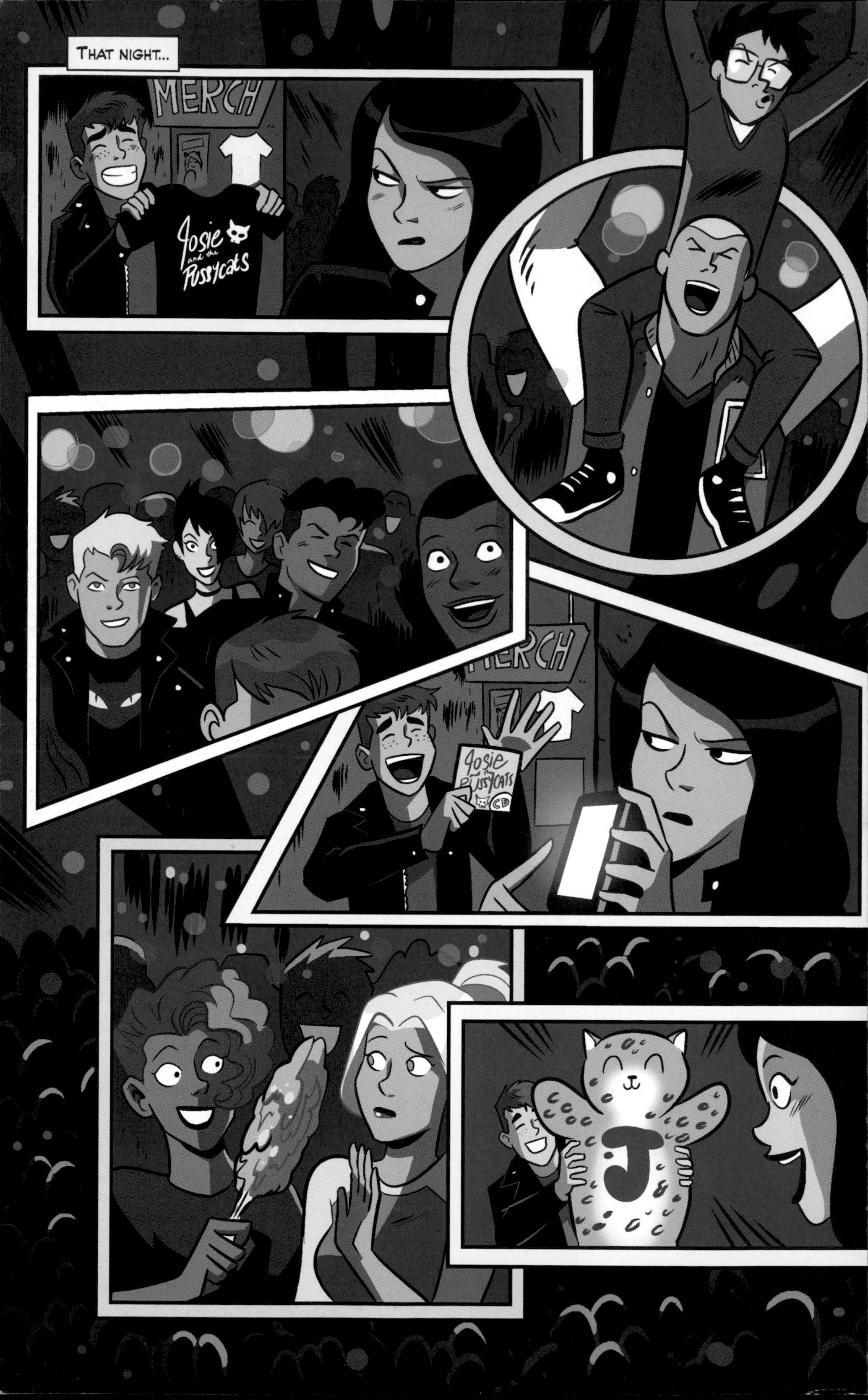
THAT NIGHT...
MERCH
Josie and the Pussycats
MERCH
Josie and the Pussycats
CD
J

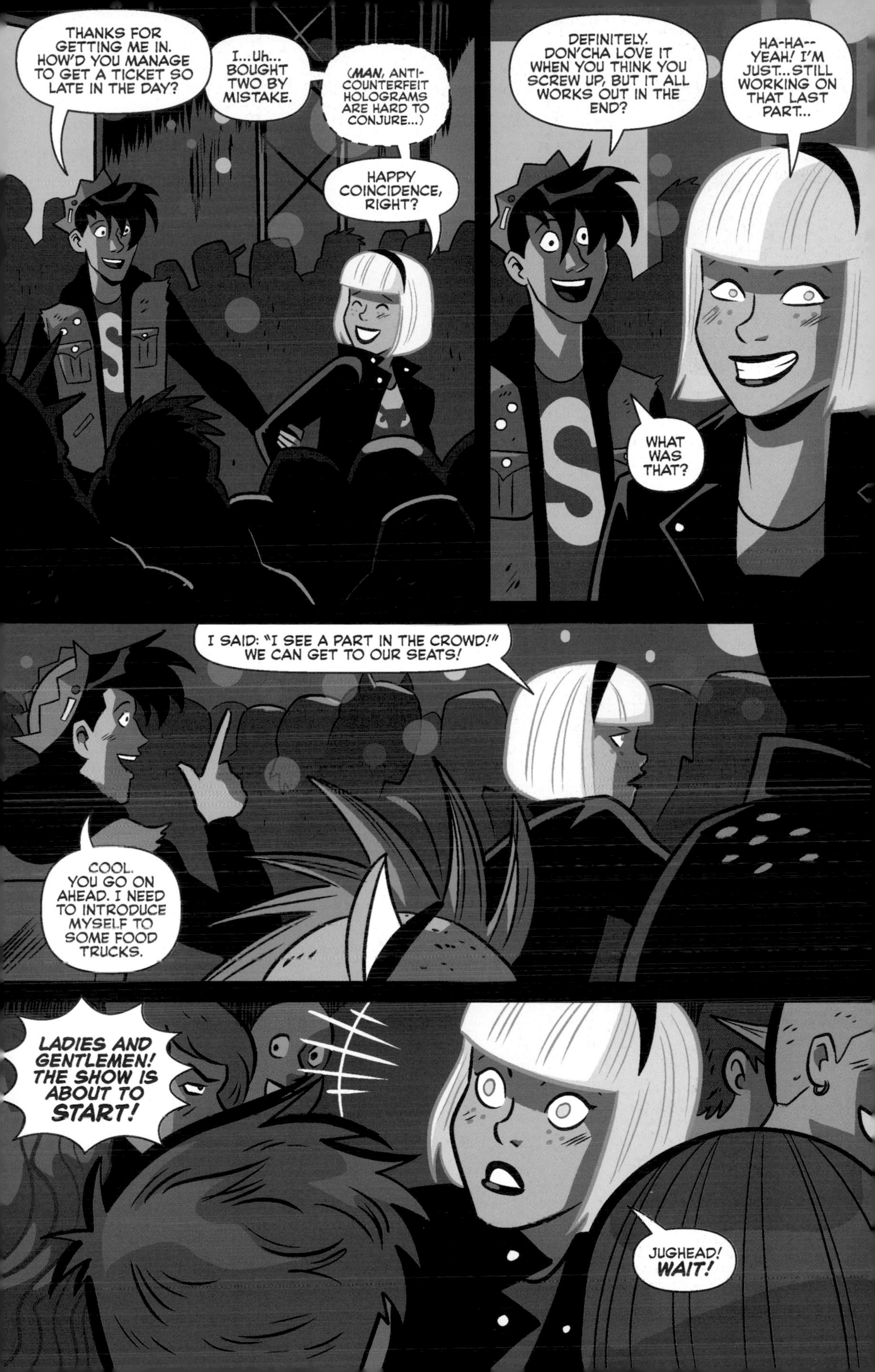
THANKS FOR GETTING ME IN. HOW'D YOU MANAGE TO GET A TICKET SO LATE IN THE DAY?
I...UH... BOUGHT TWO BY MISTAKE.
(MAN, ANTI-COUNTERFEIT HOLOGRAMS ARE HARD TO CONJURE...)
HAPPY COINCIDENCE, RIGHT?
DEFINITELY. DON'CHA LOVE IT WHEN YOU THINK YOU SCREW UP, BUT IT ALL WORKS OUT IN THE END?
HA-HA--YEAH! I'M JUST...STILL WORKING ON THAT LAST PART...
WHAT WAS THAT?
I SAID: "I SEE A PART IN THE CROWD!" WE CAN GET TO OUR SEATS!
COOL. YOU GO ON AHEAD. I NEED TO INTRODUCE MYSELF TO SOME FOOD TRUCKS.
LADIES AND GENTLEMEN! THE SHOW IS ABOUT TO START!
JUGHEAD! WAIT!

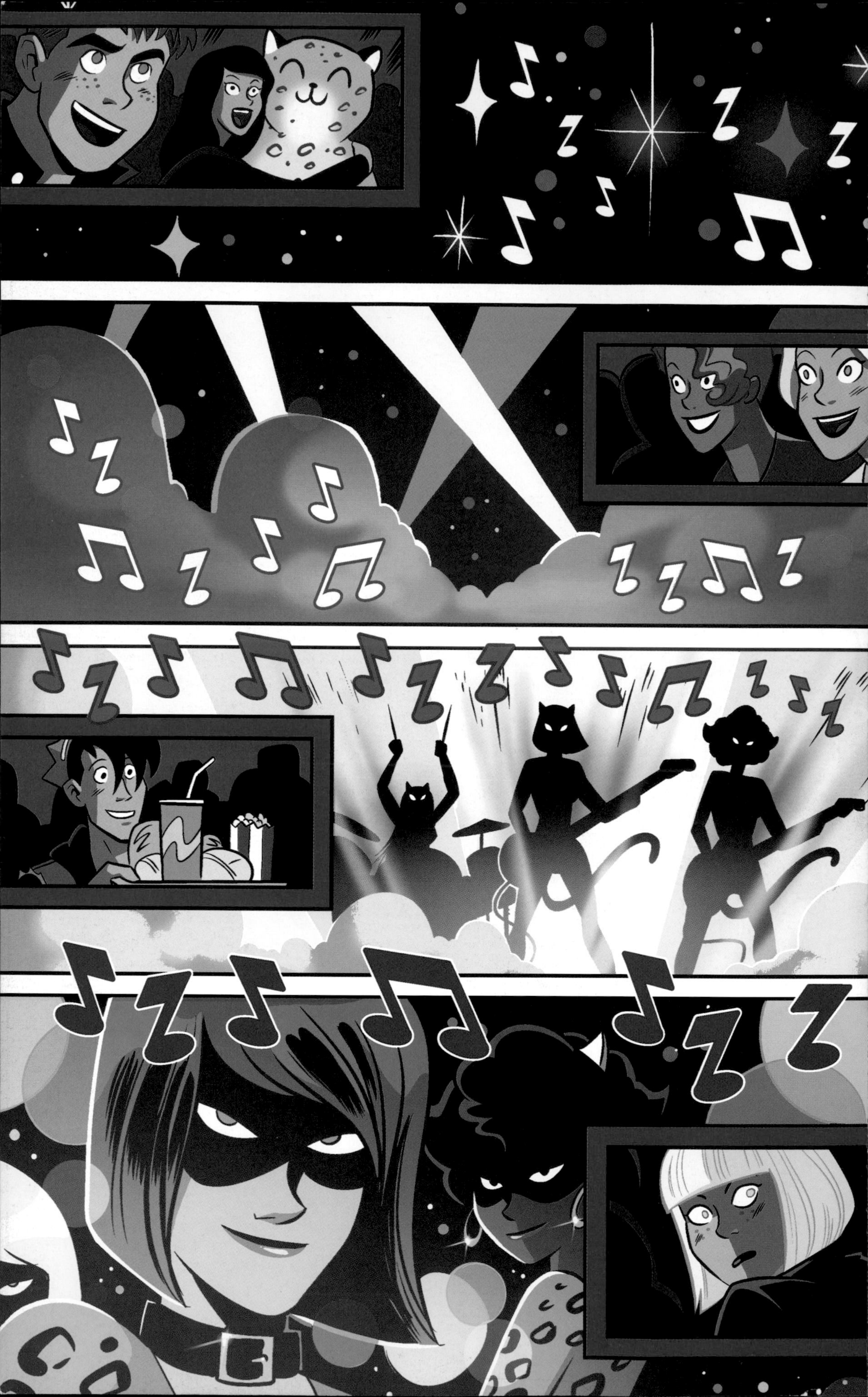

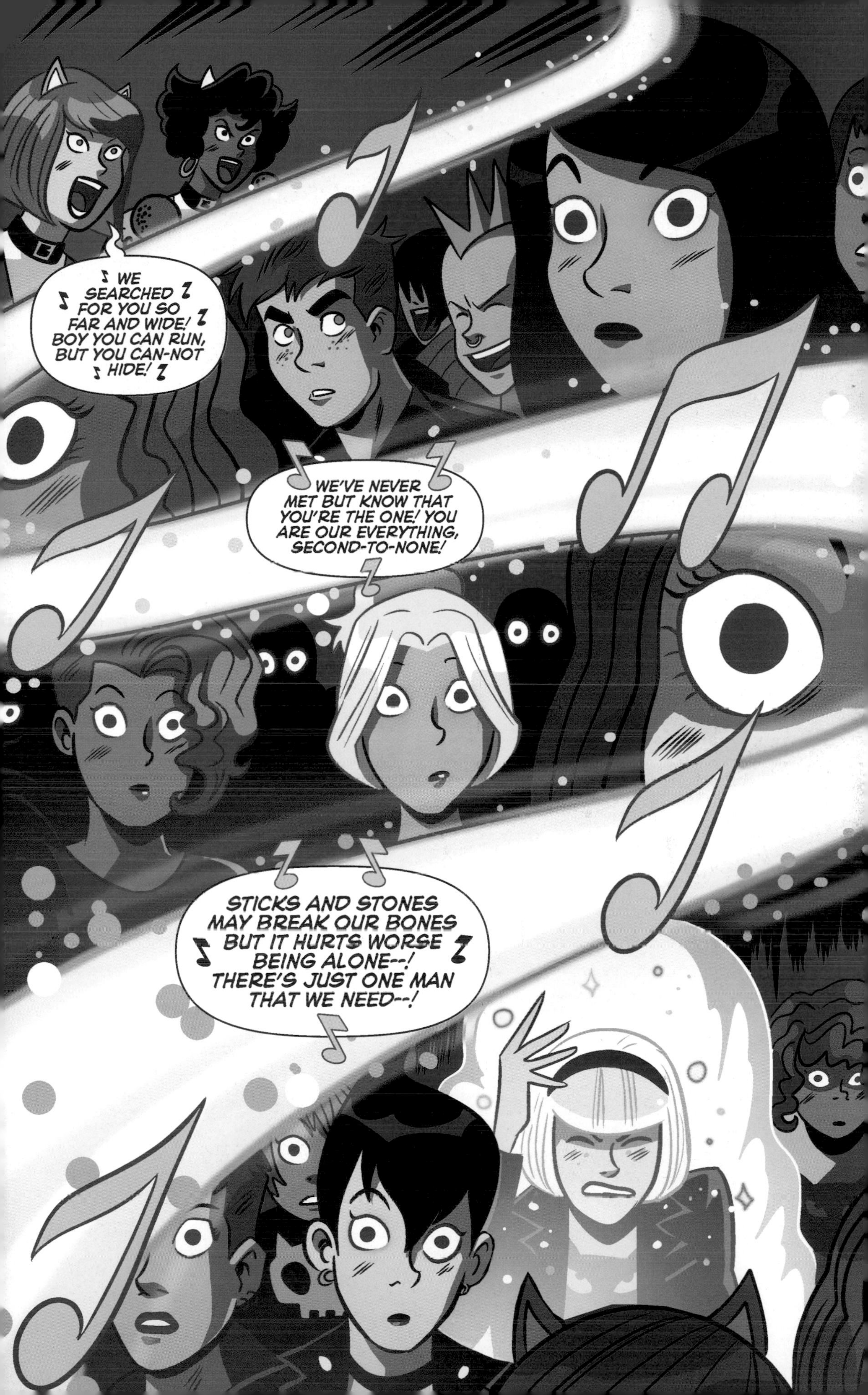
WE SEARCHED FOR YOU SO FAR AND WIDE! BOY YOU CAN RUN, BUT YOU CAN-NOT HIDE!
WE'VE NEVER MET BUT KNOW THAT YOU'RE THE ONE! YOU ARE OUR EVERYTHING, SECOND-TO-NONE!
STICKS AND STONES MAY BREAK OUR BONES BUT IT HURTS WORSE BEING ALONE--! THERE'S JUST ONE MAN THAT WE NEED--!

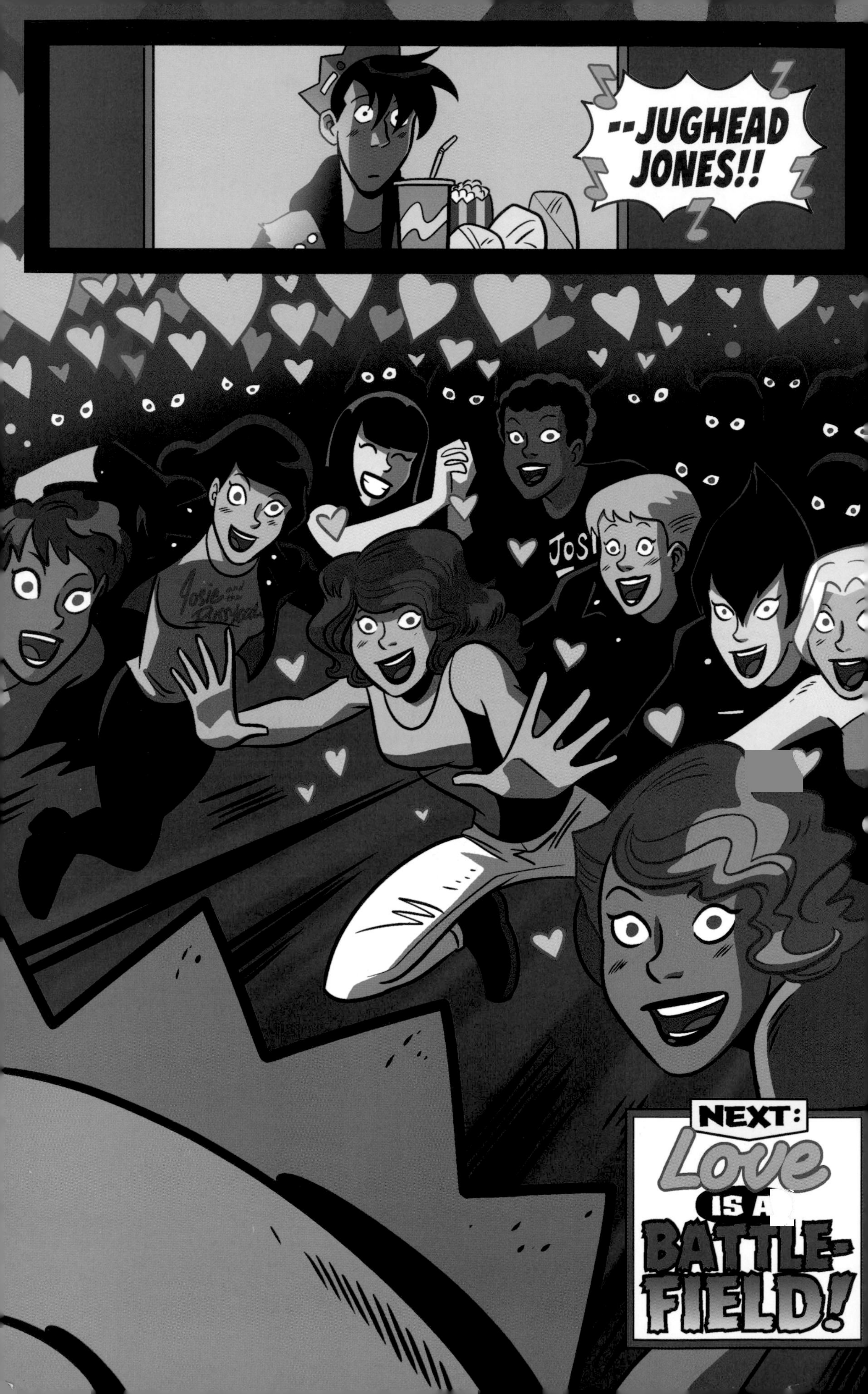
--JUGHEAD JONES!!
NEXT:
Love IS A BATTLE-FIELD!

TO BE
CONTINUED...

ISSUE SIXTEEN

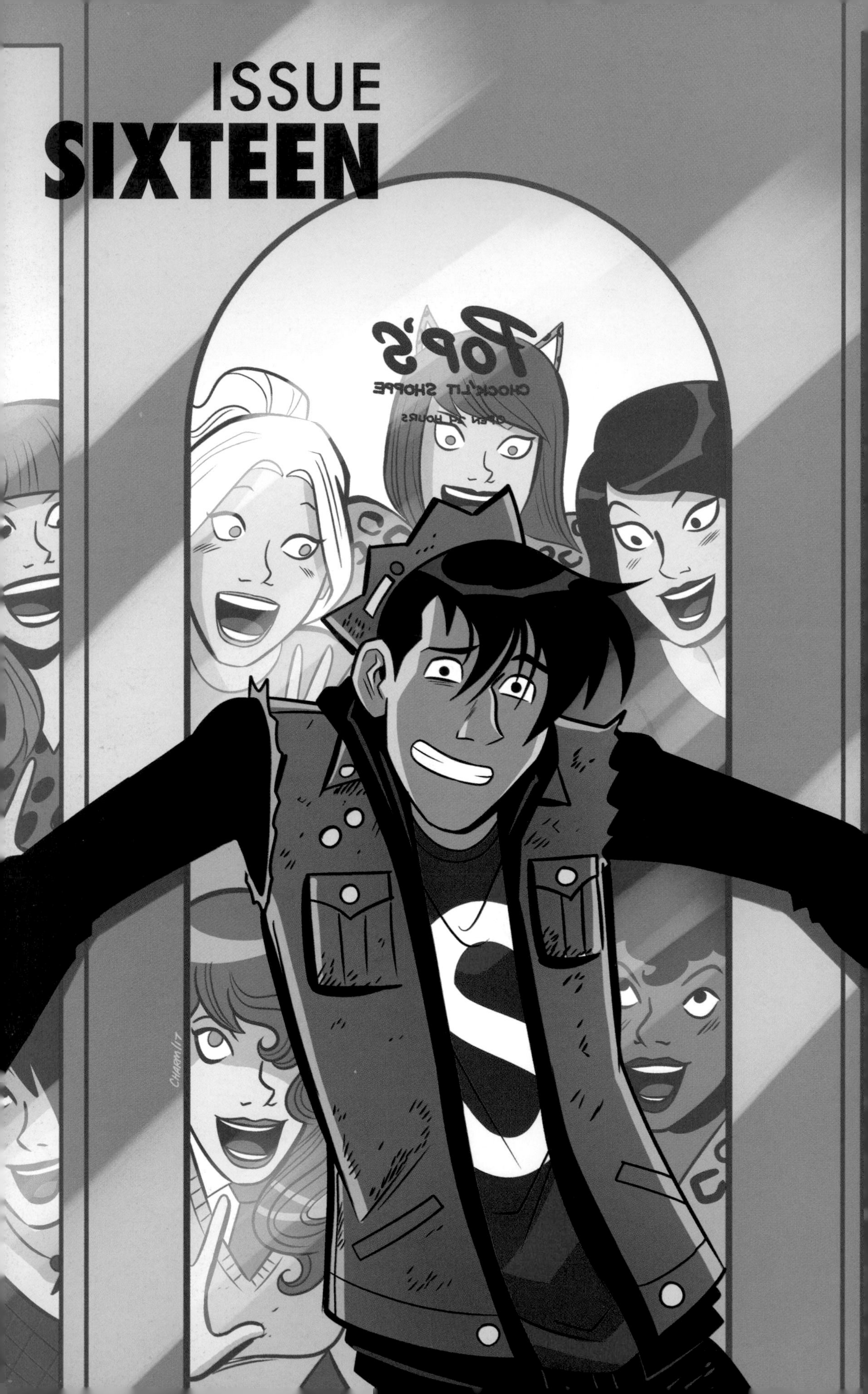
Pop's
CHOCK'LIT SHOPPE
OPEN 24 HOURS

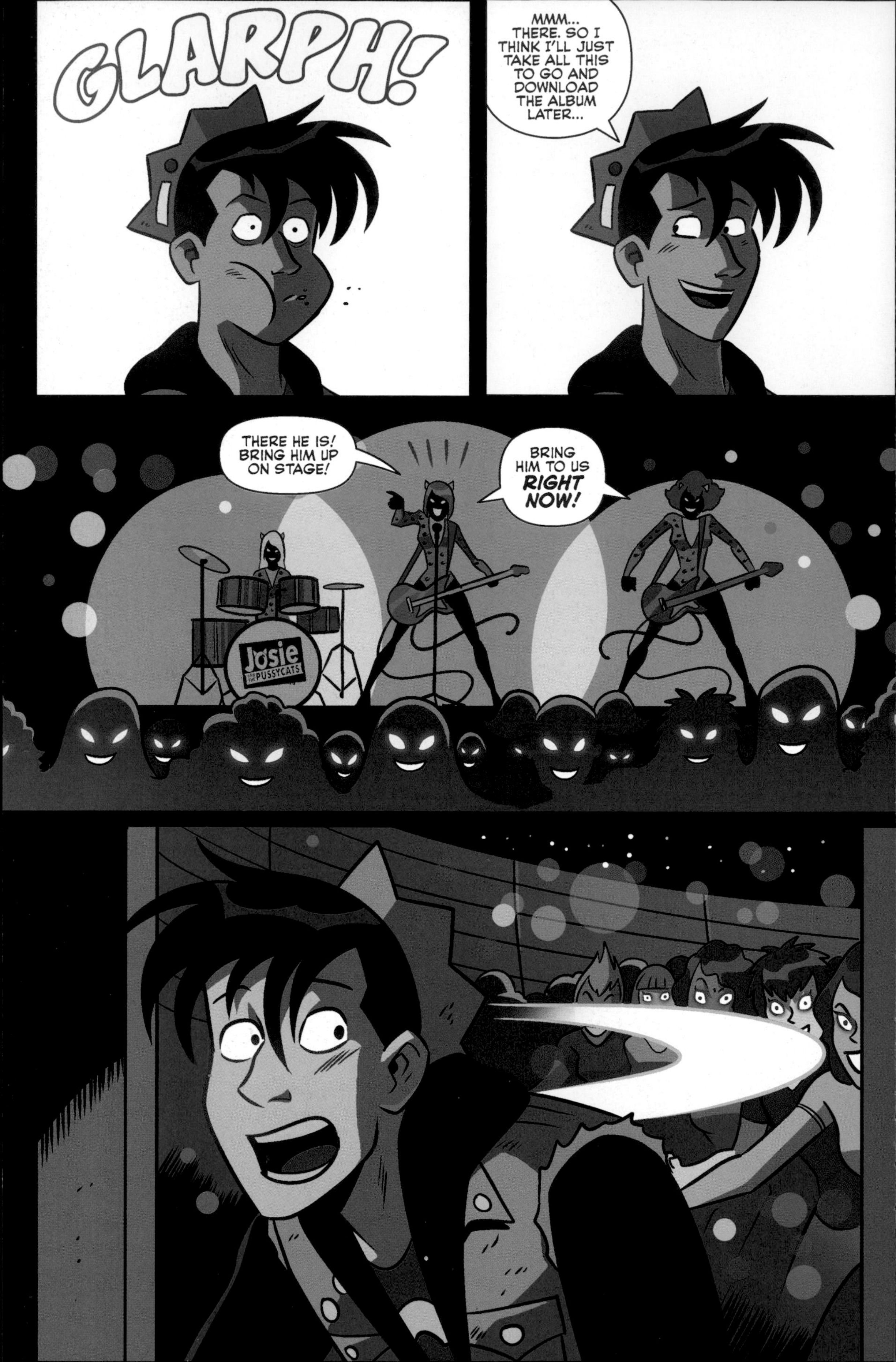
GLARPH!
MMM... THERE. SO I THINK I'LL JUST TAKE ALL THIS TO GO AND DOWNLOAD THE ALBUM LATER...
THERE HE IS! BRING HIM UP ON STAGE!
BRING HIM TO US RIGHT NOW!
Josie AND THE PUSSYCATS

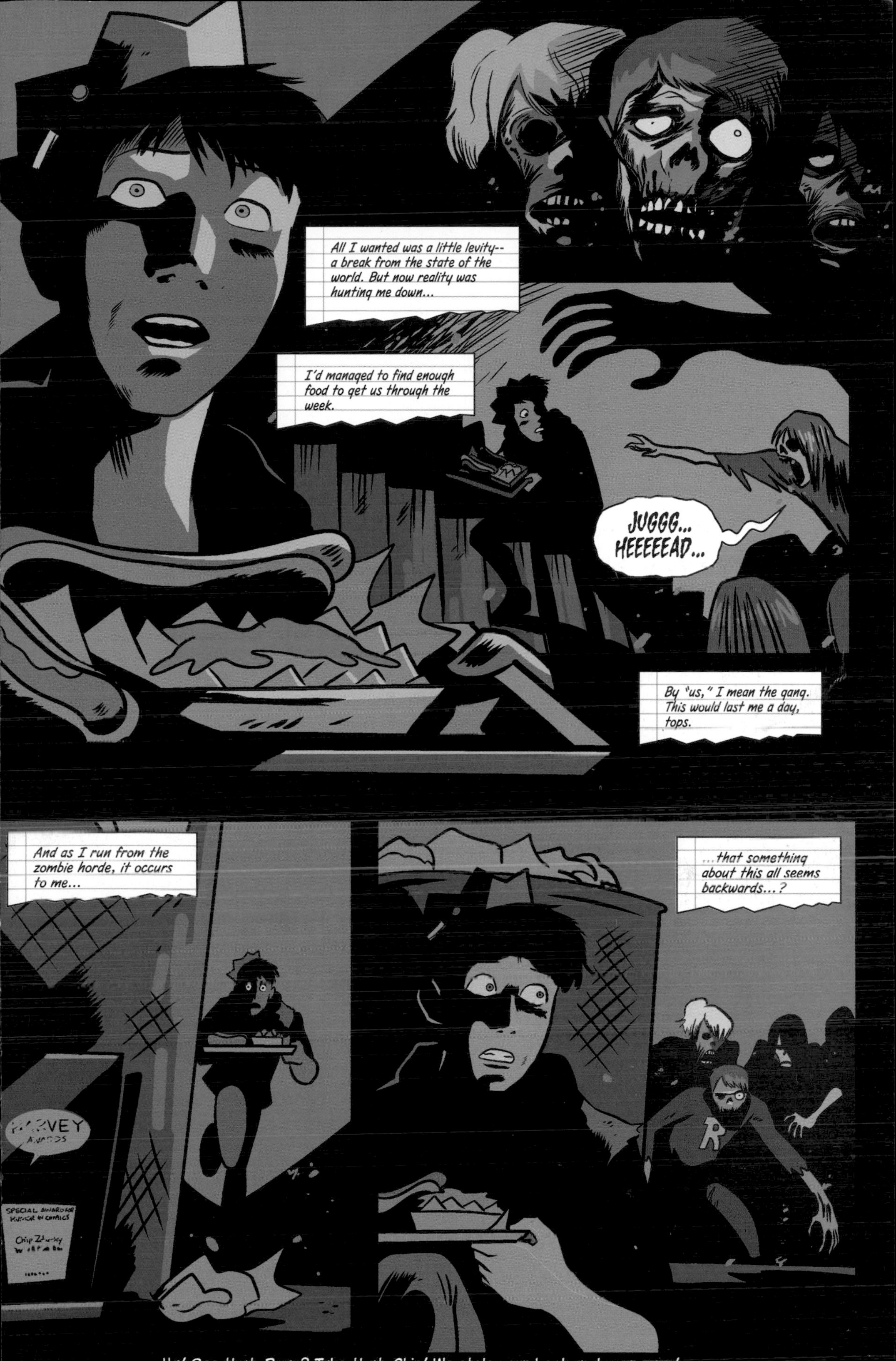
All I wanted was a little levity--a break from the state of the world. But now reality was hunting me down...
I'd managed to find enough food to get us through the week.
JUGGG... HEEEEEAD...
By "us," I mean the gang. This would last me a day, tops.
And as I run from the zombie horde, it occurs to me...
...that something about this all seems backwards...?
HARVEY AWARDS
SPECIAL AWARD FOR HUMOR IN COMICS

Ha! See that, Ryan? Take that, Chip! We stole your book and your gags!
(No, seriously, this is an homage. Also, that's your Harvey Award, Chip.)

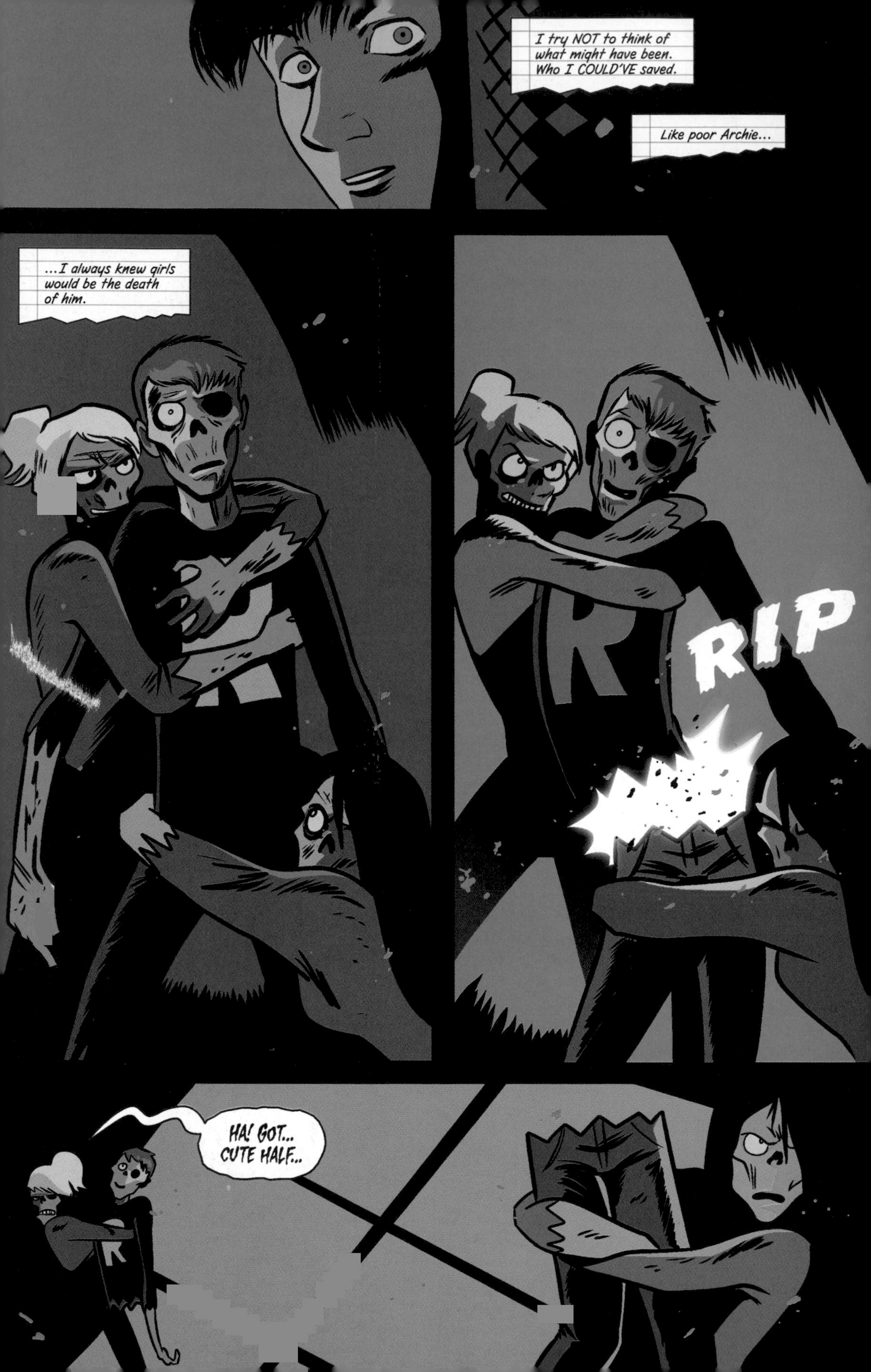
I try NOT to think of what might have been. Who I COULD'VE saved.
Like poor Archie...
...I always knew girls would be the death of him.
RIP
HA! GOT... CUTE HALF...

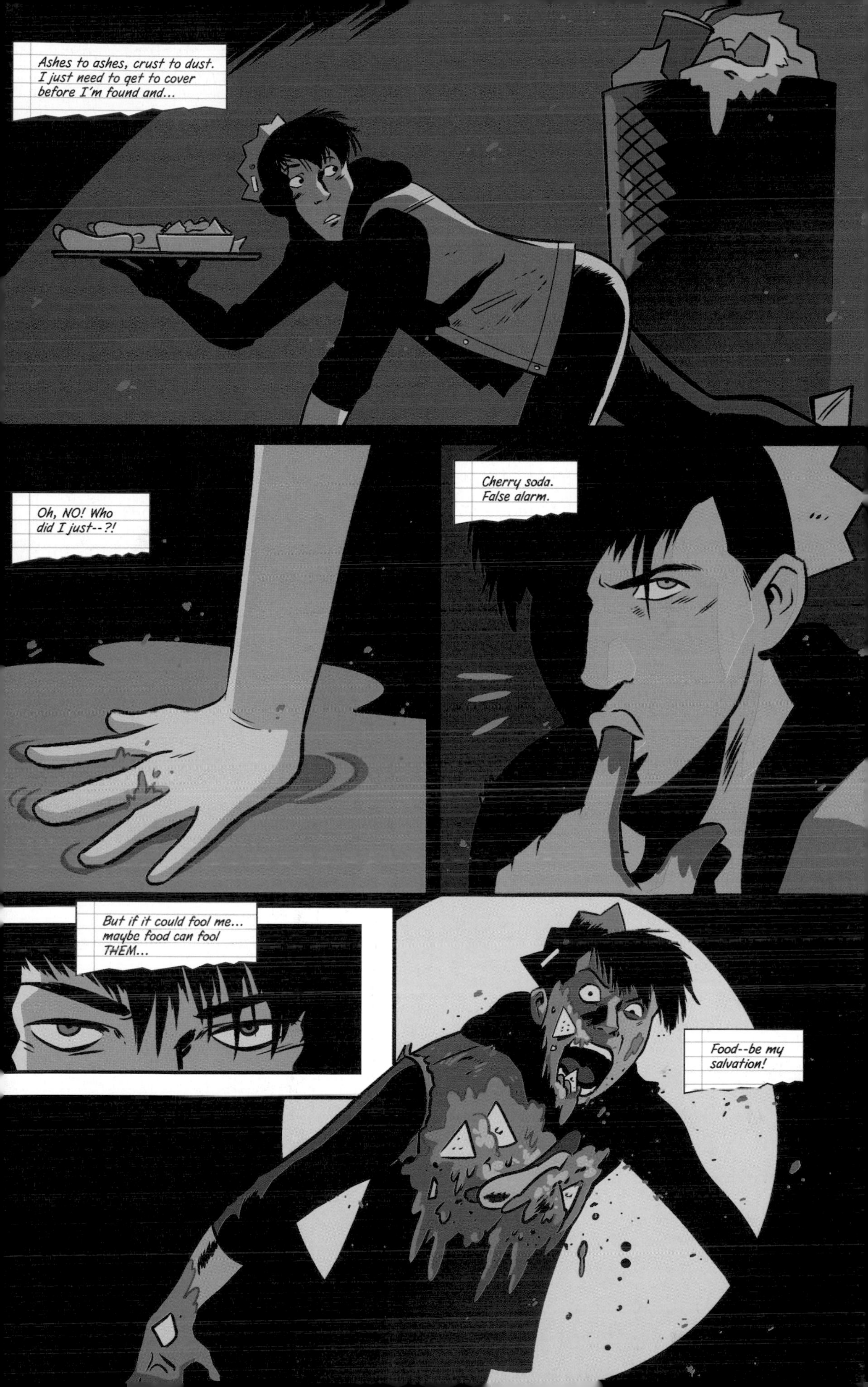
Ashes to ashes, crust to dust. I just need to get to cover before I'm found and...
Oh, NO! Who did I just--?!
Cherry soda. False alarm.
But if it could fool me... maybe food can fool THEM...
Food--be my salvation!

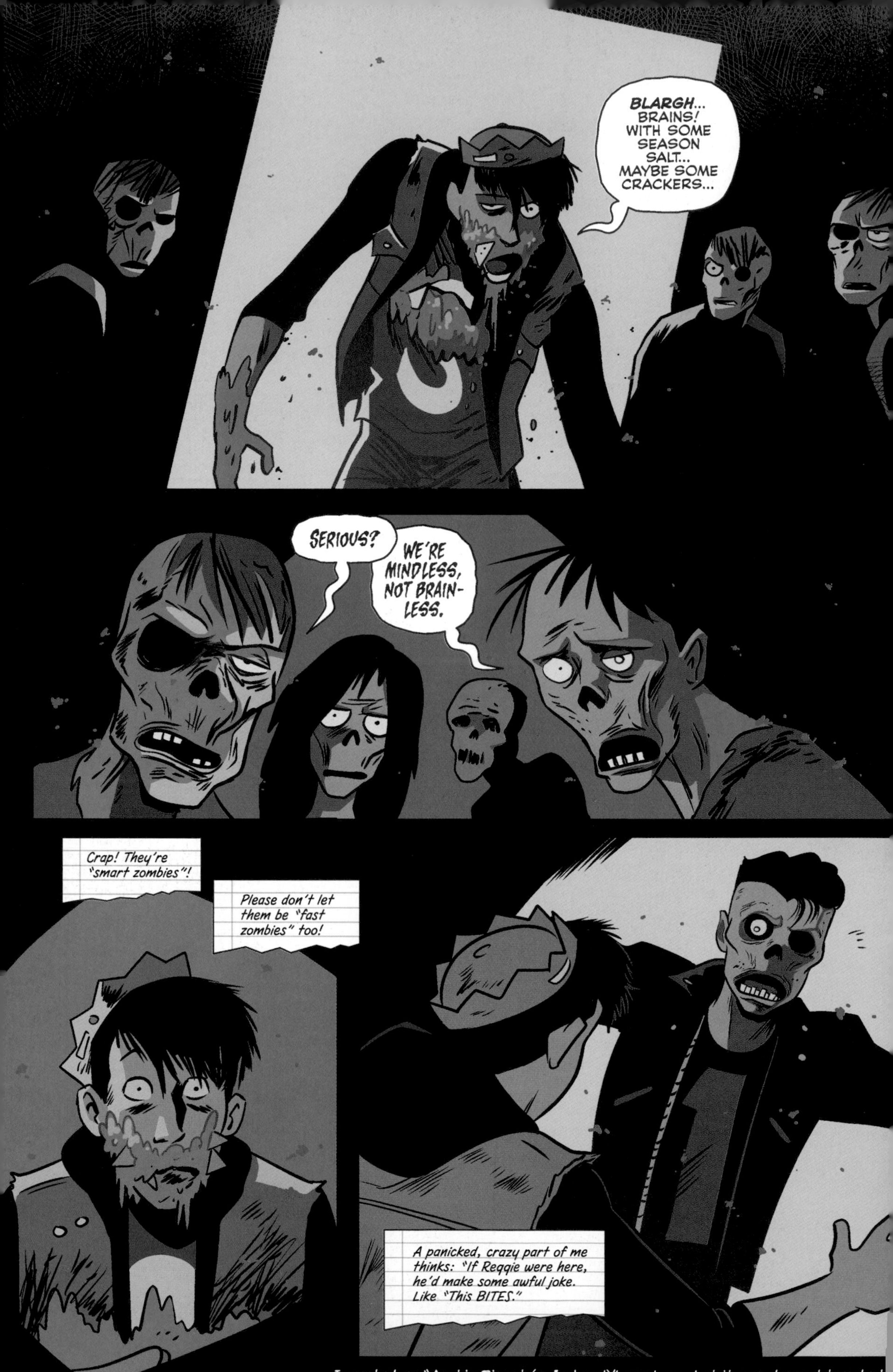
BLARGH... BRAINS! WITH SOME SEASON SALT... MAYBE SOME CRACKERS...
SERIOUS?
WE'RE MINDLESS, NOT BRAIN-LESS.
Crap! They're "smart zombies"!
Please don't let them be "fast zombies" too!
A panicked, crazy part of me thinks: "If Reggie were here, he'd make some awful joke. Like "This BITES."

I wanted an "Archie Digest (c. Jughead)" gag here, but it was deemed too dark

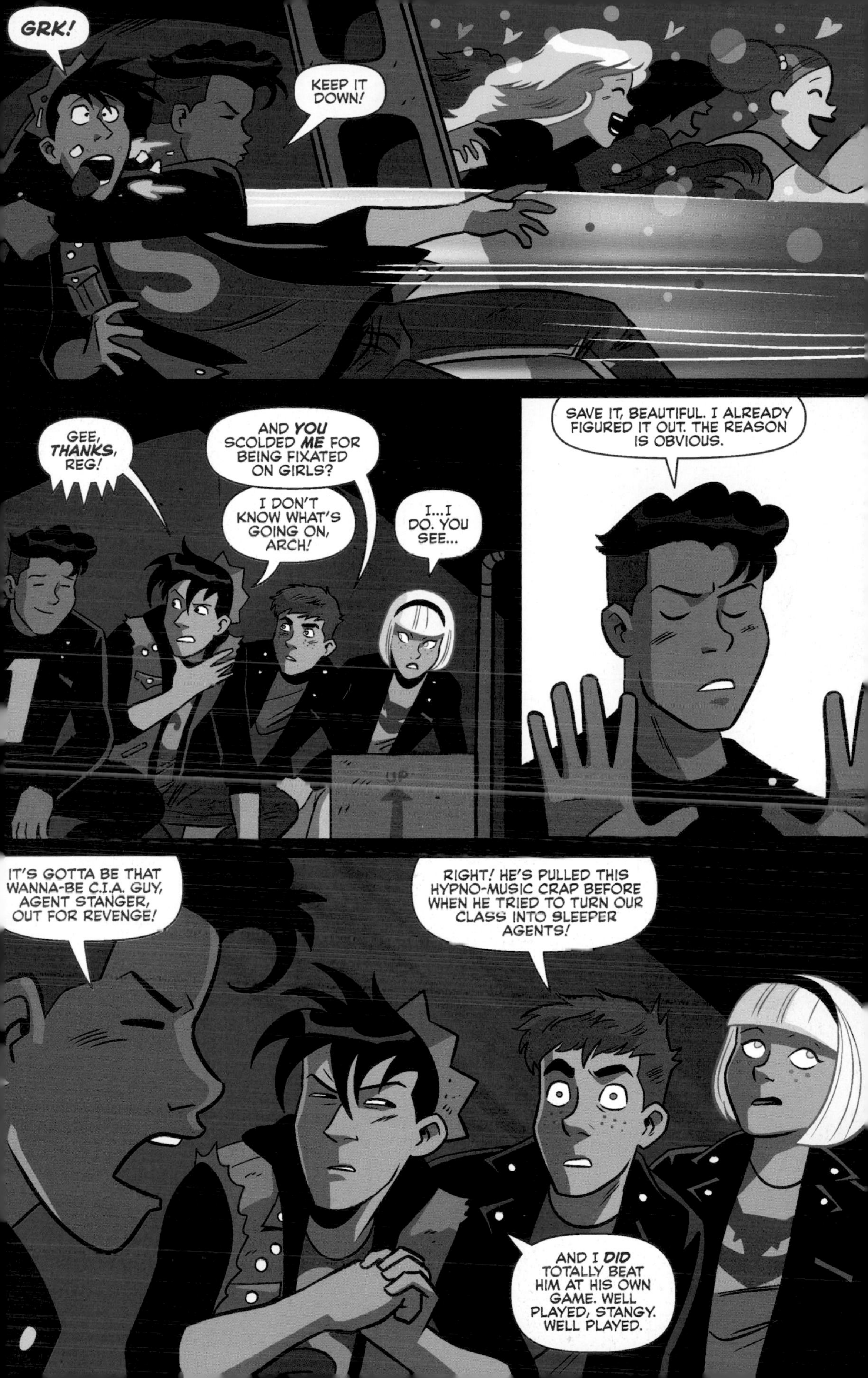
GRK!
KEEP IT DOWN!
GEE, THANKS, REG!
AND YOU SCOLDED ME FOR BEING FIXATED ON GIRLS?
I DON'T KNOW WHAT'S GOING ON, ARCH!
I...I DO. YOU SEE...
SAVE IT, BEAUTIFUL. I ALREADY FIGURED IT OUT. THE REASON IS OBVIOUS.
IT'S GOTTA BE THAT WANNA-BE C.I.A. GUY, AGENT STANGER, OUT FOR REVENGE!
RIGHT! HE'S PULLED THIS HYPNO-MUSIC CRAP BEFORE WHEN HE TRIED TO TURN OUR CLASS INTO SLEEPER AGENTS!
AND I DID TOTALLY BEAT HIM AT HIS OWN GAME. WELL PLAYED, STANGY. WELL PLAYED.

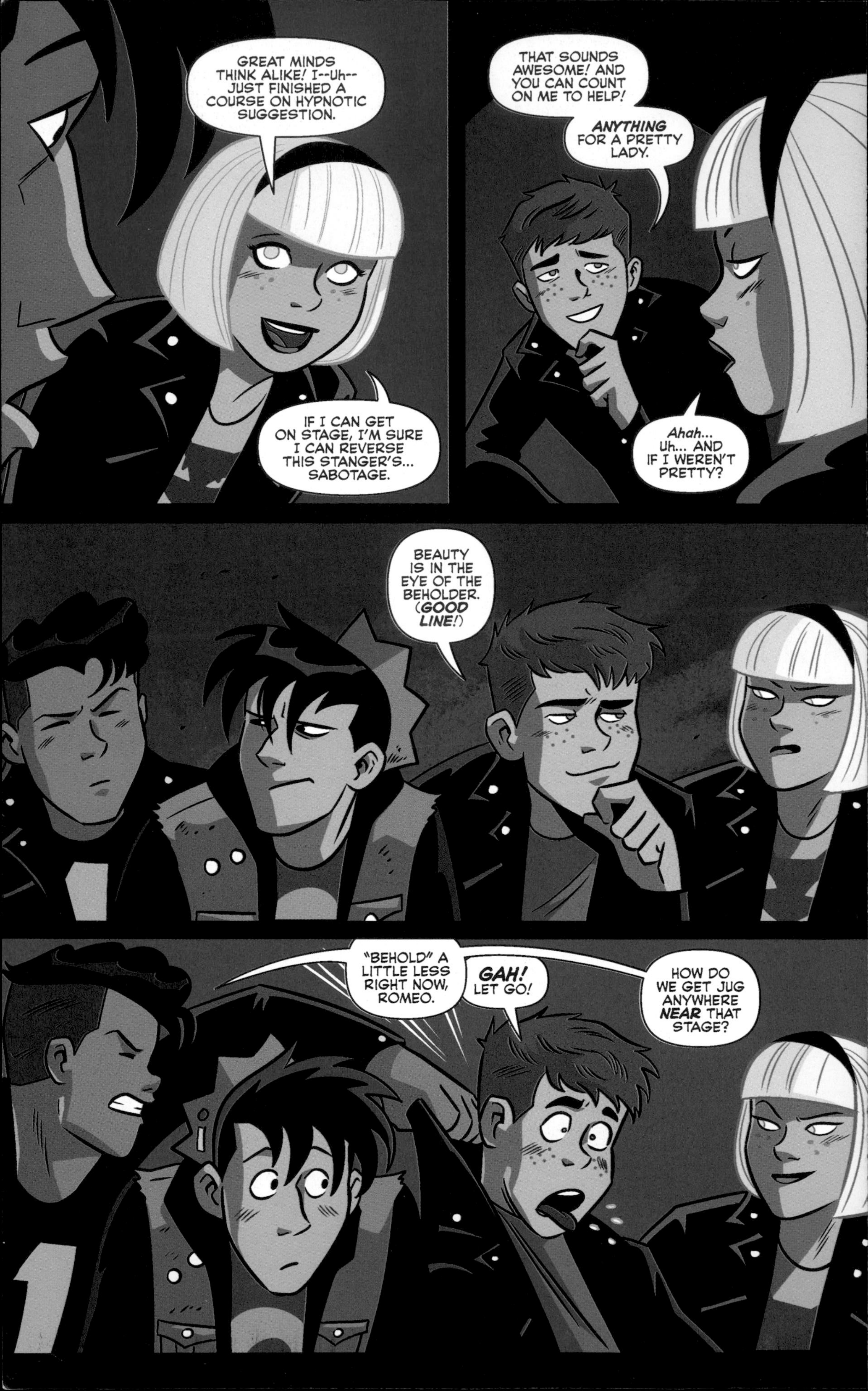
GREAT MINDS THINK ALIKE! I--Uh-- JUST FINISHED A COURSE ON HYPNOTIC SUGGESTION.
IF I CAN GET ON STAGE, I'M SURE I CAN REVERSE THIS STANGER'S... SABOTAGE.
THAT SOUNDS AWESOME! AND YOU CAN COUNT ON ME TO HELP!
ANYTHING FOR A PRETTY LADY.
Ahah... Uh... AND IF I WEREN'T PRETTY?
BEAUTY IS IN THE EYE OF THE BEHOLDER. (GOOD LINE!)
"BEHOLD" A LITTLE LESS RIGHT NOW, ROMEO.
GAH! LET GO!
HOW DO WE GET JUG ANYWHERE NEAR THAT STAGE?

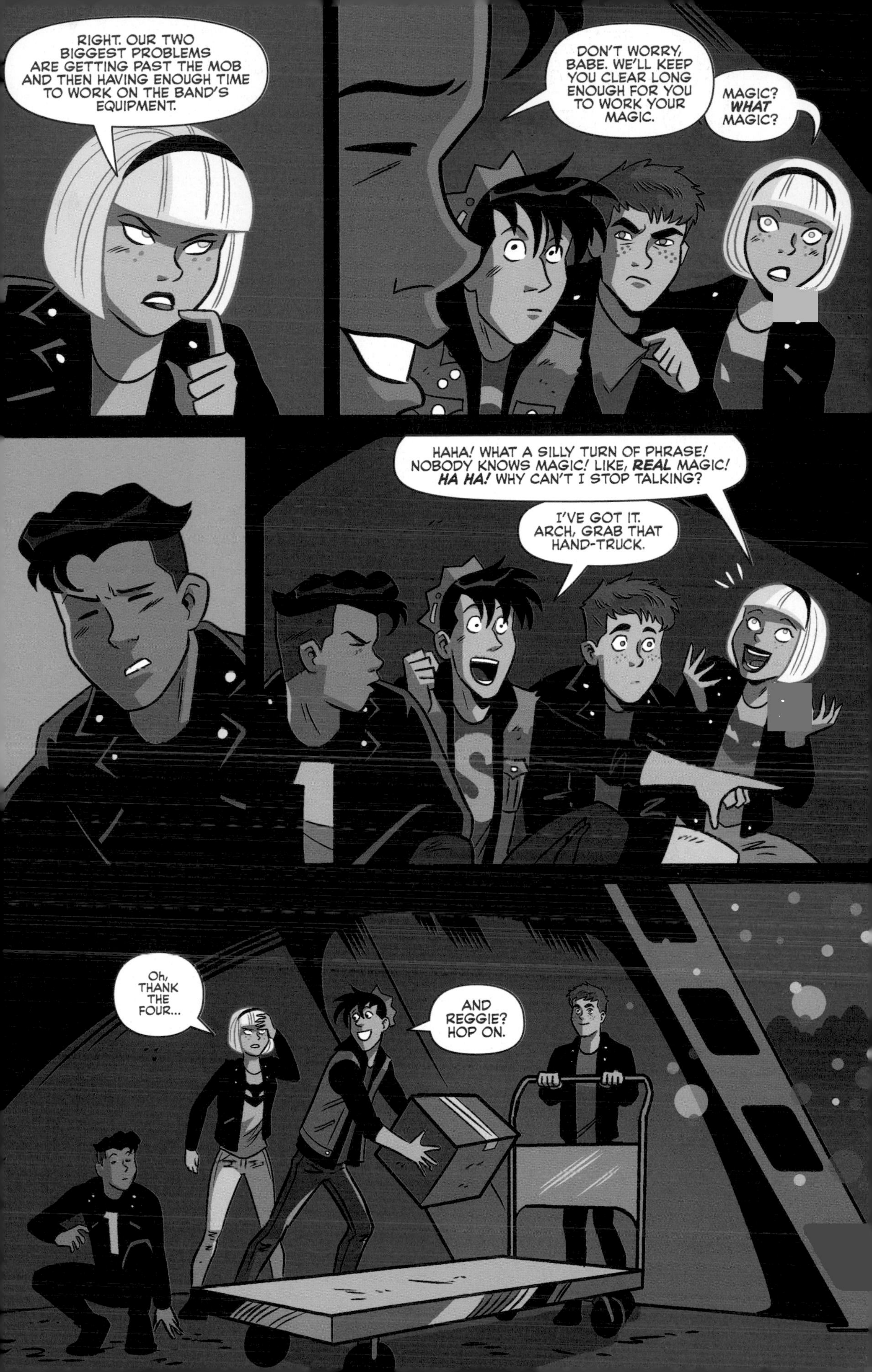
RIGHT. OUR TWO BIGGEST PROBLEMS ARE GETTING PAST THE MOB AND THEN HAVING ENOUGH TIME TO WORK ON THE BAND'S EQUIPMENT.
DON'T WORRY, BABE. WE'LL KEEP YOU CLEAR LONG ENOUGH FOR YOU TO WORK YOUR MAGIC.
MAGIC? WHAT MAGIC?
HAHA! WHAT A SILLY TURN OF PHRASE! NOBODY KNOWS MAGIC! LIKE, REAL MAGIC! HA HA! WHY CAN'T I STOP TALKING?
I'VE GOT IT. ARCH, GRAB THAT HAND-TRUCK.
Oh, THANK THE FOUR...
AND REGGIE? HOP ON.

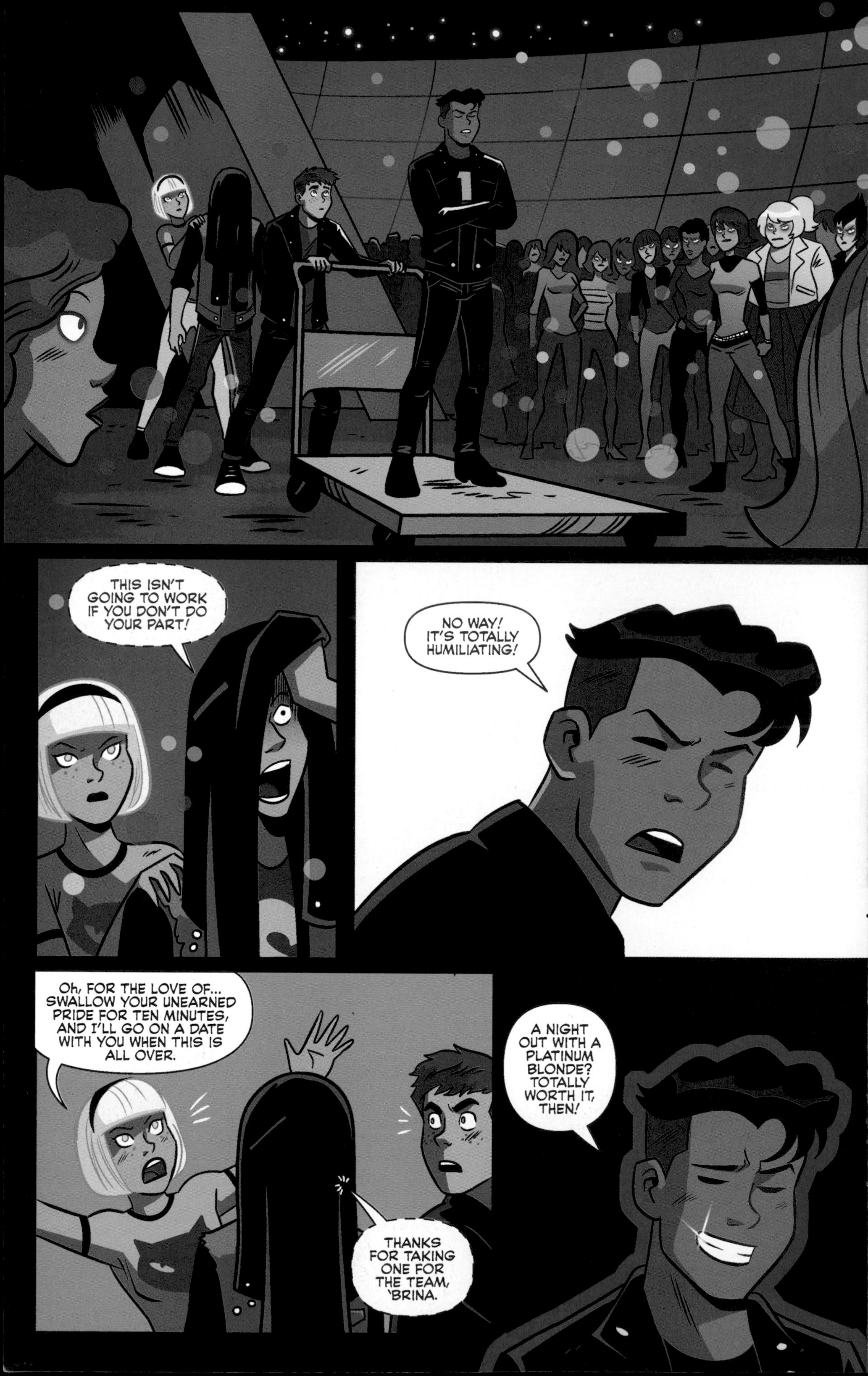
THIS ISN'T GOING TO WORK IF YOU DON'T DO YOUR PART!
NO WAY! IT'S TOTALLY HUMILIATING!
Oh, FOR THE LOVE OF... SWALLOW YOUR UNEARNED PRIDE FOR TEN MINUTES, AND I'LL GO ON A DATE WITH YOU WHEN THIS IS ALL OVER.
THANKS FOR TAKING ONE FOR THE TEAM, 'BRINA.
A NIGHT OUT WITH A PLATINUM BLONDE? TOTALLY WORTH IT, THEN!

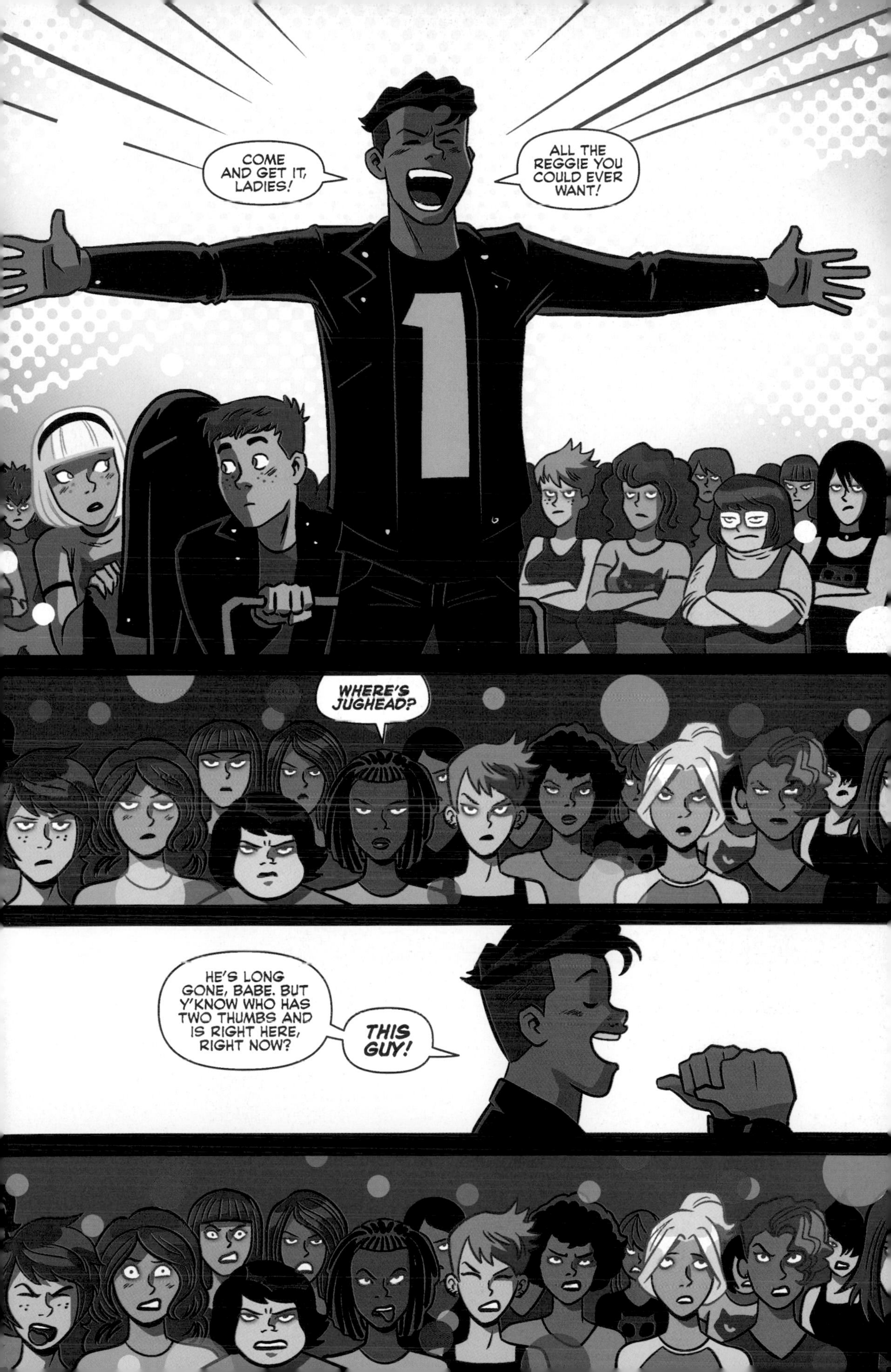
COME AND GET IT, LADIES!
ALL THE REGGIE YOU COULD EVER WANT!
WHERE'S JUGHEAD?
HE'S LONG GONE, BABE. BUT Y'KNOW WHO HAS TWO THUMBS AND IS RIGHT HERE, RIGHT NOW?
THIS GUY!

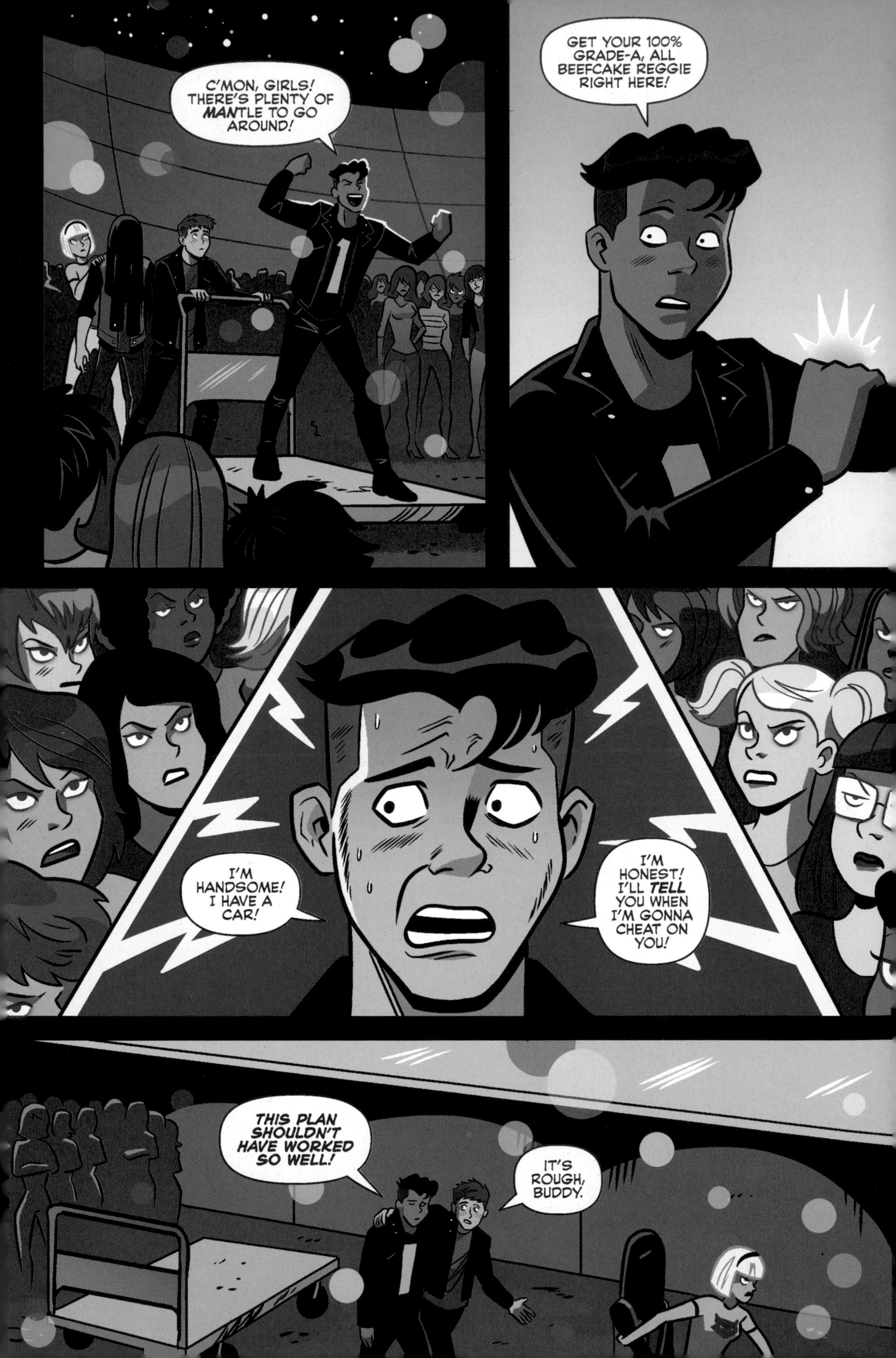
C'MON, GIRLS! THERE'S PLENTY OF MANTLE TO GO AROUND!
GET YOUR 100% GRADE-A, ALL BEEFCAKE REGGIE RIGHT HERE!
I'M HANDSOME! I HAVE A CAR!
I'M HONEST! I'LL TELL YOU WHEN I'M GONNA CHEAT ON YOU!
THIS PLAN SHOULDN'T HAVE WORKED SO WELL!
IT'S ROUGH, BUDDY.

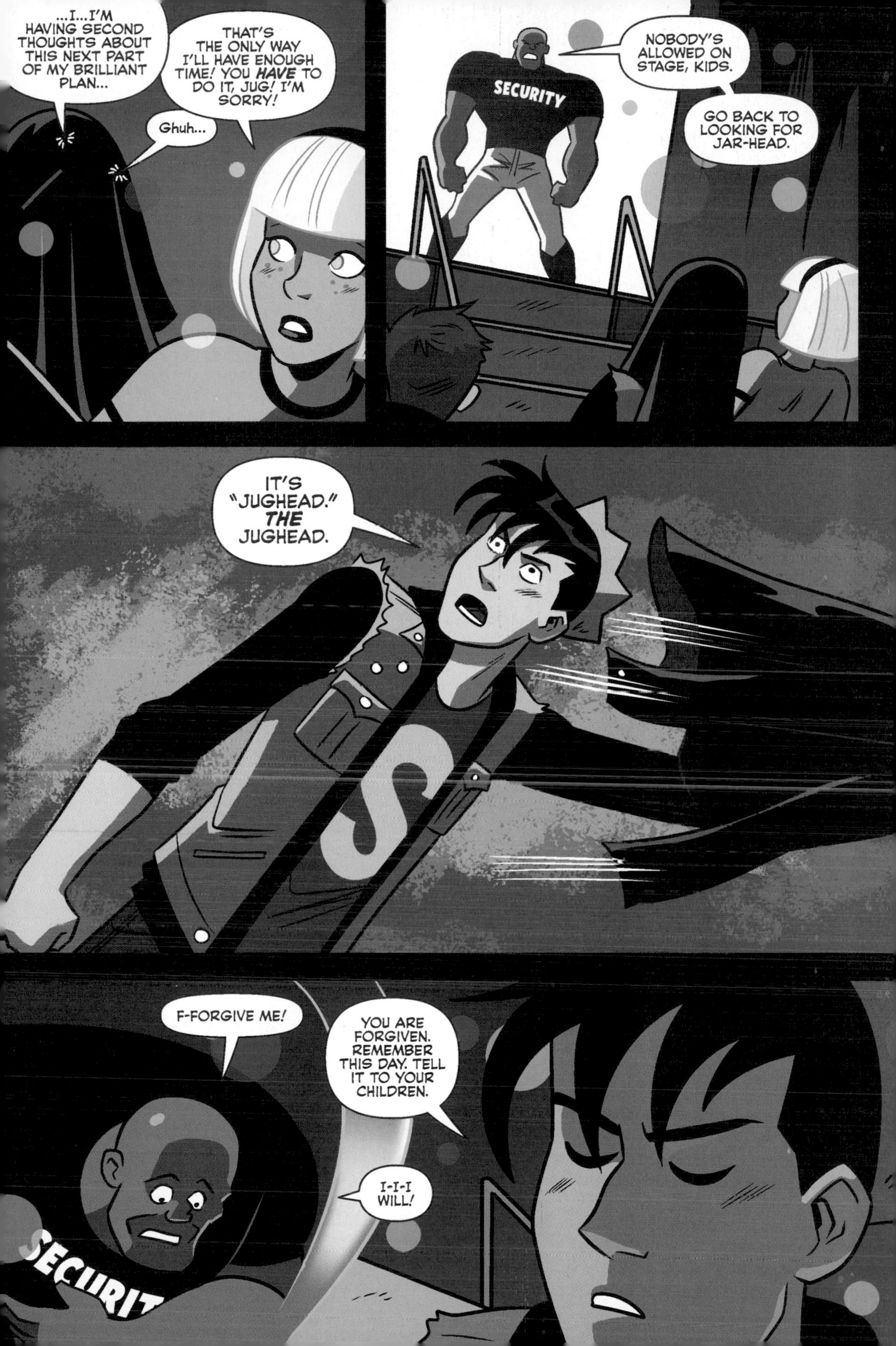
...I...I'M HAVING SECOND THOUGHTS ABOUT THIS NEXT PART OF MY BRILLIANT PLAN...
THAT'S THE ONLY WAY I'LL HAVE ENOUGH TIME! YOU HAVE TO DO IT, JUG! I'M SORRY!
Ghuh...
NOBODY'S ALLOWED ON STAGE, KIDS.
GO BACK TO LOOKING FOR JAR-HEAD.
SECURITY
IT'S "JUGHEAD." THE JUGHEAD.
F-FORGIVE ME!
YOU ARE FORGIVEN. REMEMBER THIS DAY. TELL IT TO YOUR CHILDREN.
I-I-I WILL!
SECURIT

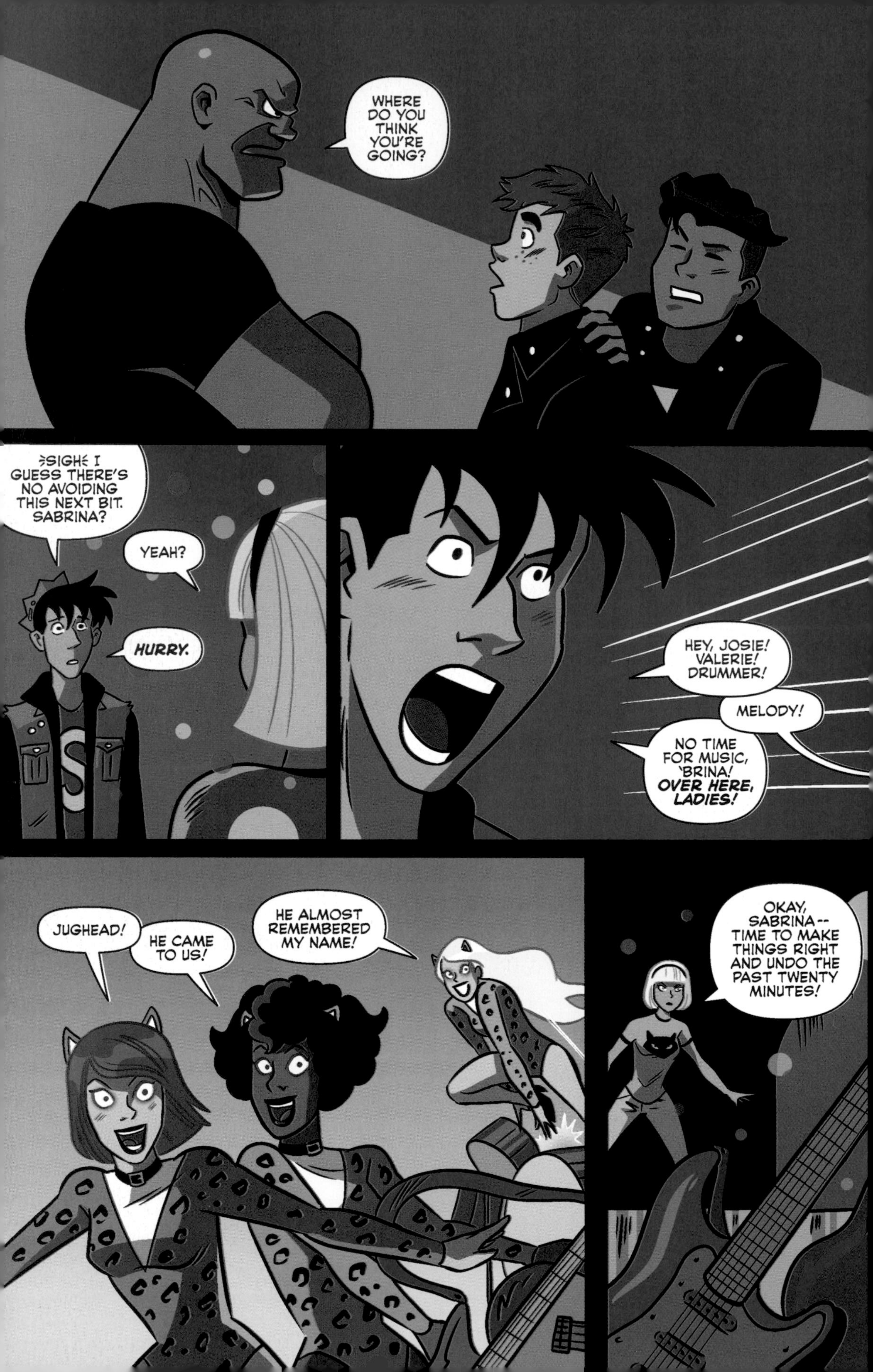
WHERE DO YOU THINK YOU'RE GOING?
⋟SIGH⋞ I GUESS THERE'S NO AVOIDING THIS NEXT BIT. SABRINA?
YEAH?
HURRY.
HEY, JOSIE! VALERIE! DRUMMER!
MELODY!
NO TIME FOR MUSIC, 'BRINA! OVER HERE, LADIES!
JUGHEAD!
HE CAME TO US!
HE ALMOST REMEMBERED MY NAME!
OKAY, SABRINA-- TIME TO MAKE THINGS RIGHT AND UNDO THE PAST TWENTY MINUTES!

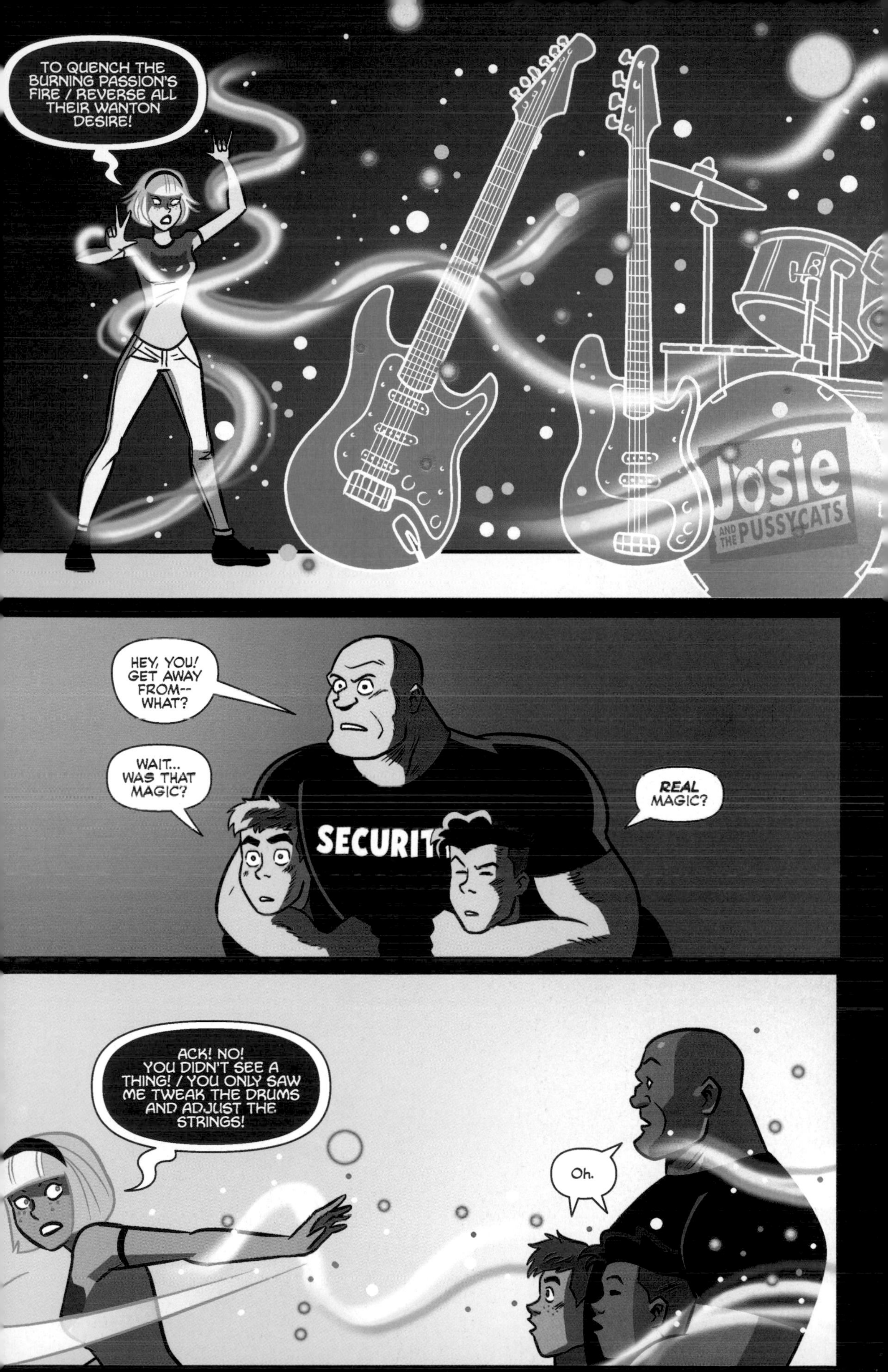
TO QUENCH THE BURNING PASSION'S FIRE / REVERSE ALL THEIR WANTON DESIRE!
Josie AND THE PUSSYCATS
HEY, YOU! GET AWAY FROM-- WHAT?
WAIT... WAS THAT MAGIC?
SECURIT
REAL MAGIC?
ACK! NO! YOU DIDN'T SEE A THING! / YOU ONLY SAW ME TWEAK THE DRUMS AND ADJUST THE STRINGS!
Oh.

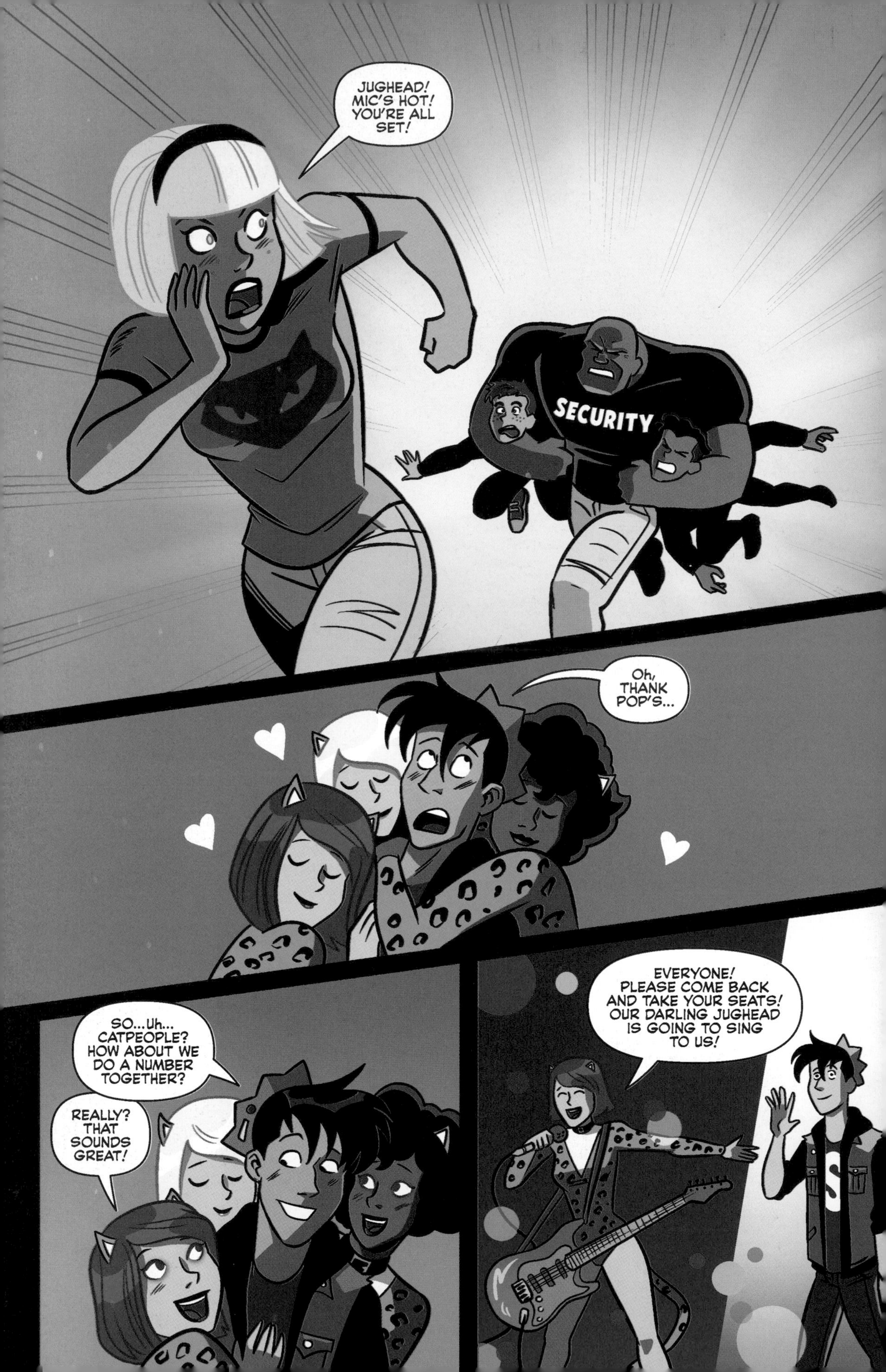
JUGHEAD! MIC'S HOT! YOU'RE ALL SET!
SECURITY
Oh, THANK POP'S...
SO...Uh... CATPEOPLE? HOW ABOUT WE DO A NUMBER TOGETHER?
REALLY? THAT SOUNDS GREAT!
EVERYONE! PLEASE COME BACK AND TAKE YOUR SEATS! OUR DARLING JUGHEAD IS GOING TO SING TO US!

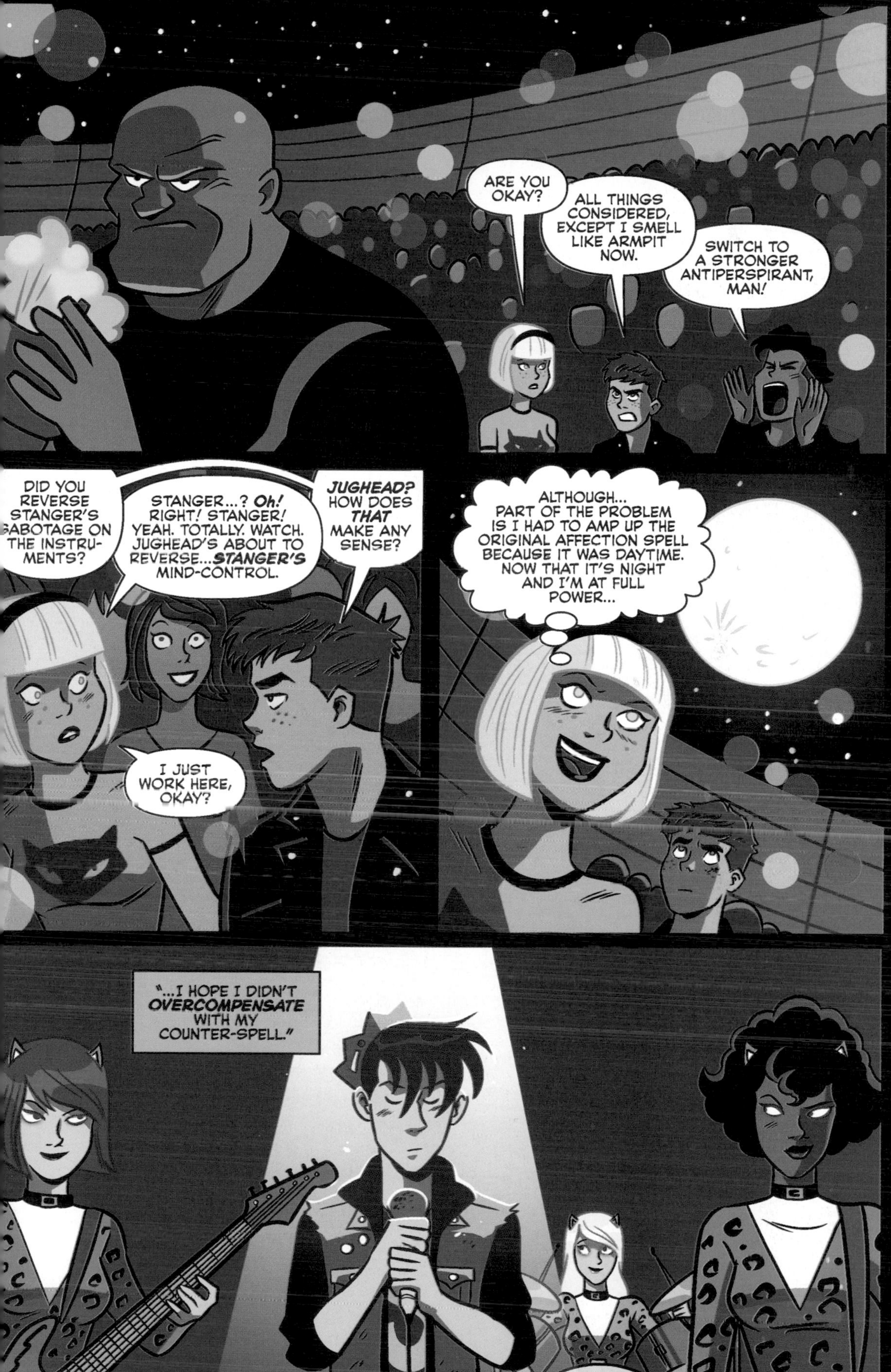
ARE YOU OKAY?
ALL THINGS CONSIDERED, EXCEPT I SMELL LIKE ARMPIT NOW.
SWITCH TO A STRONGER ANTIPERSPIRANT, MAN!
DID YOU REVERSE STANGER'S SABOTAGE ON THE INSTRU-MENTS?
STANGER...? Oh! RIGHT! STANGER! YEAH. TOTALLY. WATCH. JUGHEAD'S ABOUT TO REVERSE...STANGER'S MIND-CONTROL.
JUGHEAD? HOW DOES THAT MAKE ANY SENSE?
I JUST WORK HERE, OKAY?
ALTHOUGH... PART OF THE PROBLEM IS I HAD TO AMP UP THE ORIGINAL AFFECTION SPELL BECAUSE IT WAS DAYTIME. NOW THAT IT'S NIGHT AND I'M AT FULL POWER...
"...I HOPE I DIDN'T OVERCOMPENSATE WITH MY COUNTER-SPELL."
Josie

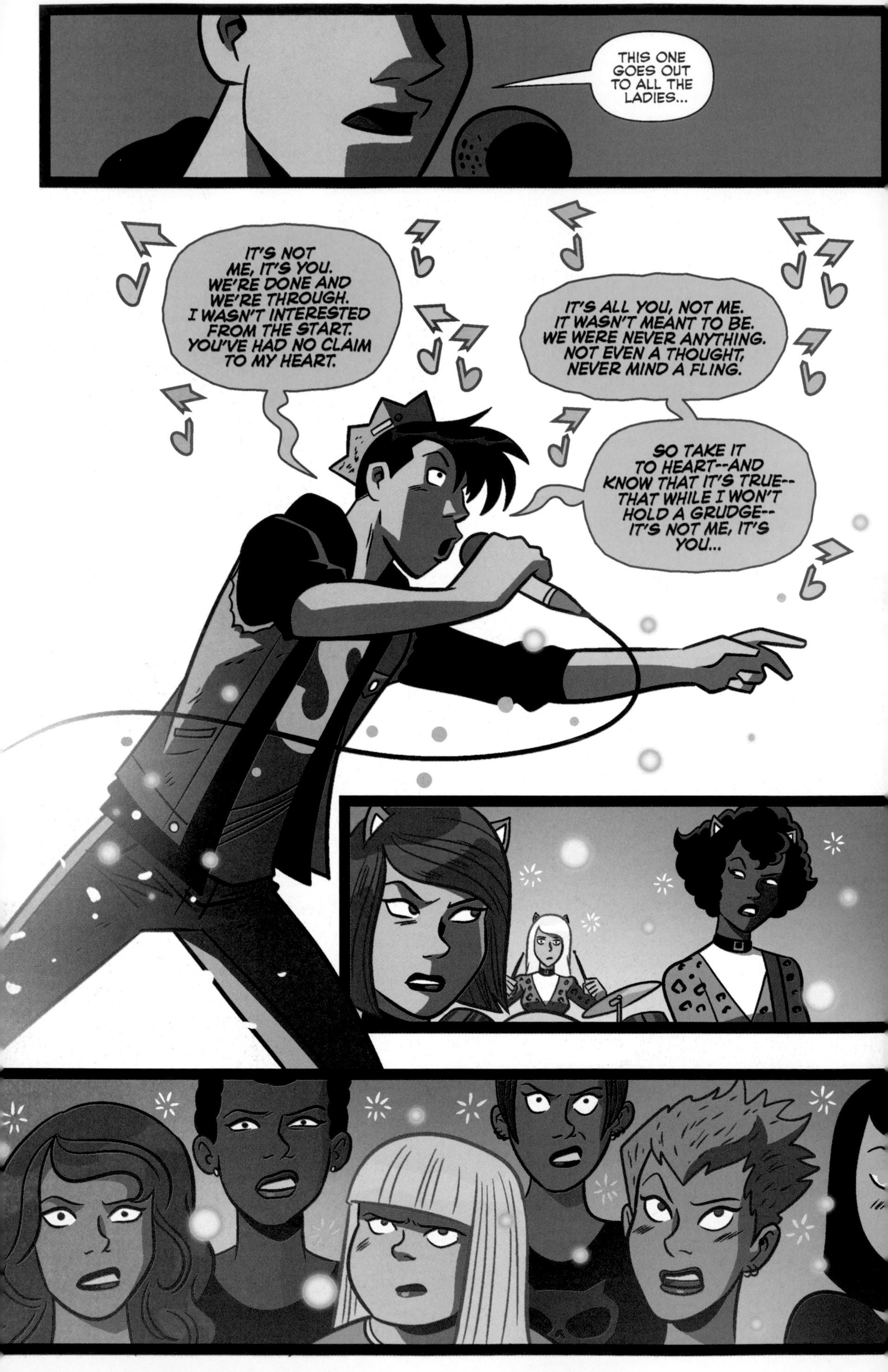
THIS ONE GOES OUT TO ALL THE LADIES...
IT'S NOT ME, IT'S YOU. WE'RE DONE AND WE'RE THROUGH. I WASN'T INTERESTED FROM THE START. YOU'VE HAD NO CLAIM TO MY HEART.
IT'S ALL YOU, NOT ME. IT WASN'T MEANT TO BE. WE WERE NEVER ANYTHING. NOT EVEN A THOUGHT, NEVER MIND A FLING.
SO TAKE IT TO HEART--AND KNOW THAT IT'S TRUE--THAT WHILE I WON'T HOLD A GRUDGE--IT'S NOT ME, IT'S YOU...

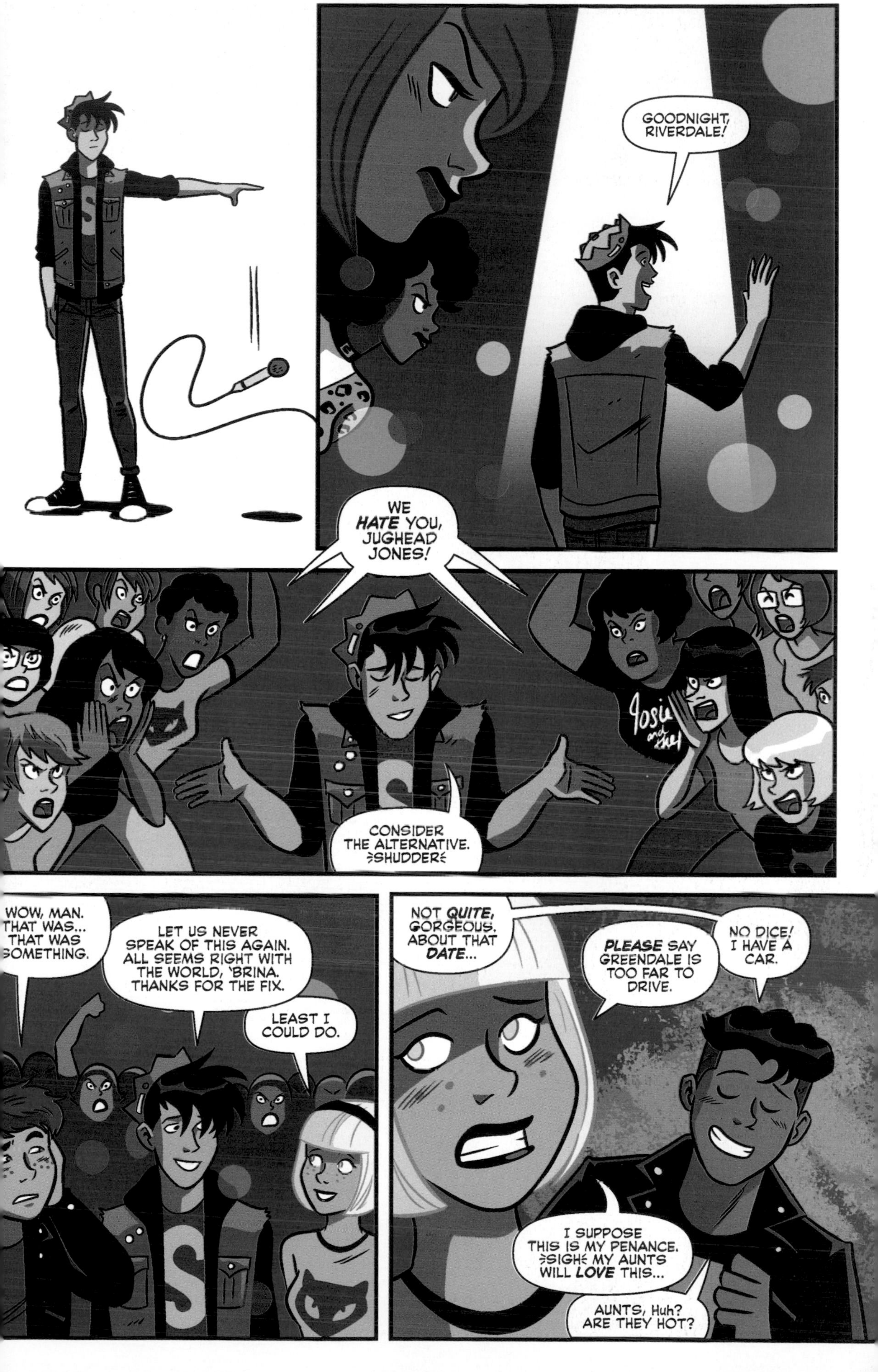
GOODNIGHT, RIVERDALE!
WE HATE YOU, JUGHEAD JONES!
CONSIDER THE ALTERNATIVE. ⁝SHUDDER⁝
WOW, MAN. THAT WAS... THAT WAS SOMETHING.
LET US NEVER SPEAK OF THIS AGAIN. ALL SEEMS RIGHT WITH THE WORLD, 'BRINA. THANKS FOR THE FIX.
LEAST I COULD DO.
NOT QUITE, GORGEOUS. ABOUT THAT DATE...
PLEASE SAY GREENDALE IS TOO FAR TO DRIVE.
NO DICE! I HAVE A CAR.
I SUPPOSE THIS IS MY PENANCE. ⁝SIGH⁝ MY AUNTS WILL LOVE THIS...
AUNTS, Huh? ARE THEY HOT?

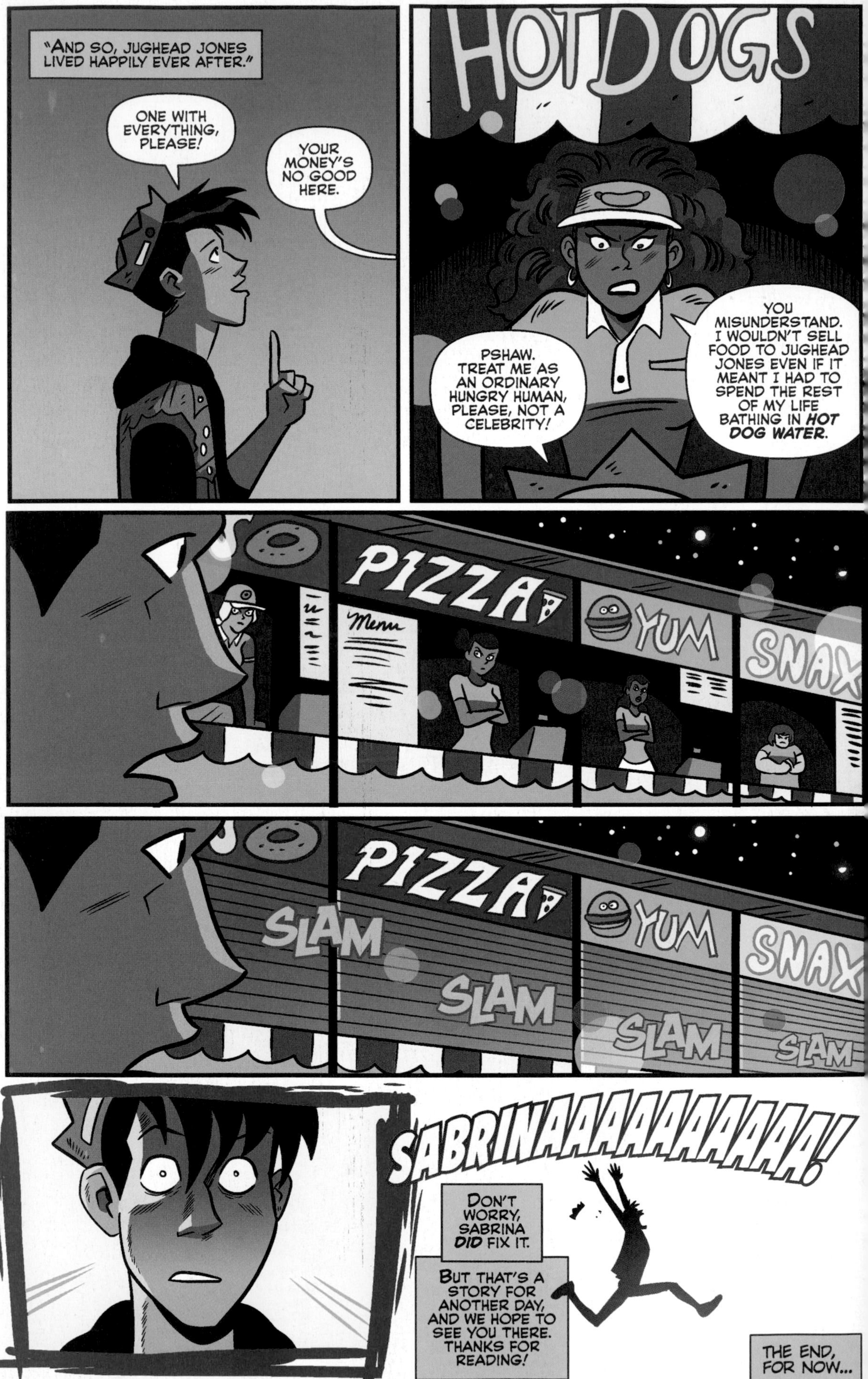
"AND SO, JUGHEAD JONES LIVED HAPPILY EVER AFTER."
ONE WITH EVERYTHING, PLEASE!
YOUR MONEY'S NO GOOD HERE.
HOT DOGS
PSHAW. TREAT ME AS AN ORDINARY HUNGRY HUMAN, PLEASE, NOT A CELEBRITY!
YOU MISUNDERSTAND. I WOULDN'T SELL FOOD TO JUGHEAD JONES EVEN IF IT MEANT I HAD TO SPEND THE REST OF MY LIFE BATHING IN HOT DOG WATER.
PIZZA
Menu
YUM
SNAX
PIZZA
YUM
SNAX
SLAM
SLAM
SLAM
SLAM
SABRINAAAAAAAAAA!
DON'T WORRY, SABRINA DID FIX IT.
BUT THAT'S A STORY FOR ANOTHER DAY, AND WE HOPE TO SEE YOU THERE. THANKS FOR READING!
THE END, FOR NOW...

Jughead®

SPECIAL FEATURES

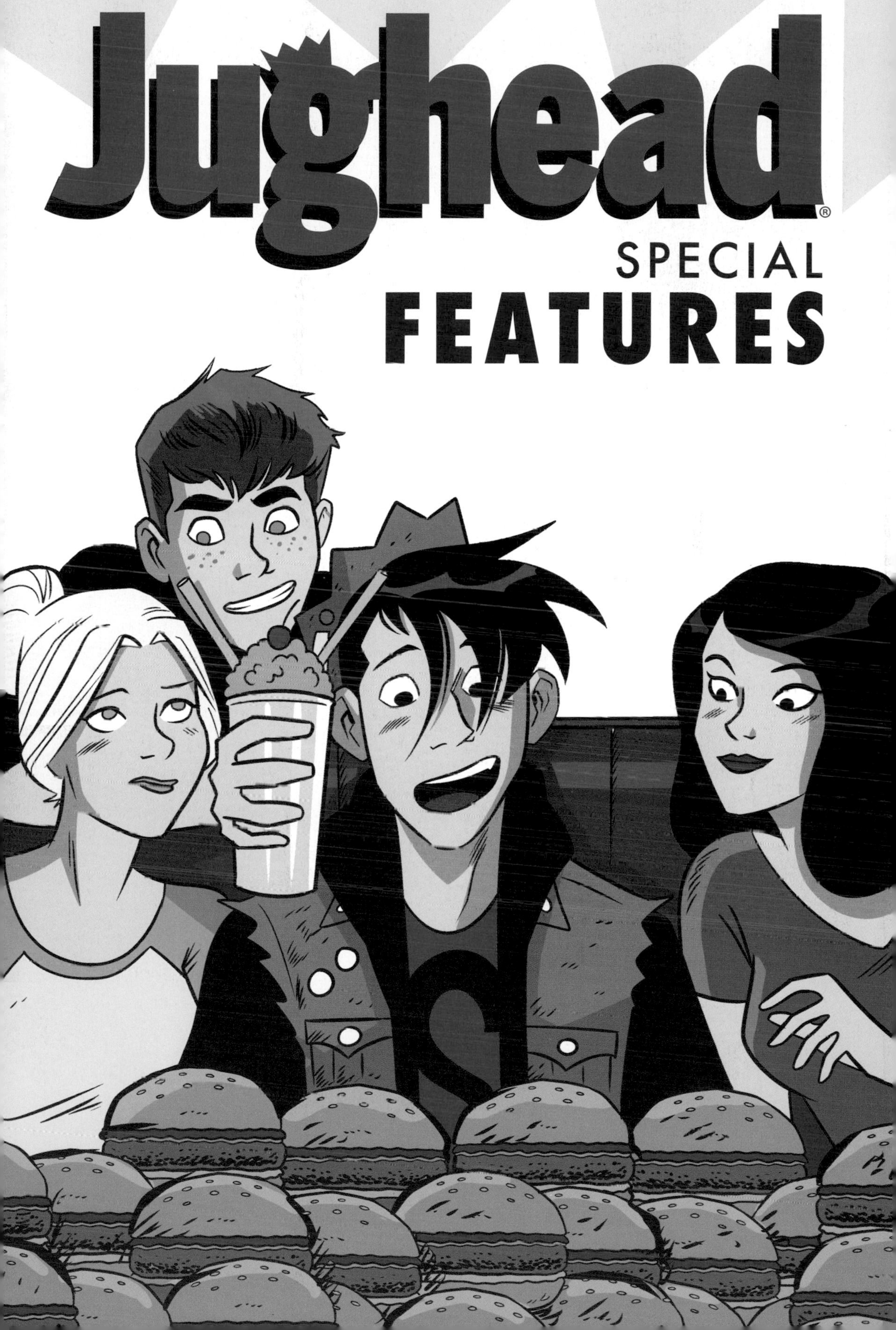

Jughead® COVER GALLERY

In addition to the amazing main covers we have for each issue, we feature special variant covers from a variety of talented artists. Here are all of the main and variant covers for each of the five issues in *Jughead Volume Three*.

ISSUE FIFTEEN VARIANT
BY MARGUERITE SAUVAGE

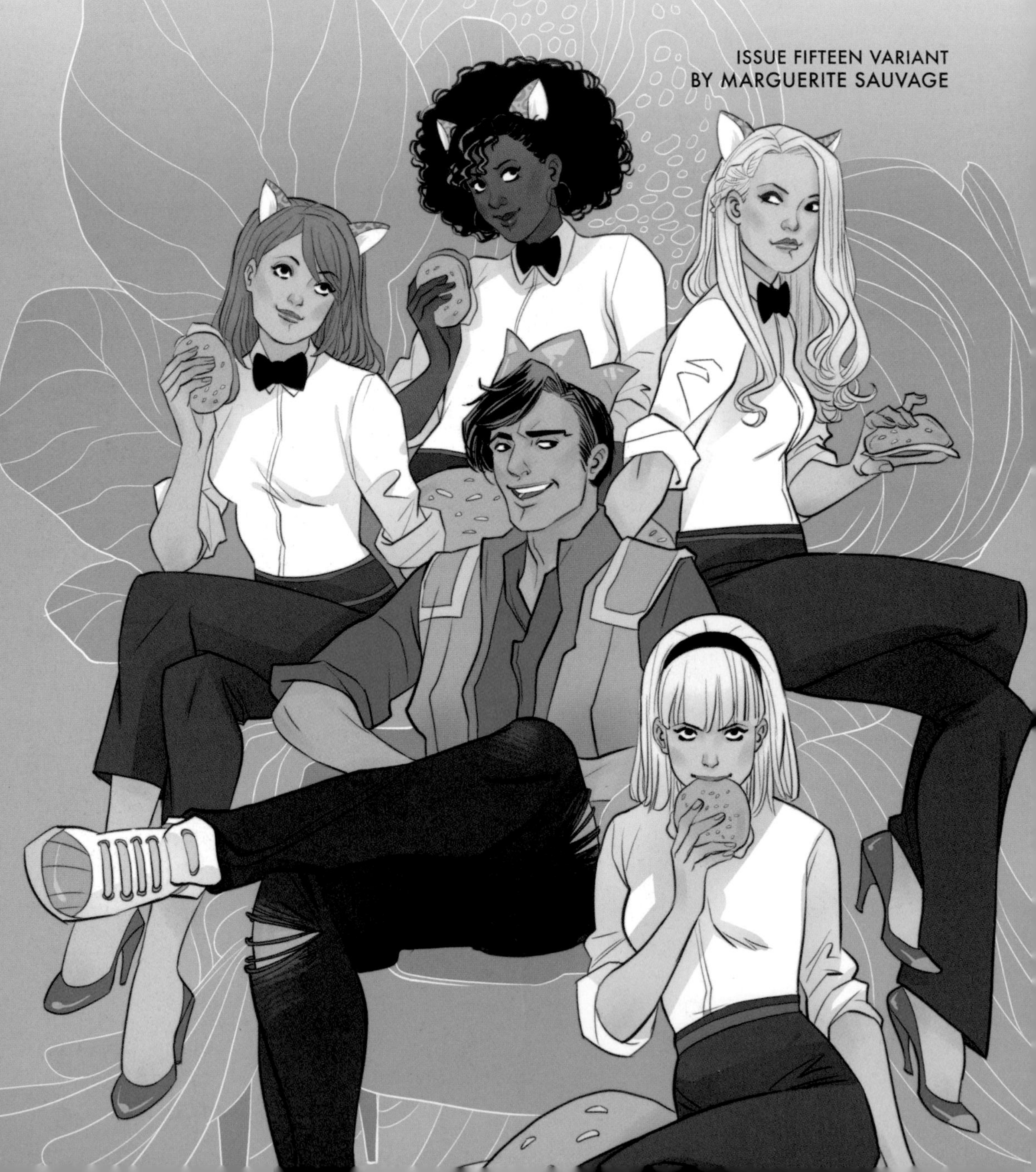

ISSUE **TWELVE**

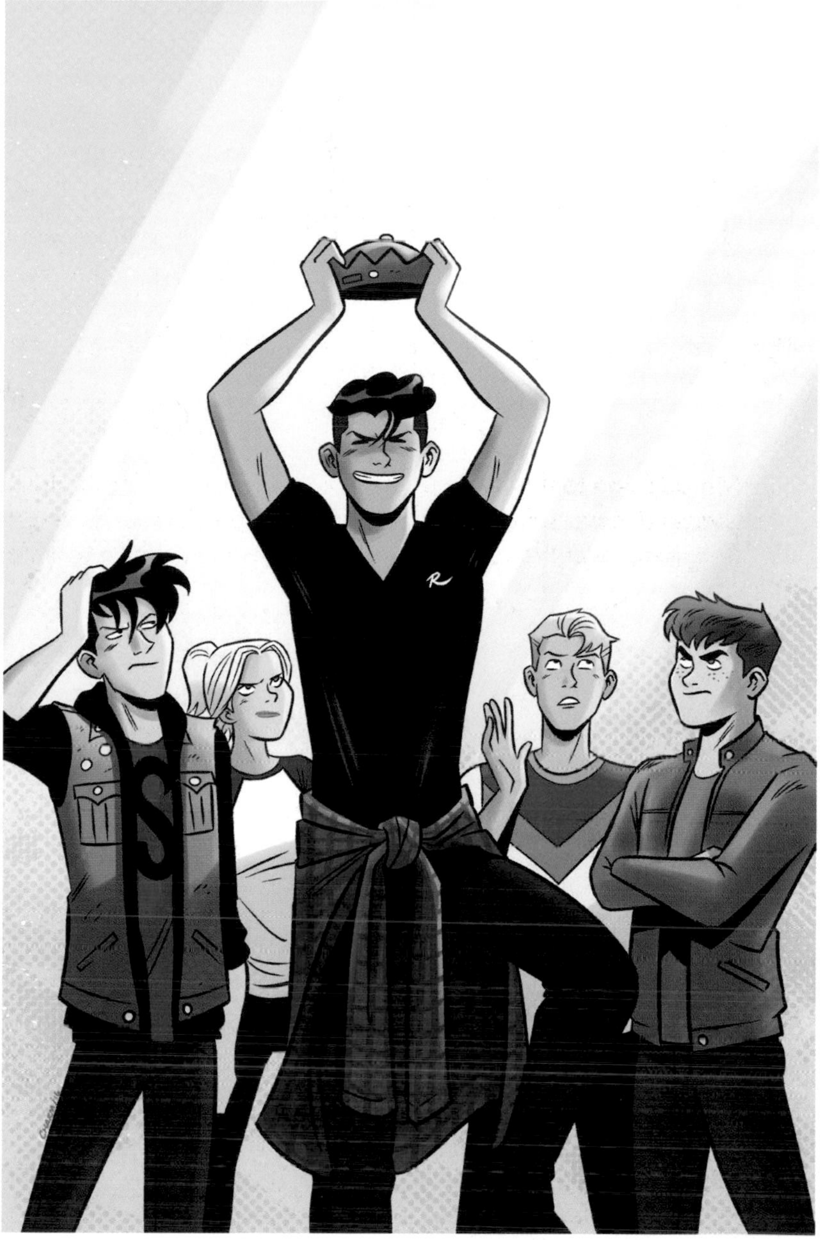

DEREK
CHARM

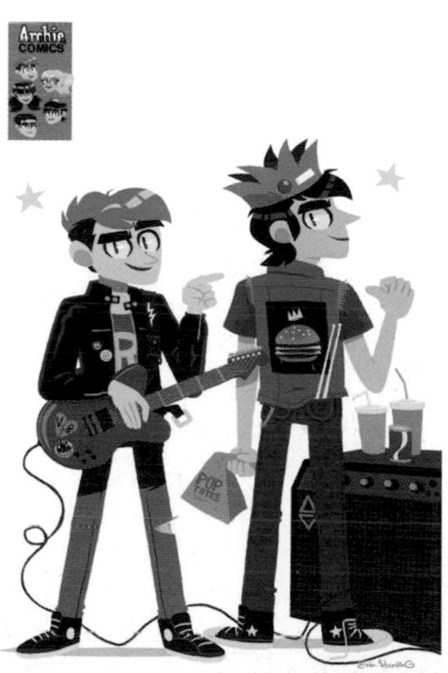
Archie
COMICS

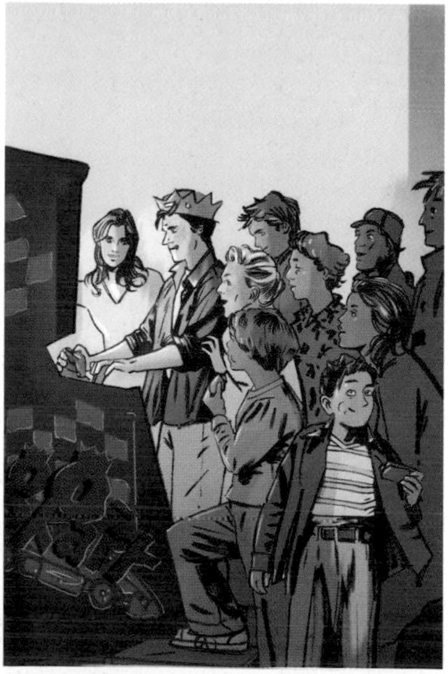

(L)
ERIN
HUNTING

(R)
TULA
LOTAY

ISSUE
THIRTEEN

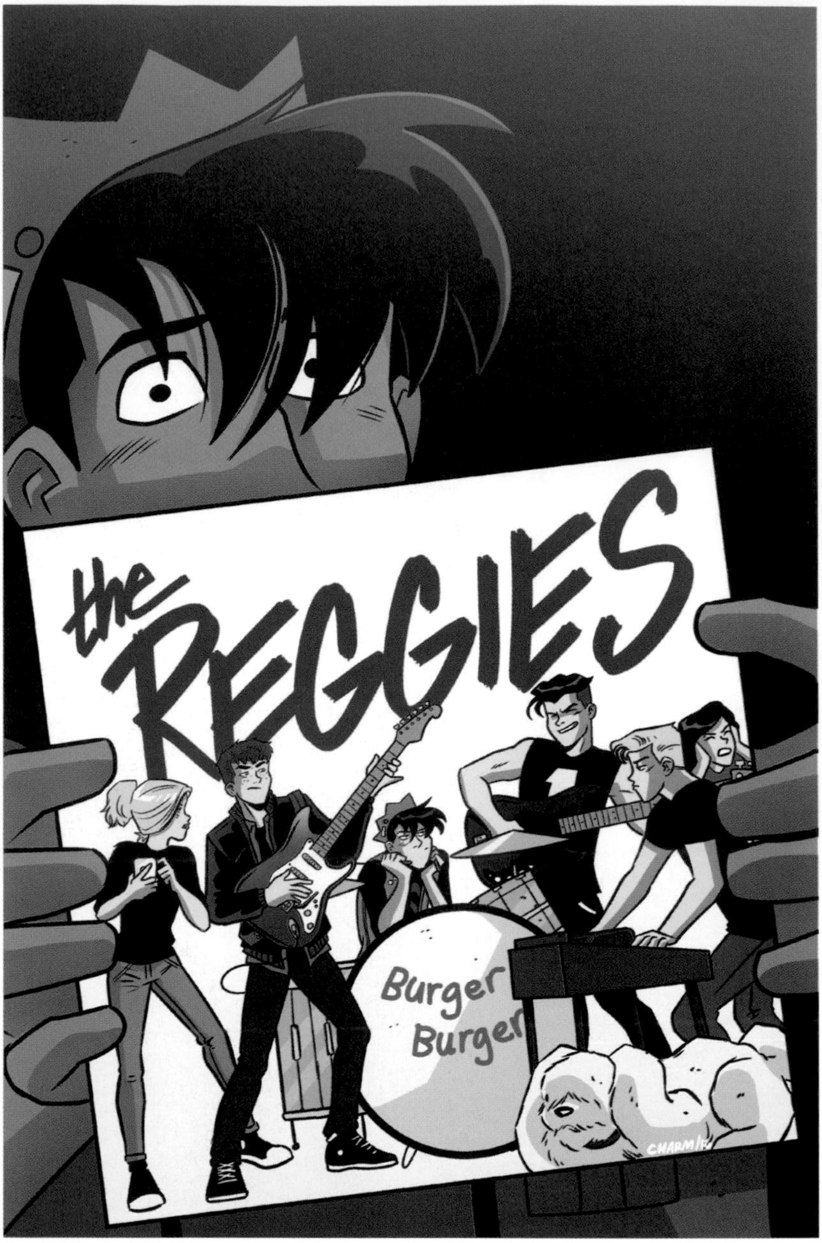
the REGGIES
Burger Burger
CHARM

DEREK
CHARM

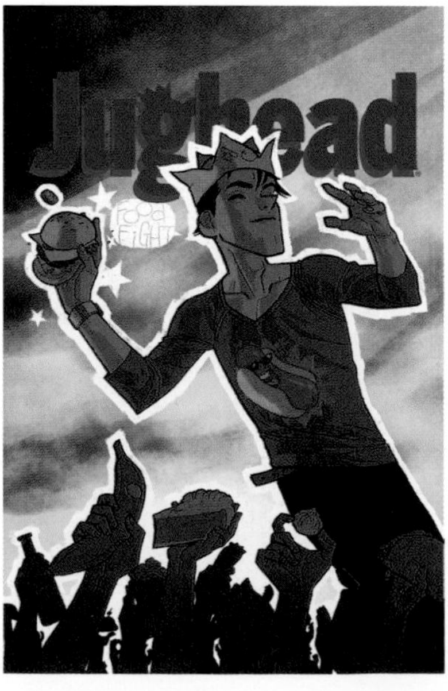
Jughead

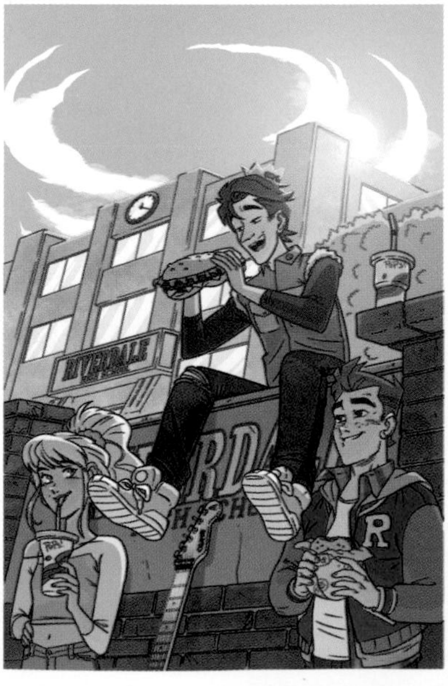
R

(L)
BEN
CALDWELL

(R)
RYAN
JAMPOLE

ISSUE
FOURTEEN

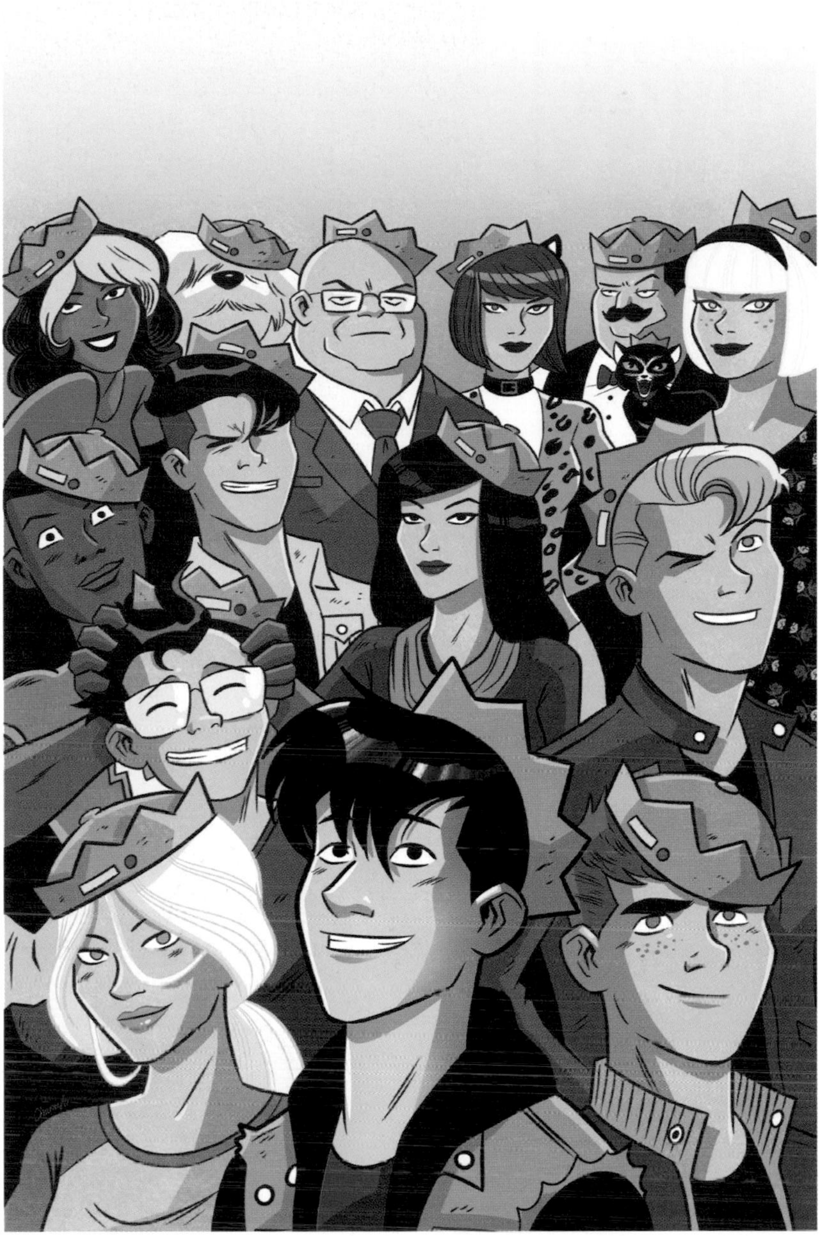

DEREK
CHARM

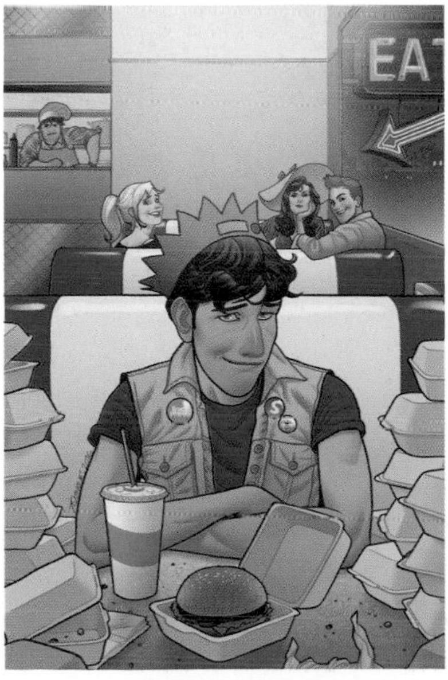
EAT

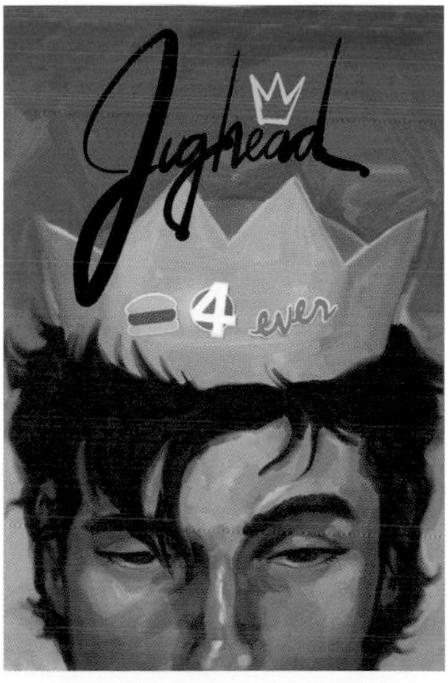
Jughead
4 ever

(L)
JOE
QUINONES

(R)
CHIP
ZDARSKY

ISSUE
FIFTEEN

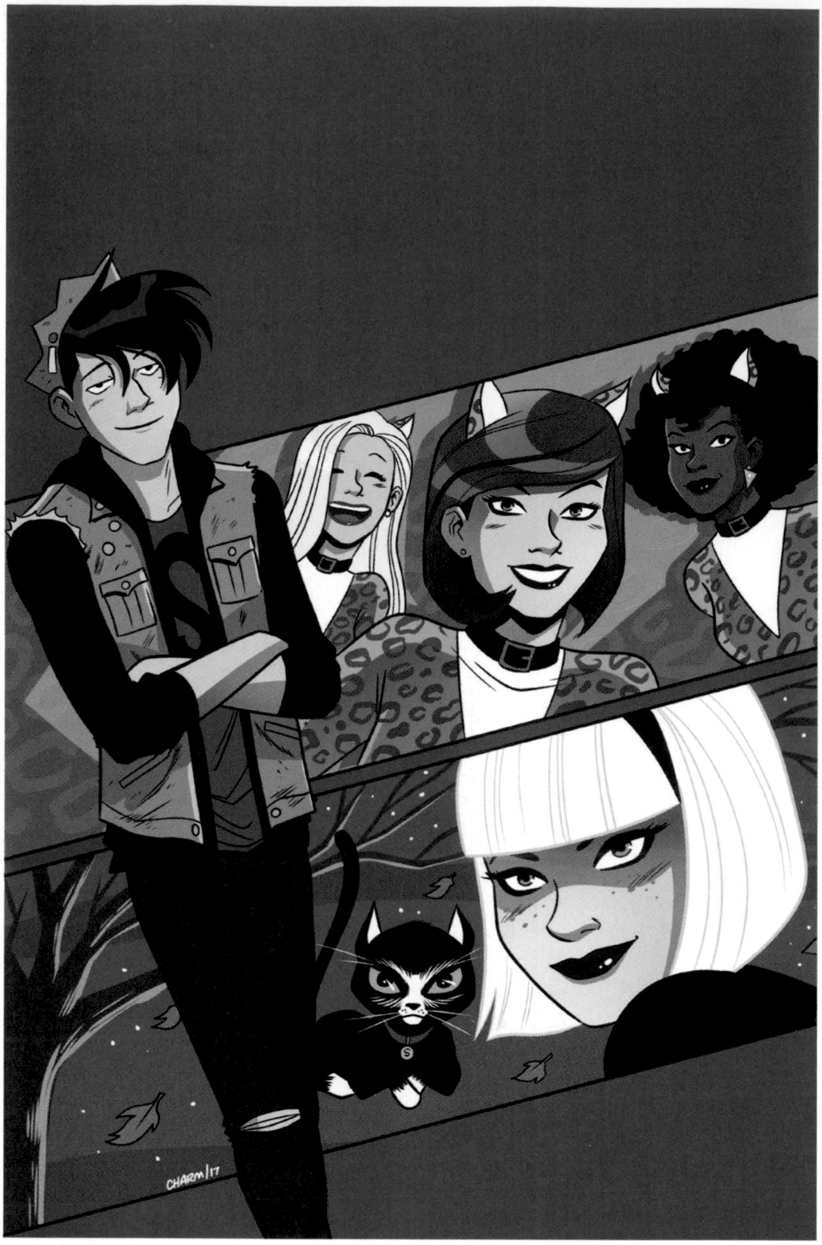

DEREK
CHARM

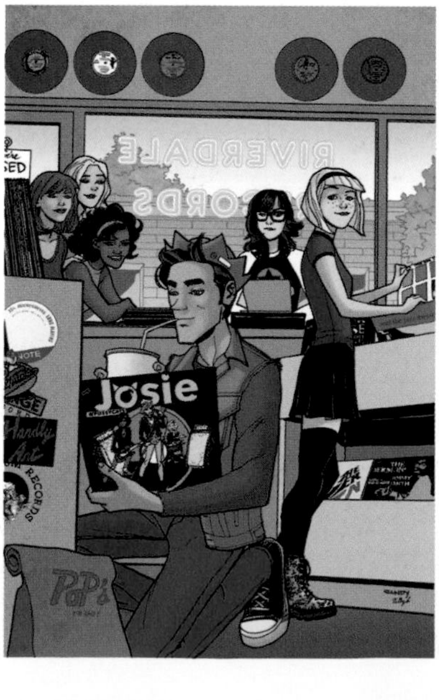
Josie

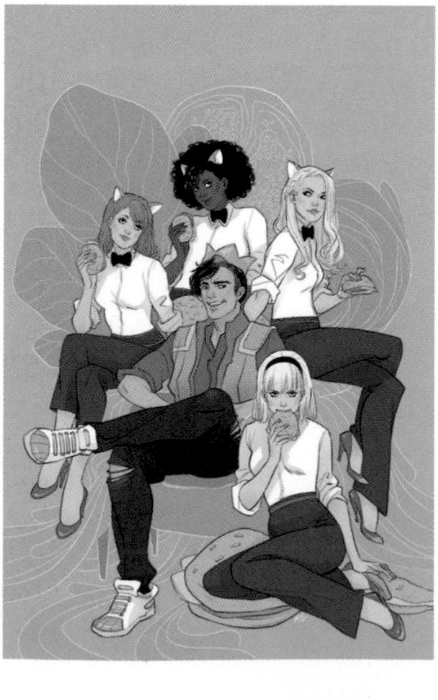

(L)
SANDY
JARRELL
WITH KELLY
FITZPATRICK

(R)
MARGUERITE
SAUVAGE

ISSUE
SIXTEEN

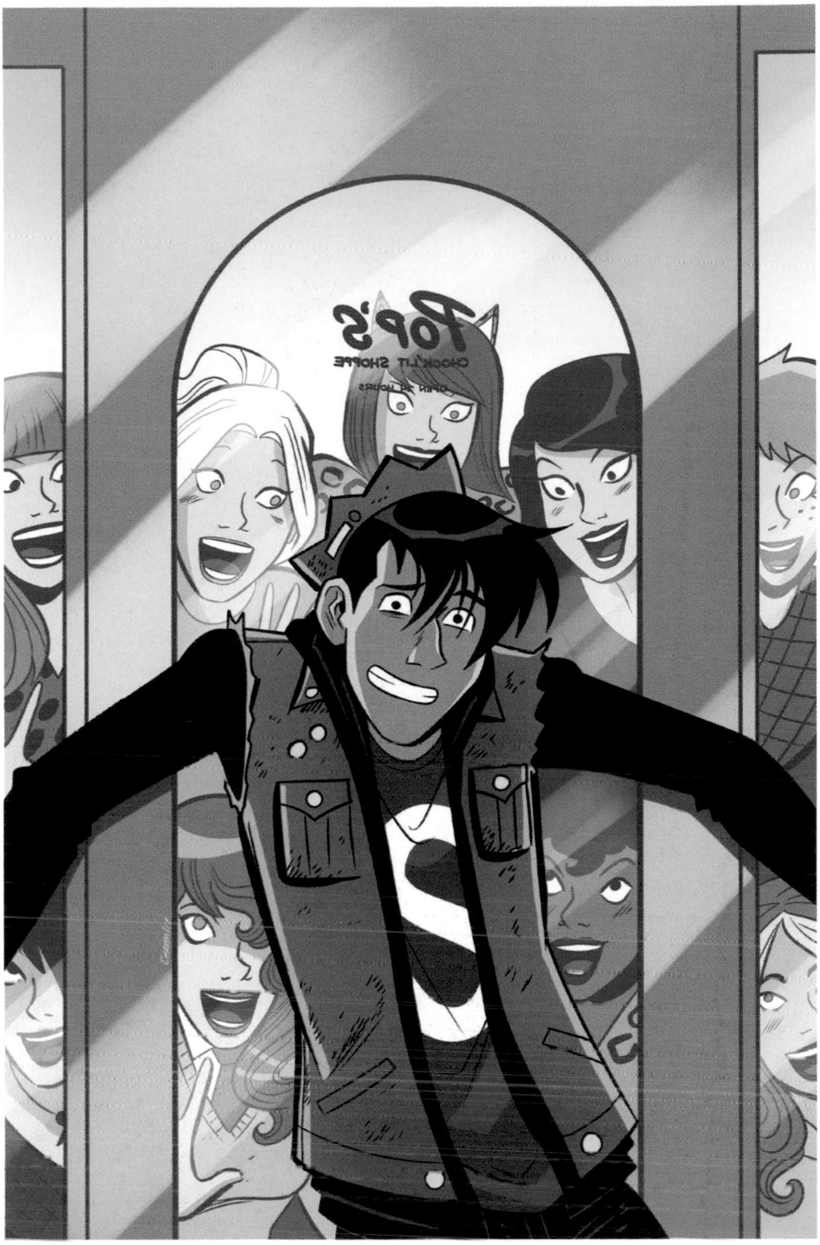
Pop's
CHOCK'LIT SHOPPE
OPEN 24 HOURS

DEREK
CHARM

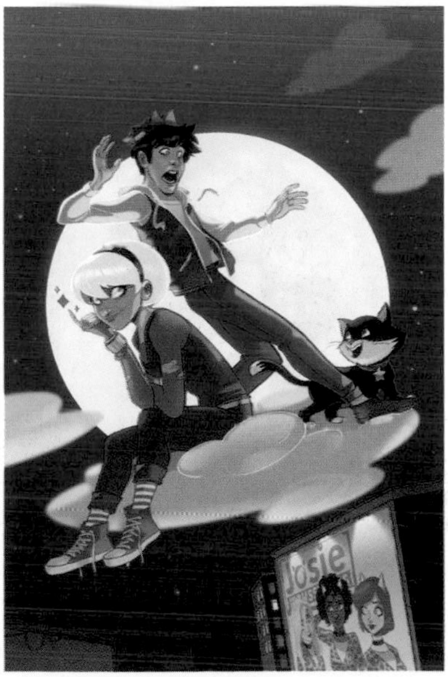
Josie

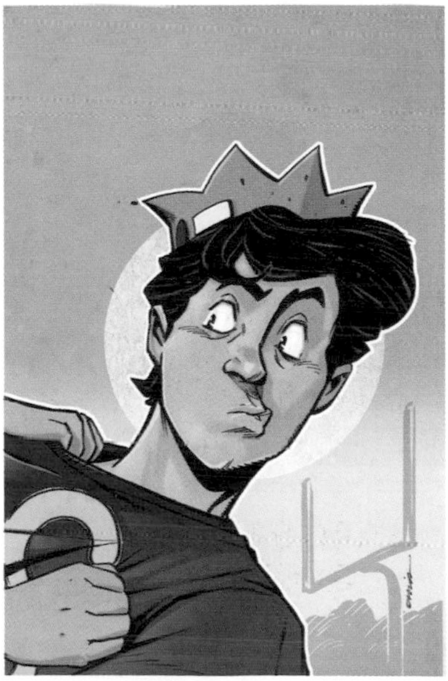

(L)
STEPHEN
BYRNE

(R)
ELLIOT
FERNANDEZ

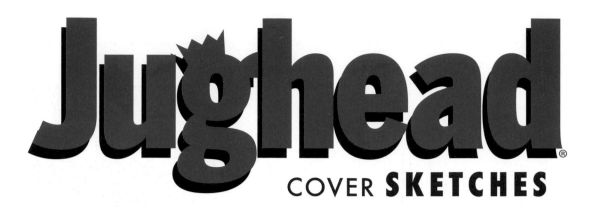

Jughead®
COVER **SKETCHES**

Before each issue goes through the Diamond Previews solicitation process, our esteemed writers give us a synopsis of what will occur in each upcoming issue, and from that our talented interior artist will come up with some main cover ideas and send in rough drafts of how they would like the cover to appear. Then the Editor/President will choose one of the options, and then a finalized version will be routed to Archie Comics Publisher/Co-CEO for final approval.

Here are a few of DEREK CHARM's brilliant cover sketch options along with how they appeared in the final versions.

ISSUE **TWELVE**

COVER SKETCHES

Jughead

Jughead
Reggie

FINAL COVER

Archie COMICS
'12
RYAN NORTH
DEREK CHARM
ALL NEW!
Jughead

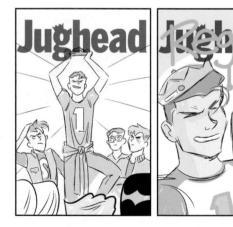

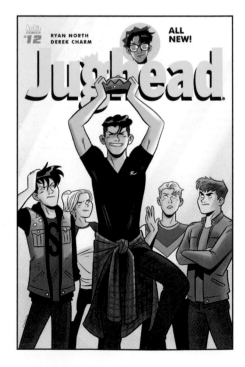

ISSUE **THIRTEEN**

COVER SKETCHES

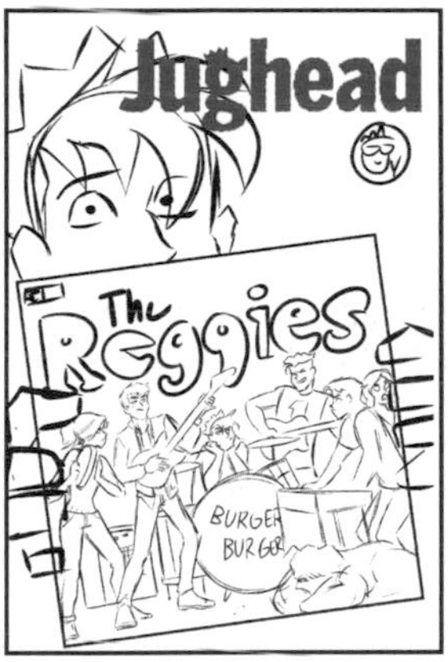
Jughead
The Reggies
BURGER
BURGER

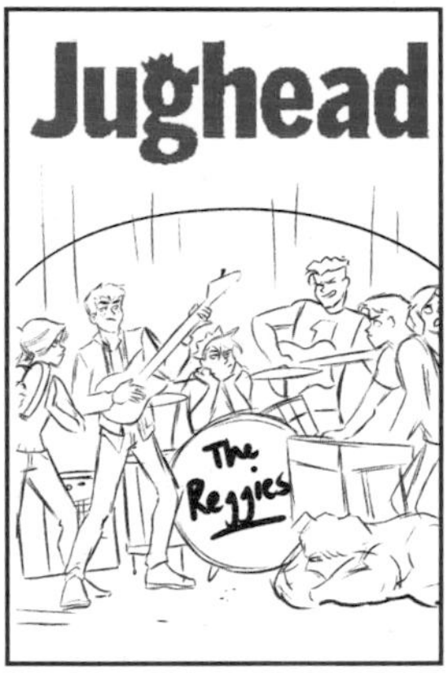
Jughead
The Reggies

FINAL COVER

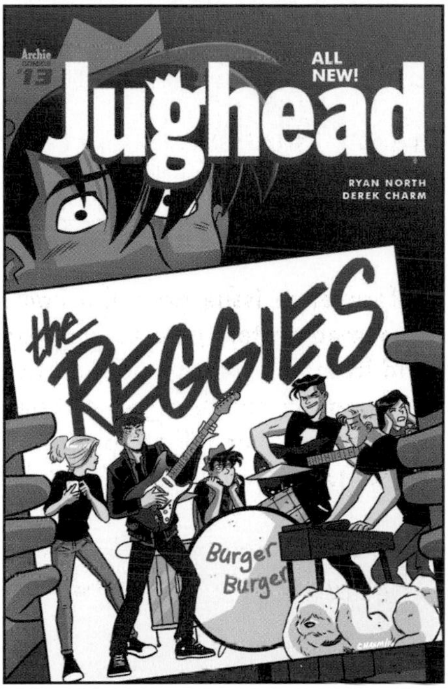
Archie
#13
ALL NEW!
Jughead
RYAN NORTH
DEREK CHARM
the REGGIES
Burger
Burger

ISSUE **FOURTEEN**

COVER SKETCHES

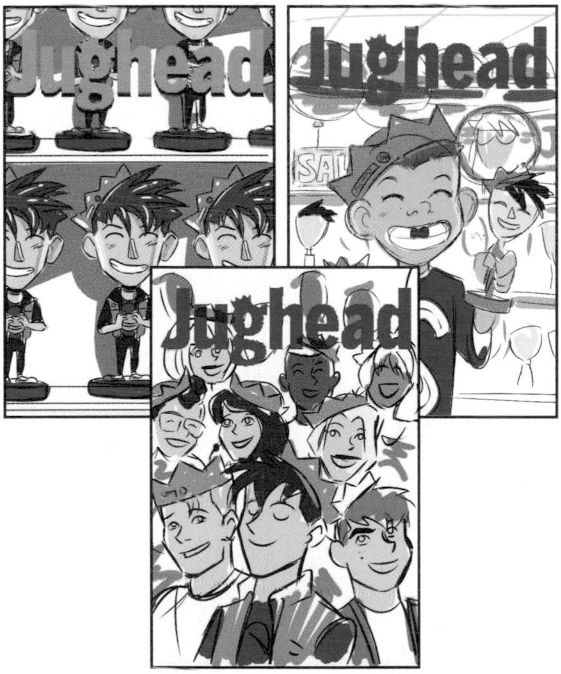
Jughead
Jughead
Jughead

FINAL COVER

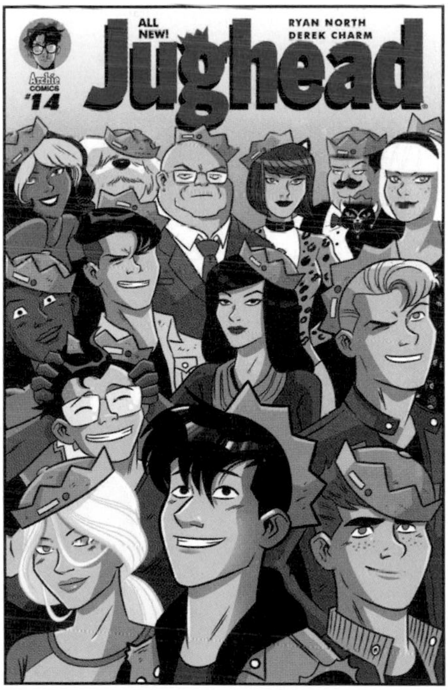
ALL NEW!
RYAN NORTH
DEREK CHARM
Archie COMICS
#14
Jughead

ISSUE **FIFTEEN**

COVER SKETCHES

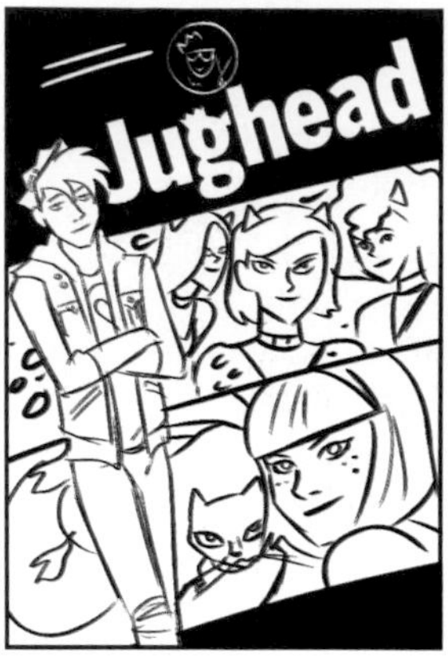
Jughead

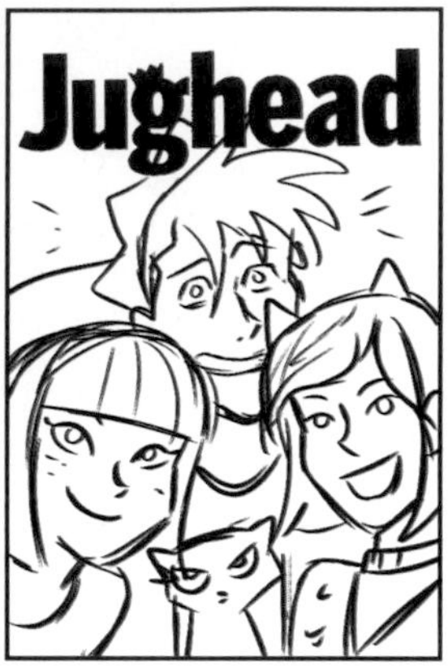
Jughead

FINAL COVER

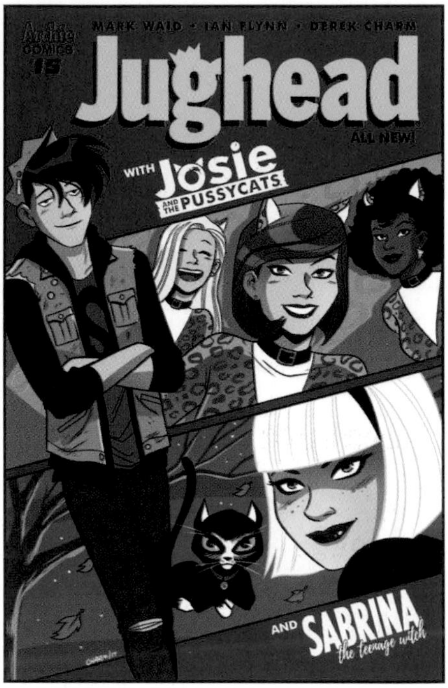
Archie
COMICS
#15
MARK WAID • IAN FLYNN • DEREK CHARM
Jughead
ALL NEW!
WITH Josie AND THE PUSSYCATS
AND SABRINA the teenage witch

ISSUE **SIXTEEN**

COVER SKETCHES

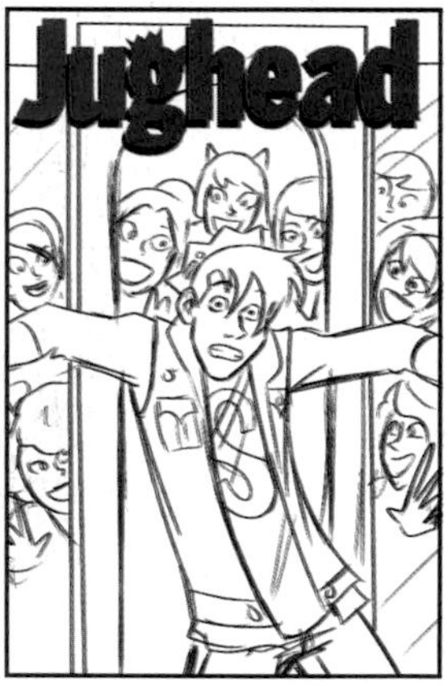
Jughead

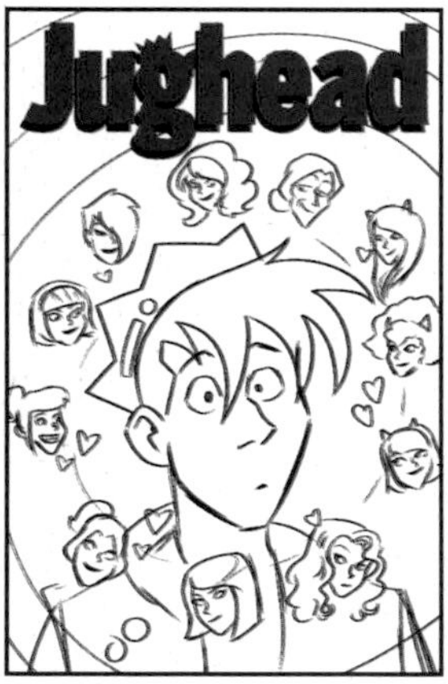
Jughead

FINAL COVER

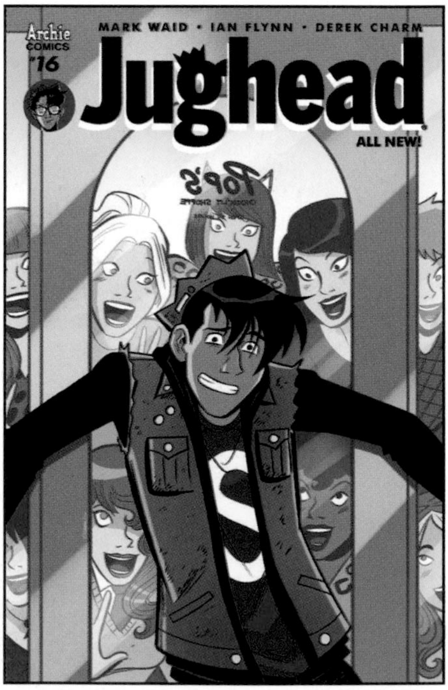
Archie
COMICS
#16
MARK WAID • IAN FLYNN • DEREK CHARM
Jughead
ALL NEW!
Pop's

SPECIAL **BONUS ISSUE**

Josie and the Pussycats #6

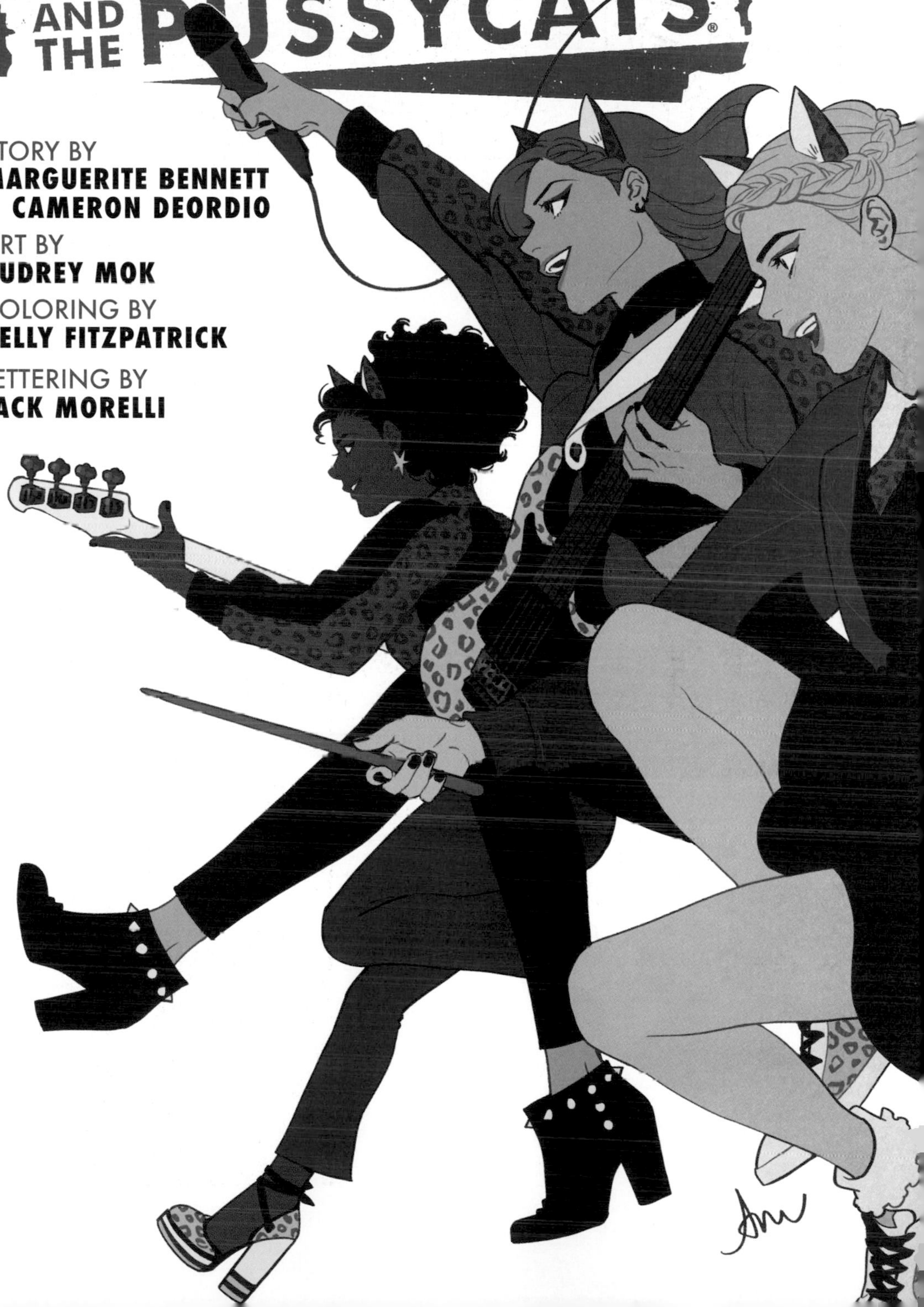

STORY BY
MARGUERITE BENNETT
& **CAMERON DEORDIO**

ART BY
AUDREY MOK

COLORING BY
KELLY FITZPATRICK

LETTERING BY
JACK MORELLI

ISSUE **SIX**

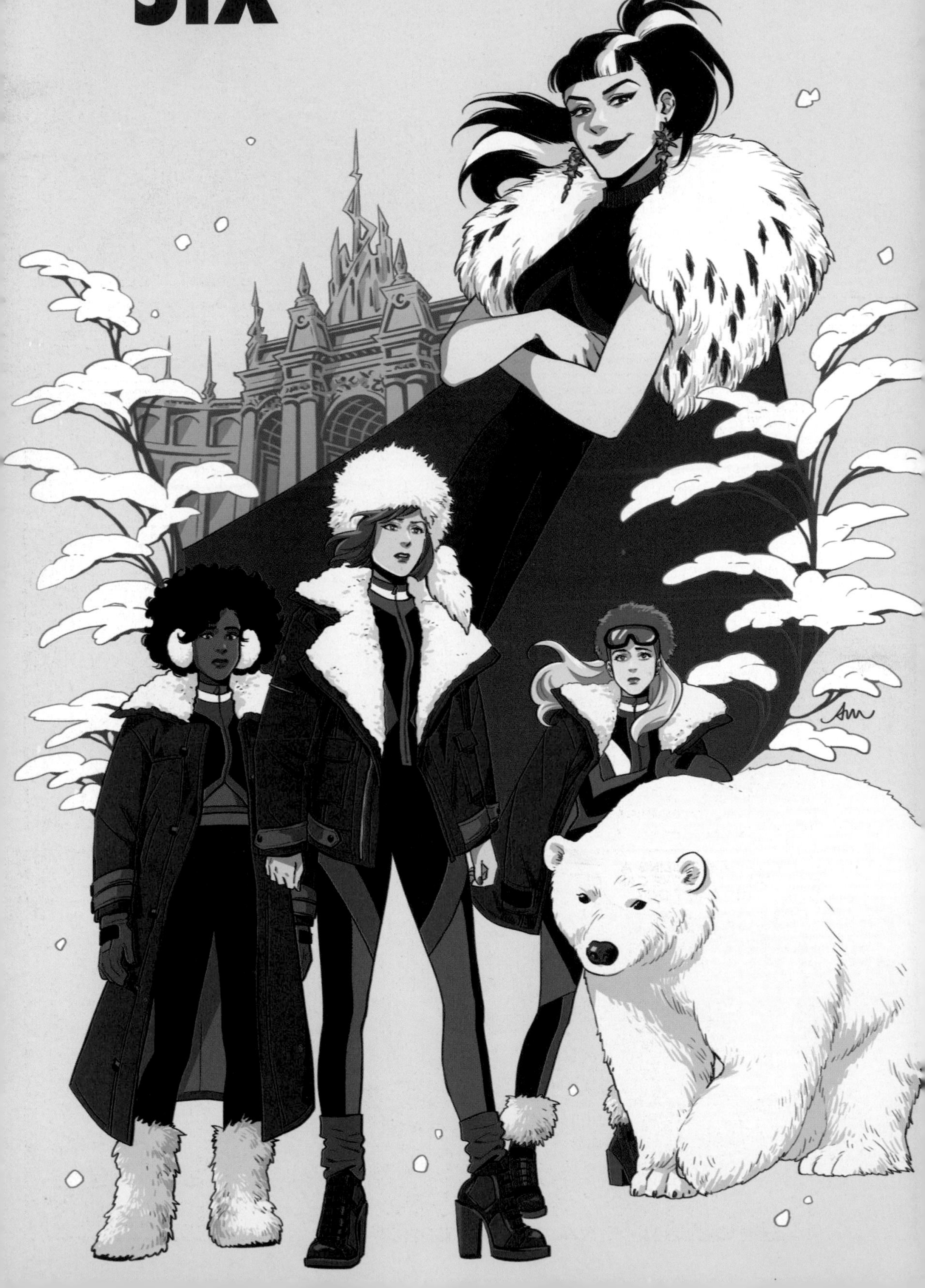

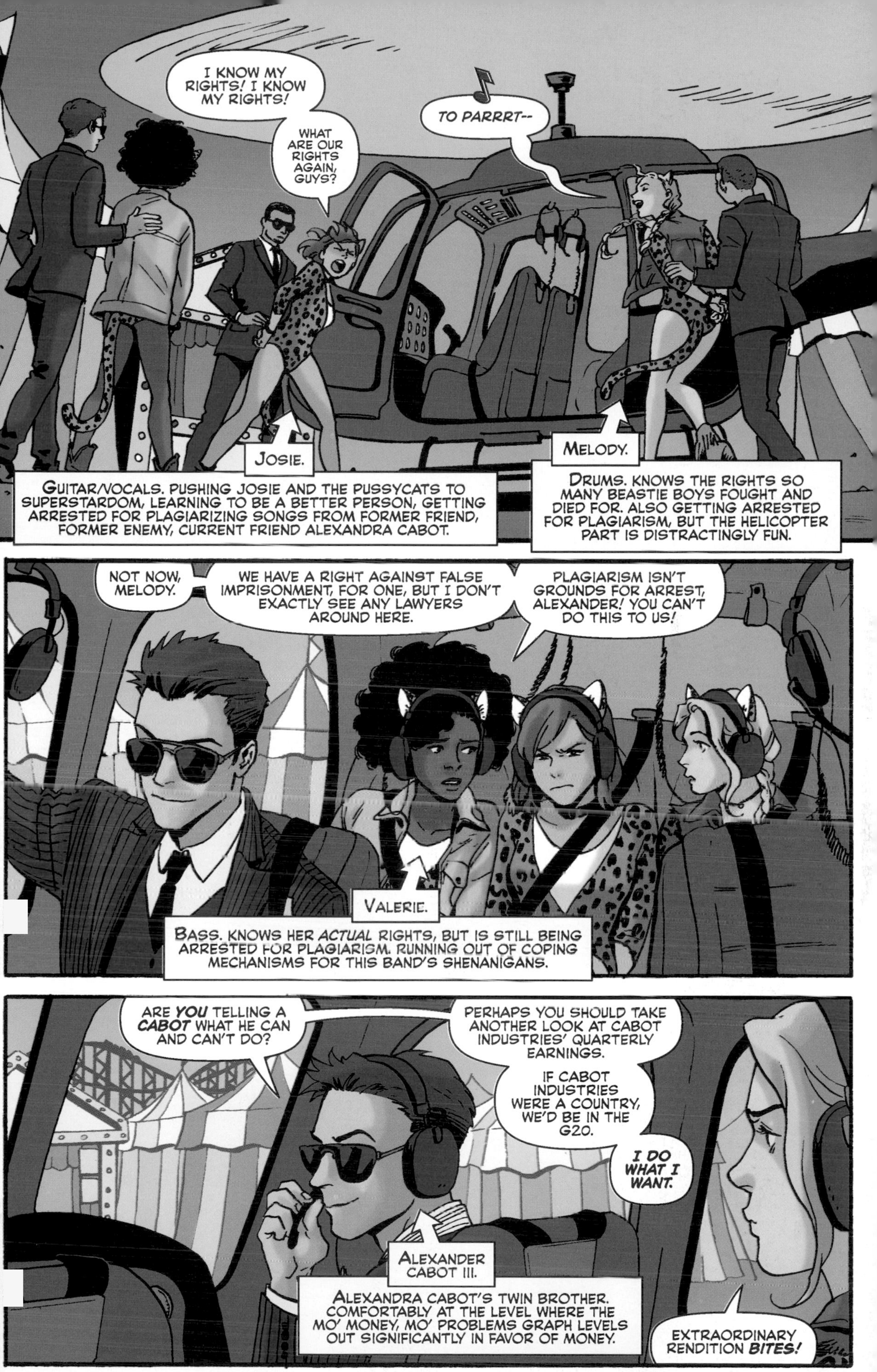

I KNOW MY RIGHTS! I KNOW MY RIGHTS!
WHAT ARE OUR RIGHTS AGAIN, GUYS?
TO PARRRT--
JOSIE.
GUITAR/VOCALS. PUSHING JOSIE AND THE PUSSYCATS TO SUPERSTARDOM, LEARNING TO BE A BETTER PERSON, GETTING ARRESTED FOR PLAGIARIZING SONGS FROM FORMER FRIEND, FORMER ENEMY, CURRENT FRIEND ALEXANDRA CABOT.
MELODY.
DRUMS. KNOWS THE RIGHTS SO MANY BEASTIE BOYS FOUGHT AND DIED FOR. ALSO GETTING ARRESTED FOR PLAGIARISM, BUT THE HELICOPTER PART IS DISTRACTINGLY FUN.
NOT NOW, MELODY.
WE HAVE A RIGHT AGAINST FALSE IMPRISONMENT, FOR ONE, BUT I DON'T EXACTLY SEE ANY LAWYERS AROUND HERE.
PLAGIARISM ISN'T GROUNDS FOR ARREST, ALEXANDER! YOU CAN'T DO THIS TO US!
VALERIE.
BASS. KNOWS HER *ACTUAL* RIGHTS, BUT IS STILL BEING ARRESTED FOR PLAGIARISM. RUNNING OUT OF COPING MECHANISMS FOR THIS BAND'S SHENANIGANS.
ARE *YOU* TELLING A *CABOT* WHAT HE CAN AND CAN'T DO?
PERHAPS YOU SHOULD TAKE ANOTHER LOOK AT CABOT INDUSTRIES' QUARTERLY EARNINGS.
IF CABOT INDUSTRIES WERE A COUNTRY, WE'D BE IN THE G20.
I DO WHAT I WANT.
ALEXANDER CABOT III.
ALEXANDRA CABOT'S TWIN BROTHER. COMFORTABLY AT THE LEVEL WHERE THE MO' MONEY, MO' PROBLEMS GRAPH LEVELS OUT SIGNIFICANTLY IN FAVOR OF MONEY.
EXTRAORDINARY RENDITION *BITES!*

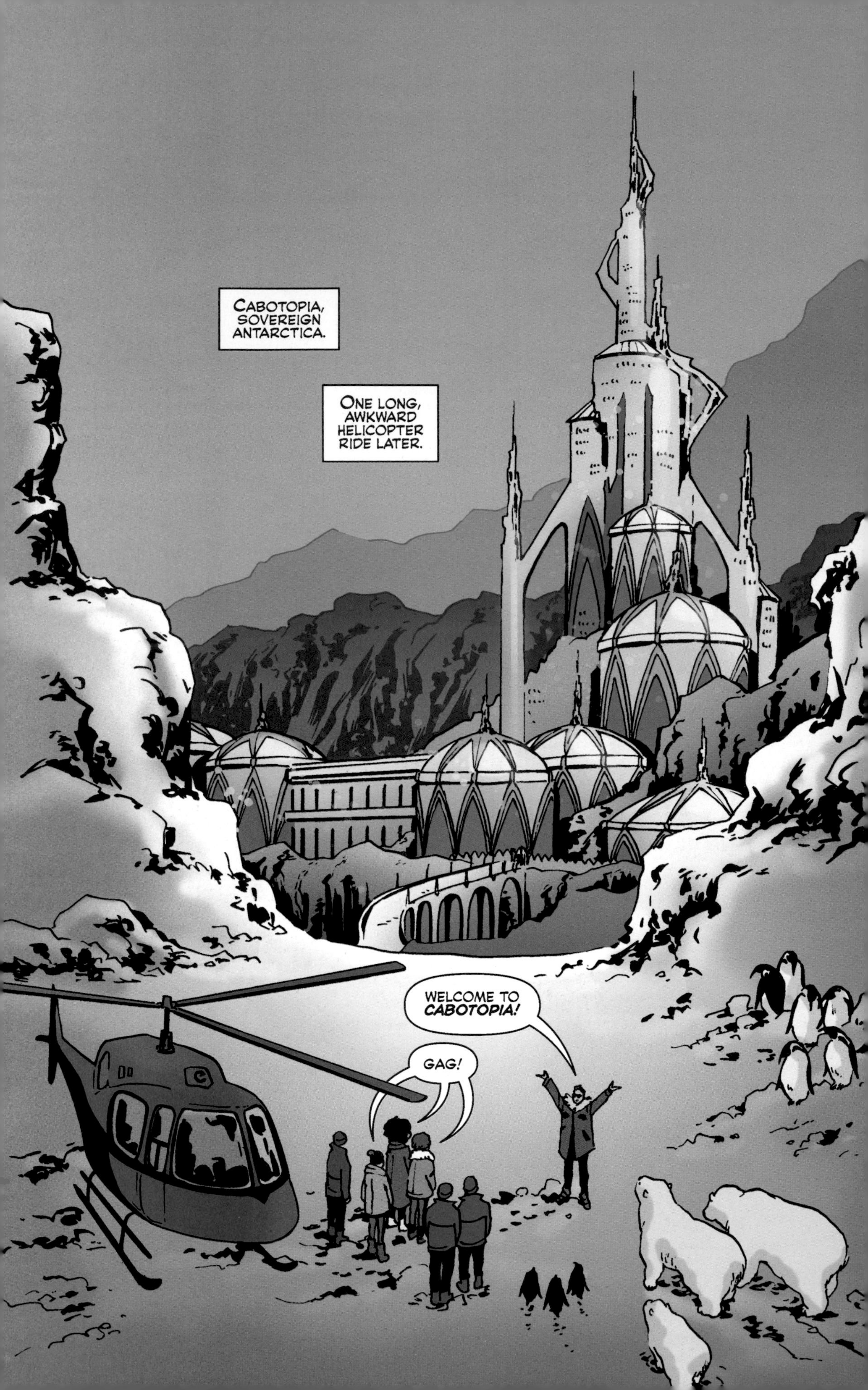
CABOTOPIA, SOVEREIGN ANTARCTICA.
ONE LONG, AWKWARD HELICOPTER RIDE LATER.
WELCOME TO *CABOTOPIA!*
GAG!

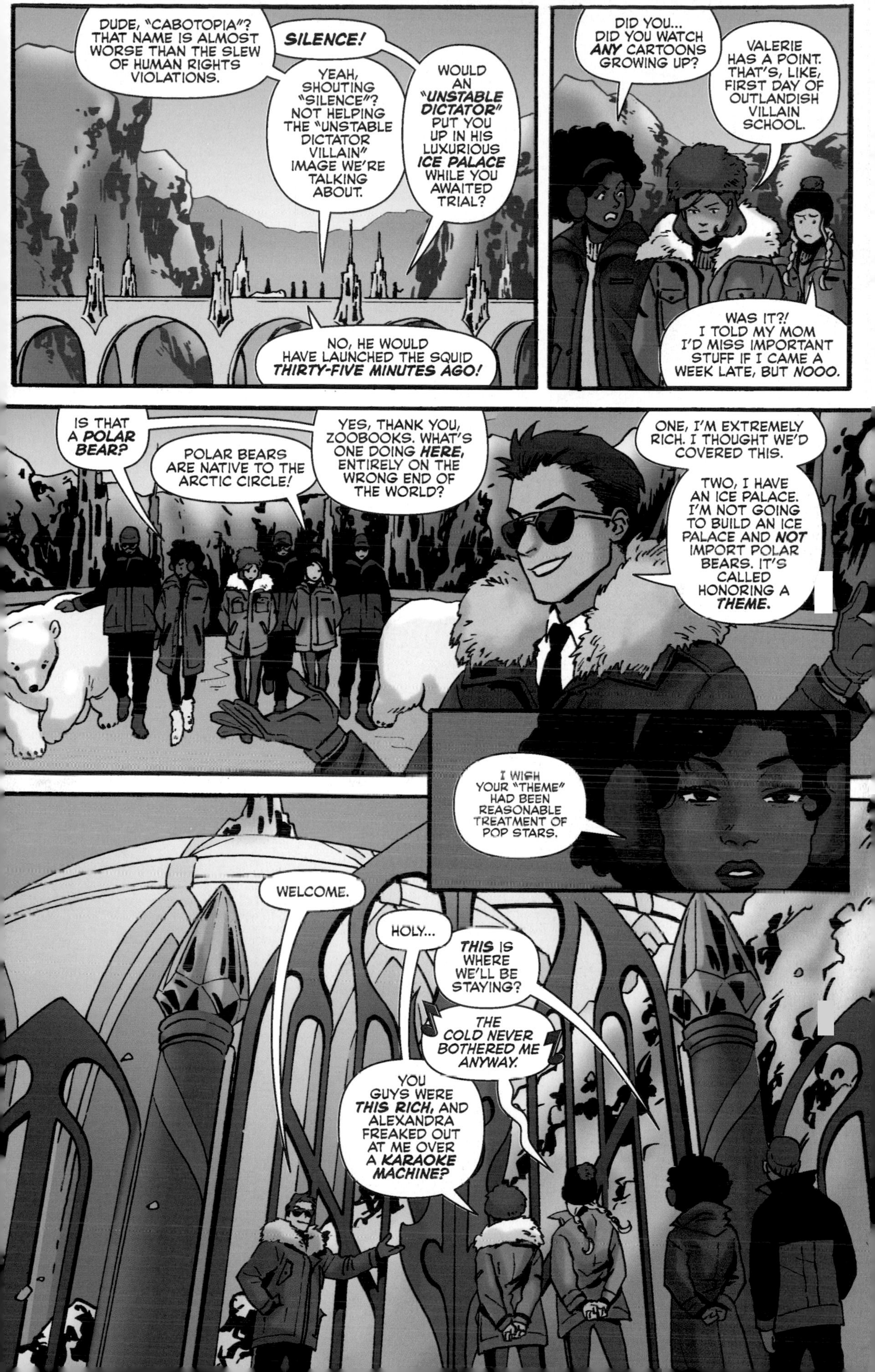
DUDE, "CABOTOPIA"? THAT NAME IS ALMOST WORSE THAN THE SLEW OF HUMAN RIGHTS VIOLATIONS.
SILENCE!
YEAH, SHOUTING "SILENCE"? NOT HELPING THE "UNSTABLE DICTATOR VILLAIN" IMAGE WE'RE TALKING ABOUT.
WOULD AN "UNSTABLE DICTATOR" PUT YOU UP IN HIS LUXURIOUS ICE PALACE WHILE YOU AWAITED TRIAL?
NO, HE WOULD HAVE LAUNCHED THE SQUID THIRTY-FIVE MINUTES AGO!
DID YOU... DID YOU WATCH ANY CARTOONS GROWING UP?
VALERIE HAS A POINT. THAT'S, LIKE, FIRST DAY OF OUTLANDISH VILLAIN SCHOOL.
WAS IT?! I TOLD MY MOM I'D MISS IMPORTANT STUFF IF I CAME A WEEK LATE, BUT NOOO.
IS THAT A POLAR BEAR?
POLAR BEARS ARE NATIVE TO THE ARCTIC CIRCLE!
YES, THANK YOU, ZOOBOOKS. WHAT'S ONE DOING HERE, ENTIRELY ON THE WRONG END OF THE WORLD?
ONE, I'M EXTREMELY RICH. I THOUGHT WE'D COVERED THIS.
TWO, I HAVE AN ICE PALACE. I'M NOT GOING TO BUILD AN ICE PALACE AND NOT IMPORT POLAR BEARS. IT'S CALLED HONORING A THEME.
I WISH YOUR "THEME" HAD BEEN REASONABLE TREATMENT OF POP STARS.
WELCOME.
HOLY...
THIS IS WHERE WE'LL BE STAYING?
THE COLD NEVER BOTHERED ME ANYWAY.
YOU GUYS WERE THIS RICH, AND ALEXANDRA FREAKED OUT AT ME OVER A KARAOKE MACHINE?

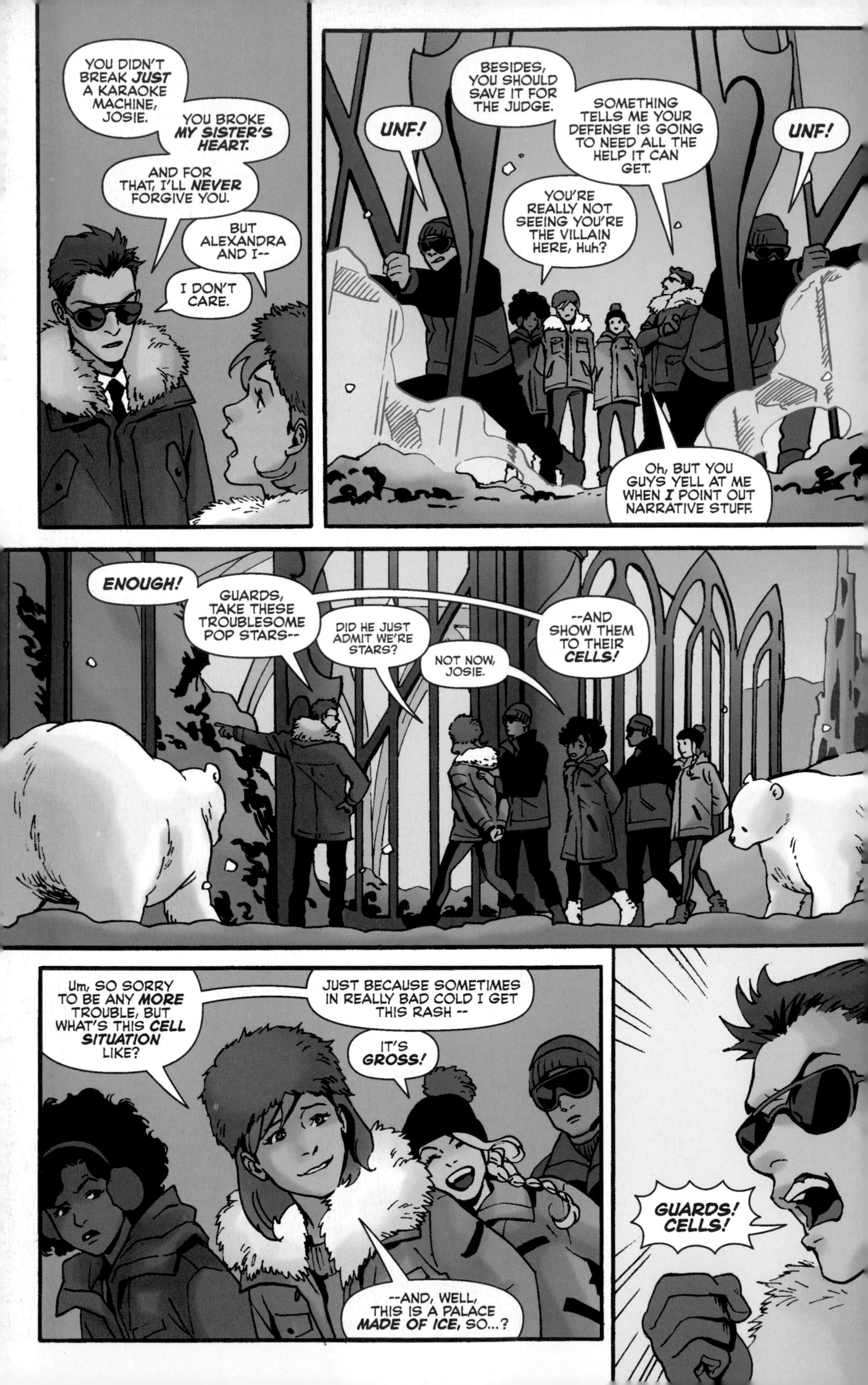

YOU DIDN'T BREAK JUST A KARAOKE MACHINE, JOSIE.
YOU BROKE MY SISTER'S HEART.
AND FOR THAT, I'LL NEVER FORGIVE YOU.
BUT ALEXANDRA AND I--
I DON'T CARE.
UNF!
BESIDES, YOU SHOULD SAVE IT FOR THE JUDGE.
SOMETHING TELLS ME YOUR DEFENSE IS GOING TO NEED ALL THE HELP IT CAN GET.
UNF!
YOU'RE REALLY NOT SEEING YOU'RE THE VILLAIN HERE, Huh?
Oh, BUT YOU GUYS YELL AT ME WHEN I POINT OUT NARRATIVE STUFF.
ENOUGH!
GUARDS, TAKE THESE TROUBLESOME POP STARS--
DID HE JUST ADMIT WE'RE STARS?
NOT NOW, JOSIE.
--AND SHOW THEM TO THEIR CELLS!
Um, SO SORRY TO BE ANY MORE TROUBLE, BUT WHAT'S THIS CELL SITUATION LIKE?
JUST BECAUSE SOMETIMES IN REALLY BAD COLD I GET THIS RASH --
IT'S GROSS!
--AND, WELL, THIS IS A PALACE MADE OF ICE, SO...?
GUARDS! CELLS!

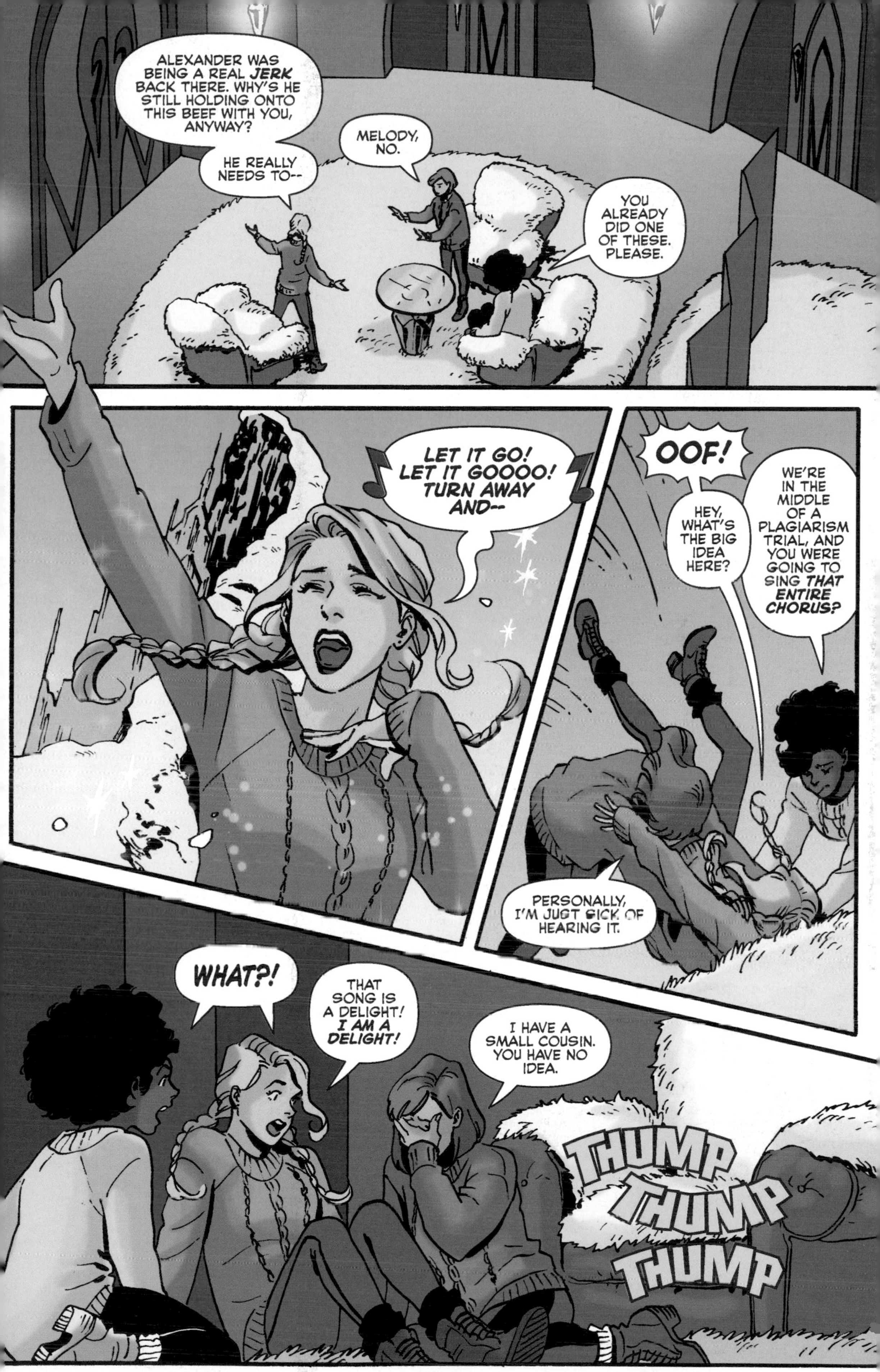
ALEXANDER WAS BEING A REAL JERK BACK THERE. WHY'S HE STILL HOLDING ONTO THIS BEEF WITH YOU, ANYWAY?
HE REALLY NEEDS TO--
MELODY, NO.
YOU ALREADY DID ONE OF THESE. PLEASE.
LET IT GO! LET IT GOOOO! TURN AWAY AND--
OOF!
HEY, WHAT'S THE BIG IDEA HERE?
WE'RE IN THE MIDDLE OF A PLAGIARISM TRIAL, AND YOU WERE GOING TO SING THAT ENTIRE CHORUS?
PERSONALLY, I'M JUST SICK OF HEARING IT.
WHAT?!
THAT SONG IS A DELIGHT! I AM A DELIGHT!
I HAVE A SMALL COUSIN. YOU HAVE NO IDEA.
THUMP
THUMP
THUMP

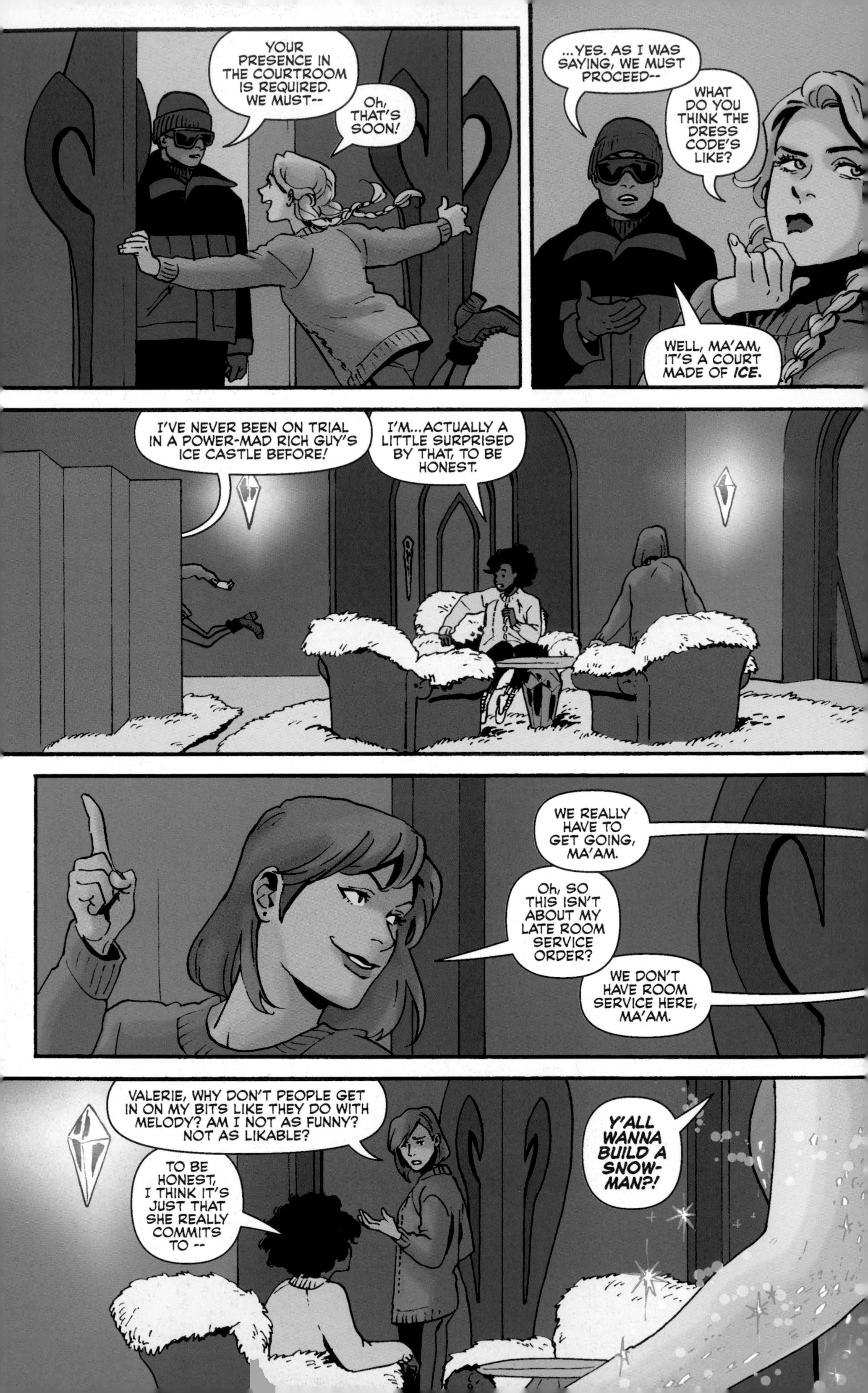
YOUR PRESENCE IN THE COURTROOM IS REQUIRED. WE MUST--
Oh, THAT'S SOON!
...YES. AS I WAS SAYING, WE MUST PROCEED--
WHAT DO YOU THINK THE DRESS CODE'S LIKE?
WELL, MA'AM, IT'S A COURT MADE OF ICE.
I'VE NEVER BEEN ON TRIAL IN A POWER-MAD RICH GUY'S ICE CASTLE BEFORE!
I'M...ACTUALLY A LITTLE SURPRISED BY THAT, TO BE HONEST.
WE REALLY HAVE TO GET GOING, MA'AM.
Oh, SO THIS ISN'T ABOUT MY LATE ROOM SERVICE ORDER?
WE DON'T HAVE ROOM SERVICE HERE, MA'AM.
VALERIE, WHY DON'T PEOPLE GET IN ON MY BITS LIKE THEY DO WITH MELODY? AM I NOT AS FUNNY? NOT AS LIKABLE?
TO BE HONEST, I THINK IT'S JUST THAT SHE REALLY COMMITS TO --
Y'ALL WANNA BUILD A SNOW-MAN?!

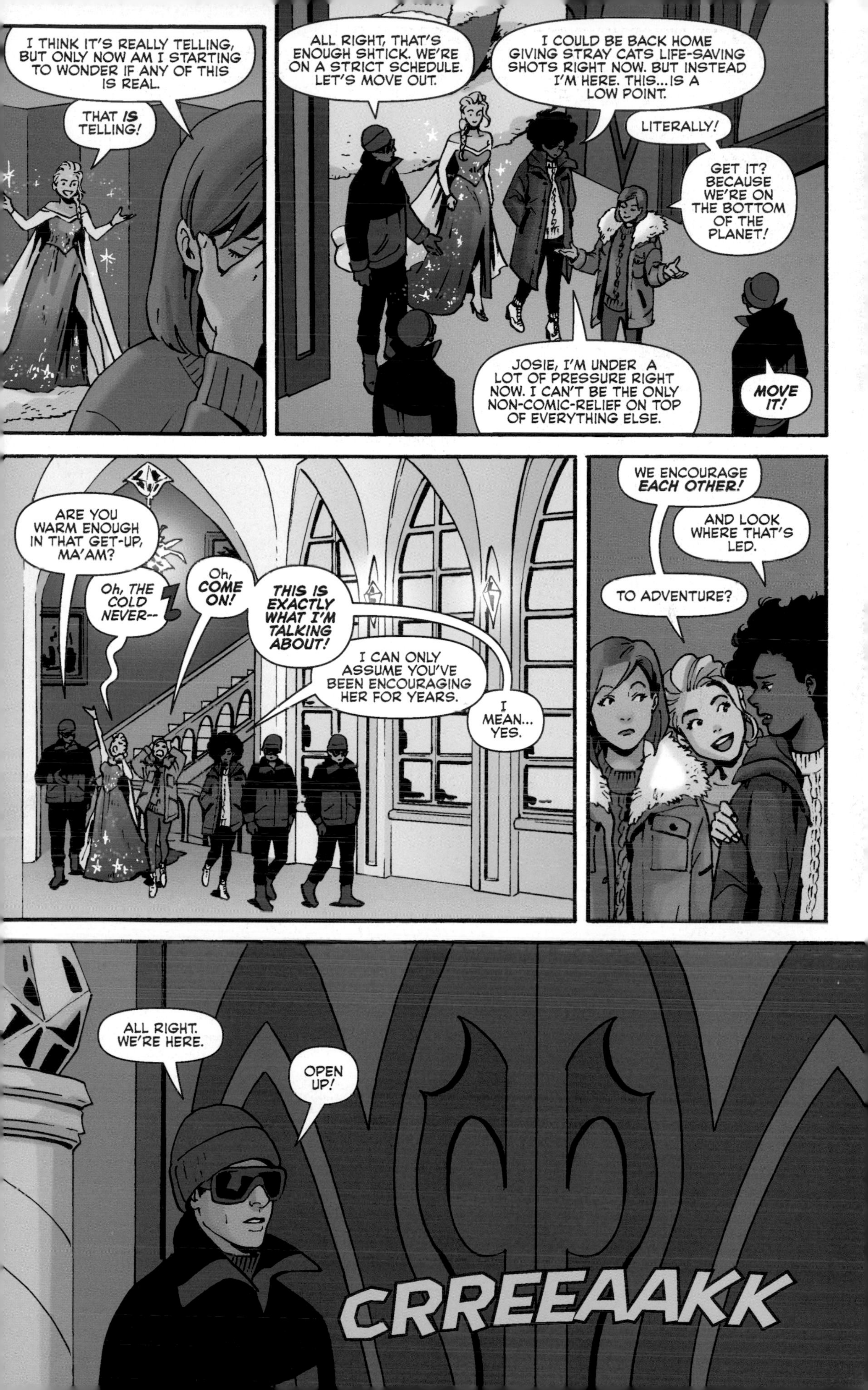
I THINK IT'S REALLY TELLING, BUT ONLY NOW AM I STARTING TO WONDER IF ANY OF THIS IS REAL.
THAT *IS* TELLING!
ALL RIGHT, THAT'S ENOUGH SHTICK. WE'RE ON A STRICT SCHEDULE. LET'S MOVE OUT.
I COULD BE BACK HOME GIVING STRAY CATS LIFE-SAVING SHOTS RIGHT NOW. BUT INSTEAD I'M HERE. THIS...IS A LOW POINT.
LITERALLY!
GET IT? BECAUSE WE'RE ON THE BOTTOM OF THE PLANET!
JOSIE, I'M UNDER A LOT OF PRESSURE RIGHT NOW. I CAN'T BE THE ONLY NON-COMIC-RELIEF ON TOP OF EVERYTHING ELSE.
MOVE IT!
ARE YOU WARM ENOUGH IN THAT GET-UP, MA'AM?
Oh, THE COLD NEVER--
Oh, COME ON!
THIS IS EXACTLY WHAT I'M TALKING ABOUT!
I CAN ONLY ASSUME YOU'VE BEEN ENCOURAGING HER FOR YEARS.
I MEAN... YES.
WE ENCOURAGE *EACH OTHER!*
AND LOOK WHERE THAT'S LED.
TO ADVENTURE?
ALL RIGHT. WE'RE HERE.
OPEN UP!
CRREEAAKK

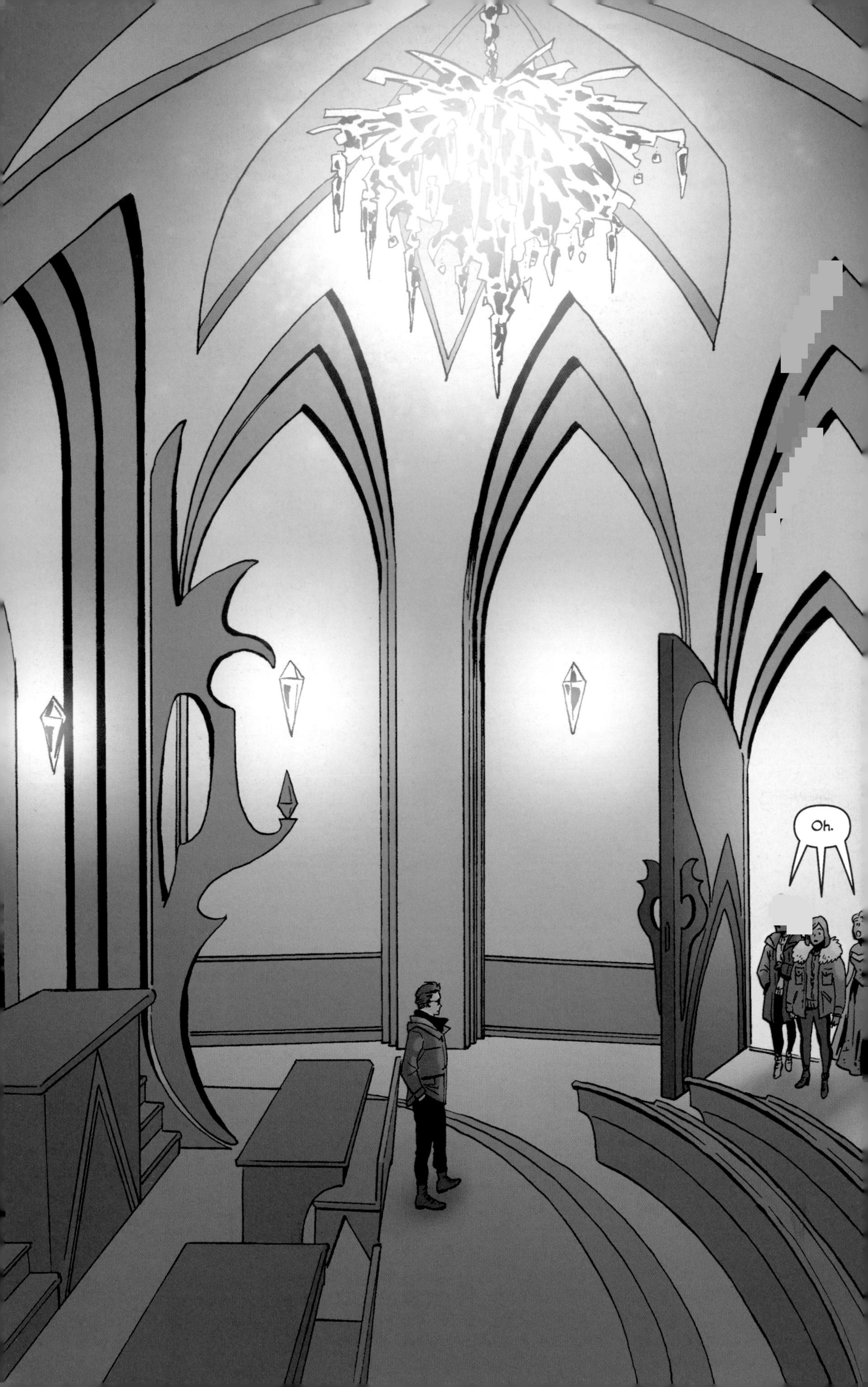
Oh.

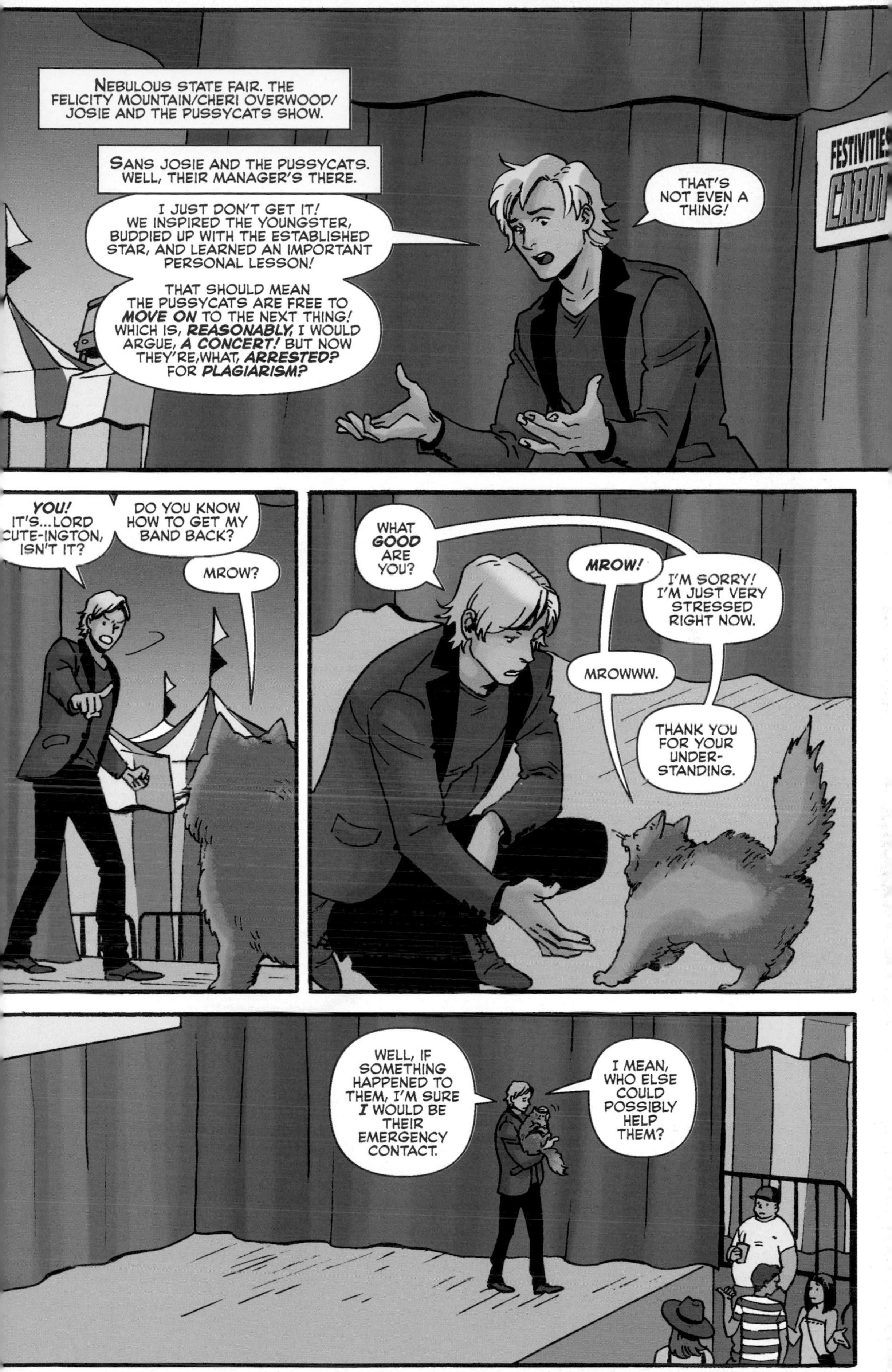
NEBULOUS STATE FAIR. THE FELICITY MOUNTAIN/CHERI OVERWOOD/ JOSIE AND THE PUSSYCATS SHOW.
SANS JOSIE AND THE PUSSYCATS. WELL, THEIR MANAGER'S THERE.
FESTIVITIES
CABOT
I JUST DON'T GET IT! WE INSPIRED THE YOUNGSTER, BUDDIED UP WITH THE ESTABLISHED STAR, AND LEARNED AN IMPORTANT PERSONAL LESSON!
THAT SHOULD MEAN THE PUSSYCATS ARE FREE TO MOVE ON TO THE NEXT THING! WHICH IS, REASONABLY, I WOULD ARGUE, A CONCERT! BUT NOW THEY'RE,WHAT, ARRESTED? FOR PLAGIARISM?
THAT'S NOT EVEN A THING!
YOU! IT'S...LORD CUTE-INGTON, ISN'T IT?
DO YOU KNOW HOW TO GET MY BAND BACK?
MROW?
WHAT GOOD ARE YOU?
MROW!
I'M SORRY! I'M JUST VERY STRESSED RIGHT NOW.
MROWWW.
THANK YOU FOR YOUR UNDER-STANDING.
WELL, IF SOMETHING HAPPENED TO THEM, I'M SURE I WOULD BE THEIR EMERGENCY CONTACT.
I MEAN, WHO ELSE COULD POSSIBLY HELP THEM?

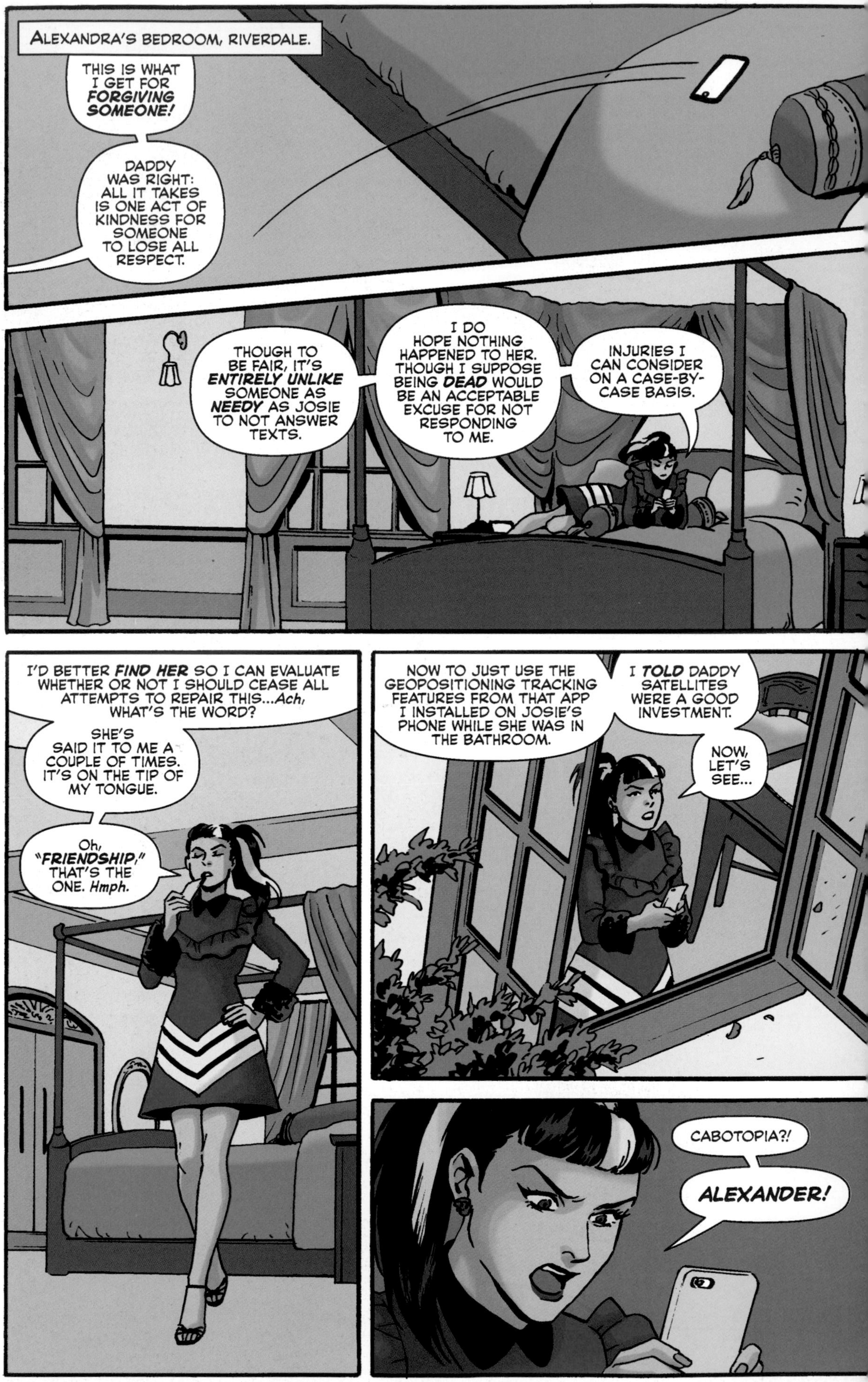
ALEXANDRA'S BEDROOM, RIVERDALE.
THIS IS WHAT I GET FOR FORGIVING SOMEONE!
DADDY WAS RIGHT: ALL IT TAKES IS ONE ACT OF KINDNESS FOR SOMEONE TO LOSE ALL RESPECT.
THOUGH TO BE FAIR, IT'S ENTIRELY UNLIKE SOMEONE AS NEEDY AS JOSIE TO NOT ANSWER TEXTS.
I DO HOPE NOTHING HAPPENED TO HER. THOUGH I SUPPOSE BEING DEAD WOULD BE AN ACCEPTABLE EXCUSE FOR NOT RESPONDING TO ME.
INJURIES I CAN CONSIDER ON A CASE-BY-CASE BASIS.
I'D BETTER FIND HER SO I CAN EVALUATE WHETHER OR NOT I SHOULD CEASE ALL ATTEMPTS TO REPAIR THIS...Ach, WHAT'S THE WORD?
SHE'S SAID IT TO ME AT COUPLE OF TIMES. IT'S ON THE TIP OF MY TONGUE.
Oh, "FRIENDSHIP," THAT'S THE ONE. Hmph.
NOW TO JUST USE THE GEOPOSITIONING TRACKING FEATURES FROM THAT APP I INSTALLED ON JOSIE'S PHONE WHILE SHE WAS IN THE BATHROOM.
I TOLD DADDY SATELLITES WERE A GOOD INVESTMENT.
NOW, LET'S SEE...
CABOTOPIA?!
ALEXANDER!

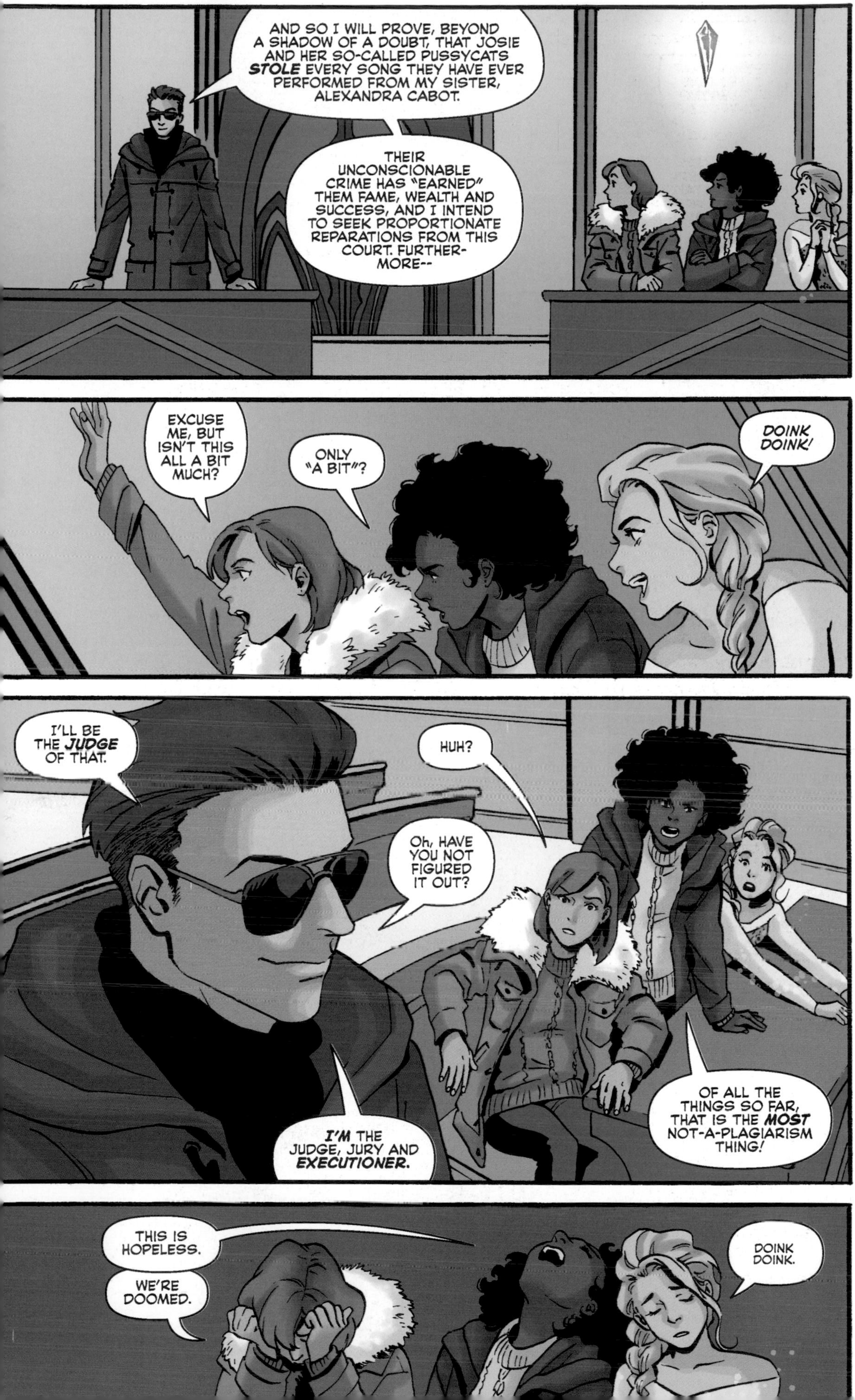
AND SO I WILL PROVE, BEYOND A SHADOW OF A DOUBT, THAT JOSIE AND HER SO-CALLED PUSSYCATS *STOLE* EVERY SONG THEY HAVE EVER PERFORMED FROM MY SISTER, ALEXANDRA CABOT.
THEIR UNCONSCIONABLE CRIME HAS "EARNED" THEM FAME, WEALTH AND SUCCESS, AND I INTEND TO SEEK PROPORTIONATE REPARATIONS FROM THIS COURT. FURTHER-MORE--
EXCUSE ME, BUT ISN'T THIS ALL A BIT MUCH?
ONLY "A BIT"?
DOINK DOINK!
I'LL BE THE *JUDGE* OF THAT.
HUH?
Oh, HAVE YOU NOT FIGURED IT OUT?
I'M THE JUDGE, JURY AND *EXECUTIONER.*
OF ALL THE THINGS SO FAR, THAT IS THE *MOST* NOT-A-PLAGIARISM THING!
THIS IS HOPELESS.
WE'RE DOOMED.
DOINK DOINK.

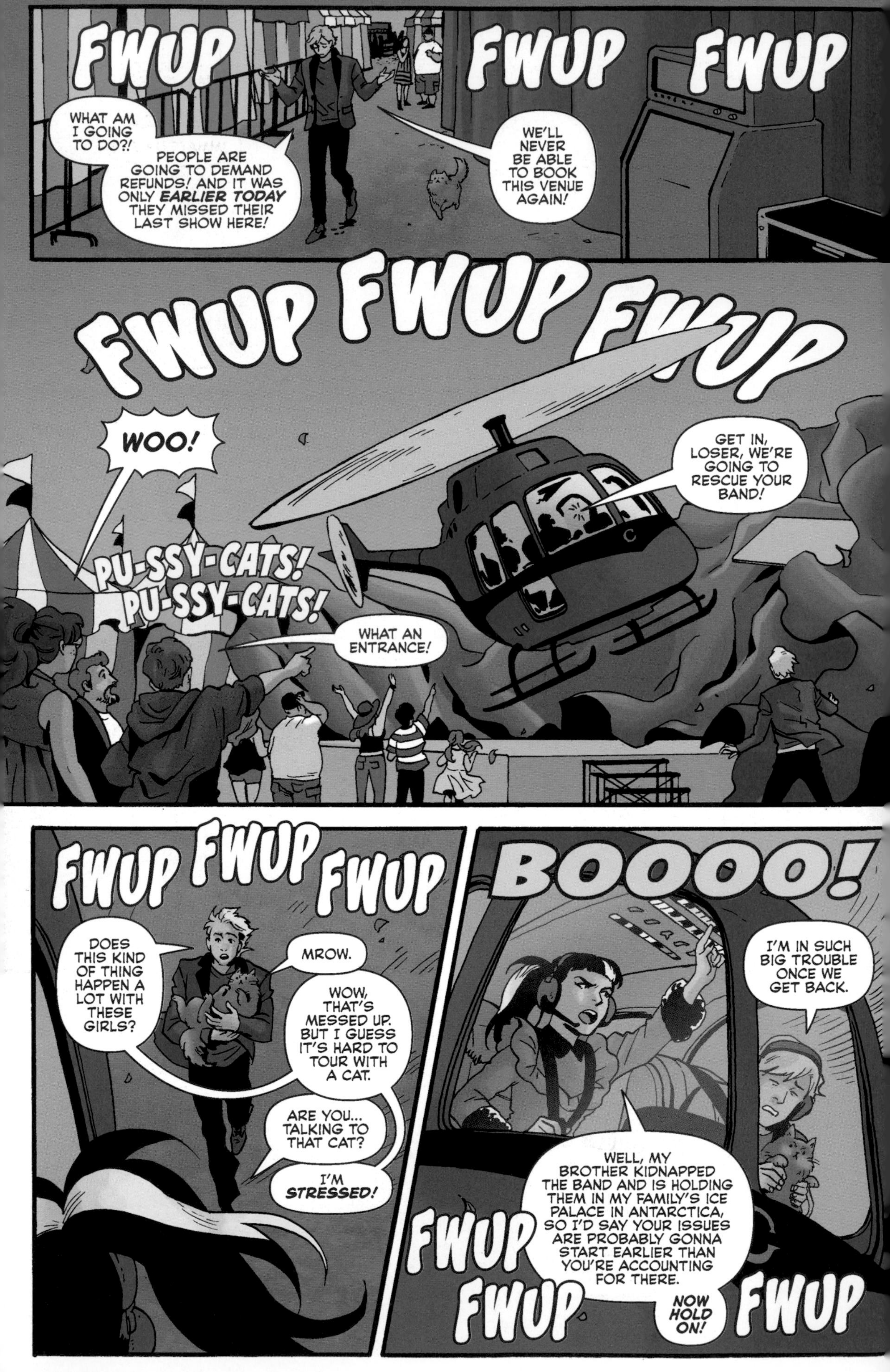
FWUP
FWUP
FWUP
WHAT AM I GOING TO DO?!
PEOPLE ARE GOING TO DEMAND REFUNDS! AND IT WAS ONLY EARLIER TODAY THEY MISSED THEIR LAST SHOW HERE!
WE'LL NEVER BE ABLE TO BOOK THIS VENUE AGAIN!
FWUP FWUP FWUP
WOO!
PU-SSY-CATS! PU-SSY-CATS!
GET IN, LOSER, WE'RE GOING TO RESCUE YOUR BAND!
WHAT AN ENTRANCE!
FWUP FWUP FWUP
DOES THIS KIND OF THING HAPPEN A LOT WITH THESE GIRLS?
MROW.
WOW, THAT'S MESSED UP. BUT I GUESS IT'S HARD TO TOUR WITH A CAT.
ARE YOU... TALKING TO THAT CAT?
I'M STRESSED!
BOOOOO!
I'M IN SUCH BIG TROUBLE ONCE WE GET BACK.
WELL, MY BROTHER KIDNAPPED THE BAND AND IS HOLDING THEM IN MY FAMILY'S ICE PALACE IN ANTARCTICA, SO I'D SAY YOUR ISSUES ARE PROBABLY GONNA START EARLIER THAN YOU'RE ACCOUNTING FOR THERE.
NOW HOLD ON!
FWUP FWUP FWUP

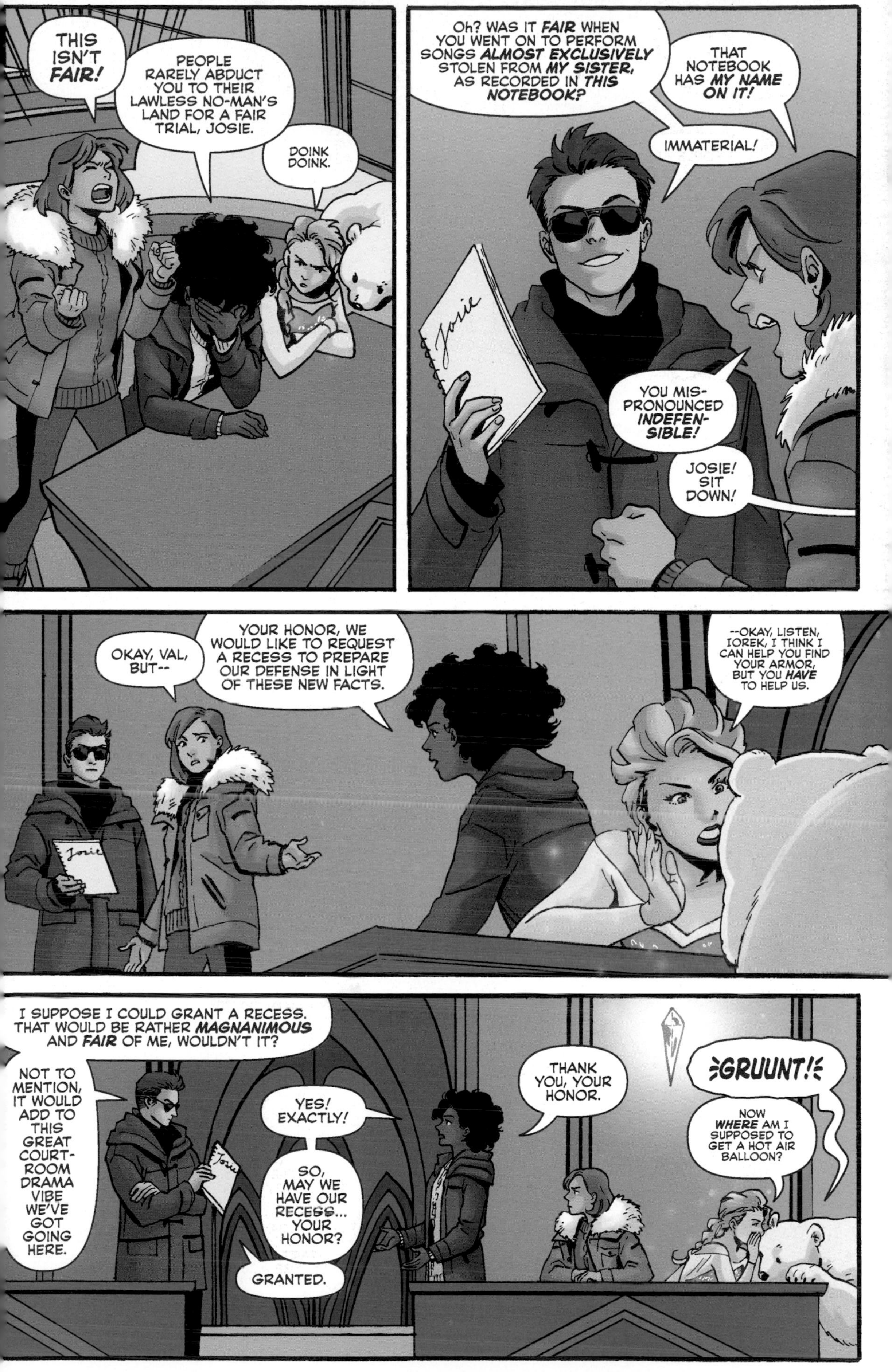
THIS ISN'T FAIR!
PEOPLE RARELY ABDUCT YOU TO THEIR LAWLESS NO-MAN'S LAND FOR A FAIR TRIAL, JOSIE.
DOINK DOINK.
Oh? WAS IT FAIR WHEN YOU WENT ON TO PERFORM SONGS ALMOST EXCLUSIVELY STOLEN FROM MY SISTER, AS RECORDED IN THIS NOTEBOOK?
THAT NOTEBOOK HAS MY NAME ON IT!
IMMATERIAL!
Josie
YOU MIS-PRONOUNCED INDEFEN-SIBLE!
JOSIE! SIT DOWN!
OKAY, VAL, BUT--
YOUR HONOR, WE WOULD LIKE TO REQUEST A RECESS TO PREPARE OUR DEFENSE IN LIGHT OF THESE NEW FACTS.
--OKAY, LISTEN, IOREK, I THINK I CAN HELP YOU FIND YOUR ARMOR, BUT YOU HAVE TO HELP US.
Josie
I SUPPOSE I COULD GRANT A RECESS. THAT WOULD BE RATHER MAGNANIMOUS AND FAIR OF ME, WOULDN'T IT?
NOT TO MENTION, IT WOULD ADD TO THIS GREAT COURT-ROOM DRAMA VIBE WE'VE GOT GOING HERE.
YES! EXACTLY!
SO, MAY WE HAVE OUR RECESS... YOUR HONOR?
GRANTED.
THANK YOU, YOUR HONOR.
GRUUNT!
NOW WHERE AM I SUPPOSED TO GET A HOT AIR BALLOON?

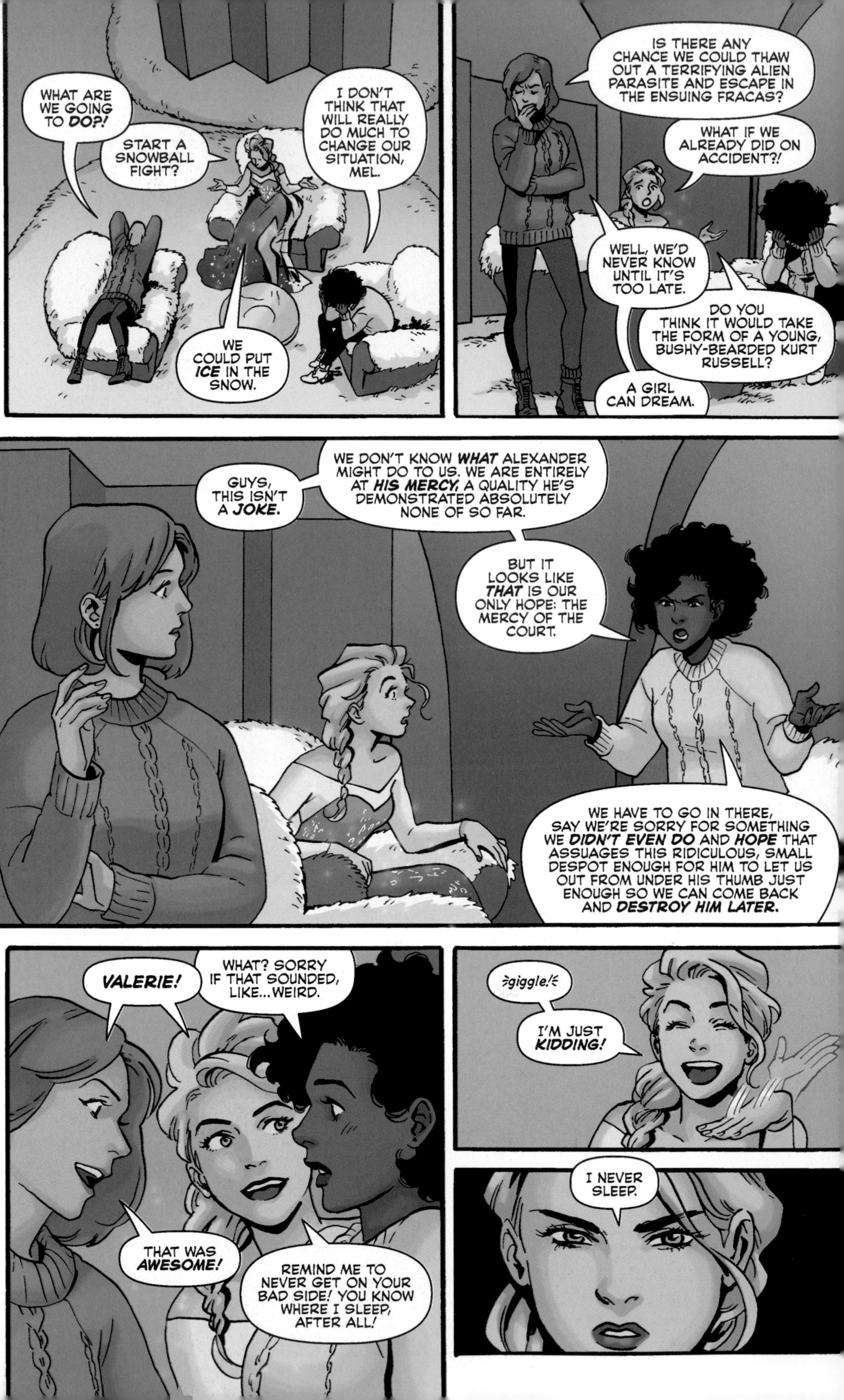
WHAT ARE WE GOING TO DO?!
START A SNOWBALL FIGHT?
I DON'T THINK THAT WILL REALLY DO MUCH TO CHANGE OUR SITUATION, MEL.
WE COULD PUT ICE IN THE SNOW.
IS THERE ANY CHANCE WE COULD THAW OUT A TERRIFYING ALIEN PARASITE AND ESCAPE IN THE ENSUING FRACAS?
WHAT IF WE ALREADY DID ON ACCIDENT?!
WELL, WE'D NEVER KNOW UNTIL IT'S TOO LATE.
DO YOU THINK IT WOULD TAKE THE FORM OF A YOUNG, BUSHY-BEARDED KURT RUSSELL?
A GIRL CAN DREAM.
GUYS, THIS ISN'T A JOKE.
WE DON'T KNOW WHAT ALEXANDER MIGHT DO TO US. WE ARE ENTIRELY AT HIS MERCY, A QUALITY HE'S DEMONSTRATED ABSOLUTELY NONE OF SO FAR.
BUT IT LOOKS LIKE THAT IS OUR ONLY HOPE: THE MERCY OF THE COURT.
WE HAVE TO GO IN THERE, SAY WE'RE SORRY FOR SOMETHING WE DIDN'T EVEN DO AND HOPE THAT ASSUAGES THIS RIDICULOUS, SMALL DESPOT ENOUGH FOR HIM TO LET US OUT FROM UNDER HIS THUMB JUST ENOUGH SO WE CAN COME BACK AND DESTROY HIM LATER.
VALERIE!
WHAT? SORRY IF THAT SOUNDED, LIKE...WEIRD.
THAT WAS AWESOME!
REMIND ME TO NEVER GET ON YOUR BAD SIDE! YOU KNOW WHERE I SLEEP, AFTER ALL!
giggle!
I'M JUST KIDDING!
I NEVER SLEEP.

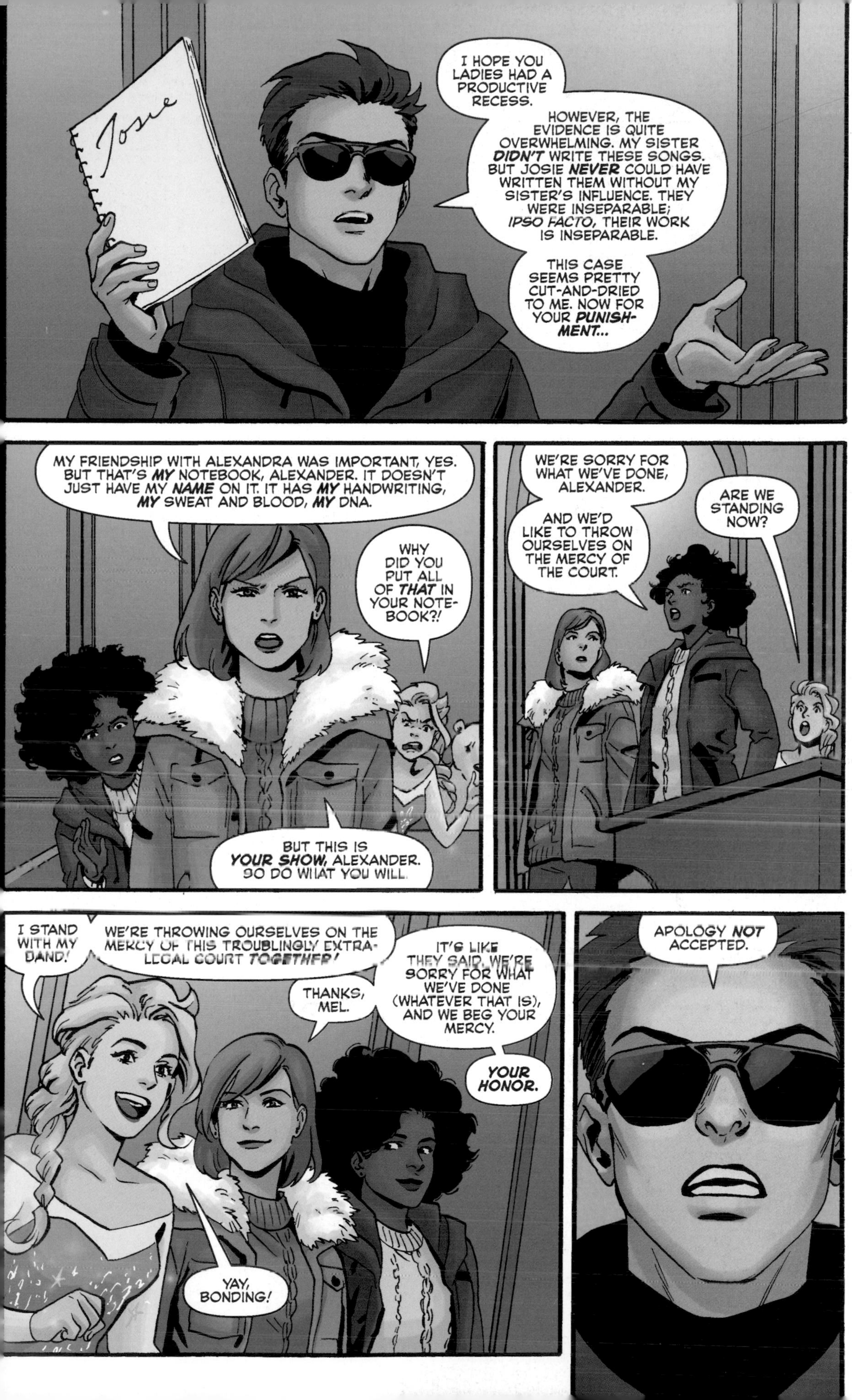

I HOPE YOU LADIES HAD A PRODUCTIVE RECESS.
HOWEVER, THE EVIDENCE IS QUITE OVERWHELMING. MY SISTER ***DIDN'T*** WRITE THESE SONGS. BUT JOSIE ***NEVER*** COULD HAVE WRITTEN THEM WITHOUT MY SISTER'S INFLUENCE. THEY WERE INSEPARABLE; *IPSO FACTO*, THEIR WORK IS INSEPARABLE.
THIS CASE SEEMS PRETTY CUT-AND-DRIED TO ME. NOW FOR YOUR ***PUNISHMENT...***
MY FRIENDSHIP WITH ALEXANDRA WAS IMPORTANT, YES. BUT THAT'S ***MY*** NOTEBOOK, ALEXANDER. IT DOESN'T JUST HAVE MY ***NAME*** ON IT. IT HAS ***MY*** HANDWRITING, ***MY*** SWEAT AND BLOOD, ***MY*** DNA.
WHY DID YOU PUT ALL OF ***THAT*** IN YOUR NOTEBOOK?!
BUT THIS IS ***YOUR SHOW,*** ALEXANDER. SO DO WHAT YOU WILL.
WE'RE SORRY FOR WHAT WE'VE DONE, ALEXANDER.
AND WE'D LIKE TO THROW OURSELVES ON THE MERCY OF THE COURT.
ARE WE STANDING NOW?
WE'RE THROWING OURSELVES ON THE MERCY OF THIS TROUBLINGLY EXTRA-LEGAL COURT ***TOGETHER!***
I STAND WITH MY BAND!
THANKS, MEL.
YAY, BONDING!
IT'S LIKE THEY SAID. WE'RE SORRY FOR WHAT WE'VE DONE (WHATEVER THAT IS), AND WE BEG YOUR MERCY.
YOUR HONOR.
APOLOGY ***NOT*** ACCEPTED.

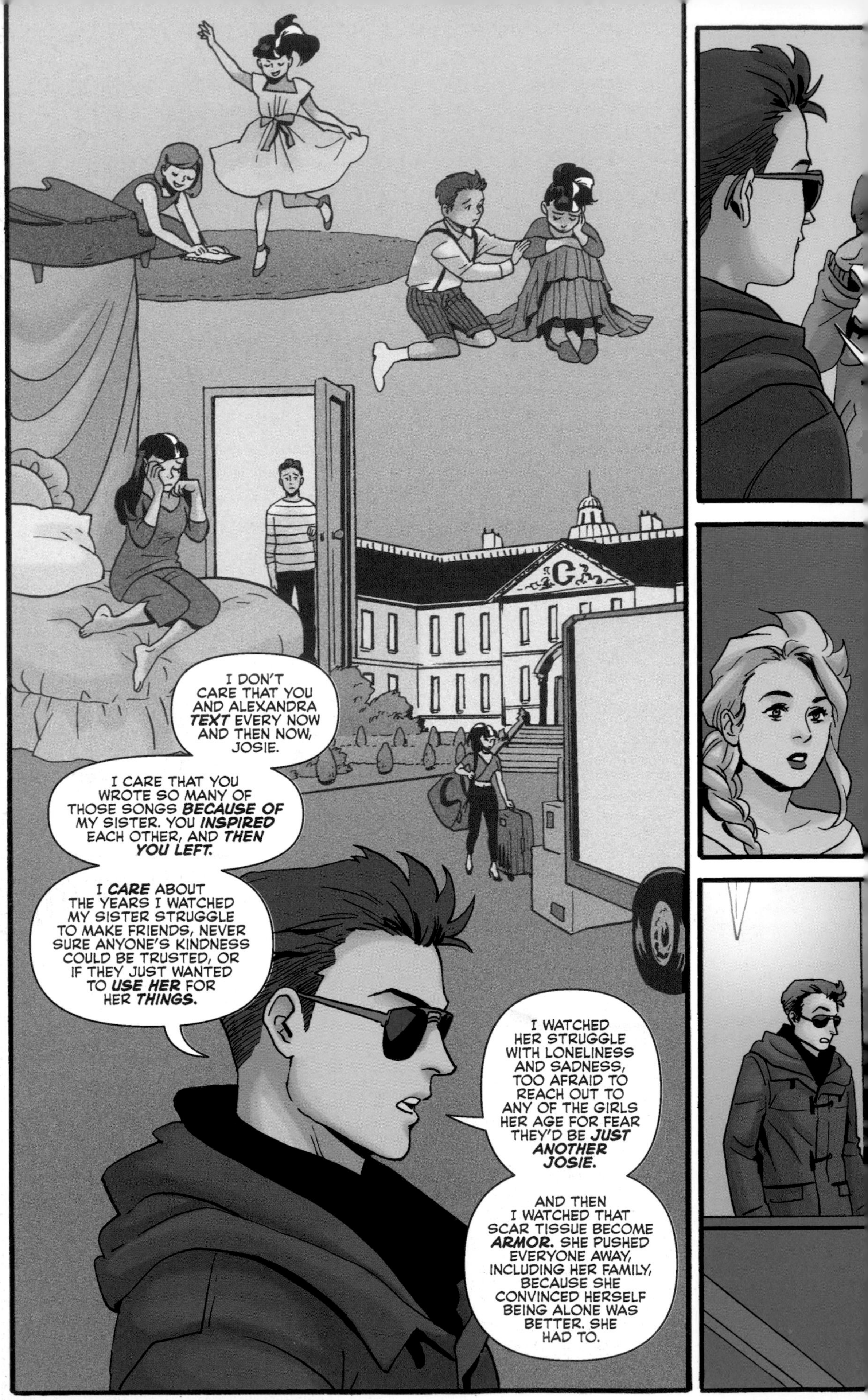
I DON'T CARE THAT YOU AND ALEXANDRA TEXT EVERY NOW AND THEN NOW, JOSIE.
I CARE THAT YOU WROTE SO MANY OF THOSE SONGS BECAUSE OF MY SISTER. YOU INSPIRED EACH OTHER, AND THEN YOU LEFT.
I CARE ABOUT THE YEARS I WATCHED MY SISTER STRUGGLE TO MAKE FRIENDS, NEVER SURE ANYONE'S KINDNESS COULD BE TRUSTED, OR IF THEY JUST WANTED TO USE HER FOR HER THINGS.
I WATCHED HER STRUGGLE WITH LONELINESS AND SADNESS, TOO AFRAID TO REACH OUT TO ANY OF THE GIRLS HER AGE FOR FEAR THEY'D BE JUST ANOTHER JOSIE.
AND THEN I WATCHED THAT SCAR TISSUE BECOME ARMOR. SHE PUSHED EVERYONE AWAY, INCLUDING HER FAMILY, BECAUSE SHE CONVINCED HERSELF BEING ALONE WAS BETTER. SHE HAD TO.

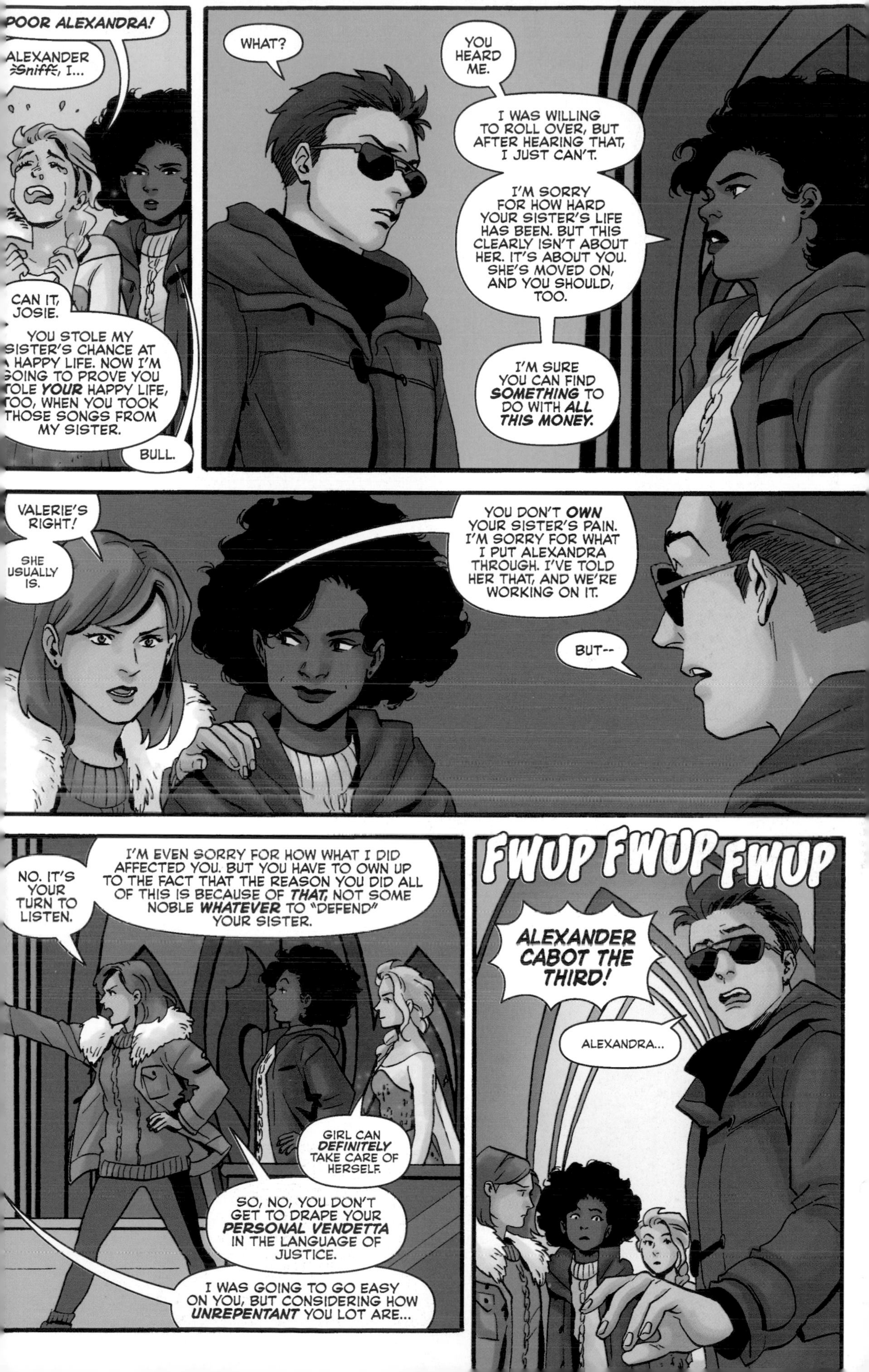
POOR ALEXANDRA!
ALEXANDER *Sniff*, I...
CAN IT, JOSIE.
YOU STOLE MY SISTER'S CHANCE AT A HAPPY LIFE. NOW I'M GOING TO PROVE YOU STOLE YOUR HAPPY LIFE, TOO, WHEN YOU TOOK THOSE SONGS FROM MY SISTER.
BULL.
WHAT?
YOU HEARD ME.
I WAS WILLING TO ROLL OVER, BUT AFTER HEARING THAT, I JUST CAN'T.
I'M SORRY FOR HOW HARD YOUR SISTER'S LIFE HAS BEEN. BUT THIS CLEARLY ISN'T ABOUT HER. IT'S ABOUT YOU. SHE'S MOVED ON, AND YOU SHOULD, TOO.
I'M SURE YOU CAN FIND SOMETHING TO DO WITH ALL THIS MONEY.
VALERIE'S RIGHT!
SHE USUALLY IS.
YOU DON'T OWN YOUR SISTER'S PAIN. I'M SORRY FOR WHAT I PUT ALEXANDRA THROUGH. I'VE TOLD HER THAT, AND WE'RE WORKING ON IT.
BUT--
NO. IT'S YOUR TURN TO LISTEN.
I'M EVEN SORRY FOR HOW WHAT I DID AFFECTED YOU. BUT YOU HAVE TO OWN UP TO THE FACT THAT THE REASON YOU DID ALL OF THIS IS BECAUSE OF THAT, NOT SOME NOBLE WHATEVER TO "DEFEND" YOUR SISTER.
GIRL CAN DEFINITELY TAKE CARE OF HERSELF.
SO, NO, YOU DON'T GET TO DRAPE YOUR PERSONAL VENDETTA IN THE LANGUAGE OF JUSTICE.
I WAS GOING TO GO EASY ON YOU, BUT CONSIDERING HOW UNREPENTANT YOU LOT ARE...
FWUP FWUP FWUP
ALEXANDER CABOT THE THIRD!
ALEXANDRA...

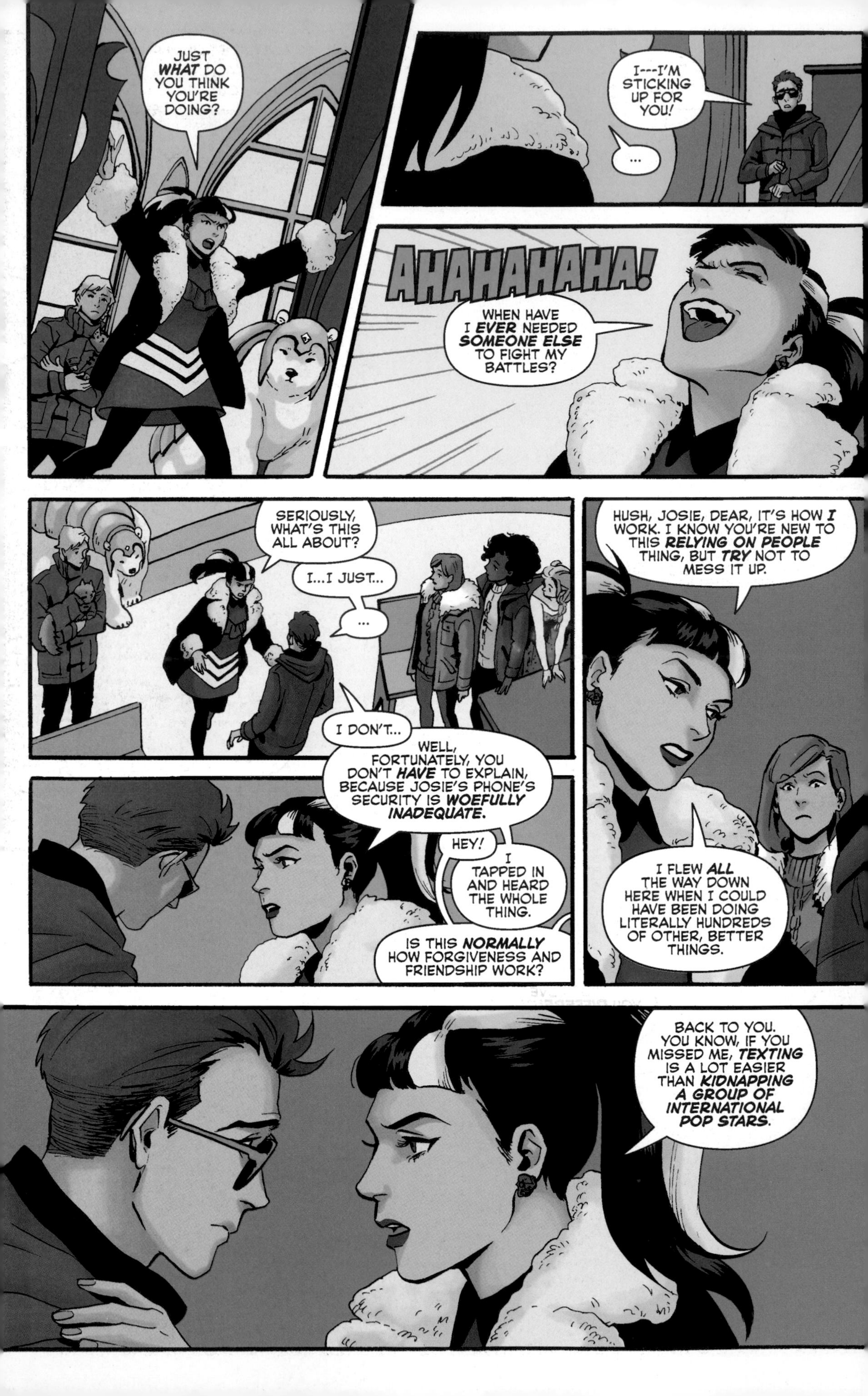
JUST WHAT DO YOU THINK YOU'RE DOING?
I---I'M STICKING UP FOR YOU!
...
AHAHAHAHA!
WHEN HAVE I EVER NEEDED SOMEONE ELSE TO FIGHT MY BATTLES?
SERIOUSLY, WHAT'S THIS ALL ABOUT?
I...I JUST...
...
I DON'T...
HUSH, JOSIE, DEAR, IT'S HOW I WORK. I KNOW YOU'RE NEW TO THIS RELYING ON PEOPLE THING, BUT TRY NOT TO MESS IT UP.
WELL, FORTUNATELY, YOU DON'T HAVE TO EXPLAIN, BECAUSE JOSIE'S PHONE'S SECURITY IS WOEFULLY INADEQUATE.
HEY!
I TAPPED IN AND HEARD THE WHOLE THING.
IS THIS NORMALLY HOW FORGIVENESS AND FRIENDSHIP WORK?
I FLEW ALL THE WAY DOWN HERE WHEN I COULD HAVE BEEN DOING LITERALLY HUNDREDS OF OTHER, BETTER THINGS.
BACK TO YOU. YOU KNOW, IF YOU MISSED ME, TEXTING IS A LOT EASIER THAN KIDNAPPING A GROUP OF INTERNATIONAL POP STARS.

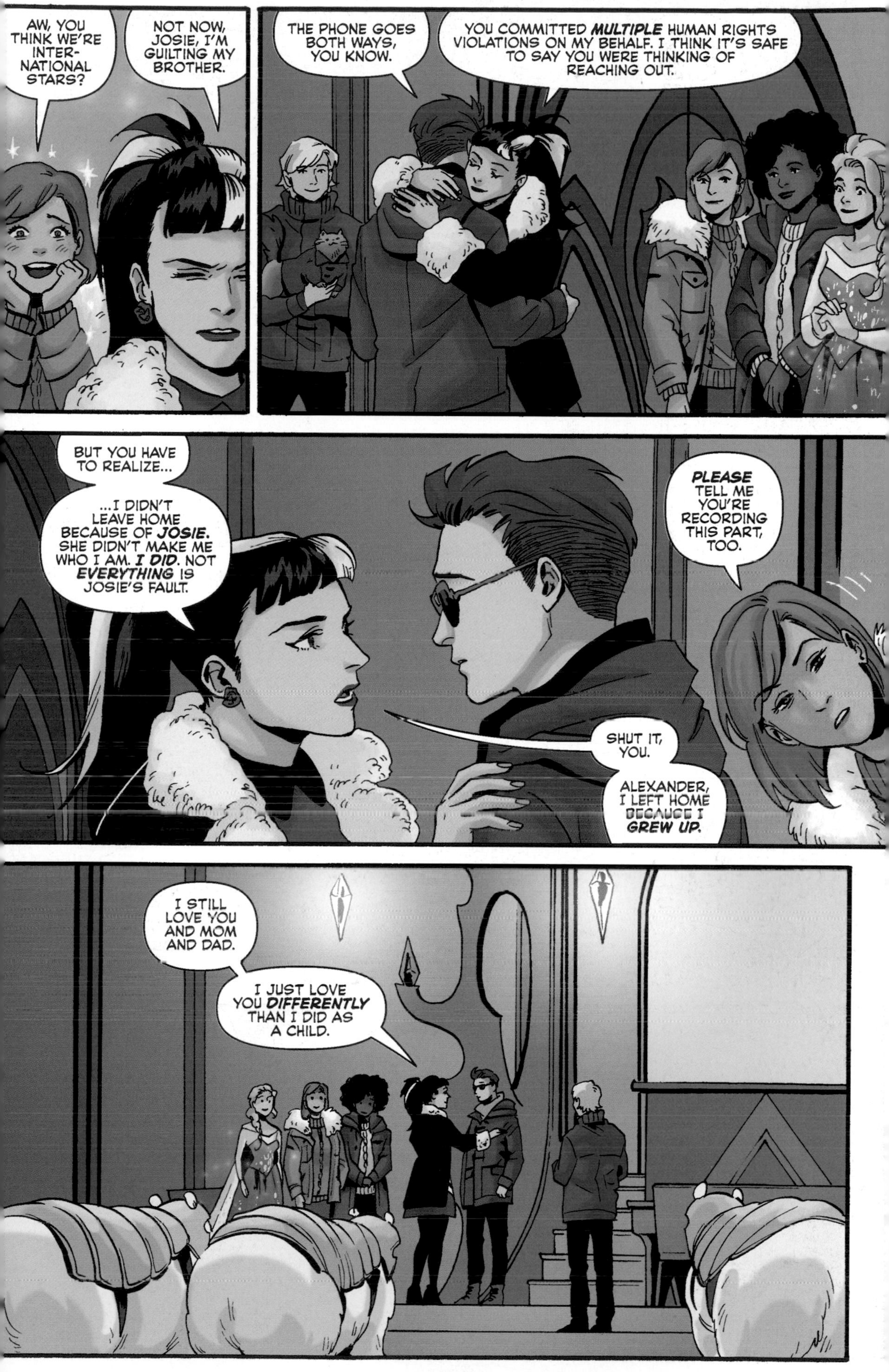
AW, YOU THINK WE'RE INTER-NATIONAL STARS?
NOT NOW, JOSIE, I'M GUILTING MY BROTHER.
THE PHONE GOES BOTH WAYS, YOU KNOW.
YOU COMMITTED MULTIPLE HUMAN RIGHTS VIOLATIONS ON MY BEHALF. I THINK IT'S SAFE TO SAY YOU WERE THINKING OF REACHING OUT.
BUT YOU HAVE TO REALIZE...
...I DIDN'T LEAVE HOME BECAUSE OF JOSIE. SHE DIDN'T MAKE ME WHO I AM. I DID. NOT EVERYTHING IS JOSIE'S FAULT.
PLEASE TELL ME YOU'RE RECORDING THIS PART, TOO.
SHUT IT, YOU.
ALEXANDER, I LEFT HOME BECAUSE I GREW UP.
I STILL LOVE YOU AND MOM AND DAD.
I JUST LOVE YOU DIFFERENTLY THAN I DID AS A CHILD.

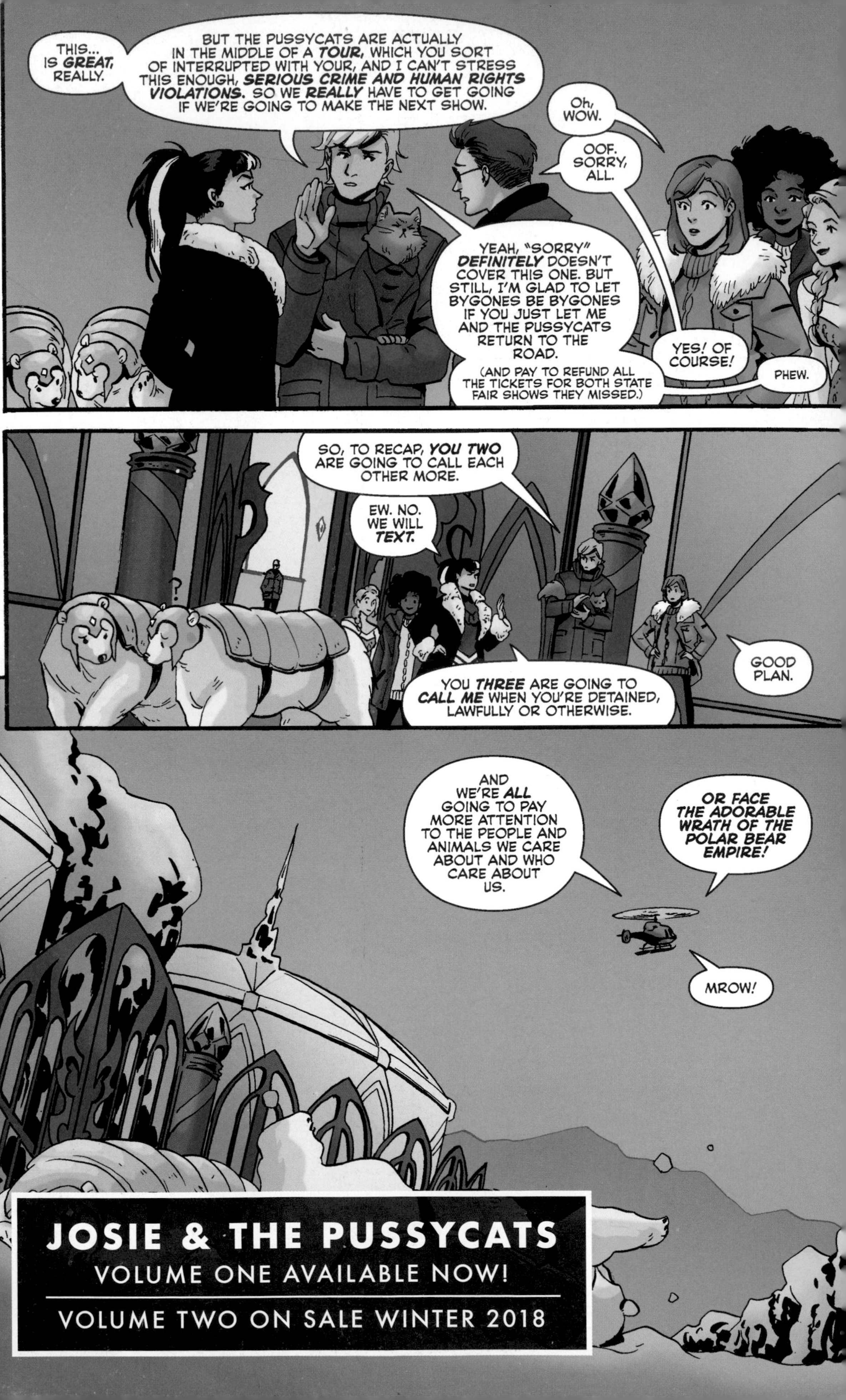
THIS... IS GREAT, REALLY.
BUT THE PUSSYCATS ARE ACTUALLY IN THE MIDDLE OF A TOUR, WHICH YOU SORT OF INTERRUPTED WITH YOUR, AND I CAN'T STRESS THIS ENOUGH, SERIOUS CRIME AND HUMAN RIGHTS VIOLATIONS. SO WE REALLY HAVE TO GET GOING IF WE'RE GOING TO MAKE THE NEXT SHOW.
Oh, WOW.
OOF. SORRY, ALL.
YEAH, "SORRY" DEFINITELY DOESN'T COVER THIS ONE. BUT STILL, I'M GLAD TO LET BYGONES BE BYGONES IF YOU JUST LET ME AND THE PUSSYCATS RETURN TO THE ROAD.
(AND PAY TO REFUND ALL THE TICKETS FOR BOTH STATE FAIR SHOWS THEY MISSED.)
YES! OF COURSE!
PHEW.
SO, TO RECAP, YOU TWO ARE GOING TO CALL EACH OTHER MORE.
EW. NO. WE WILL TEXT.
YOU THREE ARE GOING TO CALL ME WHEN YOU'RE DETAINED, LAWFULLY OR OTHERWISE.
GOOD PLAN.
AND WE'RE ALL GOING TO PAY MORE ATTENTION TO THE PEOPLE AND ANIMALS WE CARE ABOUT AND WHO CARE ABOUT US.
OR FACE THE ADORABLE WRATH OF THE POLAR BEAR EMPIRE!
MROW!
JOSIE & THE PUSSYCATS
VOLUME ONE AVAILABLE NOW!
VOLUME TWO ON SALE WINTER 2018